TAKING SIDES

Clashing Views
on Controversial Issues
in Family
and Personal Relationships

Edited, Selected, and with Introductions by

Gloria W. Bird
Virginia Polytechnic Institute and State University

and

Michael J. Sporakowski
Virginia Polytechnic Institute and State University

The Dushkin Publishing Group, Inc.

To my parents, Vincent B. and Marjorie J. Wanager, whose acceptance of four children with decidedly clashing views has always amazed and inspired me (G. W. B.)

To Walter A. Garrett, the consummate facilitator of clashing views on controversial issues (J. J. S.)

Taking Sides ® is a registered trademark of The Dushkin Publishing Group, Inc.

Library of Congress Catalog Card Number: 90-84860

Manufactured in the United States of America

First Edition, First Printing
ISBN: 1-56134-001-4

 Printed on Recycled Paper

The Dushkin Publishing Group, Inc.
Sluice Dock, Guilford, CT 06437

**Clashing Views
on Controversial Issues
in Family
and Personal Relationships**

PREFACE

This text contains thirty-four essays, arranged in *pro* and *contra* pairs, that address seventeen controversial issues relating to family and personal relationships. Each of the seventeen issues is expressed in terms of a single question in order to draw the lines of debate more clearly.

Some issues cover familiar topics but ask you to look at them in previously unexplored ways. See, for example, Issue 4: *Is Marriage Good for You?* This issue explores the implications of marriage for the individual and for society. Some issues focus on newly emerging topics that reflect and consider recent changes in society. See, for example, Issue 3: *Have Men's Family Roles Changed?* In this issue, each side considers the emergence of the dual-career family and whether or not men's family roles within such families have changed. The articles selected for inclusion in this volume introduce recent empirical research in the field of marriage and family studies, and in many cases the authors of the selections are well known for making contributions to research, theory, or critical thinking in the area of focus.

Today, approximately 90 percent of individuals in the United States will eventually marry. Most of them, as well as those who do not marry, will interact daily for much of their lives with the members of their families of origin. It is within the family that people gain many of their insights into the nature and context of personal relationships—what a relationship is, how it works, and the range of appropriate and inappropriate behavior. But family and personal relationships are inevitably influenced by the larger social context in which they occur. The social context impinges on individual and family choices and the freedom to exercise such choices. Throughout this book you will find essays and reports that will challenge you to think about personal and family issues.

Plan of the book   Our book is primarily designed for courses in marriage and the family, and the issues are such that they can be easily incorporated into any marriage and family course regardless of organization or emphasis. The selections have been taken from a variety of sources—books, journals, magazines—and were chosen because of their usefulness in defending a position and for their accessibility to students.

Each issue in this volume is self-contained: Each issue has an issue *introduction*, which sets the stage for the debate as it is argued in the YES and NO selections. Each issue concludes with a *postscript* that makes some final observations about the selections, points the way to other questions related to the issue, and offers suggestions for further reading on the issue. The introductions and postscripts do not preempt what is the reader's own task: to achieve a critical and informed view of the issues at stake.

As you read an issue and form your own opinion, you should not feel confined to adopt one or the other of the positions presented. Some readers may see important points on both sides of an issue and may construct for themselves a new and creative approach. Such an approach might incorporate the best of both sides, or it might provide an entirely new vantage point for understanding.

At the back of the book (beginning on page 340) is a listing of all the *contributors to this volume*, which will give you additional information on the scholars, practitioners, and social critics whose views are debated here.

Supplements   An *Instructor's Manual with Test Questions* (multiple-choice and essay) is available through the publisher. A general guidebook, called *Using Taking Sides in the Classroom*, which discusses methods and techniques for integrating the pro-con approach into any classroom setting, is also available.

Acknowledgments   For their great assistance in performing the research for this project, we wish to thank Paula A. DuPrey and Martyn L. Bird.

Gloria W. Bird
Michael J. Sporakowski
Virginia Polytechnic Institute and State University

CONTENTS IN BRIEF

PART 1   GENDER ROLES AND FAMILY RELATIONSHIPS 1

Issue 1.   Are Gender Differences Present at Birth? **2**

Issue 2.   Are Women Only Victims in Their Roles as Social Support Providers? **16**

Issue 3.   Have Men's Family Roles Changed? **36**

PART 2   MAKING A COMMITMENT: THE DECISION TO MARRY 51

Issue 4.   Is Marriage Good for You? **52**

Issue 5.   Should Gays and Lesbians Fight for the Right to Marry? **74**

PART 3   PARENTHOOD 87

Issue 6.   Is It Possible to Be Pro-Life and Pro-Choice? **88**

Issue 7.   Is Parenthood Necessary for a Good Marriage? **110**

Issue 8.   Should Surrogate Parenting Be Permitted for Infertile Couples? **136**

Issue 9.   Should Pregnant Teens Marry the Fathers of Their Babies? **154**

PART 4   STRESS IN THE FAMILY 177

Issue 10.   Does Arrest Reduce Domestic Violence? **178**

Issue 11.   Would a "Mommy Track" Benefit Employed Women? **192**

Issue 12.   Should the Government Establish Special Programs and Policies for Black Youths and Their Families? **208**

Issue 13.   Husband Battering: Is It a Social Problem? **224**

Issue 14.   Are Extramarital Relationships Becoming More Frequent? **242**

PART 5   FORMING NEW RELATIONSHIPS: DIVORCE AND REMARRIAGE 265

Issue 15.   Children of Divorce: Are They at Greater Risk? **266**

Issue 16.   Do Stepchildren Need Special Policies and Programs on Their Behalf? **292**

Issue 17.   Is the Success of Remarriage Doomed? **310**

CONTENTS

Preface   i

Introduction: The Study of Marriage and the Family   x

PART 1   GENDER ROLES AND FAMILY RELATIONSHIPS   1

ISSUE 1. Are Gender Differences Present at Birth?   2
YES: Steven Goldberg, from "Reaffirming the Obvious," *Society*   4
NO: Cynthia Fuchs Epstein, from "Inevitabilities of Prejudice," *Society*   9

Sociologist Steven Goldberg argues that there are basic physiological differences between women and men that lead men to do whatever is necessary to attain dominance in society. Sociologist Cynthia Fuchs Epstein counters that Goldberg's thesis ignores the pervasive societal constraints on women's lives as well as evidence of historical changes in women's status and roles despite such constraints.

ISSUE 2. Are Women Only Victims in Their Roles as Social Support Providers?   16
YES: Deborah Belle, from "Gender Differences in the Social Moderators of Stress," in Rosalind Barnett et al., eds., *Gender and Stress*   18
NO: Micaela di Leonardo, from "The Female World of Cards and Holidays: Women, Families, and the Work of Kinship," *Signs: Journal of Women in Culture and Society*   28

Assistant professor of psychology Deborah Belle maintains that, in comparison to men, women are more highly involved as support providers. She claims that women often suffer from "support gap" stress. Micaela di Leonardo, an associate professor of anthropology and women's studies, asserts that women's involvement with kin and friends, despite its drawbacks, provides them with satisfaction as well as power within the family.

ISSUE 3. Have Men's Family Roles Changed?   36
YES: Joseph H. Pleck, from "The Contemporary Man," in Murry Scher et al., eds., *Handbook of Counseling and Psychotherapy with Men*   38
NO: Steven L. Nock and Paul William Kingston, from "Time With Children: The Impact of Couples' Work-Time Commitments," *Social Forces*   42

Professor of sociology Joseph H. Pleck argues that men married to employed women have substantially increased their involvement in housework and child care. Professors of sociology Steven L. Nock and Paul William Kingston contend that the emergence of the dual-earner family has not influenced men to increase their participation in family life.

PART 2 MAKING A COMMITMENT: THE DECISION TO MARRY 51

ISSUE 4. Is Marriage Good for You? 52

YES: **Bryce J. Christensen,** from "The Costly Retreat from Marriage," *The Public Interest* 54

NO: **Liz Hodgkinson,** from *Unholy Matrimony: The Case for Abolishing Marriage* 60

Bryce J. Christensen, director of The Rockford Institute Center on the Family in America, argues that being married has positive mental and physical health benefits for individuals and society. Free-lance writer Liz Hodgkinson asserts that modern marriage should be abolished because it is dysfunctional for individuals and society as a whole.

ISSUE 5. Should Gays and Lesbians Fight for the Right to Marry? 74

YES: **Andrew Sullivan,** from "Here Comes the Groom," *The New Republic* 76

NO: **Paula L. Ettelbrick,** from "Since When Is Marriage a Path to Liberation?" *OUT/LOOK* 80

Andrew Sullivan, a former editor of *The New Republic,* proposes that allowing gay couples to marry would have social and legal advantages. Gay rights activist Paula L. Ettelbrick argues that marriage would further constrain lesbians and gay men, making it easier for society to refuse to validate relationships that do not include marriage.

PART 3 PARENTHOOD 87

ISSUE 6. Is It Possible to Be Pro-Life and Pro-Choice? 88

YES: **Carl Sagan and Ann Druyan,** from "Is It Possible to Be Pro-Life and Pro-Choice?" *Parade Magazine* 90

NO: **Orrin G. Hatch,** from *The Value of Life* 99

Astronomer Carl Sagan and writer Ann Druyan argue that the abortion issue is not a simple dichotomy, pro-life *or* pro-choice, but one that has many facets worth considering. They explore the reasons to uphold the view that it is possible to value life and support abortion. Senator Orrin G. Hatch, a supporter of a constitutional amendment to overturn the Supreme Court *Roe v. Wade* decision on abortion, argues that the pro-choice position is morally and legally without foundation and goes against biblical injunctions.

ISSUE 7. Is Parenthood Necessary for a Good Marriage?   110

YES: Irving Sarnoff and Suzanne Sarnoff, from *Love-Centered Marriage in a Self-Centered World*   112

NO: J. E. Veevers, from *Childless by Choice*   126

Psychologists Irving Sarnoff and Suzanne Sarnoff discuss their holistic model of love-centered marriage and argue that the satisfaction of love needs through marriage and parenthood is essential to self-realization and fulfillment. Sociologist J. E. Veevers describes the stages that lead to childlessness and concludes that having children is not a solution for an unhappy marriage nor a necessity for a happy marriage.

ISSUE 8. Should Surrogate Parenting Be Permitted for Infertile Couples?   136

YES: John A. Robertson, from "Surrogate Mothers: Not So Novel After All," *Hastings Center Report*   138

NO: Herbert T. Krimmel, from "The Case Against Surrogate Parenting," *Hastings Center Report*   145

Professor of law John A. Robertson argues that the legal and ethical problems associated with surrogate motherhood are not significantly different from those that already exist with artificial insemination by a donor and adoption. Professor of law Herbert T. Krimmel questions the morality of bearing children for the purpose of giving them up, especially for payment.

ISSUE 9. Should Pregnant Teens Marry the Fathers of Their Babies?   154

YES: P. Lindsay Chase-Lansdale and Maris A. Vinovskis, from "Should We Discourage Teenage Marriage?" *The Public Interest*   156

NO: Naomi Farber, from "The Significance of Race and Class in Marital Decisions Among Unmarried Adolescent Mothers," *Social Problems*   164

Family researcher P. Lindsay Chase-Lansdale and professor of history Maris A. Vinovskis call for a reexamination of research findings and current policies that cast doubt on the benefits of having adolescent mothers and fathers rear their own children. Human services educator Naomi Farber replies that, although adolescent mothers value marriage, they express legitimate concerns about rushing into marriage simply because they are pregnant or have given birth.

PART 4   STRESS IN THE FAMILY   177

ISSUE 10. Does Arrest Reduce Domestic Violence?   178

YES: Joan Meier, from "Battered Justice," *The Washington Monthly*   180

NO: Franklyn W. Dunford, David Huizinga, and Delbert S. Elliott, from "The Role of Arrest in Domestic Assault: The Omaha Police Experiment," *Criminology*   186

Attorney Joan Meier, after reviewing several reports on domestic violence, maintains that arrest is the most effective deterrent to continued assault. Criminologists Franklyn W. Dunford, David Huizinga, and Delbert S. Elliott argue that there is no clear-cut best approach to minimizing the continuation of wife abuse.

ISSUE 11. Would a "Mommy Track" Benefit Employed Women?   192

YES: Felice N. Schwartz, from "Management Women and the New Facts of Life," *Harvard Business Review*   194

NO: Barbara Ehrenreich and Deirdre English, from "Blowing the Whistle on the 'Mommy Track,' " *Ms.*   202

Felice N. Schwartz, president and founder of an organization that consults with corporations on the leadership development of women, argues that it is in the best interests of corporations to retain valued managerial women by creating two career paths within the organization, one for "career-primary" women and the other for "career-and-family" women. Journalists Barbara Ehrenreich and Deirdre English maintain that the "mommy track" notion is based on stereotypical assumptions about women and ignores the real issue of why corporations continue to promote work policies that are incompatible with family life.

ISSUE 12. Should the Government Establish Special Programs and Policies for Black Youths and Their Families?   208

YES: Ronald L. Taylor, from "Black Youth: The Endangered Generation," *Youth and Society*   210

NO: Jean M. Granger, from "African American Family Policy or National Family Policy: Are They Different?" *Urban League Review*   215

Sociologist Ronald L. Taylor argues that black youths and their families are disproportionately affected by poverty, crime, and unemployment and should therefore be targeted for federal and state support. Jean M. Granger, a professor of social work, asserts that the needs of black families should not be separated and distinguished from the needs of all American families. Singling out black families would only perpetuate negative myths concerning the black family.

ISSUE 13. Husband Battering: Is It a Social Problem?   **224**

YES: Suzanne K. Steinmetz and Joseph A. Lucca, from "Husband Battering," in Vincent B. Van Hasselt et al., eds., *Handbook of Family Violence*   **226**

NO: R. Emerson Dobash and Russell P. Dobash, from "Research as Social Action: The Struggle for Battered Women," in Kersti Yllö and Michele Bograd, eds., *Feminist Perspectives on Wife Abuse*   **233**

Professor of sociology Suzanne K. Steinmetz and professor of physical therapy Joseph A. Lucca contend that the detrimental consequences of husband battering are real but are being ignored because wives' violence against husbands is not considered a serious social problem. R. Emerson Dobash and Russell P. Dobash, professors at the University of Stirling in Scotland, argue that husband battering is not a real social problem because women do not typically evidence patterns of severe, persistent, and intimidating violence against their husbands.

ISSUE 14. Are Extramarital Relationships Becoming More Frequent?   **242**

YES: Lynn Atwater, from *The Extramarital Connection: Sex, Intimacy, and Identity*   **244**

NO: Andrew M. Greeley, Robert T. Michael, and Tom W. Smith, from "Americans and Their Sexual Partners," *Society*   **254**

Associate professor of sociology Lynn Atwater argues that the incidence of extramarital involvement has been increasing over the past half-century in the United States. Sociologist Andrew M. Greeley, economist Robert T. Michael, and survey researcher Tom W. Smith critique research purporting an increased frequency of extramarital affairs and provide data indicating that extramarital liaisons are at a relatively low level.

PART 5 FORMING NEW RELATIONSHIPS: DIVORCE AND REMARRIAGE   **265**

ISSUE 15. Children of Divorce: Are They at Greater Risk?   **266**

YES: Judith S. Wallerstein, from "Children of Divorce: The Dilemma

of a Decade," in Elam W. Nunnally, Catherine S. Chilman, and Fred
M. Cox, eds., *Troubled Relationships*   268

NO: David H. Demo and Alan C. Acock, from "The Impact of Divorce on Children," *Journal of Marriage and the Family*   276

Clinician and researcher Judith S. Wallerstein contends that children whose parents divorce are at greater risk of mental and physical health problems than are children whose families are intact. Sociologists David H. Demo and Alan C. Acock argue that much of the research on children of divorce is theoretically or methodologically flawed and, consequently, the findings cannot always be trusted.

**ISSUE 16. Do Stepchildren Need Special Policies and Programs on
    Their Behalf?**   292

YES: Margaret Crosbie-Burnett and Ada Skyles, from "Stepchildren in Schools and Colleges: Recommendations for Educational Policy Changes," *Family Relations*   294

NO: Lawrence H. Ganong and Marilyn Coleman, from "A Comparison of Clinical and Empirical Literature on Children in Stepfamilies," *Journal of Marriage and the Family*   301

Margaret Crosbie-Burnett, associate professor of education and psychology, and Ada Skyles, a J.D. candidate, maintain that stepchildren face uniquely stressful problems related to their family situations that require special educational policies and programs. Professors of family studies Lawrence H. Ganong and Marilyn Coleman argue that the information currently available on stepchildren and their families is theoretically and methodologically flawed. As a consequence, inaccurate images of stepchildren and their families as deviant and dysfunctional are perpetuated.

ISSUE 17. Is the Success of Remarriage Doomed?   310

YES: Andrew Cherlin, from "Remarriage as an Incomplete Institution," *American Journal of Sociology*   312

NO: Ann Goetting, from "The Six Stations of Remarriage: Developmental Tasks of Remarriage After Divorce," *Family Relations*   326

Sociologist Andrew Cherlin discusses why remarriage is less successful than marriage and proposes that this is primarily because remarriage in its present form has not been accepted by society. Professor of sociology Ann Goetting argues that remarriage is a process and that for it to be successful it must progress through a series of developmental stages.

Contributors   340
Index   346

INTRODUCTION

The Study of Marriage and the Family

Gloria W. Bird

Michael J. Sporakowski

Most of us were raised in families and have had the chance to observe a variety of marriages and families throughout our lives—kin, friends, neighbors, and so on. This is valuable life experience that generally serves us well as we relate to others. Attempts to take this personal life experience, however, and apply it to all American families distorts the reality of what *most* marriages and families are like. Some of our own memories and hopes of "the way things ought to be" mesh with what we actually see around us, creating assumptions that are selective and generally inaccurate.

HISTORY OF FAMILY STUDIES

Serious study of marriage and family life began only relatively recently, although readings and commentaries about marriage and family life can be traced throughout much of recorded history in religious and other historical literature. Family scientists now rely on a multitude of research methods, including mailed surveys, personal interviews, observational studies, and content analysis of historical documents, to produce accurate information about what families are like today and were like in the past. One of the more recent trends is the study of family history through the examination of personal journals and diaries, census reports, and other artifacts of earlier times. By these means we have gained valuable insights into American family life from the early 1600s through the 1800s. These attempts to reconstruct an accurate historical record have resulted in a greater understanding of American families over the past three centuries.

Not only are there family sociologists, but psychologists, economists, lawyers, and physicians also have groups within their larger professional organizations that specialize in research, counseling, and other work with families. The contributions to the field by this varied group of professionals continue to be useful in theory development and practical application, as evidenced by some of the many articles offered in such journals as *Journal of Marriage and the Family, American Journal of Family Therapy, Journal of Divorce and Remarriage, Family Law Quarterly,* and *Marriage and Family Review.*

Anthropologists, psychologists, sociologists, and historians have all addressed aspects of marriage and family development both within the United States and internationally. Examples of these works include Edward Westermarck's *A History of Human Marriage* (1896) and G. E. Howard's *A History of Matrimonial Institutions* (1904). Both of these books looked at marriage from a longitudinal perspective. Works by Bronislaw Malinowski and Margaret Mead provided insight into the cultural variations of marriages and families around the world. Havelock Ellis and Sigmund Freud provided not only cross-cultural but also intrapersonal perspectives on how families function.

Family-focused literature in the 1920s, 1930s, and 1940s in the United States explored issues such as intermarriage, the effects of the Great Depression on families, and factors promoting marital success and failure. More recently, family demography, marriage and family therapy, family life education, and family research have been prominent topics in the literature.

FAMILY STUDIES AS A FORMAL DISCIPLINE

Since the beginning of the 1960s there has been a concerted effort to organize and synthesize each decade of research on marriage and family life. In 1964, Harold Christensen edited a *Handbook of Marriage and the Family*, which provided, among other things, a historical perspective on the evolution of the marriage and family field. More recently, the *Journal of Marriage and the Family* published three decade reviews that examine what has occurred in the marriage and family field during the periods of 1960–1969, 1970–1979, and 1980–1989. In 1987, Marvin Sussman and Suzanne Steinmetz edited a second *Handbook on Marriage and the Family*. All the chapters in this book were written by prominent scholars on their specialized areas of family studies.

Decade Reviews: 1970–1990
The first decade review (1970) was edited by Carl Broderick. He asked the authors to provide an overview of preselected, family-relevant topics. In the 1980 review, sociologist Felix Berardo introduced the volume by discussing Clark Vincent's 1966 opinion that the family acts as a sponge, adapting to what is going on in the larger society for the benefit of its members, and mediating between individual family members and the larger society. Many of the topics covered in this second review, such as family violence, sex roles, family stress and coping, and nontraditional family forms, were relatively new to the family field, but had been researched often in the 1970s. The third decade review (1990), edited by Alan Booth, begins with Felix Berardo's commentary on trends in family research during the 1980s and suggestions for future research directions.

Notable Changes Since 1960
In the latest decade review the following changes were noted: sex roles became gender roles, reflecting more recent changes in thinking and language; domestic violence, which had previously focused on wife abuse, expanded to include the specific topic of child sexual abuse; racial and cultural family variations more specifically concentrated on black and His-

panic families; articles on divorce and remarriage were more numerous; and issues such as kinship, cross-societal research, family power, and family stress and coping were integrated into other topic areas and not presented separately. Topical additions to the 1990 review include religion and families, feminism, parental and nonparental child care, family policy, family economic stress, and family relationships in later life.

FAMILY STUDIES—AN EVOLVING DISCIPLINE

The National Council on Family Relations (NCFR) is the primary professional organization for researchers, educators, therapists, and others who study and provide services to families. It was organized in 1938 as an interdisciplinary professional association interested in family research, education, counseling, and social action. The NCFR continues to be vital today, with membership that uniquely cuts across lines of professional training and education with integrative programs, publications, and public policy actions for the benefit of families.

Sociologist Wesley R. Burr, in his 1982 NCFR presidential address, discussed the evolution of the identity of the family as a profession, from the contributions of Ernest Groves, credited with teaching the first college-level course on marriage and the family in Boston in the 1930s, through the development and proliferation of graduate programs related to family, and most recently through the throes of the professional identity struggles the NCFR and related organizations have been experiencing. Burr pushed very hard for the use of *famology* as the best word to describe the study of the family. His presentation defended the maturity of the field of study and suggested that it had met all of the criteria that would make it distinctive in the larger world of disciplines and professions. Although there is general agreement that the study of marriage and the family is indeed a discipline, the issue of what to call this discipline is not yet resolved. Various groups within the NCFR promote various names, including famology, family studies, and family science.

RECENT TRENDS IN AMERICAN FAMILY LIFE

Living Arrangements
The 1990 census provides recent data that attest to the continuing demographic changes in American family life. For example, more individuals now postpone marriage until later in life, but cohabitation has increased among adults aged 21 to 35. There seems to be a need among these individuals for intimate relationships, but not necessarily within the bounds of marriage.

Also, more young adults aged 18 to 24 are choosing to live with their parents—an increase of over 25 percent since 1960. Some young people are finding that their jobs do not pay well enough to allow independent living arrangements and that parents may actually make good housemates. Also, with the rising costs of higher education, some young adults are living with their parents and attending colleges and universities closer to home.

Furthermore, census figures show an increase in the number of adults aged 25 to 34 who live with their parents. Some move home out of economic necessity after going through a divorce—sometimes accompanied by young children. Or, like younger adults, they are single and find that their paychecks are inadequate to meet living expenses.

Marriage and Divorce

The median age of marriage is now 26 years for men and 24 years for women. Postponement of marriage is related to other trends, such as the increased number of people who are seeking advanced education and higher annual incomes. More highly educated women postpone marriage and, when they do marry, form dual-career families. These women also delay childbearing and have fewer children than do other women. The average family today is smaller than ever before—less than two children per family.

Another trend that affects marriage and family life is the growing divorce rate, which remains high despite a recent leveling off in the late 1980s. It is projected that one-half to two-thirds of today's marriages will eventually end in divorce. One result of divorce is more single-parent families. This family type has increased by 36 percent since 1980, and women and children make up the vast majority of such families. Because women often have less education than their husbands and earn less money than men do, and because divorced fathers generally pay child support for an average of about two years, many single-parent families are at greater risk of economic hardship than are other families.

Single and Working Mothers

Black women are especially vulnerable to economic pressures due to their high rate of out-of-wedlock childbearing as well as their greater propensity to live in single-parent families than to marry. All unwed mothers are less disposed than were their counterparts in the 1970s to wed the fathers of their children. Many say that they would rather live as single parents than risk marriage and later divorce to men they describe as unprepared for marriage and family life. In single-parent households, where 26 percent of children under age 18 now reside, 39 percent live with a divorced parent (usually the mother) and 31 percent live with a parent who has never married (also usually the mother). Families headed by women who have never married increased 1,000 percent during the past two decades.

The majority of mothers today are employed outside the home. In fact, the largest increases in employed mothers have been among those families with preschool children. In addition to the increasing numbers of single-parent and dual-worker families, the high rate of divorce has led some social commentators to express special concern for the children in today's families and to question whether we as a society are doing enough to help families with children.

IMPLICATIONS OF CHANGE IN AMERICAN FAMILIES

Though it is becoming increasingly popular to discuss the "traditional" American family as being an endangered entity, the truth is that American families have been changing since the first settlers arrived on the shores of the New World. Unlike today, however, there used to be laws that clearly defined and enforced the roles of family members. Family matters were actually seen as community matters—the greater good outweighed individual needs and desires.

In the book *Habits of the Heart: Individualism and Commitment in American Life* (1985), sociologists Bellah, Madsen, Sullivan, Swidler, and Tipton describe individuals today as caring less about community and family matters and being more concerned with personal autonomy. The authors point out that because marriage and family life are now typically viewed as sources of emotional fulfillment rather than of instrumental need and moral obligation, marriages, families, and communities are in danger of becoming increasingly unstable. Bellah and his colleagues agree that the people interviewed for their book discussed their marriages in the context of how they were different from those of their parents. Those interviewed found that expressing intimacy, sharing feelings, and solving marital problems was much easier for them than they perceived it was for their parents. Yet, the overall assessment of these authors was one of caution about individual autonomy, fragile and vulnerable relationships, and waning commitment to community.

An opposing view is offered by sociologist Francesca Cancian in *Love in America: Gender and Self-Development* (1987). Cancian traces the changing definitions of love across time in America and concludes that the current conception of love involves a "weness"—the expectation that individuals must be connected to others for maximum well-being. She also discusses ways that couples are bonded and provides research findings to support her thesis. Cancian contends that individualism and autonomy were ideals of the late 1970s and early 1980s that were never really reached. More recently she has seen a movement toward commitment to relationships through marriage, kinship, friendship, and community.

Recent polls evidence the changes in how Americans view marriage and family life. They indicate that men are more committed than in the past to family roles and to women's needs in the workplace, and that women are more willing to negotiate gender roles within the family, though they still feel stress because husbands do not share as much of the housework and child care as is needed (Virginia Slims/Roper, 1990). Polls also provide evidence of some stability in American family life. For example, most American families make major efforts to eat their evening meals together, and community volunteerism in the United States has become prominent (New York Times/ CBS News, 1991).

The two recent books we have mentioned and the current polls are but a few examples of the many informational sources on the topic of American families that are published each year. Changing trends in marriage and family life have become points of contention between various private and public organizations and among the major political groups, and the ensuing debates are becoming increasingly bitter.

Those who seek a return to "true family values," for example, characterize present families as rootless, troubled, and often dysfunctional. This group sometimes describes the parents within what they term "broken" or "unhealthy" families as selfish, undisciplined, and lacking in commitment, and sometimes even portray such family members as bereft of spiritual values. Others deplore this labeling of individuals and families as biased and unscientific and as based on nostalgia rather than on what family life was really like in the past. This camp argues for the importance of acknowledging the adaptive strengths of today's diverse family forms and for helping such families find the resources to cope with contemporary life.

CONTEMPORARY ISSUES IN MARRIAGE AND THE FAMILY

Sociologists, psychologists, historians, and other professionally trained students of family studies are becoming increasingly concerned with providing accurate accounts of what marriage and family life is like today as well as giving accurate descriptions of families from a historical perspective. Each group necessarily proceeds from their own unique view of the world, providing different and sometimes contradictory answers to the same questions. In professional circles as well as among the larger public audience, books, research studies, speeches, and other informational presentations are more often being debated and argued.

The self-appointed family authority, typically with little or no formal training, who "tells it like it is," will find it more difficult to find a believing audience in the 1990s. The family field is comprised of individuals with various kinds of expertise and training; however, the vast majority of these diverse groups is interested in research-based conclusions that have application to "real-life families."

The issues in this book are now being discussed and debated among people considering the current state of marriage and the family. Some of the questions posed may not have been previously seen by readers as having multiple sides to them. Part of your task is to critically examine your thinking about these issues in light of contemporary knowledge. Sometimes the readings will reinforce what you believe; other times you may find yourself rethinking your position; and sometimes you may wish to read more about a particular topic before you form your final opinion.

Steiner/DPG

PART 1

Gender Roles and Family Relationships

Society's view of the family and the roles each member must assume is constantly changing. Basic questions on the nature of gender differences lead to specific questions on the expected behaviors of men and women within the familial boundaries. For example, is male superiority genetically determined, or does society perpetuate attitudes and stereotypes that subordinate women? Are men becoming more involved with their families, or do financial responsibilities still take precedence in men's lives? Are expectations of women to foster social relationships with extended family and friends harmful or beneficial to their physical and emotional well-being? The discussions in this section will help define what it means to be male and female in today's society.

Are Gender Differences Present at Birth?

Are Women Only Victims in Their Roles as Social Support Providers?

Have Men's Family Roles Changed?

ISSUE 1

Are Gender Differences Present at Birth?

YES: Steven Goldberg, from "Reaffirming the Obvious," *Society* (September/October 1986)

NO: Cynthia Fuchs Epstein, from "Inevitabilities of Prejudice," *Society* (September/October 1986)

ISSUE SUMMARY

YES: Sociologist Steven Goldberg argues that there are basic biological differences between women and men that explain the emotions and behaviors common to each, and that physiological differences lead men to do whatever is necessary to attain dominance in society.
NO: Sociologist Cynthia Fuchs Epstein counters that Goldberg's thesis ignores the pervasive societal constraints on women's lives as well as evidence of historical changes in women's statuses and roles despite such constraints.

Are women and men different? Most people now agree that women and men are indeed different, though they share many of the same characteristics and behaviors. The primary argument currently centers on what is most responsible for the differences between the sexes: anatomical, chromosomal, and hormonal features that are specific to each sex or learned and socially reinforced feminine and masculine behaviors?

Those who maintain that cultural influences are predominantly responsible for gender differences assume that women and men are born with relatively equal potentials for most behavior—that how people behave is ultimately influenced by others around them, such as parents, teachers, friends, and peers, as well as by the personal choices they make in particular life situations. Those who insist that biology sufficiently explains human behavior reject the influence of nurturing and personal choice and extol the pervasive involvement of genes and hormones in determining gender differences.

In the past few years, as the division between these two camps of theorists and researchers has widened, a language refinement has occurred that takes ideological and empirical differences into consideration. The terms *sex* and *gender* have been redefined so that *sex* is now used to indicate the biological or physiological characteristics unique to being either male or female. *Gender,* in contrast, is used to describe the cultural and psychological aspects of being male or female. So today it is more appropriate to discuss gender roles rather than sex roles when referring to the rules and norms that are learned through the socialization process—the preferred ways for men and women to behave as prescribed by society. The term *sex difference* is more often reserved for instances when people are referring to biological differences between women and men.

Societies often have sets of opinions and beliefs about what it means to be male and female called "gender belief systems." These systems include attitudes about appropriate roles and behaviors for women and men. They also perpetuate some negative stereotypes, such as women cannot be effective leaders and men are incapable of preparing meals or caring for children, that have been disproved by many empirical studies. Nevertheless, individuals who deviate from what is expected according to these prevailing gender beliefs are often punished or censured in some way. Though gender belief systems are slow to change, they incorporate new information from time to time. For example, in the United States it is much more acceptable for women to be in the labor force today; there is increasing pressure for men to be more involved in childrearing; and women are more likely now than in the past to negotiate for greater equity at home and at work.

In the following selections, Steven Goldberg argues that there are obvious immutable differences between women and men that are driven by biological destiny. These differences, explains Goldberg, manifest themselves in the inevitable social dominance of men over women. Men are psycho-physiologically driven to seek out high-status positions in society and are genetically predisposed to sacrifice all other rewards, including personal and family satisfactions, to achieve status and dominance in society.

Cynthia Fuchs Epstein counters that the historical dominance of men over women is not a natural phenomenon but a social exaggeration. She challenges Goldberg to reevaluate his thesis in light of recent research findings and the obvious movement of women into more powerful societal positions. Women, contends Epstein, have made impressive advances despite centuries of disadvantage and pervasive legal, educational, and social barriers to their progress.

YES   Steven Goldberg

REAFFIRMING THE OBVIOUS

That anyone doubted it, was astonishing from the start. All experience and observation seemed to attest to the presence of core-deep differences between men and women, differences of temperament and emotion we call masculinity and femininity. All analyses of such differences were, it seemed obvious, empty or incoherent unless they saw the differences as related to substrative differences between men and women, differences that gave masculine and feminine direction to the emotions and behavior of men and women. The question to be answered, it seemed, was how these substrative differences manifest themselves on a social and institutional level—not whether the differences exist.

Yet there it was. A generation of educated people was jettisoning the evidence of both experience and intellect in order to propound a clearly indefensible hypothesis: emotional and behavioral differences between men and women, and the social expectations associated with them, are primarily the result of environmental factors to which physiology is of little relevance. Proponents supported this view with arguments ranging from the confused to the misrepresentative. Individuals who are exceptions were invoked as somehow refuting the possibility of physiological roots of behavior, a maneuver that makes about as much sense as arguing that a six-foot-tall woman somehow demonstrates the social causation of height. Myths about matriarchies were introduced as historical evidence, an approach that would justify a belief in cyclopses. The primary argument supporting this view, an argument accepted even in college textbooks, was the argument that emotional and behavioral differences between men and women were caused primarily by socialization.

The central problem with this approach is that it does not explain anything; it merely begs the question: Why does not one of the thousands of disparate societies on which we have evidence reverse male and female expectations? Why does every society from that of the Pygmy to that of the

Published by permission of Transaction Publishers from *Society*, vol. 23, no. 6. Copyright © 1986 by Transaction Publishers.

Swede associate dominance and attainment with males? To say that males are more aggressive because they have been socialized that way is like saying that men can grow moustaches because boys have been socialized toward that end. There is no outside experimenter for society, setting up whatever rules seem desirable. Possible social values are limited by observation of reality; if male physiology is such that males have a lower threshold for the elicitation of dominance behavior, then social expectations denying this cannot develop.

Ten years ago it was not clear to all that there had never been a society reversing the sexual expectations I discuss. Social science texts, out of ignorance or tendentiousness, misrepresented ethnographic studies and asserted the existence of societies that reversed the sexual expectations. Recourse to the original ethnography on every alleged exception demonstrated beyond the possibility of reasonable dispute that not one of the thousands of societies (past and present) on which we have any sort of evidence lacks any of three institutions: patriarchy, male attainment, and male dominance.

All societies that have ever existed have associated political dominance with males and have been ruled by hierarchies overwhelmingly dominated by men. A society may have a titular queen or a powerful queen when no royal male is available; there were more female heads of state in the first two-thirds of the sixteenth century than the first two-thirds of the twentieth. An occasional woman may gain the highest position in a modern state; the other eighteen ministers in Golda Meir's cabinet, and all other Israeli prime ministers, were male. In every society from the most primitive to the most modern—whatever the yardstick—it is the case that political dominance, in particular, and hierarchical dominance, in general, are overwhelmingly in the hands of men.

Whatever the nonmaternal roles that are given highest status—whichever these are and whatever the reasons they are given high status in any given society—these roles are associated with males. A modern example describes the situation that obtains in every society: if being a medical doctor is given high status (as in the United States), most doctors are male; if being an engineer is given high status and being a doctor relatively low status (as in the Soviet Union), then most engineers are male and most nonhierarchical doctors may be female. There are societies—although modern societies, by their nature, could not be among them—in which women perform objectively far more important economic functions while working harder and longer outside the home than do men. Indeed, save for political and hierarchical leadership, internal and external security, and nurturance of the young, every task is seen as male in some societies and female in others. However, in every society that which is given highest status is associated with men. It is tempting to explain this as a residue of male political dominance, but this view gets things backwards. Male roles do not have high status because they are male; nor do high-status roles have high status because they are male. Many male roles have low status and many low-status roles are male. High-status roles are male because they have (for different reasons in different societies) high status; this high-status motivates males to attain the roles—for psychophysiological reasons— more strongly than it does females (statistically-speaking). Social expectations conform to limits set by this reality.

The emotions of both males and females of all societies associate dominance with the male in male-female relationships and encounters. The existence of this reality is evidenced by the ethnographies of every society; the observations and statements of the members of every society; the values, songs, and proverbs of every society; and, in our own society, also by feminists who abhor this reality and incorrectly attribute it primarily to social and environmental causes. We might argue that in the family the women of some or all societies have greater power, attributable to either a male abdication or a female psychological acuity that enables women to get around men. But the question relevant to universality is why both the men and women have the emotional expectation of a male dominance that must be gotten around.

The social sciences have discovered precious few nontrivial institutions that are both universal and sufficiently explicable with direct physiological evidence. The three institutions I discuss require explanation and this explanation must be simple. I mention this in anticipation of the inevitable, however wrongheaded, criticism that any physiologically-rooted theory is simplistic, determinist, or reductionist. Were we to attempt to explain variation in the forms of these institutions in physiological terms, an explanation would, in all likelihood, be simplistic. Physiology is in all likelihood irrelevant to differences between, say, American patriarchy and Arabic patriarchy. An explanation sufficient to explain the universal limits within which all variation takes place, if it is to be at all persuasive, requires a single factor common to, and imposing limits on, all societies that have ever existed. Indeed, the very extensiveness of the cross-cultural variation in most institutions emphasizes the need to explain why the institutions we discuss always work in the same direction. No reality is inevitable simply because it is universal, but when an institution is universal we must ask why. If the reason for universality is a physiological factor giving direction to the motivations that make us what we are, then we must entertain the possibility that the institution is an inevitable social resolution of the psychophysiological reality. . . .

Differences between the male and female endocrine/central nervous systems are such that—statistically speaking—males have a greater tendency to exhibit whatever behavior is necessary in any environment to attain dominance in hierarchies and male-female encounters and relationships, and a greater tendency to exhibit whatever behavior is necessary for attainment of nonmaternal status. Using somewhat unrigorous terms, we might say that males are more strongly motivated by the environmental presence of hierarchy, by a member of the other sex, or by status to do what is necessary to attain dominance. It is irrelevant whether we conceptualize this as a lower male threshold for the release of dominance behavior, a greater male drive for dominance, a greater male need for dominance, or a weaker male ego that needs shoring up by attainment of dominance and status. It is the reality of the male-female difference that matters, not the model used to explain the difference that any model must explain. Likewise, it is irrelevant why our species (and those from which we are descended) evolved the psychophysiological differentiation;

all that matters for an explanation of universality is that the differentiation exists. . . .

Physiology does not determine the actual behavior required for dominance and attainment in any given society: that is socially determined. What physiology accounts for is the male's greater willingness to sacrifice the rewards of other motivations—the desire for affection, health, family life, safety, relaxation, vacation and the like—in order to attain dominance and status. This model makes clear why physiology need not be considered in a causal analysis of the behavior of a given individual exception. At the same time physiology is necessary for an analysis of the existence on a societal level of the universal institutions I discuss. Even the effects of virtually pure physiology expect many exceptions (as the six-foot-tall woman demonstrates). Dominance motivation no doubt has other causes—experiential and familial—in addition to the physiological causes and, for the exception, these may counteract the physiological factors.

When we speak of an entire society, the law of large numbers becomes determinative. The statistical, continuous, and quantitative reality of the male's greater dominance tendency becomes concretized on the social level in absolute, discrete, and qualitative terms. The statistical reality of the male's greater aggression becomes in its pure and exaggerated form: "men are aggressive (or dominant); women are passive (or submissive)." This leads to discrimination, often for the woman who is an exception and occasionally for every woman. Discrimination is possible precisely because the statistical reality makes the exception an exception, exposed to the possibility of discrimination. The six-foot-tall girl who wishes she were short lives in a world of boys who are praised for being six feet tall.

As long as societies have hierarchies, differentiated statuses, and intermixing of men and women, they will possess the only environmental cues necessary to elicit greater dominance and attainment behavior from males. In utopian fantasy a society lacking hierarchy, status, and male-female relationships may be possible, but in the real world it is not. In the real world, societies have cultures. These cultures will value some things more than others and—particularly in the modern, bureaucratic society—some positions more than others. If male physiology is such that males are willing to sacrifice more for these things and positions, they will learn what is necessary and do what is necessary—whatever that may be in any given society—for dominance and attainment. There are other necessary conditions: it is not only gender that keeps a black woman from ruling the Republic of South Africa. Nevertheless, within any group possessing the other necessary conditions, dominance will go to those most willing to sacrifice for dominance and status (and social values will lead to such expectations). . . .

The male-female differentiation that I have discussed is the one for which the evidence is by far the most overwhelming. There are other differences that may well be functions of endocrine-central nervous system differentiation. The stereotype that sees logically abstract thinking as "thinking like a man" and psychological perception as "woman's intuition" without question reflect empirical realities; it is only the cause of these realities that is open to question. A score on the SAT mathematics aptitude section that puts a girl in the ninetieth percentile among girls places a boy in only the sixty-eighth percentile among boys; among mathematically-precocious students (thirteen years old), a score of 700 is thirteen times more likely to be attained by a boy than by a girl (with equal numbers of boys and girls with similar mathematical backgrounds taking the test). There also seems to be a linear relationship between the importance of logical abstraction to an area and the percentage of those at the highest levels who are men; there has never been a woman at the highest level of mathematics, chess, or composing music (which is not thought of as a macho enterprise), while there have been many women of genius in literature and the performing arts. . . .

Nothing I have written about patriarchy, male attainment, or male dominance implies (or precludes) males' better performing roles once they attain them. Whether the male tendencies increase performance or retard it is another issue (save for the fact that a position must be attained before it can be performed). Similarly, nothing I have written implies the desirability of any particular social or political program. "Is cannot imply ought," and no scientific analysis of how the world works can entail a subjective decision on which of two programs is preferable. We might accept all that I have written and see this as demonstrating the need for an equal rights law limiting the male physiological advantage for attainment. Or we might see the same evidence as justifying a socialization system that provides clear role models by emphasizing the sex differences I discuss. Science is silent on such a choice.

NO
Cynthia Fuchs Epstein

INEVITABILITIES OF PREJUDICE

Is there any reason to believe that patriarchy is more inevitable than anti-Semitism, child abuse, or any other mode of oppression that has been around for as long as anyone can remember? On the basis of his own experience, Aristotle believed that slavery was inevitable; and although it is still around in some countries, few reasonable people now believe it must be inevitable. Unfortunately, people with credentials for reasonableness, such as a new school of sociobiologists and their popularizers—among them Steven Goldberg—feel comfortable believing that the subordination of women is inevitable, programmed into human nature.

Many forms of oppression seem inevitable because they are so difficult to dislodge. History shows us that. It is easier to maintain oppression than to overthrow it. This is because when a group has a power advantage (which may emerge by chance, or historical accident), even if it is small, it may escalate rapidly if those in power can monopolize not only material resources but the avenues of communication as well. The Nazis did so effectively. Karl Marx cautioned that the owners of production were also the owners of the production of ideas. This means that the values and knowledge of a society usually reflect the views of those who rule, often by convincing those in subordinate statuses that they deserve what they get. The Nazis argued that they belonged to the "master race" and tried to build a science to prove it. They were less subtle than other rulers, but their case is instructive: beware the thesis of any powerful group that claims its power is derived solely from "divine right" or from its genes.

If anything is inevitable, it is change. Change in history is characteristic of human experience and reflects the human capacity to order and reorder it, to understand the processes of its ordering, and to sweep away old superstitions. As Robert K. Merton pointed out in the *American Journal of Sociology* in 1984: "What everyone should know from the history of thought is that what everyone knows turns out not to be so at all."

Some twelve years have passed since Steven Goldberg published his book, *The Inevitability of Patriarchy,* more than a decade which has produced thousands of studies of gender differences and similarities, an extensive reanalysis of the relationship and applicability of primate behavior to human behavior, and debate and analysis of sociobiological interpretation. Goldberg has offered us once again, a view of women's subordination as inevitable simply because it has always existed. The thesis, unchanged from his formulation of a decade ago, is uninformed about the rich body of scholarship that has been published—much of it disproving his assumptions about significant differences in men's and women's emotions, cognitive capacities, and situation in the structure of the social hierarchy. In these intervening years, there have also been changes in the statuses and roles of women in the United States and in other parts of the world—these also invalidate Goldberg's perspective on the constancy and universality of his observations about the subordination of women.

Women in the United States, as elsewhere, have been elected and appointed to positions of power. They have joined the ranks of the prestigious and the powerful in the domains of law and medicine, and are entering specialties and practices to which they were denied admission and discouraged from pursuing only a decade ago. Women are now judges at every level of the judiciary in the United States, as well as prosecutors in the courts engaging in adversarial and assertive behavior, exhibiting what may be termed as "dominant behavior." There is considerable evidence that women perform well, sometimes even better than do men, in examinations that determine admission to all fields in professional and graduate schools, where women constitute from a third to half of all students. Each year sees an increase in the number of women admitted to schools of engineering and science in spite of men's supposed greater social orientation toward careers in these fields.

Women have also become university professors and researchers and have thus been empowered to challenge many biased views about human nature and to fill gaps left by male scholars who have characteristically had little interest or inclination to do research in this field. Therefore, a revised view of what is "natural" or "inevitable" is part of the contemporary intellectual agenda.

Women are also making inroads in blue-collar technical work, heretofore denied them because of restrictions in apprenticeship programs made yet more difficult because of personal harassment. Women have experienced the same exclusionary mechanisms exercised against all minority groups who have had the audacity to compete with white males for the privileged positions guarded by "covenants" instituted by unions and ethnic clusters. According to a 1985 Rand Corporation research study by Linda Waite and Sue Berryman, *Women in Non-Traditional Occupations: Choice and Turnover*, women behave similarly to men in that they exhibit similar work force commitment and turnover rates once involved in nontraditional jobs such as those of the blue-collar crafts or in the army. These researchers emphasize that policies equalizing work conditions for men and women also equalize commitment to the job.

Increasing convergence of gender role behavior is also seen in studies of crime. Girls' crime rates show increasing similarity to that of boys. Girls and boys both commit violent crimes and exhibit increasingly similar criminal histories.

Certainly much of the challenge and change is due to the women's movement and the insistence of women on their rights to equality. Sizable numbers of women in every sphere of society have taken an aggressive role in contesting the domination of men in personal, political, and intellectual life. Given the short period of time in which women have been active on their own behalf and in which they have succeeded in engaging the support of sympathetic men, their strides have been great both with regard to social rank and intellectual accomplishment.

This movement has evolved within the historical context still affected by centuries of oppression that have created and perpetuated the sense that women's inequality is natural. Yet no society, no social group, and especially no ruling group, has ever left gender hierarchy (nor any other form of hierarchy) to nature. It has not been women's incompetence or inability to read a legal brief, to perform brain surgery, to predict a bull market, or to make an intonation to the gods that has kept them from interesting and highly paid jobs. The root of discrimination against women, preventing their access to a variety of fields, has been a rule system replete with severe punishments for those who deviate from "traditional" roles. Access is now achieved through political and social action, and not at all through genetic engineering.

Sociobiologists, on the other hand, argue that the division of labor by sex is a biological rather than a social response. If this were so, sex-role assignments would not have to be coercive. Social groups do not actually depend on instinct or physiology to enforce social arrangements because they cannot reliably do so. Societies assign groups to be responsible for such social needs as food, shelter, and child care; nowhere do they depend on nature to meet these requirements. The types of work that men and women perform in each society are stipulated by society, allowing few individuals to make choices outside the prescribed range. The assignments are justified on the basis of ideologies claiming that they are just and reflect popular, cultural opinions that the arrangement is good (or that, if not, little can be done about it).

Such ideologies and popular views suppose that a fit exists between the job and worker—a fit that makes sense. This argument relies on the maintenance of gender differences. Division according to sex is reinforced by requirements that men and women dress differently (whether it is to don the veil or a skirt if female; and trousers or a *doti* if male), learn different skills (women's literacy rates are considerably lower than those of males in the Third World; in the Western world males and females still are "encouraged" to choose "sex-appropriate" subjects) and engage in different forms of activity. Violators are punished for infractions. Sometimes a raised eyebrow will keep a woman in line; in the extreme she may even face being stoned to death or burned alive (as in the recent outbreak of deaths over dowries in India).

The literal binding of women's feet or the constraint of their minds by law and social custom is part of the process by which the gender division of human beings perpetuates a two-class system. The hierarchy is kept in place subtly by the insistence that people behave in the way society's opinion molders say they should. Thus, "ideal" roles mask real behavior. If we look at what men and women actually do—or *can* do without the distorting mirror of "ideal" gender roles—there is a fundamental similarity in personalities, behavior, and competence, given equal opportunity and social conditions. This is what the vast array of scholarship in psychology, sociology, and physiology has revealed in the last decade.

The research has been so extensive that it is impossible to summarize it here, although I shall review it in my forthcoming book, *Deceptive Distinctions*. By now, reviewers have reanalyzed thousands of articles on gender differences in every attribution and behavior imaginable. Despite what everyone believes, the similarities far outweigh the differences, even in considering aggression. As for the differences that census takers count —frequencies of women and men in different jobs and leisure activities—these clearly seem to be a result of social rules and habits. . . .

SEX HORMONES

. . . The question relevant to gender in society is the meaning of differences. For Goldberg, there is an unbroken line between "androgen binding sites in the brain, rough and tumble play in infants, and the male domination of state, industry and the nuclear family." E. O. Wilson is more cautious: "we can go against it if we wish, but only at the cost of some efficiency." If the hormone testosterone is supposed to make men aggressive and thus fit for public office, "female" hormones and the cycles attached to them are seen as detrimental to women's participation in public life. Edgar Berman, medical adviser to the late Senator (and Vice President) Hubert Humphrey, warned against women's participation in public affairs because of their "raging hormones." (Berman later published a book, *The Compleat Chauvinist*, in which he provided "biological evidence" for his views that menopausal women might create havoc if they held public office. Chapter titles from his book are: "The Brain That's Tame Lies Mainly in the Dame," "Testosterone, Hormone of Champions," and "Meno: The Pause that Depresses.") More recently, United Nations Ambassador Jeane Kirkpatrick reported that White House critics resisted her advancement into a higher political post because of the "temperament" she exhibited as a woman. No similar attributions of hormonal barriers to decision-making posts have been offered for men, although they have been excused from infidelity that is explained in popular culture by "male menopause," or by the sociobiologists who see it as an evolutionary response of men.

Many sociobiologists of the Wilson school have been committed to a model of inequity as a product of the natural order, arguing that male domination (patriarchy) is the most adaptive form of society, one that has conferred an advantage on individuals who operate according to its precepts. This thesis—put forth by E. O. Wilson, Lionel Tiger, Robin Fox, and Steven Goldberg—maintains that the near universality of male dominance arose because of the long dependence of the human infant and as a result of hunting and gathering, the early modes of obtaining food. Male-based cooperation was expressed through dominance relations. Men guarded the bands and thus ensured survival. There was pressure on men to perfect hunting skills and on women to stay home and mind the children. Each sex would have developed cognitive abilities attached to these activities. A socially imposed hierarchical division of labor between the sexes gradually became genetically fixed. . . .

MAN THE HUNTER; WOMAN THE GATHERER

In recent years, anthropologists have reevaluated the perspective of "man the hunter," which long served as a model of the origins of human society. . . . Using this model, primatologists and anthropologists such as Sherwood Washburn and Irven De Vore in *The Social Life of Early Man* and Desmond Morris in *The Naked Ape* had reasoned that hunting, a male activity, was a creative turning point in human evolution—that it required intelligence to plan and to stalk game, and to make hunting and other tools. It also required social bonding of men, the use of language to cooperate in the hunt, and then the distribution of meat and the development of tools for hunting and cutting the meat. According to Washburn and Lancaster in Lee and De Vore's *Man the Hunter*, "In a very real sense our intellect, interests, emotions and basic social life—all are evolutionary products of the success of the hunting adaptation." . . . The question is, what merit is there to the model and the explanations derived from it?

Among others, Frances Dahlbert in *Woman the Gatherer* suggests the account can only be considered a "just-so story" in the light of new scholarship. Beginning in the 1960s, research on primates, on hunter-gatherer societies, and archaeological and fossil records made this story obsolete. For example, the paleoanthropological myth of man the hunter was deflated when the "killer ape" of Robert Ardrey's *The Hunting Hypothesis*, the presumed australopithecine forebear of humans, turned out to be predomi-

nantly vegetarian. . . . A greater challenge to the man the hunter model came from Sally Linton in Sue Ellen Jacobs's *Women in Cross-Cultural Perspective*. Linton attacked the validity of theories of evolution that excluded or diminished women's contributions to human culture and society. She noted that women contribute the bulk of the diet in contemporary hunting and gathering societies, that small-game hunting practiced by both sexes preceded large-game hunting practiced by men, and that females as well as males probably devised tools for their hunting and gathering and some sort of carrying sling or net to carry babies. According to this view, the collaboration and cooperation of women was probably as important to the development of culture as that of men. . . .

People persist in wanting to view the world in terms of sex differences. They insist that individuals conform to ideal roles and turn away from their real roles, common interests, and goals, and from their mutual fate. These people disregard the obvious truth that most things that most people do most of the time can be performed equally well by either sex. The persistence of the view, as well as the persistence of physical and symbolic sex segregation, is created and maintained for a purpose, which is to maintain the privileges of men who predictably resist claims to the contrary. I suspect that the debates will continue and may do so as long as one group derives advantage from suppressing another. But evidence is mounting that supports equality between the sexes and which no truly reasonable people can continue to deny.

POSTSCRIPT

Are Gender Differences Present at Birth?

Are women's and men's roles and statuses the products of a natural, biological order or are they due to the persistence of a cultural perspective that excludes and devalues women's contributions to society? Goldberg maintains that his book *The Inevitability of Patriarchy* (William Morrow, 1973), published almost 20 years ago, is still relevant to life in the 1990s. Over the intervening years, explains Goldberg, nothing has changed to shake the main focus of his argument that male dominance is inevitable and universal. According to Goldberg, the few women who display leadership characteristics are only occasional anomalies in a centuries-old pattern of male dominance. Attempts to socialize men and women into more egalitarian roles only serve to mask the realities of biological determinism. These attempts are not realistic, nor are they necessarily in the best interests of society.

Epstein derides Goldberg's thesis and claims that his book is dated. She points out that thousands of studies have been completed since Goldberg's book was published that suggest how women's roles have begun to change. Women are now better educated than they have ever been, and such large numbers of women are engaged in economic, educational, and judicial pursuits that it would be difficult to call their collective accomplishments occasional or minimal. Epstein urges readers to consider the structural constraints on women's progress through the ages.

Are there signs that women's and men's social roles are changing? According to a poll reported in the *Gallup Poll Monthly* (February 1990), younger men and women are dividing household chores, such as laundry, dishwashing, cooking, and cleaning, more equitably among themselves than did their fathers and mothers. Women are also protesting more about the unfairness of the current gender belief system. The pollsters asked social historian Donald Bell, author of *Being a Man: The Paradox of Masculinity* (Harcourt Brace Jovanovich, 1984), and sociologist Pepper Schwartz, coauthor with Philip Blumstein of *American Couples* (Paul R. Branch, 1985), for their comments on this and other recent social trends. They replied that women today are more likely to expect family and work roles to be equitable and to push for changes in that direction. "Women used to be too far down to see the ceiling. Now they're smarter, they understand the system better, and they don't feel they've gotten a fair deal," said Schwartz.

A recent Roper poll substantiates this perception. After interviewing 3,000 women nationwide, Bickley Townsend, a vice president in the Roper Organization, told BettiJane Levine of the *Los Angeles Times* (September 25, 1990) that women have two main issues that they are angry about. First, women believe that a "glass ceiling" and a sexist "old boy network" hold them back from making even greater career strides. They also believe that they are not being paid according to their worth. If they were, women say, the extra money would make their lives less stressful and more manageable. Second, women say that men do not share enough of the housework. They rank this issue as the "single biggest source of resentment" in their lives. Levine asked Ellen Galinsky of the Work and Family Institute for her comments on these poll results. Galinsky replied, "Men are getting angry, too. They say that anytime they do something, it gets criticized."

These comments signify that gender roles are changing. Change is typically accompanied by stress and resentment. Normalcy is resumed as people get used to the new ways of doing things. In this case, women are chafing at the traditional gender belief system, which forces them into work and family situations that cause role overload, anxiety, and frustration. They are lobbying supervisors at work and husbands at home for structural changes in the way roles are viewed and conditioned. Men in families and in the workplace are generally comfortable with tradition and show resistance to change.

According to the Roper poll, men do express empathy and support for women's positions and say that change is needed. As sociologist William Goode points out in "Why Men Resist," in Barrie Thorne and Marilyn Yolm, eds., *Rethinking the Family: Some Feminist Questions* (Longman, 1982), men see the problems but cannot quite bring themselves to change a system that favors them. Why should those in a traditionally superordinate societal position voluntarily take on more responsibilities and make changes that would add to their workloads?

Some questions regarding changing gender roles to consider are: What are the pluses and minuses of a more androgynous society? Are there other prevalent trends that support either gender equality or male superiority? In what ways does society perpetuate gender differences in the workplace, at home, and in the community? Who are some of the exemplary women and men from past or recent history who have modeled less stereotypically masculine or feminine gender roles? Did these individuals suffer any psychological, economic, or political costs because of the choices they made? What benefits did they gain?

SUGGESTED READINGS

C. F. Epstein, *Deceptive Distinctions: Sex, Gender, and the Social Order* (Yale University Press, 1988).

S. Ioanilli, "Changing Perspectives on a Man's World," *The Humanist* (January/February, 1990).

L. L. Lindsey, *Gender Roles: A Sociological Perspective* (Prentice Hall, 1990).

L. Thompson and A. Walker, "Gender in Families: Women and Men in Marriage, Work, and Parenthood," *Journal of Marriage and the Family*, 51 (1989): 845–871.

ISSUE 2

Are Women Only Victims in Their Roles as Social Support Providers?

YES: Deborah Belle, from "Gender Differences in the Social Moderators of Stress," in Rosalind Barnett et al., eds., *Gender and Stress* (The Free Press, 1987)

NO: Micaela di Leonardo, from "The Female World of Cards and Holidays: Women, Families, and the Work of Kinship," *Signs: Journal of Women in Culture and Society,* vol. 12, no. 3 (Spring 1987)

ISSUE SUMMARY

YES: Assistant professor of psychology Deborah Belle maintains that, in comparison to men, women are more highly involved as support providers. She claims that women often suffer from "support gap" stress, which is fatigue, anxiety, and depression caused by giving more support than they receive.

NO: Micaela di Leonardo, an associate professor of anthropology and women's studies, asserts that women's involvement with kin and friends, despite its drawbacks, provides them with satisfaction as well as power within the family.

In earlier times, before U.S. education and health care systems and the service industries became institutionalized, women were regularly relied upon to deliver babies, care for the sick, and provide whatever emotional support was needed to keep families, neighbors, and communities functioning. Women of the middle class often formed women's clubs, which bonded their kin and friend networks into a cohesive body that operated for the collective good. Regardless of race or class, women's friendships were typically warm and affectionate as well as instrumentally supportive. The diaries and letters of some of these women of earlier generations indicate that women's roles as nurturers and social support providers were burdensome but also critically important to personal and family well-being.

In more modern times the focus of women's support has been redefined and has shifted from the broader neighborhood and community perspective to a narrower family perspective. In the nuclear family, as the roles of mother and wife have grown to incorporate expectations for employment outside the home and as visits with and aid to friends and kin have become more of a choice than a "must," the value of such roles has diminished or at least has been questioned.

The woman who works an eight-hour day and then goes home to prepare dinner and take care of parenting responsibilities without much support from her husband is also the person who usually takes care of social, kin, and friend obligations. Because tending to this group of people, called the *social support network*, has in the past been seen as having only positive psychological and physical health benefits for women, and because women's roles have traditionally included this expectation for caregiving, very few people have suggested that any negative aspects exist. Until a handful of recent studies began to find detrimental consequences for such women, guilt was usually the only negative feeling associated with obligatory caregiving that implied such expectations might contain some elements of burden and risk.

One recent study pertaining to women and social support was reported by Mary Ann Stripling and Gloria W. Bird at the 1990 annual meeting of the National Council on Family Relations. They surveyed a sample of 277 employed women in intact marriages. The average respondent had two children and was employed 43 hours per week. Women who were under greater pressure from the demands of job and family roles indicated that they found it difficult to maintain sources of social support. For this group of women, maintaining a social support network was costly in terms of time depletion, physical energy loss, and the psychological burden involved in taking on the problems and attendant emotional pain of others. Women who are employed in demanding jobs and who also have heavy family responsibilities, conclude Stripling and Bird, may not be able to reach out to others in their social network.

In the following selections, Deborah Belle compares women's to men's involvement in social support networks and discusses gender differences in the costs and benefits of such caregiving. After exploring the positive and negative consequences of social network obligations, she cautions that for many women the negatives far outweigh any derived satisfactions. Micaela di Leonardo says that kin work, such as paying visits, writing letters, making phone calls, giving gifts, and organizing family events, is a valuable asset for women. She asserts that kin work keeps nuclear families connected to other nuclear families. Moreover, she emphasizes that such work takes skill and time, and that the women who do it gain power and satisfaction from it.

YES

Deborah Belle

GENDER DIFFERENCES IN THE SOCIAL MODERATORS OF STRESS

Involvement in supportive human relationships has been hypothesized to protect stressed individuals against a variety of ills, from depression (Belle, 1982a; Brown, Bhrolchain, & Harris, 1975; Pearlin & Johnson, 1977) to complications of pregnancy (Barrera & Balls, 1983; Nuckolls, Cassell, & Kaplan, 1972) to ill health following job loss (Gore, 1978). Emotionally intimate, confiding relationships appear to be particularly powerful in some circumstances (Brown et al., 1975; Lowenthal & Haven, 1968), while less intimate connections with acquaintances, workmates, and neighbors are often also associated with positive outcomes (Miller & Ingham, 1976; Pearlin & Johnson, 1977). Theorists have argued that members of our social networks can provide us with social support resources such as assistance in problem solving and reassurance of worth, and can support a "repertoire of satisfactory social identities" (Hirsch, 1981, p. 163) that are critical to our self-concept and self-esteem. Such resources, in turn, help to prevent demoralization in times of stress, increase our options when confronting change and loss, and often facilitate a more active style of problem solving (Antonucci & Depner, 1982; Cobb, 1976; Hirsch, 1981).

Social networks can also have negative impacts on individuals, as several recent studies have demonstrated (Belle, 1982a, 1982b; Cohler & Lieberman, 1980; Eckenrode & Gore, 1981; Fiore, Becker, & Coppel, 1983; Fischer, 1982; Kessler & McLeod, 1984; Riley & Eckenrode, 1986; Rook, 1984; Wahler, 1980). The theoretical links between the social network and stress reactions have been less fully developed than those between the social network and beneficial social support.

Research does suggest that networks can create or exacerbate psychological distress when network members convey disrespect or disapproval, betray confidences, or fail to fulfill expectations for aid (Belle, 1982a; Fiore et al., 1983; Wahler, 1980), when network members place heavy demands on individuals to provide assistance and support (Cohler & Lieberman, 1980;

Stack, 1974), and when the stressful life circumstances of network members produce a "contagion of stress" (Wilkins, 1974) from sufferer to network member (Eckenrode & Gore, 1981; Belle, 1982a). As I have argued elsewhere, "one cannot receive support without also risking the costs of rejection, betrayal, burdensome dependence, and vicarious pain" (Belle, 1982a, p. 143). Studies that have separated the social network into stressful and supportive components have found evidence that the stressful components are actually more strongly related to mental health status than are the supportive ones (Belle, 1982a; Fiore, Becker, & Coppel, 1983; Rook, 1984).

Furthermore, research suggests that the supportive aspects of social ties are more pronounced among those from subgroups favored with high levels of personal resources, such as income, education, and internal locus of control (Eckenrode, 1983; Lefcourt, Martin, & Saleh, 1984; Sandler & Lakey, 1982), while the costs of social ties are greater among those with fewer such resources (Belle, 1983; Riley & Eckenrode, 1986). For instance, in a recent study of the impact of social ties on women with differing levels of material and psychological resources, Riley and Eckenrode found that maintaining a large support network was beneficial only for the women with higher levels of resources. Such networks actually appeared more harmful than helpful for low-resource women, who presumably had greater difficulty in responding to the needs of network members and who were more distressed by the stressful experiences of network members than were high-resource women.

While research on the social network as a stress moderator has proliferated in recent years, gender differences in this area have received little attention. This is surprising, since gender differences in interpersonal behavior and interpersonal relationships are evident throughout the life cycle, suggesting that men and women differ in the ways they participate in social relationships and in the resources they seek in such relationships. Throughout life, the norms for appropriate male behavior tend to promote self-reliance and inhibit emotional expressiveness, self-disclosure, and help-seeking (DePaulo, 1982; Jourard, 1971; Lowenthal & Haven, 1968), while females are encouraged to value close relationships and even to define themselves in terms of the close relationships in which they participate (Chodorow, 1974; Gilligan, 1982; Miller, 1976). Given such differences, it is likely that social moderators of stress function differently for males and females. . . .

PARTICIPATION IN SOCIAL NETWORKS

Some researchers have characterized male participation in social networks across the life cycle as more "extensive" but less "intensive" than that of females. There is ample evidence that males tend to participate in more activity-focused relationships than do females, while females at all ages maintain more emotionally intimate relationships than do males. . . .

The relative size of men's and women's networks seems to be strongly affected by many factors. Fischer (1982) found, for instance, that having children restricted the social involvements of mothers more than those of fathers. Mothers more than fathers differed from childless adults in having fewer friends and associates, fewer social activities, less reliable social supports, and more localized networks.

Age and ill health, however, restricted the size of men's networks more than those of women. Social class and employment status have also been shown to affect differentially the size of men's and women's networks (Booth, 1972; Depner & Ingersoll, 1982; Lowenthal & Haven, 1968).

While the relative size of men's and women's networks varies with many factors, women's greater investment in close, confiding relationships seems to endure throughout life. . . . Candy, Troll, and Levy (1981), in an exploration of friendship among women from age 14 to 80, were struck by the consistency with which disclosing private feelings and offering emotional and instrumental support were named as functions of women's friendships. Booth and Hess (1974) found that women's interactions were more dyadic and intimate and that women seemed to have more close personal relationships than did men. In middle age and old age, women are more likely than men to have close relationships (Depner & Ingersoll, 1982) and confidants (Lowenthal & Haven, 1968).

While women's relationships tend to emphasize emotional intimacy, men's friendships tend to center around shared activities and experiences, such as sports (Caldwell & Peplau, 1982; Weiss & Lowenthal, 1975), repeating the gender differences observed in childhood.

MOBILIZATION OF SUPPORT IN TIMES OF STRESS

Throughout the life cycle, females show a greater propensity to mobilize social supports in times of stress. Females are more likely than males to seek out such support, to receive such support, and to be pleased with the support they receive.

In childhood, girls are more likely than boys to seek help when facing problems (Nelson-LeGall, Gumerman, & Scott-Jones, 1983) and are more likely to confide their experiences to at least one other person than are boys (Belle & Longfellow, 1984). In a study of 8- to 15-year-old children whose parents had divorced, Wolchik, Sandler, and Braver (1984) found that girls reported more family members who provided emotional support and positive feedback and more individuals from outside the family who provided advice, goods and services, and supportive feedback than did boys. Girls also felt more positively than did boys about the individuals who provided this support.

Among adolescents, girls name more informal sources of support, such as friends and other adults, than do boys (Cauce, Felner, & Primavera, 1982) and are more likely to turn to their peers for support than are boys (Burke & Weir, 1978). Among college students, females report more available helpers, receive more support, and rate other people more helpful in dealing with problematic events than do males (Cohen, McGowan, Fooskas, & Rose, 1984). . . .

Women were more likely than men to utilize both formal and informal sources of help, more likely than men to turn to more than one friend or family member in times of crisis, and more likely to turn to friends and to children in times of unhappiness.

What is most striking about men's mobilization of support is that it is so heavily focused on one support provider—the wife. Among an elderly population sample, wives were the most frequently mentioned confidants of men, while women were about twice as likely as men to mention a child or other relative and more likely to name a friend as a confidant (Lowenthal & Haven, 1968). Veroff, Douvan, and Kulka (1981) found that married men were more likely than married women to turn solely to their spouses in times of stress. Even following divorce, men were significantly more likely than women to report that in the ideal situation the most helpful person to them would be their spouse (Chiriboga et al., 1979).

Not only do men and women tend to differ in their utilization of potential support figures in times of stress, there is also suggestive evidence for gender differences in the particular support resources sought by men and women. . . . In a projective study with college students, only women envisioned a troubled person who confided in a friend as gaining relief from stress, enhanced insight, or strength through sharing her worry with the friend (Mark & Alper, 1985). Men, on the other hand, typically depicted the friend giving advice or the two friends working on a solution to the problem together. However, "none of the men imagined any kind of self-enhancement, growth, strengthening, or relief as a result of confiding" (p. 86). . . .

McMullen and Gross (1983), who conducted a major review of gender differences in help-seeking, concluded that "our culture has included help-seeking among the behaviors that are designated as more appropriate for females than males" (p. 251). Men may regard help-seeking as a threat to their competence or independence, while women may view help-seeking as a means of creating or sustaining interpersonal relationships, and thus a desirable experience in its own right (DePaulo, 1982).

Men may also refrain from help-seeking because of explicit social sanctions against such behavior, particularly in the workplace. Weiss (1985) found in an interview study of upper-income men in administrative and business-related occupations that the occupational setting seemed to prohibit or punish the display of emotions other than anger. "Failing to maintain the proper facade of self-assurance could be penalized in the world of work" (p. 57). For the men Weiss studied, this prohibition often seemed to extend beyond the workplace into the home, so that men concealed their "weaker" emotions from their wives and even from themselves.

McMullen and Gross (1983) have also argued that because help-seeking has been considered a feminine activity, and because the male role is more highly valued in our culture, there has probably been "a general cultural devaluation of this activity and the person who seeks help" (p. 252). As men and women increasingly move away from such traditional sex role norms, we may well see a lessening of the stigma against seeking help in times of stress and more appropriate help-seeking by both men and women (McMullen & Gross, 1983).

RESPONSE TO NETWORK MEMBERS WHO EXPERIENCE STRESS

Women's place in man's life cycle has been that of nurturer, caretaker, and helpmate, the weaver of those networks of relationships on which she in turn relies (Gilligan, 1982, p. 17).

Just as females are more frequent utilizers of social support, they appear to be utilized more often than males as *providers* of social support when others are under stress. Fischer (1982) found that while men and women tended to name persons of their own gender for most support, women were named disproportionately as counselors and companions by both men and women. In their family roles as wives, mothers, and "kin keepers," and in their community roles as neighbors and friends, women provide considerable social support to others. What has sometimes been called women's "expressive function" (Parsons & Bales, 1955) can also be viewed as the provision of social support to others (Vanfossen, 1981).

Within marriage, husbands more than wives report being understood and affirmed by their spouses (Campbell, Converse, & Rodgers, 1976; Vanfossen, 1981), and husbands have generally been found to confide in their wives more frequently than wives do in their husbands. . . . In a study of upper-income married men, Weiss (1985) found that, while husbands typically told their wives little of the events of the workday, men did communicate their feelings about their work through their moods and through the "leakage" of information, such as overheard telephone conversations. Thus wives could often guess the issues which were preoccupying their husbands, while at the same time they were discouraged from talking about them. Whatever the extent or nature of their confiding behavior, husbands are much more likely than wives to rely solely on the spouse as confidant, as discussed above (Veroff, Douvan, & Kulka, 1981).

While adult gender roles are changing to some extent, mothers still retain more responsibility for the care of children than do fathers, and are still named more frequently as confidants by children (Belle & Longfellow, 1984) and adolescents (Rivenbark, 1971). Hunter and Youniss (1982) found that mothers exceeded both fathers and friends as sources of inti-

macy and nurturance to children at the fourth-grade level, and studies have shown that mothers are major sources of advice, guidance, and intimacy to their adolescent children as well (Kandel & Lesser, 1972; Kon & Losenkov, 1978). Even when children are themselves adult, mothers may be more knowledgeable about and more emotionally involved in children's problems than are fathers (Loewenstein, 1984). . . .

Studies of black families, white working-class families, white ethnic families, and low-income families emphasize the importance of the instrumental assistance and emotional support shared among female kin, friends and neighbors, particularly around child rearing (Belle, 1982a; Cohler & Lieberman, 1980; McAdoo, 1980; Stack, 1974; Young & Willmott, 1957). The importance of such female networks in ensuring day-to-day survival and maintaining family solidarity has been noted by many.

There is also evidence that females tend to be more supportive friends than are males. Wheeler, Reis, and Nezlek (1983) found that among both male and female college seniors, loneliness was negatively related to the amount of time spent with females, while time spent with males did not appear to buffer loneliness. Only when the "meaningfulness" of interactions with males was taken into consideration did contact with males appear to stave off loneliness. In an ingenious role-play study of friendships (Caldwell & Peplau, 1982), women who role-played a friend calling to congratulate another on a recent success made more supportive statements than did men. They were more likely than men to say they were happy for the successful person, were more likely to express enthusiasm for the friend's success, and were more likely to ask about the friend's own feelings than were men role-playing the same conversation. Perhaps, however, this study's criteria for supportiveness simply reflect a feminine style of support provision. It would be interesting to know whether other, more indirect statements, such as humor, irony, or mock criticism actually served to convey support between male role-players.

In addition to the support women provide informally to their husbands, children, other relatives, neighbors, and friends, many women are professionally involved in the provision of support to those under stress. Many predominantly female occupations, such as teaching, nursing, and social work, require empathic attention to the needs of others and the ability to provide emotional support to those in distress. While a full discussion of women's professional involvement in providing social support is beyond the scope of this [article], it should be noted that many women "already gave at the office" when they come home to provide support to members of their informal social networks.

What accounts for the tendency of both males and females to turn to females disproportionately in times of stress and for women to offer support to so many others? Wheeler et al. (1983) have argued that women are simply more effective as social partners than are men. Men, in contrast, tend to lack training in supportiveness skills (Bernard, 1971), so that their attempts at providing social support are not as effective as those of women. . . .

Miller (1976) has argued that women's socialization and especially their subordinate status, which requires attention to others, better prepares them "to first recognize others' needs and then to be-

lieve strongly that others' needs can be served" so much so that women organize their lives around the principle of nurturing others and promoting their growth. This is consistent with Gilligan's argument (1982) that women's moral sense tends to presume responsibility for the well-being of others. . . .

POSITIVE AND NEGATIVE IMPLICATIONS OF INVOLVEMENT IN SOCIAL NETWORKS

. . . As indicated, women tend to (1) maintain more emotionally intimate relationships than do men, (2) mobilize more social supports in times of stress than do men while relying less heavily than men on the spouse as a source of social support, and (3) provide more frequent and more effective social support to others than do men. . . .

Women Maintain More Emotionally Intimate Relationships Than Do Men

. . . [W]omen's propensity for intimate social involvements may predispose women to the "contagion of stress" that is felt when troubling life events afflict those to whom they are emotionally close. Dohrenwend (1976) found, for instance, that when men and women were asked to list recent events that had occurred to themselves, family members, and other people important to them, a higher proportion of the events women reported had happened to family members or friends rather than to the respondents themselves. Eckenrode and Gore (1981) reported that women whose relatives and friends experienced stressful life events such as burglaries and illnesses found these events stressful to themselves, and reflected this vicarious stress in their own poor health. Kessler and McLeod (1984) argue that this sensitivity to the undesirable life events of others actually accounts for women's greater vulnerability to stressful life events in comparison to men. Wethington, McLeod, and Kessler were able to show that while men are distressed by events that happen to their children and spouses, women are distressed not only by these events but by events which occur to other members of the social network. Thus, it is women's greater "range of caring" that seems to expose them to additional vicarious stress.

Women Mobilize More Varied Social Supports in Times of Stress Than Do Men

Research on bereavement provides the most impressive evidence that men's and women's differential investment in social support figures has consequences for their well-being. In particular, a man's heavy investment in his wife as confidant and support figure may account for the higher mortality rates of widowers versus widows in the months and years following bereavement. . . .

While men appear particularly vulnerable when they lose a spouse to death, other research suggests that differences in the actual supportiveness of the spouse when alive may be more important to women than to men. Husaini, Neff, Newbrough, and Moore (1982) studied the stress-buffering properties of social support among rural married men and women and found that various aspects of the marital relationship (marital satisfaction, spouse satisfaction, spouse as confidant) were more powerfully associated with mental health status among women than among men.

Why should the mere presence of a wife be beneficial, while only the supportiveness of a husband is protective? . . . Such findings are open to different interpretations but may reflect a ceiling effect: the average wife (or female friend) may provide such a high level of support that further increments in supportiveness make little difference to health and mental health outcomes. It may also be that since the role of wife is so central to a woman's social status and self-concept, a nonsupportive spouse is particularly devastating to a woman's well-being. . . .

When we turn from the marital relationship to other network ties, there is evidence that men and women may be differentially protected by their involvements. In their prospective study of mortality, Berkman and Syme (1979) found that overall the protective effects of social contacts were stronger for women than for men. While, as discussed earlier, marriage was much more protective for men, it was women who benefited more from contact with friends and relatives and from involvement in formal and informal groups. Holahan and Moos (1981) reported that the quality of family relationships was associated with well-being for women but not for men, while the quality of work relationships was more strongly related to well-being for men than for women.

Women Provide More Frequent and More Effective Social Support to Others Than Do Men

Several authors have pointed to women's heightened vulnerability to stress resulting from women's propensity to take care of needy and stressed network members. Fischer (1982) found that women, especially mothers of young children, were much more likely than others to report too many demands from members of their households.

In general women and parents, especially parents of infants and toddlers, were most likely to feel pressed by their households, but the combination of being a woman and being a parent was especially deadly. . . . The general point is clear: children demand and women respond to those demands, as well as to the demands of others (p. 136).

Similarly, Cohler and Lieberman (1980) discovered that among first and second generation adult members of three European ethnic groups, the women who were more involved with relatives and friends experienced *more* psychological distress than their less involved peers, while network involvement among the men was either unrelated to mental health or showed small positive associations with morale. Cohler and Lieberman noted that, particularly within the ethnic communities they studied, women are socialized from childhood to care for others. Such socialization may then contribute to the contagion of stress women experience from the disasters and disappointments of others. In addition to the vicarious pain they feel, women may also find themselves burdened with new tasks and obligations to aid the suffering individual. The close contact experienced in such kin-keeping may then keep the sufferer's pain vivid to the person who aids him or her.

Women's specialization as support providers and men's relative neglect of this activity may also have consequences for cross-sex friendships and for romantic and marital relationships. In a male-female relationship, the female may experience a "support gap" (Belle, 1982b) when she receives less support from a significant male figure than she provides to him. If the flow of supportive provisions is highly unequal, and if the woman is heavily involved in providing support to children, needy friends, or relatives while receiving little support in return, the result may well be demoralization and depression. . . .

While most network studies emphasize the benefits to be gained by network involvement, a new line of research is demonstrating that the costs of network ties may, if anything, be greater than the benefits. Studies have also shown, as noted earlier, that the costs and benefits of networks are not distributed randomly among the population, but tend to vary with gender and with access to personal resources (which also tends to vary with gender).

In addition to the gender differences in network involvements that have been discussed thus far, it is important to note the impact of society-wide inequalities in access to crucial resources as these affect men's and women's utilization of support resources. A growing body of research has shown, ironically, that those most in need of supportive provisions from their social networks are those least likely to receive them, while they are also most likely to experience the costs of network involvement (Belle, 1983; Eckenrode, 1983; Lefcourt, Martin, & Saleh, 1984; Riley & Eckenrode, 1986; Sandler & Lakey, 1982). In American society at large, women are more likely than men to fall into the ranks of the impoverished, to hold relatively powerless positions in the workplace, and to lack the independent resources that can give bargaining advantages within marriage.

REFERENCES

Antonucci, T., & Depner, C. (1982). Social support and informal relationships. In T. Wills (Ed.), *Basic processes in helping relationships*. New York: Academic Press.

Barrera, M., & Balls, P. (1983). Assessing social support as a prevention resource: An illustrative study. *Prevention in Human Services, 2,* 59–74.

Belle, D. (1982a). Social ties and social support. In D. Belle (Ed.), *Lives in stress: Women and depression.* Beverly Hills, CA: Sage.

———. (1982b). The stress of caring: Women as providers of social support. In L. Goldberger & S. Breznitz (Eds.), *Handbook of stress: Theoretical and clinical aspects.* New York: Free Press.

———. (1983). The impact of poverty on social networks and supports. *Marriage and Family Review, 5,* 89–103.

Belle, D., & Longfellow, C. (1984). *Turning to others: Children's use of confidants.* Paper presented at the annual meeting of the American Psychological Association, Toronto.

Berkman, L. F., & Syme, L. (1979). Social networks, host resistance, and mortality: A nine-year follow-up study of Alameda County residents. *American Journal of Epidemiology, 109,* 186–204.

Bernard, J. (1971). *Women and the public interest.* Chicago: Aldine.

Booth, A. (1972). Sex and social participation. *American Sociological Review, 37* 183–193.

Booth, A., & Hess, E. (1974). Cross-sex friendship. *Journal of Marriage and the Family, 36,* 38–47.

Brown, G., Bhrolchain, M., & Harris, T. (1975). Social class and psychiatric disturbance among women in an urban population. *Sociology, 9,* 225–254.

Burke, R. J., & Weir, T. (1978). Sex differences in adolescent life stress, social support, and well-being. *Journal of Psychology, 98,* 277–288.

Caldwell, M. A., & Peplau, L. A. (1982). Sex differences in same-sex friendship. *Sex Roles, 8,* 721–732.

Campbell, A., Converse, P., & Rodgers, W. (1976). *The quality of American life: Perceptions, evaluations, and satisfactions.* New York: Russell Sage.

Candy, S. G., Troll, L. W., & Levy, S. G. (1981). A developmental exploration of friendship functions in women. *Psychology of Women Quarterly, 5,* 456–472.

Cauce, A. M., Felner, R. D., & Primavera, J. (1982). Social support in high-risk adolescents: Structural components and adaptive impact. *American Journal of Community Psychology, 10* 417–428.

Chiriboga, D. A., Coho, A., Stein, J. A., & Roberts, J. (1979). Divorce, stress and social supports: A study in help-seeking behavior. *Journal of Divorce, 3* 121–135.

Chodorow, N. (1974). Family structure and feminine personality. In M. Rosaldo & L. Lamphere (Eds.), *Women, culture, and society.* Stanford: Stanford University Press.

Cobb, S. (1976). Social support as a moderator of life stress. *Psychosomatic Medicine, 38,* 300–314.

Cohen, L. H., McGowan, J., Fooskas, S., & Rose, S. (1984). Positive life events and social support and the relationship between life stress and psychological disorder. *American Journal of Community Psychology, 12,* 567–587.

Cohler, B. M., & Lieberman, M. A. (1980). Social relations and mental health: Middle-aged and older men and women from three European ethnic groups. *Research on Aging, 2,* 445–469.

DePaulo, B. (1982). Social-psychological processes in informal help seeking. In T. A. Wills (Ed.), *Basic processes in helping relationships.* New York: Academic Press.

Depner, C., & Ingersoll, B. (1982). Employment status and social support: The experience of the mature woman. In M. Szinovacz (Ed.), *Women's retirement: Policy implications of recent research.* Beverly Hills, CA: Sage Yearbooks in Women's Policy Studies, Vol. 6.

Dohrenwend, B. S. (1976). *Anticipation and control of stressful life events: An exploratory analysis.* Paper presented to the annual meeting of the Eastern Psychological Association, New York City.

Eckenrode, J. (1983). The mobilization of social supports: Some individual constraints. *American Journal of Community Psychology, 11,* 509–528.

Eckenrode, J., & Gore, S. (1981). Stressful events and social support: The significance of context. In B. Gottlieb (Ed.), *Social networks and social support.* Beverly Hills, CA: Sage.

Fiore, J., Becker, J., & Coppel, D. B. (1983). Social network interactions: A buffer or a stress? *American Journal of Community Psychology, 11,* 423–439.

Fischer, C. (1982). *To dwell among friends: Personal networks in town and city.* Chicago: University of Chicago Press.

Gilligan, C. (1982). *In a different voice.* Cambridge, MA: Harvard University Press.

Gore, S. (1978). The effect of social support in moderating the Health consequences of unemployment. *Journal of Health and Social Behavior, 19,* 157–165.

Hirsch, B. J. (1981). Social networks and the coping process: Creating personal communities. In B. H. Gottlieb (Ed.), *Social networks and social support.* Beverly Hills, CA: Sage.

Holahan, C., & Moos, R. (1981). Social support and psychological distress: A longitudinal analysis. *Journal of Abnormal Psychology, 90,* 365–370.

Hunter, F. T., & Youniss, J. (1982). Changes in functions of three relations during adolescence. *Developmental Psychology, 18,* 806–811.

Husaini, B. A., Neff, J. A., Newbrough, J. R., & Moore, M. C. (1982). The stress-buffering role of social support and personal competence among the rural married. *Journal of Community Psychology, 10,* 409–426.

Jourard, S. (1971). Some lethal aspects of the male role. In J. Pleck & J. Sawyer (Eds.), *Men and masculinity.* Englewood Cliffs, NJ: Prentice-Hall.

Kandel, D. B., & Lesser, G. S. (1972). *Youth in two worlds: U.S. and Denmark.* San Francisco: Jossey-Bass.

Kessler, R. C., & McLeod, J. D. (1984). Sex differences in vulnerability to undesirable life events. *American Sociological Review, 49,* 620–631.

Kon, I. S., & Losenkov, V. A. (1978). Friendship in adolescence: Values and behavior. *Journal of Marriage and the Family, 40,* 143–155.

Lefcourt, H. M., Martin, R. A., & Saleh, W. E. (1984). Locus of control and social support: Interactive moderators of stress. *Journal of Personality and Social Psychology, 47,* 378–389.

Loewenstein, S. F. (1984). *Fathers and mothers in midlife.* Presentation to the Family Track Seminar of the Boston University Department of Psychology, Boston.

Lowenthal, M. J., & Haven, C. (1968). Interaction and adaptation: Intimacy as a critical variable. *American Sociological Review, 33,* 20–30.

Mark, E. W., & Alper, T. G. (1985). Women, men, and intimacy motivation. *Psychology of Women Quarterly, 9,* 81–88.

McAdoo, H. (1980). Black mothers and the extended family support network. In L. Rodgers-Rose (Ed.), *The black woman.* Beverly Hills, CA: Sage.

McMullen, P. A., & Gross, A. E. (1983). Sex differences, sex roles, and health-related help-seeking. In B. DePaulo, A. Nadler, & J. Fisher (Eds.), *New directions in helping* (Vol. 2). New York: Academic Press.

Miller, J. (1976). *Toward a new psychology of women.* Boston: Beacon.

Miller, P. M., & Ingham, J. G. (1976). Friends, confidants, and symptoms. *Social Psychiatry, 11,* 51–58.

Nelson-Le Gall, S., Gumerman, R. A., & Scott-Jones, D. (1983). Instrumental help-seeking and everyday problem-solving: A developmental perspective. In B. DePaulo, A. Nadler, & J. Fisher (Eds.), *New directions in helping* (Vol. 2). New York: Academic Press.

Nuckolls, K. B., Cassel, J., & Kaplan, B. H. (1972). Psychosocial assets, life crisis and the prognosis of pregnancy. *American Journal of Epidemiology, 95,* 431–441.

Parsons, T., & Bales, R. (1955). *Family, socialization, and interaction process.* New York: Free Press.

Pearlin, L., & Johnson, J. (1977). Marital status, life-strains, and depression. *American Sociological Review, 42,* 704–715.

Riley, D., & Eckenrode, J. (1986). Social ties: Subgroup differences in costs and benefits. *Journal of Personality and Social Psychology, 51,* 770–778.

Rivenbark, W. H. (1971). Self-disclosure patterns among adolescents. *Psychological Reports, 28,* 35–42.

Rook, K. S. (1984). The negative side of social interaction: Impact on psychological well-being. *Journal of Personality and Social Psychology, 46,* 1097–1108.

Sandler, I. N., & Lakey, B. (1982). Locus of control as a stress moderator: The role of control perceptions and social support. *American Journal of Community Psychology, 10,* 65–80.

Stack, C. (1974). *All our kin: Strategies for survival in a Black community.* New York: Harper & Row.

Vanfossen, B. E. (1981). Sex differences in the mental health effects of spouse support and equity. *Journal of Health and Social Behavior, 22,* 130–143.

Veroff, J., Douvan, E., & Kulka, R. (1981). *The inner American: A self-portrait from 1957–1976.* New York: Basic Books.

Wahler, R. (1980). The insular mother: Her problems in parent-child treatment. *Journal of Applied Behavior Analysis, 13,* 207–219.

Weiss, R. S. (1985). Men and the family. *Family Process, 24,* 49–58.

Wheeler, L., Reiss, H., & Nezlek, J. (1983). Loneliness, social interaction, and sex roles. *Journal of Personality and Social Psychology, 45,* 943–953.

Wilkins, W. (1974). Social stress and illness in industrial society. In E. Gunderson & R. Rahe (Eds.), *Life stress and illness.* Springfield, IL: Charles C. Thomas.

Wolchik, S. A., Sandler, I. N., & Braver, S. L. (1984). *The social support networks of children of divorce.* Paper presented at the American Psychological Association meeting, Toronto.

Young, M., & Willmott, P. (1957). *Family and kinship in East London.* London: Routledge and Kegan Paul.

NO

Micaela di Leonardo

THE FEMALE WORLD OF CARDS AND HOLIDAYS: WOMEN, FAMILIES, AND THE WORK OF KINSHIP

Why is it that the married women of America are supposed to write all the letters and send all the cards to their husbands' families? My old man is a much better writer than I am, yet he expects me to correspond with his whole family. If I asked him to correspond with mine, he would blow a gasket. [LETTER TO ANN LANDERS]

Women's place in man's life cycle has been that of nurturer, caretaker, and helpmate, the weaver of those networks of relationships on which she in turn relies. [CAROL GILLIGAN, *In a Different Voice*]

Feminist scholars in the past fifteen years have made great strides in formulating new understandings of the relations among gender, kinship, and the larger economy. As a result of this pioneering research, women are newly visible and audible, no longer submerged within their families. We see households as loci of political struggle, inseparable parts of the larger society and economy, rather than as havens from the heartless world of industrial capitalism. And historical and cultural variations in kinship and family forms have become clearer with the maturation of feminist historical and social-scientific scholarship.

Two theoretical trends have been key to this reinterpretation of women's work and family domain. The first is the elevation to visibility of women's nonmarket activities—housework, child care, the servicing of men, and the care of the elderly—and the definition of all these activities as *labor*, to be enumerated alongside and counted as part of overall social reproduction. The second theoretical trend is the nonpejorative focus on women's domestic or kin-centered networks. We now see them as the products of conscious strategy, as crucial to the functioning of kinship systems, as sources of women's autonomous power and possible primary sites of emotional fulfillment, and, at times, as the vehicles for actual survival and/or political resistance.

From Micaela di Leonardo, "The Female World of Cards and Holidays: Women, Families, and the Work of Kinship," *Signs: Journal of Women in Culture and Society*, vol. 12, no. 3 (Spring 1987). Copyright © 1987 by the University of Chicago. Reprinted by permission. Notes omitted.

Recently, however, a division has developed between feminist interpreters of the "labor" and the "network" perspectives on women's lives. Those who focus on women's work tend to envision women as sentient, goal-oriented actors, while those who concern themselves with women's ties to others tend to perceive women primarily in terms of nurturance, other-orientation—altruism. . . .

I shall argue that we need to fuse, rather than to oppose, the domestic network and labor perspectives. . . .

In my recent field research among Italian-Americans in Northern California, I found myself considering the relations between women's kinship and economic lives. As an anthropologist, I was concerned with people's kin lives beyond conventional American nuclear family or household boundaries. To this end, I collected individual and family life histories, asking about all kin and close friends and their activities. I was also very interested in women's labor. As I sat with women and listened to their accounts of their past and present lives, I began to realize that they were involved in three types of work: housework and child care, work in the labor market, and the work of kinship.

By kin work I refer to the conception, maintenance, and ritual celebration of cross-household kin ties, including visits, letters, telephone calls, presents, and cards to kin; the organization of holiday gatherings; the creation and maintenance of quasi-kin relations; decisions to neglect or to intensify particular ties; the mental work of reflection about all these activities; and the creation and communication of altering images of family and kin vis-à-vis the images of others, both folk and mass media. Kin work is a key element that has been missing in the

synthesis of the "household labor" and "domestic network" perspectives. In our emphasis on individual women's responsibilities within households and on the job, we reflect the common picture of households as nuclear units, tied perhaps to the larger social and economic system, but not to *each other*. We miss the point of telephone and soft drink advertising, of women's magazines' holiday issues, of commentators' confused nostalgia for the mythical American extended family: it is kinship contact *across households*, as much as women's work within them, that fulfills our cultural expectation of satisfying family life.

Maintaining these contacts, this sense of family, takes time, intention, and skill. We tend to think of human social and kin networks as the epiphenomena of production and reproduction: the social traces created by our material lives. Or, in the neoclassical tradition, we see them as part of leisure activities, outside an economic purview except insofar as they involve consumption behavior. But the creation and maintenance of kin and quasi-kin networks in advanced industrial societies is *work*; and, moreover, it is largely women's work.

The kin-work lens brought into focus new perspectives on my informants' family lives. First, life histories revealed that often the very existence of kin contact and holiday celebration depended on the presence of an adult woman in the household. When couples divorced or mothers died, the work of kinship was left undone; when women entered into sanctioned sexual or marital relationships with men in these situations, they reconstituted the men's kinship networks and organized gatherings and holiday celebrations. Middle-aged businessman Al Bertini, for example, recalled the death of his mother in his early adolescence: "I think that's probably one of the biggest losses in losing a family—yeah, I remember as a child when my Mom was alive . . . the holidays were treated with enthusiasm and love . . . after she died the attempt was there but it just didn't materialize." Later in life, when Al Bertini and his wife separated, his own and his son Jim's participation in extended-family contact decreased rapidly. But when Jim began a relationship with Jane Bateman, she and he moved in with Al, and Jim and Jane began to invite his kin over for holidays. Jane single-handedly planned and cooked the holiday feasts.

Kin work, then, is like housework and child care: men in the aggregate do not do it. It differs from these forms of labor in that it is harder for men to substitute hired labor to accomplish these tasks in the absence of kinswomen. Second, I found that women, as the workers in this arena, generally had much greater kin knowledge than did their husbands, often including more accurate and extensive knowledge of their husbands' families. This was true both of middle-aged and younger couples and surfaced as a phenomenon in my interviews in the form of humorous arguments and in wives' detailed additions to husbands' narratives. Nick Meraviglia, a middle-aged professional, discussed his Italian antecedents in the presence of his wife, Pina:

> *Nick:* My grandfather was a very outspoken man, and it was reported he took off for the hills when he found out that Mussolini was in power.
> *Pina:* And he was a very tall man; he used to have to bow his head to get inside doors.
> *Nick:* No, that was my uncle.

> *Pina:* Your grandfather too, I've heard your mother say.
> *Nick:* My mother has a sister and a brother.
> *Pina:* Two sisters!
> *Nick:* You're right!
> *Pina:* Maria and Angelina.

Women were also much more willing to discuss family feuds and crises and their own roles in them; men tended to repeat formulaic statements asserting family unity and respectability. (This was much less true for younger men.) Joe and Cetta Longhinotti's statements illustrate these tendencies. Joe responded to my question about kin relations: "We all get along. As a rule, relatives, you got nothing but trouble." Cetta, instead, discussed her relations with each of her grown children, their wives, her in-laws, and her own blood kin in detail. She did not hide the fact that relations were strained in several cases; she was eager to discuss the evolution of problems and to seek my opinions of her actions. Similarly, Pina Meraviglia told the following story of her fight with one of her brothers with hysterical laughter: "There was some biting and hair pulling and choking . . . it was terrible! I shouldn't even tell you. . . ." Nick, meanwhile, was concerned about maintaining an image of family unity and respectability.

Also, men waxed fluent while women were quite inarticulate in discussing their past and present occupations. When asked about their work lives, Joe Longhinotti and Nick Meraviglia, union baker and professional, respectively, gave detailed narratives of their work careers. Cetta Longhinotti and Pina Meraviglia, clerical and former clerical, respectively, offered only short descriptions focusing on factors of ambience, such as the "lovely things" sold by Cetta's firm.

These patterns are not repeated in the younger generation, especially among younger women, such as Jane Bateman, who have managed to acquire training and jobs with some prospect of mobility. These younger women, though have *added* a professional and detailed interest in their jobs to a felt responsibility for the work of kinship.

Although men rarely took on any kin-work tasks, family histories and accounts of contemporary life revealed that kins-women often negotiated among themselves, alternating hosting, food-prepara-tion, and gift-buying responsibilities—or sometimes ceding entire task clusters to one woman. Taking on or ceding tasks was clearly related to acquiring or divest-ing oneself of power within kin networks, but women varied in their interpretation of the meaning of this power. Cetta Lon-ghinotti, for example, relied on the "fam-ily Christmas dinner" as a symbol of her central kinship role and was involved in painful negotiations with her daughter-in-law over the issue: "Last year she insisted—this is touchy. She doesn't want to spend the holiday dinner together. So last year we went there. But I still had my dinner the next day . . . I made a big dinner on Christmas Day, regardless of who's coming—candles on the table, the whole routine. I decorate the house my-self too. . . . well, I just feel that the time will come when maybe I won't feel like cooking a big dinner—she should take advantage of the fact that I feel like doing it now." Pina Meraviglia, in contrast, was saddened by the centripetal force of the developmental cycle but was unworried about the power dynamics involved in her negotiations with daughters- and mother-in-law over holiday celebrations. Kin work is not just a matter of power among women but also of the mediation of power represented by household units. Women often choose to minimize status claims in their kin work and to include numbers of households under the rubric of family. Cetta Longhinotti's sister Anna, for example, is married to a professional man whose parents have considerable economic resources, while Joe and Cetta have low incomes and no other well-off kin. Cetta and Anna re-main close, talk on the phone several times a week, and assist their adult chil-dren, divided by distance and economic status, in remaining united as cousins.

Finally, women perceived housework, child care, market labor, the care of the elderly, and the work of kinship as com-peting responsibilities. Kin work was a unique category, however, because it was unlabeled and because women felt they could either cede some tasks to kinswom-en and/or could cut them back severely. Women variously cited the pressures of market labor, the needs of the elderly, and their own desires for freedom and job enrichment as reasons for cutting back Christmas card lists, organized holiday gatherings, multifamily dinners, letters, visits, and phone calls. They expressed guilt and defensiveness about this cut-back process and, particularly, about their failures to keep families close through con-stant contact and about their failures to create perfect holiday celebrations. Cetta Longhinotti, during the period when she was visiting her elderly mother every weekend in addition to working a full-time job, said of her grown children, "I'd have the whole gang here once a month, but I've been so busy that I haven't done that for about six months." And Pina Meraviglia lamented her insufficient work on family Christmases, "I wish I had really made it traditional . . . like my sister-in-law has special stories."

Kin work, then, takes place in an arena characterized simultaneously by cooperation and competition, by guilt and gratification. Like housework and child care, it is women's work, with the same lack of clear-cut agreement concerning its proper components: How often should sheets be changed? When should children be toilet trained? Should an aunt send a niece a birthday present? Unlike housework and child care, however, kin work, taking place across the boundaries of normative households, is as yet unlabeled and has no retinue of experts prescribing its correct forms. Neither home economists nor child psychologists have much to say about nieces' birthday presents. Kin work is thus more easily cut back without social interference. On the other hand, the results of kin work—frequent kin contact and feelings of intimacy—are the subject of considerable cultural manipulation as indicators of family happiness. Thus, women in general are subject to the guilt my informants expressed over cutting back kin-work activities.

Although many of my informants referred to the results of women's kin work—cross-household kin contacts and attendant ritual gatherings—as particularly Italian-American, I suggest that in fact this phenomenon is broadly characteristic of American kinship. We think of kin-work tasks such as the preparation of ritual feasts, responsibility for holiday card lists, and gift buying as extensions of women's domestic responsibilities for cooking, consumption, and nurturance. American men in general do not take on these tasks any more than they do housework and child care—and probably less, as these tasks have not yet been the subject of intense public debate. And my informants' gender breakdown in rela-

tive articulateness on kinship and workplace themes reflects the still prevalent occupational segregation—most women cannot find jobs that provide enough pay, status, or promotion possibilities to make them worth focusing on—as well as women's perceived power within kinship networks. The common recognition of that power is reflected in Selma Greenberg's book on nonsexist child rearing. Greenberg calls mothers "press agents" who sponsor relations between their own children and other relatives; she advises a mother whose relatives treat her disrespectfully to deny those kin access to her children.

Kin work is a salient concept in other parts of the developed world as well. Larissa Adler Lomnitz and Marisol Pérez Lizaur have found that "centralizing women" are responsible for these tasks and for communicating "family ideology" among upper-class families in Mexico City. Matthews Hamabata, in his study of upper-class families in Japan, has found that women's kin work involves key financial transactions. Sylvia Junko Yanagisako discovered that, among rural Japanese migrants to the United States, the maintenance of kin networks was assigned to women as the migrants adopted the American ideology of the independent nuclear family household. Maila Stivens notes that urban Australian housewives' kin ties and kin ideology "transcend women's isolation in domestic units."

This is not to say that cultural conceptions of appropriate kin work do not vary, even within the United States. Carol B. Stack documents institutionalized fictive kinship and concomitant reciprocity networks among impoverished black American women. Women in populations characterized by intense feelings of ethnic identity may feel bound to emphasize particular occasions—Saint Patrick's or Columbus Day—with organized family feasts. These constructs may be mediated by religious affiliation, as in the differing emphases on Friday or Sunday family dinners among Jews and Christians. Thus the personnel involved and the amount and kind of labor considered necessary for the satisfactory performance of particular kin-work tasks are likely to be culturally constructed. But while the kin and quasi-kin universes and the ritual calendar may vary among women according to race or ethnicity, their general responsibility for maintaining kin links and ritual observances does not.

As kin work is not an ethnic or racial phenomenon, neither is it linked only to one social class. Some commentators on American family life still reflect the influence of work done in England in the 1950s and 1960s (by Elizabeth Bott and by Peter Willmott and Michael Young) in their assumption that working-class families are close and extended, while the middle class substitutes friends (or anomie) for family. Others reflect the prevalent family pessimism in their presumption that neither working- nor middle-class families have extended kin contact. Insofar as kin contact depends on residential proximity, the larger economy's shifts will influence particular groups' experiences. Factory workers, close to kin or not, are likely to disperse when plants shut down or relocate. Small businesspeople or independent professionals may, however, remain resident in particular areas—and thus maintain proximity to kin—for generations, while professional employees of large firms relocate at their firms' behest. This pattern obtained among my informants.

In any event, cross-household kin contact can be and is effected at long distance through letters, cards, phone calls, and holiday and vacation visits. The form and functions of contact, however, vary according to economic resources. Stack and Brett Williams offer rich accounts of kin networks among poor blacks and migrant Chicano farmworkers functioning to provide emotional support, labor, commodity, and cash exchange—a funeral visit, help with laundry, the gift of a dress or piece of furniture. Far different in degree are exchanges such as the loan of a vacation home, a multifamily boating trip, or the provision of free professional services—examples from the kin networks of my wealthier informants. The point is that households, as labor- and income-pooling units, whatever their relative wealth, are somewhat porous in relation to others with whose members they share kin or quasi-kin ties. We do not really know how class differences operate in this realm; it is possible that they do so largely in terms of ideology. It may be, as David Schneider and Raymond T. Smith suggest, that the affluent and the very poor are more open in recognizing necessary economic ties to kin than are those who identify themselves as middle class.

Recognizing that kin work is gender rather than class based allows us to see women's kin networks among all groups, not just among working-class and impoverished women in industrialized societies. This recognition in turn clarifies our understanding of the privileges and limits of women's varying access to economic resources. Affluent women can "buy out" of housework, child care—and even some kin-work responsibilities. But they, like all women, are ultimately responsible, and subject to both guilt and blame, as the administrators of home, children, and kin network. Even the wealthiest women must negotiate the timing and venue of holidays and other family rituals with their kinswomen. It may be that kin work is the core women's work category in which all women cooperate, while women's perceptions of the appropriateness of cooperation for housework, child care, and the care of the elderly vary by race, class, region, and generation. . . .

Are women kin workers the nurturant weavers of the Gilligan quotation, or victims, like the fed-up woman who writes to complain to Ann Landers? That is, are we to see kin work as yet another example of "women's culture" that takes the care of others as its primary desideratum? Or are we to see kin work as another way in which men, the economy, and the state extract labor from women without a fair return? And how do women themselves see their kin work and its place in their lives?

As I have indicated above, I believe that it is the creation of the self-interest/altruism dichotomy that is itself the problem here. My women informants, like most American women, accepted their primary responsibility for housework and the care of dependent children. Despite two major waves of feminist activism in this century, the gendering of certain categories of unpaid labor is still largely unaltered. These work responsibilities clearly interfere with some women's labor force commitments at certain life-cycle stages; but, more important, women are simply discriminated against in the labor market and rarely are able to achieve wage and status parity with men of the same age, race, class, and educational background.

Thus for my women informants, as for most American women, the domestic domain is not only an arena in which much unpaid labor must be undertaken but also a realm in which one may attempt to gain human satisfactions—and power—not available in the labor market. . . . Feminists considering Western women and families have looked at the issue of power primarily in terms of husband-wife relations or psychological relations between parents and children. If we adopt Collier and Lamphere's broader canvas, though, we see that kin work is not only women's labor from which men and children benefit but also labor that women undertake in order to create obligations in men and children and to gain power over one another. Thus Cetta Longhinotti's struggle with her daughter-in-law over the venue of Christmas dinner is not just about a competition over altruism, it is also about the creation of future obligations. And thus Cetta's and Anna's sponsorship of their children's friendship with each other is both an act of nurturance and a cooperative means of gaining power over those children.

POSTSCRIPT

Are Women Only Victims in Their Roles as Social Support Providers?

As women's expanded work roles increasingly take them out of the home, will social network obligations begin to fall within the realm of *family* work and need to be negotiated like other family responsibilities?

Today, most women *must* be employed for the family to comfortably survive leaner economic times. New Gallup and Roper polls show that women are now more likely to negotiate with their husbands for shared household responsibilities. Women are willing to admit that they get angry for having such heavy schedules at home in addition to maintaining full-time jobs. Husbands today, the polls also find, are more willing than in past generations to support a renegotiation of family work.

If Belle is correct that social network obligations are more harmful than beneficial to most women's psychological and physical health, then will these women grow averse to being the network representatives for their entire families? Would extended family relationships break down completely if social responsibilities were simply dropped from a woman's and/or couple's schedule? Or, as di Leonardo suggests, do women get enough satisfaction and power from their social network roles that they would give up other obligations if necessary in order to keep these roles? In what ways have families reduced friend and kin responsibilities?

One way to reduce social support network responsibilities is to purchase services. Social commentator Jeff Ostroff, in *American Demographics* (January 1991), reports that business is already stepping in to help individuals and families provide support for one another. For example, business provides live-in caregivers for older relatives who still live at home, adult daycare for relatives who cannot stay home alone, Meals on Wheels, mail-order catalogs offering gifts to be wrapped and delivered with a hand-signed card, shopping services, cleaning services, psychological services, and so forth. In what other ways might business ease social network responsibilities?

SUGGESTED READINGS

M. Cochran, M. Larner, D. Riley, L. Gunnarsson, and C. R. Henderson, *Extending Families: The Social Networks of Parents and Their Children* (Cambridge University Press, 1990).

S. E. Hobfoll and J. R. Leiberman, "Personality and Social Resources in Immediate and Continued Stress Resistance Among Women," *Journal of Personality and Social Psychology*, 52 (1987): 18–26.

R. Milardo, ed., *Families and Social Networks* (Sage Publications, 1988).

ISSUE 3

Have Men's Family Roles Changed?

YES: Joseph H. Pleck, from "The Contemporary Man," in Murry Scher et al., eds., *Handbook of Counseling and Psychotherapy with Men* (Sage Publications, 1987)

NO: Steven L. Nock and Paul William Kingston, from "Time With Children: The Impact of Couples' Work-Time Commitments," *Social Forces* (September 1988)

ISSUE SUMMARY

YES: Professor of sociology Joseph H. Pleck argues that men married to employed women have substantially increased their involvement in housework and child care, and that men who share the family work also report less stressful lives than do other men.

NO: Professors of sociology Steven L. Nock and Paul William Kingston contend that the emergence of the dual-earner family has not influenced men to increase their participation in family life, and that only on Sundays do men with employed wives and children under age 7 spend more time with their children than do other men.

It is widely acknowledged that women in families still do much more of the housework and child care than their husbands regardless of the extent of their outside employment responsibilities. However, the question of whether or not men married to employed women are taking on a *larger* share of the domestic responsibilities still exists.

The American family has undergone substantial changes in the last few decades. The number of dual-earner families has increased dramatically. The traditional family grouping of homemaker mother, provider father, and two children now represents a distinct minority of American families—some say 15 percent of all families; others maintain that the figure is closer to 7 percent. Employment rates are increasing partly because mothers of school-age and younger children are entering the labor force in large numbers. The current rate of employment for mothers with school-age children is 73 percent. In 1990, over half of all married mothers with children under age 1 were in the work force.

In the dual-earner family, mothers who work full-time often experience an overload of responsibilities as they attend to the competing demands of employment and family roles. Pressures from striving to fulfill all responsibilities in these two areas typically lead to emotional and physical manifestations of stress. Studies show that, compared to their husbands, women employed full-time spend over twice as many hours performing household duties and almost as much time in the workplace. Mothers in particular feel responsible for the success and happiness of their families. They generally feel that, if anything goes wrong in the lives of family members, the larger community will be inclined to hold them, rather than the fathers, accountable.

Yet, despite multiple role responsibilities, employed women typically report a high level of life satisfaction and good mental health. Several recent studies conclude that employed women feel less anxiety, depression, and general overall stress than nonemployed women. Many reasons for this have been explored, but one of the most consistent findings is that women with fewer physical and psychological symptoms of stress say that the key to their greater well-being is having a supportive husband.

Various studies show that the stress of a woman's many roles is eased when her husband becomes more involved in family roles—when he takes more responsibility for household tasks and child care and is supportive of his wife's career. Moreover, there is evidence that the father's greater involvement in child care is important to a child's development. Recent research concludes that children with involved fathers are more socially and academically competent and are less likely to stereotype women's and men's roles.

In today's families what men do in the household is increasingly being recognized as important to the lives of their wives and children. In the following selections, Joseph H. Pleck discusses the results of his research in this area and asserts that men's roles in the family are changing in concert with or in response to women's expanding employment roles. Steven L. Nock and Paul William Kingston, in contrast, relate that the fathers in their study were not significantly more involved in childrearing than were other fathers, and that they did not compensate for the time that mothers spent at work.

YES

Joseph H. Pleck

THE CONTEMPORARY MAN

MEN'S INCREASING TIME IN FAMILY ROLES

In *Women's Two Roles: Home and Work* (1956), Alva Myrdal argued that women in industrial societies were, to an increasing degree, adding a new role in paid work to their traditional family role. The phrase "women's two roles" caught on as a description of this change in women's lives. A decade later, Myrdal developed her argument a step further: Women having two roles could not succeed in the long run unless men developed two roles as well. For men, having two roles meant adding a greatly enlarged family role to their customary responsibility as family economic breadwinners (Myrdal, 1967).

From this perspective, data on trends in time spent by men in their family roles provide a key social indicator of change in men. By examining data on this variable, one can objectively determine whether men are really changing. Time in the family is, in effect, the social indicator for men analogous to labor force participation for women. A surprisingly large number of studies have investigated how men's participation in family life has changed in the United States over the twentieth century. . . . This research in fact documents that men's family role has increased. Two analyses provide particularly valuable evidence.

In one of the classic American community studies, Robert and Helen Merrill Lynd investigated "Middletown" (Muncie, Indiana) in the mid-20s. Caplow and Chadwick (1979; Caplow, Bahr, Chadwick, Hill, & Williamson, 1982) replicated the study in 1978 with a similarly drawn sample from the same city. About 10% of all fathers were reported by their wives to spend *no* time with their children in 1924; in 1978, the parallel figure was 2%. Thus the proportion of completely uninvolved fathers dropped from 1 in 10 to 1 in 50. (The proportion of fathers spending more than 1 hour per day, the highest reported category of involvement reported by the researchers, rose from 66% to 76%.)

From Joseph H. Pleck, "The Contemporary Man," in Murry Scher et al., eds., *Handbook of Counseling and Psychotherapy with Men* (Sage Publications, 1987), pp. 16–20, 26. Copyright © 1987 by Sage Publications, Inc. Reprinted by permission.

Most who ask whether men are really changing are thinking not of the last 60 years, but of only the last 10 or 20, that is, since the rise of the contemporary women's movement. Juster (1985) provides data on the time spent by adult males in the United States in family work (housework and child care combined) from time diary surveys conducted with national representative samples in 1965 and 1981. Men's time in these activities rose from about 1.6 hours per day in 1965 to slightly under 2.0 hours per day in 1981, an increase of somewhat over 20%. Taking into account women's decreasing time in these activities, men's proportion of all housework and child care (that is, the total performed by the average man and the average woman combined) rose from 20% to 30% over this 16-year period.

Thus, on a key social indicator, men show clear evidence of change in their role, and to more than a trivial degree. This change is not, of course, necessarily occurring to an equal degree among all men. Aggregate figures such as these probably conceal subgroups of men who have not changed or who are doing even less family work than they used to, men who have changed only a little, and men who have changed a great deal. But if an overall generalization is needed, it must be that American men have markedly increased their family participation over the last 60 years. Further, the pace of change over the last two decades (men's proportion of total family work rising from 20% to 30%) seems substantial when one considers that these data describe the U.S. population as a whole, not just the young, the highly educated, residents of college towns, or the large East and West Coast cities. This rate of change is in fact comparable to the increase in the average woman's proportion of the paid work performed by her and the average man combined, which rose from 27% to 35% during this same period. . . .

The most important qualification to be made about these data is that they concern only the amount of time men spend in family roles, and not the degree of responsibility men take. Analyses of how spouses divide family tasks underline the importance of the distinction between simply performing an activity and being responsible for the task being done (Lein, 1984). The extent to which men are *responsible* for family work is much lower than their participation, and has probably not increased as much.

Nonetheless, men's increase in family participation is socially significant. In a similar way, women's increasing labor force participation has had tremendous social consequences, in spite of the fact that women's average earnings relative to men's have not changed. Many would argue today that any woman who aspires to, or actually has, a higher-level job than women have traditionally held (or who has a job, when traditionally she would not have) shows the effects of the changed consciousness among women stimulated by feminism. In the same way, any man who is doing more in the family than he used to, or than his father did, likewise demonstrates the effects of broader cultural change in the male role.

MEN'S INCREASING RATES OF PSYCHOLOGICAL DISTRESS RELATIVE TO WOMEN

One of the research results giving impetus to the women's movement during the 1970s was the finding that women have higher rates of mental health disorders, especially depression, than men, and that this gender difference could not be accounted for by biological factors (Chesler, 1972; Guttentag, Salasin, & Belle, 1980). Recent research, however, has documented a significant change over the last three decades in the relationship between gender and psychological distress.

Kessler and McRae (1981; see also McLanahan & Glass, 1985) analyzed five national surveys conducted between 1957 and 1976 that included measures of psychophysiological symptoms such as sleep difficulty, nervousness, headaches, and dizziness. These surveys also included items assessing symptoms such as "times you couldn't take care of things because you just couldn't get going" and "times when personal worries got you down physically." While women reported a higher rate of these stress indicators than did men in all five surveys, the average difference between women and men became steadily smaller between 1957 and 1976. Detailed analyses showed that women's rates of such symptoms increased slightly over these two decades. . . . But men's rates increased about three times more. . . . As a result, the "gender gap" in symptoms was 38% smaller at the end of the period than it was at the beginning. Over these two decades, men's mental health deteriorated relative to women's.

It is possible that men's increased reports of psychological distress may not reflect an increase in its acutal frequency, only an increasing willingness to acknowledge it. Undoubtedly, this factor contributes to some degree. However, it cannot be the only explanation, since exactly the same trend is evident in data on attempted suicide from 1960 to the present: Women still do it more, but men are catching up. Generalizing across a large group of studies, the ratio of females to males attempting suicide dropped from about 2.3 to 1 in 1960, to about 1.3 to 1 in 1980 (Kessler & McRae, 1983). (Men show substantially higher rates of successful suicide than women.) . . .

One of the main changes since the 1950s is, of course, that today more men have employed wives. The increase in wives' employment did account for some of the change in men's psychological symptoms. In the 1976 data, men with employed wives reported significantly more depression and lower self-esteem than sole-breadwinning husbands, though the size of the difference was not great. It is interesting to note that this pattern did not hold true for the youngest group, men in their twenties.

Several factors that the investigator thought might explain exactly *how* wives' employment diminished husbands' mental health were not validated. For example, husbands of employed wives did not appear to experience more symptoms because the money their wives made rendered their own breadwinner role less important. In fact, among husbands with employed wives, those with higher-earning wives reported less distress. Likewise, the problem did not seem to be that husbands of employed wives performed more housework and child care. In fact, among husbands with employed wives, those who performed more family tasks showed less, not more, distress.

Pleck (1985) found parallel results in a study focusing specifically on the impact of men performing more family work on their family satisfaction and overall well-being. Pleck's interpretation of this latter, initially puzzling finding is that husbands whose wives are employed, but who do *not* contribute significantly to household and family tasks, exhibit "learned helplessness" behavior. . . . Most two-earner families face considerable demands in maintaining the household and arranging for child care. If housework needs doing and the children need to be cared for, but the husband does not have any behavior in his repertory that will help meet these needs, he will experience low control and increased stress.

It is sometimes asked whether men actually show signs of hurting as a result of the limitations of the traditional male role, or because relationships between the sexes are changing. The question is sometimes put more pointedly: What is the evidence that men today are actually feeling pain, and are not simply happily enjoying their male privilege? Kessler and McRae's data in fact show that men as a group are experiencing more psychological distress than they did three decades ago, both absolutely and relative to women.

From one point of view, the research discussed earlier about men's increased family participation is the "good news" about contemporary men, while the data about men's increasing psychological symptoms is the "bad news." Some might interpret the two trends together as suggesting that men experience increased stress *because* of the ways they are changing their role. Actually, the data suggest the exact opposite: The increased discomfort occurs predominantly among the men whose own role (as reflected by their family behavior) is *not* changing. Current research suggests that having a nontraditional role, in the sense of an enlarged family role, is good for men's mental health.

REFERENCES

Caplow, T., Bahr, H., Chadwick, B., Hill, R., & Williamson, M. H. (1982). *Middletown families: Fifty years of change and continuity.* Minneapolis: University of Minnesota Press.

Caplow, T., & Chadwick, B. (1979). Inequality and life-styles in Middletown, 1920–1978. *Social Science Quarterly, 60,* 367–390.

Chesler, P. (1972). *Women and madness.* Garden City, NY: Doubleday.

Guttentag, M., Salasin, S., & Belle, D. (Eds.). 1980). *The mental health of women.* New York: Academic Press.

Juster, F. T. (1985). A note on recent changes in time use. In F. T. Juster and F. Stafford (Eds.), *Time, goods, and well-being* (pp. 313–332). Ann Arbor, MI: Institute for Social Research.

Kessler, R., & McRae, J. (1981). Trends in the relationship between sex and psychological distress: 1957–1976. *American Sociological Review, 46,* 443–452.

Kessler, R., & McRae, J. (1983). Trends in the relationship between sex and attempted suicide. *Journal of Health and Social Behavior, 24,* 98–110.

Lein, L. (1984). *Families without villains.* Lexington, MA: D. C. Heath.

McLanahan, S. S., & Glass, J. L. (1985). A note on the trend in sex differences in psychological distress. *Journal of Health and Social Behavior, 26,* 328–335.

Myrdal, A. (1967). Foreword. In E. Dahlstrom & E. Liljestrom (Eds.), *The changing roles of men and women* (pp. 9–15). London: Duckworth.

Myrdal, A., & Klein, V. (1956). *Women's two roles: home and work.* London: Routledge & Kegan Paul.

Pleck, J. H. (1985). *Working Wives, Working Husbands.* Newbury Park, CA: Sage.

NO

**Steven L. Nock and
Paul William Kingston**

TIME WITH CHILDREN: THE IMPACT OF COUPLES' WORK-TIME COMMITMENTS

In public and scholarly arenas the employment of married mothers has been both denounced and celebrated: children and family life are portrayed as the victims as well as the beneficiaries of this development. Thus, working wives with children are alleged—in different quarters—to shortchange their children of guidance and care, provide valuable role models for a nonsexist societal organization, give distinctive "quality time" to their children, become overloaded with responsibilities, and depend on the aid of others, including their husbands. And for their part, the husbands in dual-earner families are also portrayed in conflicting ways: the involved father, contributing to a new, shared parental concern for raising children; and the detached male, leaving the joint responsibilities of a job and children to his wife. . . .

At the same time, fathers' involvement in raising children has received little systematic attention. By implication, this neglect almost seems to suggest that fathers do not or even cannot have an important hands-on role as a parent, though their influence in child development has become increasingly recognized (Radin & Russell 1983). . . .

Our concern is to document the extent and nature of any "trade-off" between couples' time at work and time with their children. While there are many issues related to the effects of parental employment on parent-child interaction, one fundamental issue is simply how much time parents, individually and as a couple, spend with their children in various types of activities. . . .

This analysis is based on a subsample of the 1981 Study of Time Use (STU) (Juster et al. [1983]). . . .

Our subsample consists of married individuals who reported the presence of children under age 20—226 husbands and 226 wives. Dual-earner couples are defined here as those in which both spouses reported at least some time in paid employment in the same wave (137 couples). Single-earners are

From Steven L. Nock and Paul William Kingston, "Time With Children: The Impact of Couples' Work-Time Commitments," *Social Forces*, vol. 67, no. 1 (September 1988). Copyright © 1988 by The University of North Carolina Press. Reprinted by permission. Notes omitted.

defined in a parallel way: all couples in which only one spouse reported time in paid employment in at least one wave (89 couples). . . .

MEASURES

To provide a detailed picture of the time parents spend with their children, we first counted the number of minutes the husband and wife in each couple separately reported spending with at least one child in seven major sorts of activities. For both husbands and wives, we also computed an aggregate measure of time spent in the presence of at least one child in any activity.

In a similar way, to indicate the extent of a couple's time commitments *as a unit* to their children, we measured the time spent by one or both parents with the children in a family. Thus, we report the joint extent of child "coverage" by parents in a family—that is, how many minutes a day at least one parent is in the company of a child in various types of activities. . . .

We should emphasize that these measures do not indicate the intensity of parent-child interaction *per se*. For example, a parent's time at a neighborhood picnic with a child or children present does not necessarily reflect any particular level of interaction between this parent and his or her child(ren). Rather, it only indicates the amount of time this parent reported spending at the picnic in the company of a child. . . .

The seven major categories of activities are:

1. *Child Care* (baby care, child care, medical care to children, etc.)
2. *Playing with/Education of Children*
  a. Indoor and outdoor play

b. Educational activities and discipline (help with homework, reading to the child, giving orders to child, etc.)
  c. Child-family activities (PTA meetings, family organization meetings, school outings)
3. *Fun*
  a. Entertaining/being entertained (attending sporting events, going to movies, museum, theater, parties, dancing, socializing, visiting)
4. *Housekeeping*
  a. Meal preparation (securing, preparing, serving food, cleaning, washing dishes, setting tables, grocery shopping)
  b. Cleaning (washing laundry, putting clothes away, indoor cleaning, cleaning pets, etc.)
  c. Making repairs/home maintenance (yard work, home repairs, indoor repairs, car repairs, car maintenance, etc.)
  d. Household management (paying bills, balancing checkbook, large item shopping, obtaining medical/government services)
  e. Shopping (grocery shopping, getting take-out food)
5. *Watching Television*
6. *Eating Meals*
7. *Talking* (as primary activity)

RESULTS

Single vs. Dual-Earners

. . . [T]here are notable differences between single and dual-earner parents, especially the mothers, on work days. Among families with preschoolers, mothers without a job spend 525 minutes in some contact with their children, more than twice the time of those with a job. Full-time mothers without a preschooler spend 355 minutes with their children, about two hours more than their employed counterparts. In contrast, the difference in overall child contact between fathers in single and dual-earner families is insignificant, whatever the age of their children. (Indeed, their only significant difference is that fathers of preschoolers in traditional families spend more time eating meals with their children than their counterparts with an employed wife.) Thus single earner couples have much greater combined total time with their children on workdays than dual-earner couples, but this difference largely reflects what mothers do.

Especially in families with preschoolers, employed mothers spend less time with their children in a wide range of activities. Among these families, mothers with jobs spend about a quarter hour less playing with or educating their children and 39 minutes less directly caring for them than full-time mothers. In absolute terms, these differences in activities directly related to children are not large, though the proportional differences are substantial. Employed mothers with preschoolers and mothers not in the labor force also differ in child contact while pursing "fun" activities (58 minutes), and most notably while homemaking (123 minutes). Of the overall difference in child contact (525 minutes), the largest proportion (23%) is accounted for by the discrepancy while homemaking—an activity that likely involves relatively limited interaction.

Among the families with only school age children, mothers spend little time playing with, educating, talking with and directly caring for their children, and their time in these activities does not differ by employment status. What differences exist largely reflect varying child contact while homemaking (a 52 minute difference), having "fun" (a 43 minute difference), and eating meals (a 15 minute difference).

Compared to the longest workday, there appear to be few differences in parent-child contact on Sundays between single and dual-earner families. . . . [O]n Sundays fathers with an employed wife have more than two hours greater contact than fathers with an unemployed wife (453 vs 328 minutes). Thus, dual-earner couples with preschoolers spend about three hours more with children (summing the commitments of fathers and mothers) than such parents in single earner couples—perhaps a partial "compensation" for their substantially lesser workday contacts. Yet there is no indication that, on average, dual-earner couples with only school age children "compensate" on weekends for their much lesser time commitments to children on workdays. Not surprisingly, whatever the age of their children, fathers in single and dual-earner couples, as well as the employed mothers, spend much more time with their children on Sundays than on workdays. . . .

Variations in Parental Coverage

To provide a sense of the amount of time couples spend with their children as a unit, we analyzed the time spent with the children in a family by one or both spouses—what we call parental coverage. Here we move beyond the simple comparison of dual- and single earner couples and ask more specifically how variations in time allocations to work influence the amount of time couples spend with their children. . . .

[T]here is no evidence of average differences in parental coverage between these two family types beyond any associated with work schedules, socio-demographic and life cycle variables.

Very young children have an understandably large impact on the amount of coverage given by parents. . . . The number of children in the household is also a factor in parental coverage. Each additional child increases by a little over an hour . . . the time one or the other parent is estimated to be with the children. Finally, parental coverage declines slightly over the course of the family life cycle; couples married longer to one another spend less and less time with their children. . . .

[T]he time spent in specific types of activities is particularly associated with work schedule variables. Fathers' work during the 9:00 AM to 3:00 PM period reduces parental coverage in "fun" and, minimally, in eating meals. Mothers' work during the school day, and even more so in the late afternoon, cuts into parental coverage in homemaking. In general, work during evening and late night hours does not affect parental coverage, though wives' work during the late night increases parental coverage watching television.

For playing with or educating children (e.g., reading to them)—an activity unambiguously defined as child-centered —some parental time is lost when wives work during the 9:00 to 3:00 PM period, but this coefficient is very small. If a wife worked these entire six hours, the estimated "cost" in parental coverage in play/education would be not quite a half hour. Work at other times does not significantly affect this activity, and no associations are found between childcare and work time during any period of the day. . . .

[S]ingle and dual-earner couples do not spend different amounts of time with their children in any activity category. One can safely say, therefore, it is largely time at work that distinguishes such families.

In short, . . . work does influence the time parents spend with children, but it does so more in the aspects of family life in which children are relatively peripheral (i.e., homemaking, visiting or entertaining) than in specifically child-oriented activities. . . .

FATHERS

. . . [I]t is clear that fathers' time at work becomes more "costly" the later it is in the day. Thus, each hour at work during the 9:00 AM to 3:00 PM interval is associated with about 20 fewer minutes with children. By comparison, an hour during the 3:00 PM to 6:00 PM or 6:00 PM to midnight intervals is associated with an estimated half-hour less time with children.

There is some indication of husbands compensating for their wives' work at particular times. The coefficient for the effect of the wife's work after 6:00 PM indicates that every hour she works in that interval is associated with an estimated *increase* of about eighteen minutes in the father's time with children. However, wives' work time at other periods of the day has no effect on husbands' time with children.

Father-child contact is expectably greater in larger families. Each additional child is estimated to add about twenty-one minutes per day in father-child contact. . . . This result contradicts the widespread sense—or, perhaps more accurately, feminist hope—that a new, more involved male parental role has emerged with the prevalence of dual-earner families. . . .

[F]athers who themselves work in the evening watch less television with their children, while if their wives work then, they watch more. . . . [T]ime with children at meals reveals very similar, though smaller results—that is, fathers' work at night reduces paternal involvement in this activity and mothers' work increases it.

Husbands' time with children in "fun" activities is also sacrificed to time at work. . . . When husbands work between 3:00 PM and 6:00 PM, they spend marginally less time with children housekeeping. . . .

With respect to childcare, there is very minor reduction in husbands' efforts when they work between midnight and 9:00 AM. Comparable small results occur in play/education when husbands work in the after-school 3:00 PM to 6:00 PM interval. There is no indication that they are more involved in these activities in response to work demands on their wives.

In sum, work has the largest . . . effects on husbands' time with children watching TV and in those activities we have defined as fun (visiting, chatting, being entertained). Much smaller effects are noted for housekeeping and meals, and activities directly related to children are only minimally related to work. Finally, for some activities, husbands' time with children increases when wives work in the evening or late night.

MOTHERS

. . . Mothers' overall time with children is responsive to their own work in predictable fashion. . . . Working between 9:00 AM and 3:00 PM reduces time with children moderately; each hour worked is associated with an estimated 22 fewer minutes with children. By contrast, work during the 3:00 PM to 6:00 PM interval is considerably more consequential. During these after-school hours, an hour of mother's work is associated with an estimated 42 minutes less time with children. . . .

In expectable ways, both the presence of very young children and the number of children in the family are associated with mothers' time with children. Mothers with children under 3 are estimated to spend about two more hours with children than those without such children. In addition, each additional child is associated with an increase of almost an hour . . . of mothers' time with children. These large time commitments are apparently somewhat offset by marriage length. Mothers married ten years spend about a half-hour less time with children than mothers married five years. . . . for mothers greater family income is related to less time with children. Each $1,000 increase in family income is estimated to reduce by almost two minutes the time mothers spend with children. Thus, two mothers, alike on all other factors but differing in family income by $20,000, would be estimated to differ by more than half an hour (35 minutes) in the time they spend with their children—with the more affluent mother spending less time with her children. . . .

[W]ork has the greatest impact on time together while homemaking. In fact, it is in housekeeping that almost all of the time with children lost to work occurs, especially as a result of the losses associated with work during after school hours. The extent of mothers' time at a job is not significantly associated with lesser time in childcare or playing with or educating their children.

As for fathers, spouse's work time affects mothers' time with children in some activities. The more their husbands work from midnight to 9:00 AM, the less mothers watch television with their children. Also, the more their husbands work from 9:00 AM to 3:00 PM, the less time mothers spend in "fun" with children. Thus a conventional workday for men cuts into the leisure time mothers have in the company of their children. . . .

[O]nce the hours and scheduling of work as well as sociodemographic and life cycle factors are considered, there remains little to distinguish working mothers from their nonemployed counterparts. . . .

[M]others' time with children during homemaking is strongly related to the number of children in the household. Mothers with larger families are especially likely to spend their housekeeping time in double-duty—caring for the house and watching the children. Family composition is also expectably related to mothers' time in child-oriented tasks. For childcare, the presence of very young children is associated with an increase of more than an hour . . . in a mother's time devoted to such tasks. Large numbers of children also require more time by mothers; each child is associated with about eleven more minutes of mother-child contact. In those activities classified as child play/education, it is the age of children that is most important. Having children under 6 increases mothers' time in such activities by about twelve minutes, on average. And mothers' time with children in childcare declines marginally with each additional year of marriage. . . .

Finally, we note two significant coefficients for race indicating that white mothers spend less time with children while housekeeping . . . and more time in education/play. . . . As intriguing as these results are, there were only seventeen nonwhites in our sample, and hence we do not attempt to interpret these results. . . .

DISCUSSION

. . . [A]mong families with young children, the lesser contact of employed mothers involves activities that are child-oriented (playing, educating, and caring for children) as well as those in which children are generally peripheral (particularly, homemaking). The results do not suggest, then, that working mothers with young children substitute "quality" *types* of time for lesser quantities of overall contact with their children. However, since mothers with preschoolers commit relatively little time to child-centered activities no matter what their employment status, most of the total difference reflects lesser contact in activities that generally do not intimately engage children. By contrast, among mothers with school-aged children, there is no difference between those who are employed and those who do not work outside the home in the most intensive types of interaction with children (very limited for each); the differences occur only as mothers pursue the routines of their domestic life.

Our findings counter the sense that the emergence of the dual-earner family has fostered a new, involved paternal role for fathers. Whatever professions of ideology parents in single and dual-earner families may make, on workdays employed and unemployed mothers still have much more contact with children than fathers, and the men in dual-earner couples generally have not adjusted their allocations of time to "compensate" for their wives' lesser time with children. The only exception to this pattern occurs among families with young children: fathers with an employed wife appear to spend more time with their children on Sundays than those whose wife is a full-time mother.

Indeed, the presence of one or two earners *per se* does not make a difference in couples' workday allocation of time to children. Once time at work is accounted for, single and dual-earner couples as a *unit* do not differ in their parental coverage—overall or in specific activities. That is, dual-earner couples have lesser parental coverage of children for the simple, prosaic reason that they work more as a unit than their single earner counterparts. The ever-increasing prevalence of two parents with paid work has not in itself created any distinctive orientation to spending time with children. While the fact of being part of a dual-earner couple also has no net effect on the *separate* time commitments of mothers, it does so for fathers. Yet the *lesser* time commitment of fathers in dual-earner families to their children (net of work time commitments) undercuts any contention that the widespread employment of women has ushered in a more directly participative male parental role.

REFERENCES

Juster, F. Thomas, Martha Hill, Frank Stafford, and J. Parsons. 1983. Time Use Longitudinal Panel Study, 1975–1981: Vol. 4: Users' Guide. Inter-University Consortium for Political and Social Research.

Radin, Norma, and Graeme Russell. 1983. "Increased Father Participation and Child Development Outcomes." Pp. 191–218 in *Fatherhood and Family Policy,* edited by Michael Lamb and Abraham Sagi. Erlbaum.

POSTSCRIPT

Have Men's Family Roles Changed?

Lois Hoffman, in an article published in the February 1989 issue of *American Psychologist*, says that fathers now demonstrate more sharing behavior when mothers work full-time, when there is more than one child in the family, and when there are no older children in the household. Hoffman also points out that the closer their incomes are to being equal, the more fathers participate with mothers in household chores and child care. When the father is more involved in family roles, says Hoffman, women report less stress and greater well-being, and fathers report an increased sense of self-esteem.

According to a recent survey conducted for Robert Half International, nearly 8 out of 10 men would choose to advance at a slower pace in their jobs if they could get more flexible work hours and more family time. Jennifer McEnroe, in *American Demographics* (February 1991), labels this trend "father hunger."

Accordingly, Pleck argues that men have increased their involvement in the home so that they are now doing about 30 percent of the housework. He also points out that husbands of employed women evidence *less* distress than other men. He further speculates that men who are not changing with the times run the highest risk of stress-related health problems.

In contrast, Nock and Kingston found that husbands of employed women were no more involved in family life than were other husbands. They, however, studied dual-earner couples in which both spouses were involved "at least some time in paid employment," which means that the women and men studied could have been employed as little as 2 hours per week or as much as 50 or 60 hours per week. Their research may conceal subgroups of men who are doing more of the family work, such as those married to women who are employed full-time. In what ways might changing father roles affect societal gender differences?

SUGGESTED READINGS

P. Bronstein and C. P. Cowan, eds., *Fatherhood Today: Men's Changing Role in the Family* (Wiley, 1988).

S. H. Cath, A. Gurwitt, and L. Gunsberg, *Fathers and Their Families* (Analytic Press, 1989).

L. DeStefano and D. Colasanto, "Unlike 1975, Today Most Americans Think Men Have It Better," *The Gallup Poll Monthly* (February 1990).

B. Townsend and K. O'Neill, "Women Get Mad," *American Demographics*, 12 (1990): 26–32.

PART 2

Making a Commitment:
The Decision to Marry

*Among the advantages of marriage are
steady companionship, security,
procreation, and various financial benefits.
Some negative aspects include restriction to
one sex partner, restriction of personal
freedom, responsibility for others, and
sometimes a routinization of life-style. The
choice to marry or to remain single
profoundly affects the way a person lives,
and many factors must be considered before
such a decision can be made. Some believe
that the institution of marriage today
promises more than it can possibly deliver
and brings more pain than it is worth.
Others protest that marriage detracts from
the validity of alternative cohabitational
life-styles and cheats single individuals out
of certain legal benefits. Still others
maintain that marriage remains the ideal
relationship for expressing love and
devotion. This section discusses some
social, legal, and personal definitions of
marriage and explores some of the life-style
alternatives to getting married.*

Is Marriage Good for You?

Should Gays and Lesbians Fight for
the Right to Marry?

ISSUE 4

Is Marriage Good for You?

YES: Bryce J. Christensen, from "The Costly Retreat from Marriage," *The Public Interest* (Spring 1988)

NO: Liz Hodgkinson, from *Unholy Matrimony: The Case for Abolishing Marriage* (Columbus Books, 1988)

ISSUE SUMMARY

YES: Bryce J. Christensen, director of The Rockford Institute Center on the Family in America, argues that being married has positive mental and physical health benefits for individuals and that marriage should also be encouraged as a solution to skyrocketing health care costs in the United States.

NO: Free-lance writer Liz Hodgkinson asserts that modern marriage should be abolished because it is dysfunctional for individuals and society as a whole.

Because they are subject to controversy and touch everyone's lives, social institutions and their perceived failures are often the focus of television talk shows and popular literature. Schools would be one example of a social institution that receives constant media scrutiny, marriage is another. It is not unusual to come across magazine articles or morning talk show panels that address such questions as "How do you measure marital success?" "Does marriage doom loving relationships?" "Can marriages ending in divorce ever be seen as successes?" "What makes a strong marriage?" How you answer these and related questions depends in part on how you view marriage, and it is interesting to note that not only have views of marriage changed over time, but also that there are currently many, often conflicting, views of marriage.

Recently, in Western cultures, marriage has come to be viewed to a considerable extent as a means to the ends of individual growth, fulfillment, and happiness, with little or at least diminished attention to its function within and impact upon the larger society. Sociologist Jessie Bernard, in *The Future of Marriage* (Yale University Press, 1972), was one of the first researchers to explore and document the outcomes of marriage in terms of the mental and physical health of the individuals involved. Although she found that marriage usually resulted in better health indices for the married individuals who participated in her studies as compared to their unmarried cohorts (marrieds had a lower suicide rate than singles, for example), she also concluded that men received many more benefits from the married state than did women. Certainly gender is a determinant in how we characterize adaptations to and adjustments in marriage.

Although marriages may show many commonalities, it is also important to remember that no two are exactly alike. The two individuals who make up a marriage and the family and community systems each comes from (and is part of) all have an impact upon the marriage. Research literature offers few single variables or factors that account for good marital adjustment. With regard to individual marriages, the factors that work to make one marriage a success do not necessarily have positive effects on another. For example, the *quantity* of communication for one couple may be as important as *quality* is for another, even though many people might assume that quality is the more important factor.

In responding to whether or not marriage is good for your well-being, remember to be attuned to definitions: what is specifically meant by *marriage*—the state, the status, the interaction, the fantasy—and just what does *good* imply and for whom?

In the following selections, Bryce J. Christensen updates Bernard's earlier findings with recent literature, and he focuses not only on individuals but also on the larger social context—specifically the correlates of marriage and economic well-being for the United States. He outlines why being married is superior to being single, divorced, or widowed. From a health care cost perspective, he indicates that if the U.S. government would simply promote positive marriage, family, and childbearing policies, the country's economic woes would significantly lessen.

Liz Hodgkinson, on the other hand, provides a very different perspective on the condition of the marital state. She sees marriage as an institutional failure, one that prevents solid relationships in a variety of ways, both within and external to the marital bond. She, too, builds upon some of Jessie Bernard's earlier work, but she utilizes her own unique perspective and looks at more recent findings about marriage in both the United States and Great Britain.

YES

Bryce J. Christensen

THE COSTLY RETREAT FROM MARRIAGE

The costs of providing medical care in America, it is frequently noted, have skyrocketed in the recent past, and promise to continue doing so in the future. There is, of course, at least a partial solution to this problem, one involving little or no expenditure of either public or personal funds. This solution calls for an increased emphasis upon preventive medicine: exercising and dieting today help to avert heart disease tomorrow; not smoking now increases the likelihood of avoiding lung cancer later.

My purpose in writing this essay is to suggest something else that Americans can do on their own to improve their health, something that government ought to do more to encourage—Americans can get married and stay married. Quite simply, marriage, no less than jogging and lowering cholesterol intake, is good for your health. Although it is obviously up to individual Americans to decide whether to marry, stay single, or divorce, it is nevertheless past time for policymakers to acknowledge the profound health benefits of marriage: the nation's runaway medical costs could be partially controlled were government to implement policies that did more to foster and encourage longer-lasting, child-producing marriages.

The new evidence linking health to marriage and family life is voluminous. Writing . . . in *Social Science and Medicine*, Catherine K. Riessman and Naomi Gerstel observe that "one of the most consistent observations in health research is that married [people] enjoy better health than those of other marital statuses." Drs. Riessman and Gerstel note that compared with married men and women, the divorced, single, and separated suffer much higher rates of disease morbidity, disability, mental neuroses, and mortality. "This pattern has been found for every age group (20 years and over), for both men and women, and for both whites and non-whites." According to James Lynch of the University of Maryland Medical School, the health advantage enjoyed by the married over the unmarried has actually grown in recent decades.

Only a small fraction of the statistical health gap separating the married from the single and divorced can be accounted for by the common-sense

From Bryce J. Christensen, "The Costly Retreat from Marriage," *The Public Interest*, no. 91 (Spring 1988), pp. 59–66. Copyright © 1988 by National Affairs, Inc. Reprinted by permission of *The Public Interest* and the author.

observation that sick people either don't get married or don't make satisfactory marriage partners. According to Dr. Lynch, married people are healthier largely because marriage per se "influences the general life-style of the individual." In a study published . . . in the *Journal of Health and Social Behavior*, Debra Umberson of the University of Michigan finds that mortality rates are "consistently higher" for the unmarried than for the married, because marriage exerts a "deterrent effect on health-compromising behaviors" such as excessive drinking, drug use, risk-taking and disorderly living. By providing a system of "meaning, obligation, [and] constraint," family relationships markedly reduce the likelihood of unhealthy practices. Interestingly, Dr. Umberson's research also underscores the difference between the widowed and the divorced. Although both groups have poorer health habits than the married, the habits of the divorced are far worse than those of the widowed.

In his research into the effects of marriage on health, Harold Morowitz of Yale University concludes that "being divorced and a non-smoker is slightly less dangerous than smoking a pack or more a day and staying married," adding facetiously that "if a man's marriage is driving him to heavy smoking he has a delicate statistical decision to make."

HAPPILY AND HEALTHILY WED

The advantage that the married enjoy over the unmarried in death rates due to cancer and heart disease is astonishing. The lung-cancer rate for divorced men is twice that for married men, while the rates for some forms of cancer (genital, buccal, and pharyngeal) are three to four times as high among the divorced. The

pattern among divorced women, while not quite so stark, is similar. Among both men and women, the single and divorced die from hypertensive heart disease at rates between two-and-a-half and three-and-a-half times those found among the married. Dr. Lynch reports that even when their diseases are not fatal, divorced and single people stay in the hospital longer than do married men and women suffering from the same illnesses. This pattern of longer hospital stays is costing America "uncounted billions of dollars" every year.

Just as impressive are the mental-health benefits bestowed by marriage. According to Peggy A. Thoits of Indiana University, "married persons have significantly lower anxiety and depression scores than unmarried persons, regardless of gender." Dr. Thoits notes that married individuals appear to enjoy better mental health even when they have experienced more potentially traumatic experiences than the unmarried. Surprisingly, even the mentally ill sometimes find psychological benefits in marriage. The British medical journal, the *Lancet*, . . . reported that in some cases marriages between the mentally ill prove "stable and may even show improved function. . . . The support provided by a shared mental disability may have a beneficial effect."

Some feminists have claimed that marriage benefits only men; but available health statistics show otherwise. While men do realize a somewhat greater health advantage from marriage than women, both sexes are clearly healthier if married than if unmarried. The latest findings only partially confirm Emile Durkheim's famous hypothesis that marriage is more important for the mental health of men than for that of women, while raising children is more important for women than for men. According to Dr. Umberson's 1987 study, "marriage and parenting relationships work together to deter health-compromising behaviors" for both men and women. In fact, for at least one disease—breast cancer—marriage protects women's health in particular, by increasing the likelihood that they will bear two or more children: a recent study at the University of Bergen in Norway found a correlation between the number of children a woman has borne and her likelihood of developing breast cancer, with the childless and the mothers of only one most vulnerable.

Nor is it just husbands and wives whose health is affected by marriage. In a study published . . . in the *New England Journal of Medicine*, researchers at the National Center for Health Statistics found that unmarried women, compared with married women, run "a substantially higher risk of having infants with very low or moderately low birth weights." Because birth weight is one of the best predictors of infant mortality, many more illegitimate than legitimate babies die. The NCHS researchers believe that marriage exerts no "direct causal influence on the outcome of pregnancy," but that a life course that includes marriage is likely to be healthier than one that does not. (For example, unmarried mothers are more likely to smoke than married mothers.)

Though divorce is less threatening to a child's health than is illegitimacy, it still takes its toll. The *Canadian Journal of Psychiatry* reports that divorce increases the likelihood of mental disturbances among children, with over a third of children still "troubled and distressed at the five year mark" (after their parents' divorce). According to John McDermott of the University of Hawaii, "divorce is now the single largest cause of childhood depression." Dr. Lynch believes that parental divorce not only causes mental neuroses among children, but also contributes to "various physical diseases, including cardiac disorders," later in their lives. The *Journal of the Royal Society of Medicine* reports that members of single-parent families also complain more frequently of less serious maladies, including "headaches, backaches, tummy aches, listlessness, . . . depression, [and] a host of other ailments," than do those in two-parent households. Finnish health authorities at the University of Tampere find that children from non-intact families are much more likely to require medical attention for psychosomatic symptoms than children from intact families. The ailments, real and imagined, of children from single-parent homes may well persist, creating sizable public costs in the decades ahead.

THE FLIGHT FROM MARRIAGE

The latest health findings should foster concern about falling marriage rates. In recent years, as the national media have glamorized the freedom and excitement of the single "life-style," an unprecedented number of young people have decided that marriage should be avoided— or at least postponed. Since 1970 the American marriage rate has fallen 30 percent, while the divorce rate has climbed 50 percent. By 1983 the average age at first marriage had risen to 24.5 for women and to 26.8 for men. If current trends continue, one American in seven will never wed. But the statistics already cited suggest that the fern bar and health spa may serve as mere way stations for singles headed for the hospital—or the cemetery.

During the 1970s, Americans witnessed what Lenore Weitzman has called "the divorce revolution." Within a decade, legislators in almost every state replaced traditional divorce laws with new "no-fault" statutes that made it much easier to dissolve a marriage. Cultural attitudes changed, as divorce shed its stigma as a "calamity" or "tragedy" and came to enjoy widespread acceptance as a simple "uncoupling," or even a laudable act of "courage," a valuable "growth opportunity." Although the divorce rate has shown signs of leveling off, it is still 50 percent higher than it was in 1970. Demographers estimate that 44 percent of all marriages formed in 1983 will end in divorce. Weitzman has documented the harmful, if unintended, economic consequences of the divorce revolution for both women and children.

Epidemiologists are now accruing data on the harm done to health by the divorce epidemic. A 1984 study by the National Center for Health Services concluded that divorced women were not only less healthy than married women, but also more likely to rely on public assistance in securing medical care. This finding is especially striking because "the divorced population is somewhat younger than the married." . . .

Clearly, public-health officials have reason to worry about what demographer Robert Schoen has described as America's "retreat from marriage." The medical costs created by this social trend will surely strain government programs such as Medicare and Medicaid. Indirect effects ought also to be taken into account. The social retreat from marriage not only drives up the nation's future medical bills, but also reduces the number of future taxpayers available to pay those bills. In explaining why our national fertility rate has languished below replacement level for more than a decade, Ben Wattenberg points to the trend toward fewer, later, and less stable marriages. Although illegitimacy rates have risen significantly since 1950, unmarried women still bear far fewer children than do married women. While the birthrate for married women aged 18–44 stands at 92.0 per 1,000 women (an historic low), the birth rate for unmarried women in the same age group remains much lower (33.4 per 1,000). Fewer babies now mean a much smaller tax base in thirty or forty years. Wattenberg believes that the "birth dearth" could cause Social Security to fail early in the next century, if—as is widely predicted—the Social Security trust fund is combined with the Medicare trust fund.

As low fertility erodes the tax base, it simultaneously imposes higher public costs for institutionalization of the elderly. Recent surveys show that taxpayers bear the burden of institutionalizing the elderly far less frequently when they are married and have three or more children than when they are single or divorced, or when they have few or no children. Looking at statistics from 1976, Stephen Crystal concludes that "the more children an older person has had, the smaller the odds of institutional placement." Historians have noted a similar pattern in the early years of this century. A 1910 Massachusetts survey found that almost 60 percent of the aged poor then living in almshouses or benevolent homes had no living adult children; a Pennsylvania survey in 1919 found that almost two-thirds of those living in almshouses had no living children; comparable statistics were reported in a 1929 National Civic Federation Survey conducted nationwide. Clearly, if fewer American marriages ended in divorce and fewer American families were small, nursing-home care would not consume 41 percent of all Medicaid expenditures.

Worse, however, is in store. Writing in the *American Journal of Public Health*, researchers from Vanderbilt University predict that the increased future costs of providing nursing-home care for aging Americans without children able or willing to care for them in their homes will be troublesome. The anticipated increase of $6 billion (in 1982 dollars) in nursing-home expenses by the year 2012, they warn, will "exacerbate . . . intergenerational conflict."

POLICY IMPLICATIONS

Public-health officials are already beginning to rediscover the importance of marital and family relationships in their fight to contain ballooning health costs. Richard Morse of Kansas State University sees "some movement, at present, to deny welfare or Medicaid to those individuals whose families cannot prove they are unable to perform that responsibility." Alexa K. Stuifbergen of the University of Texas at Austin likewise believes that "policymakers are increasingly looking to the family as a hedge against the rising cost of health care services."

This rediscovery of family responsibility could mark a positive first step in reshaping public-health policy. Unless, however, it is matched by some policies that help intact marriages, the rediscovery of family responsibility could create economic injustices: it could push intact families to the end of the line of those eligible for federal benefits, while keeping them near the front of the line of those responsible for paying for those benefits. One possible approach would be to restructure Medicare rates so that married recipients pay a lower monthly premium than the unmarried. But it is politically unthinkable and ethically questionable for government to favor the married over the unmarried directly: millions of older Americans are unmarried because of the death of a spouse; many others either had no opportunity to marry or divorced only for the most serious of reasons, after making every effort at reconciliation.

Yet policymakers could benefit most young marriages by framing a tax policy that offers greater advantages to households with children present. First, tax reformers could raise the personal federal income-tax exemption for dependent children from $2,000 to $4,000. (Even at $4,000 the personal exemption would remain hundreds of dollars below its 1948 value, when adjusted for inflation.) Second, the income ceiling for the Earned Income Tax Credit could be raised—to perhaps $25,000 or $27,500—and the benefits could be scaled to the number of children in the home (while still restricting the credit to no more than the total payroll taxes paid by the recipient). Third, the current child-care tax credit could be universalized, allowing households with a stay-at-home mother to share the benefits now received by dual-income homes.

Admittedly, such a child-centered approach would help unwed and divorced mothers, but not childless couples and older married couples with no children at home. Yet the young married couple remains the most fertile unit and would therefore receive most of the benefits. Although married American women now bear fewer children than in past decades, only about one married couple in twenty is both childless and infertile. Even a cohabiting couple is only half as likely as a married couple to have a child in its household. Moreover, improving the economic status of the nation's children is a worthy policy objective in itself, quite apart from the gain for marriage. The two objectives of helping children and encouraging marriage could actually prove mutually reinforcing: married couples might well choose to have more children if some of the economic hardship of childrearing were eliminated, while children arguably provide the strongest cement for a marital union. It is no accident that the divorce rate dropped during the baby boom of the 1950s.

Many of the forces fueling America's retreat from marriage are ultimately cultural, hence not under the direct control of policymakers in a liberal democracy. Nonetheless, policymakers must cope with the rising medical costs created by the flight from marriage. In discharging this responsibility, simple prudence suggests the need for approaches that will reduce these medical costs by encouraging marriage. At the same time, justice dictates that those who build successful marriages and families be relieved of at least some of the public burdens created by those who repudiate marriage. Child-based tax benefits could help achieve these objectives without unfairly penalizing those who are unmarried for reasons beyond their control.

NO

Liz Hodgkinson

MARRIAGE TODAY

Modern marriage is in a bad way. Although couples may agree to love, honour and share all worldly goods at the outset, few of them stick to these vows for any length of time. Many couples end up hating and resenting each other, even resorting, in extreme cases, to violence and murder.

The condition of being married and having to live in close and intimate contact, day after day, year after year, with just one adult member of the opposite sex, encourages very strong dependencies to develop. Married people expect, and are expected, to share general interests and political persuasions, to take an active involvement in each other's work and hobbies, and to go on holiday together. Such cosy togetherness is constantly encouraged by society. Many of us get married, or form partnerships, assuming that this familiarity will make us happy, content and fulfilled. Indeed, in modern Western marriages it is almost impossible for partners to get away from each other for any length of time. Married people are expected to sleep together, in the same bed, and to live as much of their lives as is humanly possible as a unit rather than as individuals. The idea of joint mortgages and joint bank accounts, hardly heard of twenty years ago, is regarded as a good idea, and the concept of joint finances underlines the way in which we like modern couples to operate.

In the old days, and also in marriages in traditional societies, men and women did not, and do not, spend so much time together. In many traditional societies today (Muslim ones, for example), it is usual for husbands and wives to entertain separately, to eat separately and to have completely separate tasks. It has been said that this separation occurs in societies where women are kept down, but in her book *Sex and Destiny* Germaine Greer makes the wise point that it at least allows the wives a bit of a breather on occasion, time away from the spouse. It has long been received wisdom that Western marriages allow more freedom to the wife, who does not always have to be at her husband's beck and call. If this is deemed to be good, why should it be so desirable for two disparate human beings, of different sexes and possibly of quite dissimilar characters, to share everything they do?

Nowadays, we insist on shared parenthood, shared housework—even shared secrets (openness of feelings, thoughts and emotions). Men and women sometimes also dress alike, particularly if they are sporty types. Advertisements aimed at retired or soon-to-retire people reveal an assumption that, once the couple are no longer in paid employment, they will want to spend every single minute in each other's company. No wonder people who stay married for a long time end up looking alike. (There is some scientific credence for this: according to the psychologist Robert Zajonc of the University of Michigan it happens because married people mirror each other's expressions and behaviour, meeting scowls with scowls and smiles with smiles.)

Modern marriage can be stifling, because it makes it so difficult for partners to spend any time away from each other. And however much a couple may be in love when they first meet, however strong the initial 'urge to merge', in time they will most probably want to reassert their individuality. But if they start out with the idea of being mutually dependent, unable to stand on their own feet, they may actually in time be incapable of doing even the simplest tasks alone. What the psychologists call 'learned helplessness' is common in marriage, and the condition is liable to worsen as the years go by. Many women who have been adventurous and independent while single discover that, once they have been married a few years, they are nervous about changing a light-bulb, booking into a hotel alone, or making decisions about even a minor purchase. Men who have been coping excellently as bachelors suddenly forget how to cook, to sew on buttons, change bed linen or how to send trousers to the dry-cleaners.

But the more a couple merge as the years go by, the more we see this as a good thing. Kitty Muggeridge, wife of the journalist Malcolm, once admitted in an interview that over the many years of their marriage they had become 'one person'. We also have a sneaking admiration for couples who involve themselves in suicide pacts, as did the writer Arthur Koestler and his wife Cynthia, who decided she could not live without him. 'Greater love hath no woman [or man] than this,' we reflect. Yet the fact is that people do not really become more alike over the years. If anything, their differences become more apparent as the years go by. And in those marriages where they seem to have merged, what has really happened is that one partner has allowed his or her personality to become *submerged* by the greater force of the other. Where couples do appear to become 'one flesh' it will not be a case of two separate, strong individuals making a whole that is greater than the sum of the parts: instead, one person will have effectively died, become a cipher, an incomplete human being. In many cases—although not all—it is the wife who allows her personality and individuality to be sucked dry and taken over by the stronger (or more aggressive) personality of the husband.

Nowadays, we seem desperate to tidy people up into couples, so that they will move in society as a team, a unit. We forget that humans are not really designed to be parcelled up in this way. One of the main reasons why marriage tends to bring out so many violent emotions in people is because they are resisting—often without being fully aware of it—being imprisoned for life with just one other person. It is now very common for married women to become clinically depressed. Depression is really anger turned inwards. Husbands tend to turn their anger outwards, and become aggressive, demanding and bad-tempered, blaming everybody apart from themselves for what has upset them. Often, neither partner realizes that he or she is silently rebelling against the straitjacket of marriage, the institution that was supposed to make them so wonderfully happy. Many partners try to escape by having affairs—but all realize that, once married, they are in a cage from which they can never really escape. At most, they go for short sorties, but their wings have been clipped. Even people who divorce usually get married again quite soon. We are so indoctrinated into marriage that few of us can envisage a life without total symbiotic union with another human being.

Again, in the days of the extended family, there was always somebody of one's own sex to talk to, and with whom burdens could be shared. Nowadays, most women have only their husbands to talk to, most men only their wives. There is a general idea that, once married, a couple should be left alone, to sink or swim together. In-laws do not want to 'interfere', and they would rather not know if anything is going wrong. No wonder there are so many marital problems, infidelities and divorces. The institution has become stifling, yet it is constantly presented as the only way to live, the only way to relate to another human being, the only way to love. If you love somebody, so the current wisdom goes, you must want to bind them to you, permanently if possible. This bondage is usually, euphemistically, called 'commitment'.

There is little freedom in the context of marriage. Togetherness is encouraged both on an everyday social level, on

which husbands and wives who do not function as couples are deemed to be a problem, and now, increasingly, in a business context: spouses are often expected to attend office parties and similar occasions, and even, if the employer is a sizeable corporation, to go along on business conferences attended by their partners (a big business is growing up in the arrangement of 'spouses' programmes' at such junkets). And for all our talk of sexual freedom, we do not, as a society, condone sexual intercourse outside marriage. It is acceptable for single people to have as many partners as they like—or at least, it was all right before the advent of AIDS—but once married, men and women are expected to be able to channel their sexual urges into their marital partnership. Society very severely castigates anybody who strays, or rather, is caught straying.

Our current fantasy is that marriage partners should be able to satisfy each other sexually, and that neither should look around for somebody more exciting, newer, younger, unless divorce or widowhood has intervened. This concept of so-called 'serial monogamy', now generally accepted, entails getting rid of the current partner before embarking on a liaison with another.

But society still reserves its severest criticism for those who are caught having affairs with other people while they are still married. This is 'cheating', or 'being unfaithful', and those in high public office or with an otherwise high profile cannot normally escape the indignation of press-generated public opinion. For public servants, the penalty for being found out is a duty to resign immediately from their high position, and there is a general understanding that such people will have to atone in some way for what they have done, because they have broken the rules. . . .

The number of well-known men in public life who have had to atone, often for years on end, for having sexual liaisons outside their marriages, is legion: Gary Hart, the 1988 American presidential candidate; John Profumo, who has spent many years working among the deprived of London's East End since his adultery with Christine Keeler was discovered in 1963; and Lord Lambton, who went to live abroad after he too was discovered, in the early 1970s, to be having an affair with a prostitute. It is less often the case that women in high office have to step down because they are having a secret affair, but then very few women are ever in high office. Throughout history, however, the penalties for women 'caught in adultery' have been severe. One can only wonder at the level of shock and horror that would result if it were to be discovered that Mrs Thatcher or the Queen, for instance, had secretly been having affairs while in positions of authority and trust.

Marriage carries with it the notion that sexual fidelity, 'belonging' to each other, is important. This notion has never been more highly upheld than it is now, in the late twentieth century. In the eighteenth century, when marriage was regarded more lightly, both husbands and wives often had lovers and mistresses, and not always in great secrecy. In medieval times, marriage and love were almost completely separated. One married for duty and fell in love for pleasure—but rarely did one fall in love with a marriage partner. If one was lucky, fondness and respect might develop over the years spent together.

Now, as the song has it, love and marriage go together like a horse and carriage. Once we marry, we are expected to be in love with that person forever. But if we fall in love with somebody else, it is all right for us to get divorced and marry that person. However, woe betide any man and woman who choose to live together just as friends, or as brother and sister. They would be regarded as distinctly odd. A conviction prevails that it is part of nature's plan for us to be permanently united, sexually, financially and emotionally, with just one other person. Many of us believe this is what God ordained for us.

The case of the millionaire novelist Jeffrey Archer in 1987 confirmed our entrenched views of the married state. Archer felt that he had to clear his name when newspapers alleged that he had paid money to Monica Coghlan, a prostitute, to prevent her revealing the nature of their relationship. In the event, it will be remembered, Archer cleared his name, thus making himself £500,000 the richer (he gave the money to a variety of deserving causes).

Archer's case had a curious effect on the British public, and encouraged many people to analyse exactly what they thought marriage was all about. Each day throughout the hearing his wife, Mary, at that time a Cambridge don, was loyally by his side, quietly and smartly dressed. Both found themselves bathed in a plethora of publicity.

The facts of their marriage, so far as they have been made public, are these: Jeffrey and Mary Archer married in 1966, when she was 21 and he was 27. Both were Oxford graduates, heading for glittering careers. It says much for their perception of the importance of the ceremony that they had their wedding videoed, and kept a video-recording of it, part of which has subsequently been seen by millions on BBC television. Jeffrey Archer, a compact, ever-smiling confident young man, went on to become a Conservative MP and was also a keen runner. He resigned his seat when a bad business deal bankrupted him, but rapidly restored his fortunes by writing bestselling fiction.

Mary, meanwhile, though she stayed in the background, was not just a wife and mother. She continued a career of her own, as a scientist and university lecturer. As time went on, the Archers prospered mightily, had two sons and became pillars of the Church. Mary was shown on television playing the organ and singing in the choir. Jeffrey was depicted as a devoted father, and shortly after the court case had his first play successfully premièred in London.

But the main focus for the media throughout the period of the libel hearing was on the Archers' marriage. How far could they be considered the ideal modern couple? It appeared that they had everything—money, looks, a family, wonderful homes, domestic staff—and, wonder of wonders, total devotion to each other after 21 years together. Mary has a career, is good-looking, well-dressed, neat, confident. Both, indeed, are very confident. They obliged for the cameras by being photographed hand in hand, arm in arm, the archetypal modern couple, both earning, both successful, both high-profile, and both with very nice things to say about each other. 'Mary is completely honest,' said Jeffrey in his most sincere manner. 'She is the most honest person I know.'

So the story became 'How to stay married, Archer-style'. Mary and Jeffrey became instant experts on marriage and their views were sought in interview after interview. When asked how she made her marriage 'work', Mary Archer replied that she didn't rate strict sexual fidelity that highly, but thought it was important for couples to be loyal, and able to stand by each other. That statement alone made many journalists reach for their word processors. 'Do you agree that sexual fidelity is not a top priority for marriage?' asked the *Daily Express* of its readers. The columnist Helen Mason wrote in *The Daily Telegraph* that Mary Archer was 'stuck in the 'sixties' to give low priority to sexual fidelity. 'We have seen the alternative to sexual fidelity and it does not work,' Mason wrote. 'Rejection of concepts such as jealousy and possessiveness sound very noble, but in fact, cleaving unto the other only, as we all promised to do, has a sound practical value.'

Helen Mason went on to say what she thought that 'sound practical value' was, and as one might expect, fear of AIDS came top of the list. Security and trust were also mentioned.

Mary Archer was also widely castigated for saying publicly that she did not think it was possible to be 'in love' after 21 years of marriage, though she declared that she was able to love her husband dearly. This called forth the wrath of newspaper columnists, in particular Lynda Lee-Potter of the *Daily Mail*, who said she was not sure Mrs Archer was right in saying that it was impossible to be in love after many years. She asked her readers to disprove this with their own stories and, of course, they obliged in droves, saying that their husbands/wives brought them flowers, presents, declared their love, that they never spent a minute apart and missed each other deeply and inconsolably if one was absent for any length of time. What passed for being 'in love' was, of course, over-attachment and dependence, and not real love. Though we may very much enjoy spending time in the other's company, surely true love means being able to let the other person go, never wanting to bind him or her to you. Wanting to bind a person to you comes from fear, not love.

We try to maintain the fantasy that being in love is a good thing, and that passion and excitement in marriage are also a good thing. In saying that she did not believe it was possible to be in love after many years, and that strict sexual fidelity was not of prime importance, Mary Archer was simply being honest— one of her greatest qualities, as we heard from her husband himself. But honesty would now seem to be a rare commodity where marriage is concerned.

All of us conspire to keep alive the fiction that marriage works, that closeness and commitment are of paramount importance. If we were to admit what marriage is *really* like, it would be revealed as an emperor without clothes, a cloying, confining and repressive union which has the power to imprison at least one, if not both, partners. Modern marriage is, I believe, largely a pretence—a hollow state that we all pretend to like because most of us cannot envisage any other way to live. Society now moves in couples and will exclude us, we believe, if we dare to move alone. The fiction is that, so long as we have a partner, all will be well. Even if that partner causes us more anguish than happiness, it is still better, we believe, to have somebody to whom we are joined by law than to be alone.

The 'ideal' for marriage is in fact a continuing honeymoon. At this stage, although the partners may be sexy and passionate with each other, they are not allowed to be sexy with anybody else. They are also supposed to have the other's interests at heart all the time, to stay in love, to prove this with presents and acknowledgement of anniversaries, and to become mutually dependent on each other. They are not supposed to want to look elsewhere for intellectual, emotional, sexual or any other kind of personal satisfaction, but are supposed to find all they are looking for in this other partner. We seem to feel that men and women are, by themselves, incomplete and can only be 'completed' by attaching themselves permanently to a member of the opposite sex.

Even gays and lesbians are now aping the married state, and are increasingly forming lifelong liaisons of a marital type. Some homosexual couples are even getting 'married' or, rather, having their unions blessed in church. The whole world, it seems, must get married. Anybody who does not do so is considered slightly odd, somewhat eccentric, or even unlovable, and is likely to be put under pressure by his or her peers to form such a liaison.

Married people are supposed to support each other and be devoted to one another. They are not supposed to grow apart or develop their own personalities. People do, of course, all the time, but as a society we do our best to encourage the idea that, once married, a couple are welded together for all time.

The supposition is that total togetherness is a highly desirable, indeed enviable, condition. Autonomy is out.

From time to time, reports and surveys about marriage appear in the newspapers. The surveys always prove that there is still overwhelming support for the institution, and as a subject marriage fascinates everybody, not least because there is such a huge disparity between the fantasy and the reality.

There is also a widespread belief that marriage is now treated too lightly by many couples. In one survey about 75 per cent of adults interviewed felt that the institution ought to be regarded with more seriousness. The leading virtues in a married couple were listed as faithfulness, mutual respect and understanding. Sex and good housekeeping also appeared on the list, but much further down. Unsatisfactory sex was not considered a good reason for divorce, whereas sexual infidelity was. A happy sexual relationship was considered important by about 50 per cent of those questioned.

By and large, the British public showed themselves conservative in their attitudes: 76 per cent believed that women with small children should stay at home and look after them, and 19 per cent felt that women with teenagers should do the same.

An opinion poll survey carried out for the *The People* in October 1985 purported to reveal the 'intimate secrets' of 1000 married men and women. One 'intimate' secret revealed was that people now expect an awful lot from marriage. We are no longer content to co-exist with somebody towards whom we feel lukewarm or indifferent; we feel we have the right to be madly in love, and that marriage should make us happy, fulfilled and secure. If a marriage does not live up to these expectations, couples will not hesitate to head towards the divorce courts. No longer will people tolerate—as their forebears did—a miserable marriage, or one where there is no compatibility.

The newspaper spelled out, in order, the nine most important ingredients of a happy marriage, as revealed by its survey. These were give and take; treating each other as equals; liking each other as friends; staying in love; staying faithful; good sex; having individual interests; financial security; and children.

These all sound reasonable, but what do they really mean?

'Give and take' seems to be what does *not* happen in the average marriage, however much the partners hope it will. Whenever an old married couple celebrating a golden wedding is asked the secret of a successful marriage, the answer is always 'give and take'. To give and take really means to be tolerant, to have the best interests of the other person at heart. How many people do that? More often than not, individual wishes prevail and a power struggle develops, with one partner trying to dominate the other while the dominated partner struggles to assert individuality.

Very often it is the man who takes and the woman who gives. At least, that is how the wife usually sees it. The husband more often sees it the other way round. He sees himself (if the marriage follows the traditional pattern of breadwinning husband and dependent wife, as fewer and fewer do) as giving everything, providing everything, and getting precious little in return.

The main problem in modern marriage is that the majority of people are desperately hungry for love. They want constant assurances that they are loved and wanted and held in respect. When the husband comes home and finds his meal is not on the table, he becomes angry because this means he is not loved enough. When the wife discovers he has forgotten her birthday yet again, she is angry because this means he is not thinking of her. People demand respect and love from others when they have little for themselves. But you cannot demand respect. You cannot even demand give and take.

Genuine give and take in marriage can be hard to find. What often happens is that there is a trade-off: I will have sex with you tonight if you buy me that new dress tomorrow; I will have your boss to dinner if you take me to the ballet. These are crass examples, of course, but they serve to illustrate the principle. Give and take, in the average marriage, usually means bargaining positions and power struggles, in which both sides tend to end up feeling miserable and cheated. So much is expected of the other person—generally more than he or she is able to give, and we are deeply disappointed when our partners fail to come up to the mark. Yet why *should* somebody else be expected to fulfil our fantasies?

'Treating each other as equals', the second 'ingredient' of a successful marriage according to the survey, is fundamentally impossible in the context of marriage. Embedded in the marriage laws themselves is the concept that men and women are *not* the same and *not* equal. The only way in which a man and woman can stay equal is not to marry, but to remain single. Marriage, by its very nature, is an arrangement which renders the two parties unequal. It is only in the twentieth century that a married woman has even been considered a person at all. In the past, she was little more than one of her husband's goods and chattels. Her property, if she had any as a single woman, became his, while his remained his, on marriage. (Personal possessions such as clothes and jewellery did not constitute property.) We may imagine things have improved, but in reality little has changed.

As the law does not see married men and women as equals, so it is impossible for them to regard each other as equals. A woman is usually expected to join her husband wherever he goes, to support him emotionally, to believe that everything he does is right. Even today, a wife cannot be compelled to give evidence against her husband in court. Many wives will stand by their husbands even when they have been accused of cheating, consorting with prostitutes, lying, even murder. This happens because, in the majority of marriages, the woman becomes more dependent and attached than the man—and often truly imagines she cannot live without him.

If you want an equal relationship, do not get married: once married, you simply will not be allowed by society or by the law to remain equal.

'Liking each other as friends' was the third ingredient suggested by the survey.

Yes, this is really the ideal. But again, it is impossible in the average marriage. Why? Simply because you are forced to be so close, so emotionally involved, so financially entangled, that friendship becomes impossible. Many wives of famous men, when interviewed, will say, 'My husband is my best friend.' By that, they often mean that this man is their *only* friend: they have in fact forsaken everybody else and are often physically isolated, to the extent that friendship is almost impossible after marriage. Many married women simply do not go to the theatre, the pub, or any place of entertainment unless the spouse is there as well. They become actually incapable, in time, of doing anything on their own. And if their husbands work very long hours they find themselves virtual prisoners in their homes, passing whole days and evenings without seeing or speaking to anyone else.

'*Staying in love*' was the next requirement listed by the survey. The idea of being perpetually in love, in the romantic sense, is actually impossible for more than a very short space of time, as Mary Archer so rightly declared in her interview. If being 'in love' continues, it becomes an obsession, almost an illness. We like to promote the idea of being in love because we believe this emotion elevates us as human beings. It is a fine emotion to be able to love, but not to be in love. That is a selfish, high-arousal state of short duration, and it should be acknowledged as such.

'*Staying faithful*' was requirement no. 5. Most married people put a high value on sexual fidelity, because they would far rather their partner never so much as looked at another man or woman. The feeling comes from insecurity. Fidelity in marriage is now (and has always been) extremely rare. Though there are no reliable figures, newspaper surveys tend to reveal that at least 30 per cent of wives have affairs (of those who will admit to them) and the number is probably even higher for men. The problem is that it is absolutely impossible to feel both highly passionate and highly sexed and remain faithful to one person. Men and women who are sexy will almost certainly have affairs at some time in their marriage.

'*Good sex*' came next in the survey's conclusions, but although this is now seen as a vital ingredient of a happy marriage, it would not have been thus viewed in the past. Whenever people look to their marriage partners to fulfil their sexual fantasies, they are bound to be disappointed. Even the wildest, most ecstatic sex life dulls with repetition, as we all know, and the only real way to obtain 'good sex' (for those who see it as important) is to have a variety of partners—which does not quite square with the other requirements mentioned in the survey. In asking for fidelity, good sex and a good friendship, people ask for the moon. They are quite simply expecting far too much.

'*Having individual interests*', on the other hand, really is important. Contrary to what people like to believe, most married people do not become more like one another as the years go by. For partners to try to pretend they have identical interests is only a recipe for disaster. Yet many have the idea that they must share everything: they go on holidays together even when one hates the place or type of holiday chosen, and one partner will try to bamboozle the other into pursuing the interests or activities that appeal to him or her. Maintaining individual interests is a far preferable idea, though very few couples seem to manage it.

'*Financial security*' was also mentioned on the shopping list of 'ingredients' for a happy marriage. Most of us would like financial security, but we are fools if we expect marriage to provide it. Girls have traditionally dreamed of marrying rich men. Those who did often discovered there was a high price to pay for access to the riches. The Bible tells us that it is harder for a rich man to enter the kingdom of heaven than for a camel to go through the eye of a needle. The reason for this saying, which is not very popular in an age when financial success is seen as the only sort worth having, is that material riches often make people believe they have more power and influence, and are more important, than is really the case. Rich husbands often treat their wives badly, as they see them as yet another possession, as something else they can buy. There is no greater inequality in marriage than financial inequality, and one's partner's possession of wealth does not make for any kind of security for the one who has nothing. The only financial security any individual can be sure of is that provided by himself or herself. Any other assumption is dangerous and can lead to rows and disappointments.

Is financial security attained when your spouse provides for you with insurance policies and pension schemes? Not necessarily; money can always be lost, as leading financiers have often found to their cost. At least the *People* readers had the sense to put financial security in marriage near the bottom of the list.

'Children', which appeared ninth and last in priority in the results of the survey, are a contentious subject. Readers were wise to put them at the bottom of their list. As we marry for 'happiness', so we have, or say we have, children for the same reason. But all the surveys show that couples without children are at least as happy as those with, and tend to stay together longer. Children do not and cannot bring happiness; neither can they cement a disintegrating marriage, although their presence might ensure that couples stay together longer than they might otherwise have done when things have gone wrong. Children are very often seen as part of the kit, something one 'goes in for' after marrying—and sometimes before or outside wedlock. As Princess Anne bluntly put it: 'Children are an occupational hazard of being a wife.' In the old days, people married mainly in order to have children, to continue the line, to have more hands to work the land, or to provide heirs or marriageable daughters. Now, those reasons for having children have largely gone, and most people do not know why they have them. We are told by infertile couples that they 'desperately' long for children, but we rarely ask them why. Children are supposed to crown a couple's happiness, but we can see all around us glaring evidence that this is rarely the effect they have.

Children can be a joy, it is true, but are they an ingredient of a happy marriage? I doubt it. It seems to me that children, particularly nowadays, cause more problems than they solve. Certainly they can never act as adhesive, to bring couples closer together, as some erroneously imagine. . . .

OF ALL THE CRIMES THAT ARE BROUGHT TO court in any one year, a high proportion of them will be domestic. In fact, it is said that about 70 per cent of all serious crimes committed take place in the matrimonial home. Not all husbands and wives are driven to violence or murder, of course, but many are sorely tempted, and many experience moments when they feel that life would be easier and more pleasant if the spouse were permanently out of the way.

These feelings arise because we invest so much in marriage—in 'making it work'; naturally we are deeply disappointed, even enraged, when all our efforts seem to come to nothing, or are unappreciated. A husband may slave at his job for fifteen hours a day to give his wife 'everything' only to find that while he has been out building up his business she has been carrying on with her hairdresser, the lodger, an old schoolfriend or a neighbour.

A woman may consider that she has 'devoted' the best years of her life to being a good and faithful wife, giving up her own career, cooking her husband nice meals and trying to be passionate in bed, only to discover that on his late nights 'at the office' he has been having an affair with his secretary or a high-powered career woman he has met. Such discoveries usually lead to highly emotional scenes—quarrels, recriminations, anger, jealousy, resentment and lasting hostility.

It appears that modern marriage brings out far more negative than positive emotions. What is usually seen as 'love' between two people who are married is often not love at all—it is a degraded, vice-ridden form of the emotion. Those who truly love somebody else will simply let them be free to develop their own personalities, to do as they wish—even if that includes being physically unfaithful.

People are horrified when they find evidence of a spouse's affairs; the discovery makes them afraid. All through the marriage, they have thought they owned the other person and controlled his or her life: the affair is evidence that they do not. We try to cling to other people when we have little self-respect and self-confidence. We vainly hope that the other person will give us what we lack—forgetting that the other person is, like ourselves, a fallible, weak human being who is probably unable to cope with such demands.

Those who are strong, and who value themselves, will be able to see the person they have chosen to live with as a friend, as somebody who is entitled to live a life of his or her own and with whom they can be civilized and respectful at all times. Very few modern marriages fall into this category. The 'commitment' we expect from a marriage partner is similar to a commitment to jail: it prevents our being free individuals. We are serving a sentence, supposedly for life.

Of course, not all marriages follow this pattern. But the majority will have ele-ments of this negativity in them. We have come to feel it is right to be so bound up with another human being that every single thing he or she does, every twitch of the face, every fleeting expression, intimately affects us. Many wives live in constant fear of their husbands' anger, just as many husbands are terrified if their wives become depressed, or 'frigid', because these emotions mean that there is a cut-off, that communication lines are no longer open.

Modern marriage is in a parlous state, as any marriage guidance counsellor or divorce lawyer will confirm. It stifles individuality, encourages us to tell lies, to practise deceit, and to be manipulative, cunning and child-like, all because we live in fear that this (usually) rather ordinary and unremarkable individual whom we have married will do something that rocks the boat—be cross, not speak, throw things around, generally make life unpleasant, or go off with somebody else.

A moment's reflection will show that it is ridiculous that so many people should allow their lives to be ruined, even prematurely ended, as in the cases described earlier, just because they cannot see how to co-exist with somebody to whom they said, 'I do' a few years previously.

The discredited Indian guru Bhagwan Shree Rajneesh said that one reason why he never married was because 'all wives and husbands come to hate each other in time'; judging by the evidence available, this is largely true.

Marriage guidance counsellors, sex therapists, advice columnists and many others have pondered the matter of how to make marriage work better and with less acrimony and distrust between the partners. The newspapers, television and radio carry lengthy debates about what constitutes a happy, perfect marriage.

Usually, the only way we can envisage marriage working is if it 'goes back' to how we think it used to be, with bread-winning husband, dependent wife and total fidelity. It is commonly assumed by traditionalists that the main reasons why today's marriages are not working is because women these days want to be financially independent, have careers and maintain their individuality. If they were content to put their families first, goes the argument, all would be well. It is extremely unlikely that marriages of the past which did follow this pattern were happy—or even that women of previous centuries were as loving and giving as they were made out to be. Even a cursory reading of novels by famous Victorian writers will give an impression of marriage that differs substantially from the fantasy we fondly carry in our heads. . . .

Men and women, fed by romantic fantasies and illusions, both yearn for marriage to be some kind of safe haven, where they will be protected from the harsh outside world. People yearn for this in marriage as they used to pray for it in their religion.

Christian hymns abound with injunctions to the Lord to keep us safe from all the perils and dangers of the world. 'Safe in the arms of Jesus' has been translated in our modern times to being safe in the arms of a loving spouse.

It is a current cliché to say that we have substituted love in marriage for the love that used to be reserved for God. Modern marriage is in a parlous state because we want and expect so much of each other, yet never stop to consider whether our marital partner is actually capable of providing what we want. There is no way to make marriages work better

while we bring to them false hopes and expectations.

Any attempt to bind people closer together, by law or by custom, is bound to fail. People become violent and hateful towards each other when they are deeply disappointed. We buy a dream—and all too often end up with a nightmare.

In her almost painfully honest book *Deceived with Kindness*, Angelica Garnett, daughter of Vanessa Bell and Duncan Grant, describes her marriage to 'Bunny' Garnett, 26 years her senior:

> The story of our marriage could be summed up as the struggle on his side to maintain the unlooked-for realization of a private dream, about which, in spite of an almost wilful blindness, he must have had deep misgivings: and on mine of the slow emancipation from a nightmare, which was none the less painful because I thought of it as almost entirely my own fault. . . . Had I not married him, he would have been a perfect friend, one in whom I could have safely confided and who would always have given me good advice.

'At bottom,' she continues, 'my love for him was simply a delusion—a dream which I had not the strength to sacrifice . . . I saw myself being swept along by a dangerous current, but was unable to lift a finger to prevent it . . . I knew inwardly that I was doing the wrong thing.'

Angelica concludes that what she had found was not life, but a backwater. Sadly her experience is not an isolated one. When I look at the marriages of most of my friends and acquaintances, I can see all too clearly that they are living a nightmare, one which, frequently, they have the courage neither to admit nor to escape from; they are living with the consequences of a ghastly mistake.

Marriage, at least in its present form, fails all of us. How much better relationships between the sexes would be if we truly could be friends, as Angelica Garnett realized she could have been with Bunny, and did not feel this overpowering need to tie ourselves together in Gordian knots. . . .

THE INSTITUTION OF MARRIAGE CARRIES A heavy historical burden. It seems, from this brief historical survey, that it was ordained in order that communities could consolidate and strengthen their position. All the historical arguments in favour of marriage now seem to have disappeared yet, strangely, we still cling to it.

Today, large numbers of people have no religious belief, yet still we adhere to the basic Christian idea of marriage—which has to a significant degree permeated the rest of the world. Even civil weddings held in registry offices have a veneer of religiosity. It is now becoming common for those undertaking their second, or even third, marriages to have them 'blessed' in church by a priest, which would have been unthinkable even as recently as the 1950s.

It seems we are left with the empty shell of an institution which has no real purpose in the modern world. People can function and exist just as well without marriage as with it. The only reason it has survived for as long as it has seems to be that the inspiration of romantic fantasy has prolonged an otherwise superannuated institution.

At one time it was virtually a necessity for men and women to marry, and thenceforth to raise families in an established household which could defend itself against human enemies and physical disasters. There was safety and strength in numbers. Now that the state has taken over most of the former functions of the family and we no longer need older sons to inherit and to defend territory, there seems little justification for continuing marriage as an institution.

POSTSCRIPT

Is Marriage Good for You?

There are many ways to view the outcomes of marriage for the individuals involved as well as for the society at large. Statistics on divorce and remarriage seem to indicate that many people are dissatisfied with marriage and thus divorce. However, many also choose to try again, hoping that lack of success, adjustment, or happiness in one marriage does not predict the same deficiencies in a second or subsequent attempt. Some contemporary social critics say that marriage was never intended to be a lifelong institution, since the thinking that produced that idea occurred when individuals rarely lived much past 35 or 40 years of age and surviving spouses often had two or more mates.

Much of the data indicating that marriage might be "good for you" is correlative, meaning, for example, that health statistics and marital status can be related to each other; however, that is not necessarily evidence of a cause and effect relationship.

Hodgkinson's approach advocates abolishing marriage in the name of "the better good" for both individuals and society. Her views raise the question of whether or not the institution of marriage is as viable as people would like it to be. Are other forms possible?

SUGGESTED READINGS

J. Bernard, *The Future of Marriage* (Bantam Books, 1973).

J. P. Bohland, "The Relationship Between Communication and Marital Satisfaction: A Review," *Journal of Sex and Marital Therapy,* **13** (1987): 286–313.

F. D. Fincham, "The Assessment of Marital Quality: A Reevaluation," *Journal of Marriage and the Family,* **49** (1987): 797–810.

G. D. Lowe, "Gender, Marital Status and Well-Being: A Retest of Bernard's His and Her Marriages," *Sociological Spectrum,* **7** (1987): 301–307.

S. R. Marks, "Toward a Systems Theory of Marital Quality," *Journal of Marriage and the Family,* **51** (1989): 15–26.

A. J. Norton and J. E. Moorman, "Current Trends in Marriage and Divorce Among American Women," *Journal of Marriage and the Family,* **49** (1987): 3–14.

T. Smith, "Happiness: A Harvest of Shared Lives," *Marriage and Family Living,* **69** (1987): 18–20.

R. M. Stopes, "Marriage in Two Cultures," *British Journal of Social Psychology,* **27** (1988): 159–169.

ISSUE 5

Should Gays and Lesbians Fight for the Right to Marry?

YES: Andrew Sullivan, from "Here Comes the Groom," *The New Republic* (August 28, 1989)

NO: Paula L. Ettelbrick, from "Since When Is Marriage a Path to Liberation?" *OUT/LOOK* (Fall 1989)

ISSUE SUMMARY

YES: Andrew Sullivan, a former editor of *The New Republic*, proposes that allowing gay couples to marry would have social and legal advantages that new laws on "domestic partnerships" cannot provide.
NO: Gay rights activist Paula L. Ettelbrick argues that marriage would further constrain lesbians and gay men, making it easier for society to ignore evidence that there is a unique and distinctive gay identity and culture and to refuse to validate relationships that do not include marriage.

In his book *Gay and Lesbian Youth* (Hemisphere, 1990), Ritch C. Savin-Williams explains that there are two political perspectives or views on homosexuality. The first perspective advocates that gay men and lesbians are similar to everyone else. They only differ in whom they choose to love. He calls this a conservative position that promotes the benefits of accommodation. Promoters of this perspective believe that fitting in with society will lead to respectability, and that gay "people will be normal, good citizens with civic responsibilities and appropriate behavior."

The second view, which Savin-Williams refers to as the gay radical perspective, promotes the belief that gay men and lesbians are "atypical." The reasons for this uniqueness may be traced to either biological or cultural reasons. Those who advocate biological origins want society to broaden its acceptance levels of what is biologically "normal" as well as its categorization of human traits as exclusively masculine or feminine. Those who believe in the cultural origins explanation hold out little hope that society will ever be very accepting of homosexuality. This group wants an end to violence against gay men and lesbians and to have civil rights extended to them.

Marriage could be considered one of those civil rights that most people take for granted. The benefits of marriage include the right to file a joint income tax return, the right of a surviving spouse to inherit property, and the right of each spouse to share in health care insurance and pension benefits made available by many employers. In this way the law favors the marital union and helps foster and preserve the marital relationship.

In the eyes of the law, same-sex couples have none of these legal rights. Such couples are barred from forming a legal marital bond that would secure their relationship rights and publicly acknowledge their private commitments. It is true that a few states and cities recognize "domestic partnerships" and prohibit discrimination based on marital status, but such partnerships do not give gay and lesbian relationships the exact same rights as married couples. Is this an important difference? Should lesbian and gay couples have the right to marry just as heterosexual couples do? Should they want that right?

In the following selections, Andrew Sullivan argues in support of marriage between gay and lesbian couples because he feels that domestic partnership laws are inadequate and that such laws allow some heterosexual partners to escape the responsibilities and commitment implied by the marital contract. Marriage, Sullivan argues, is a much more secure and protective legal arrangement than is the domestic partnership. For lesbian and gay couples, marriage would symbolize a clear set of responsibilities and establish a more definite standard of partner commitment. This could lead to greater social approval because homosexuals would be viewed as being more family-oriented and less deviant.

Paula L. Ettelbrick strongly disagrees, asserting that marriage *would* provide greater social approval, but at too great a cost. Liberation by means of marriage would render lesbians and gay men even more invisible to the larger community and would undermine the movement to establish the existence of a separate gay and lesbian identity and culture, asserts Ettelbrick. Fervor for the notion that valid and committed relationships can exist in many forms other than in marriage would be diminished, if not lost. Justice, argues Ettelbrick, is much more important than rights. Justice means being accepted despite being different, while rights are legally dictated and morally dismissed. Ettelbrick claims that having the legal right to marry would mean that individuals in gay relationships would be expected to behave just like heterosexuals, amounting to the concession that heterosexual relationships represent the standard for what a good or successful relationship should be.

YES

Andrew Sullivan

HERE COMES THE GROOM

Last month in New York, a court ruled that a gay lover had the right to stay in his deceased partner's rent-control apartment because the lover qualified as a member of the deceased's family. The ruling deftly annoyed almost everybody. Conservatives saw judicial activism in favor of gay rent control: three reasons to be appalled. Chastened liberals (such as the *New York Times* editorial page), while endorsing the recognition of gay relationships, also worried about the abuse of already stretched entitlements that the ruling threatened. What neither side quite contemplated is that they both might be right, and that the way to tackle the issue of unconventional relationships in conventional society is to try something both more radical and more conservative than putting courts in the business of deciding what is and is not a family. That alternative is the legalization of civil gay marriage.

The New York rent-control case did not go anywhere near that far, which is the problem. The rent-control regulations merely stipulated that a "family" member had the right to remain in the apartment. The judge ruled that to all intents and purposes a gay lover is part of his lover's family, inasmuch as a "family" merely means an interwoven social life, emotional commitment, and some level of financial interdependence.

It's a principle now well established around the country. Several cities have "domestic partnership" laws, which allow relationships that do not fit into the category of heterosexual marriage to be registered with the city and qualify for benefits that up till now have been reserved for straight married couples. San Francisco, Berkeley, Madison, and Los Angeles all have legislation, as does the politically correct Washington, D.C., suburb, Takoma Park. In these cities, a variety of interpersonal arrangements qualify for health insurance, bereavement leave, insurance, annuity and pension rights, housing rights (such as rent-control apartments), adoption and inheritance rights. Eventually, according to gay lobby groups, the aim is to include federal income tax and veterans' benefits as well. A recent case even involved the right to use a family member's accumulated frequent-flier points. Gays are not the only beneficiaries; heterosexual "live-togethers" also qualify.

There's an argument, of course, that the current legal advantages extended to married people unfairly discriminate against people who've shaped their lives in less conventional arrangements. But it doesn't take a genius to see that enshrining in the law a vague principle like "domestic partnership" is an invitation to qualify at little personal cost for a vast array of entitlements otherwise kept crudely under control.

To be sure, potential DPs have to prove financial interdependence, shared living arrangements, and a commitment to mutual caring. But they don't need to have a sexual relationship or even closely mirror old-style marriage. In principle, an elderly woman and her live-in nurse could qualify. A couple of uneuphemistically confirmed bachelors could be DPs. So could two close college students, a pair of seminarians, or a couple of frat buddies. Left as it is, the concept of domestic partnership could open a Pandora's box of litigation and subjective judicial decision-making about who qualifies. You either are or are not married; it's not a complex question. Whether you are in a "domestic partnership" is not so clear.

More important, the concept of domestic partnership chips away at the prestige of traditional relationships and undermines the priority we give them. This priority is not necessarily a product of heterosexism. Consider heterosexual couples. Society has good reason to extend legal advantages to heterosexuals who choose the formal sanction of marriage over simply living together. They make a deeper commitment to one another and to society; in exchange, society extends certain benefits to them. Marriage provides an anchor, if an arbitrary and weak one, in the chaos of sex and relationships to which we are all prone. It provides a mechanism for emotional stability, economic security, and the healthy rearing of the next generation. We rig the law in its favor not because we disparage all forms of relationship other than the nuclear family, but because we recognize that not to promote marriage would be to ask too much of human virtue. In the context of the weakened family's effect upon the poor, it might also invite social disintegration. One of the worst products of the New Right's "family values" campaign is that its extremism and hatred of diversity has disguised this more measured and more convincing case for the importance of the marital bond.

The concept of domestic partnership ignores these concerns, indeed directly attacks them. This is a pity, since one of its most important objectives—providing some civil recognition for gay relationships—is a noble cause and one completely compatible with the defense of the family. But the way to go about it is not to undermine straight marriage; it is to legalize old-style marriage for gays.

THE GAY MOVEMENT HAS DUCKED THIS IS-sue primarily out of fear of division. Much of the gay leadership clings to notions of gay life as essentially outsider, anti-bourgeois, radical. Marriage, for them, is co-optation into straight society. For the Stonewall generation, it is hard to see how this vision of conflict will ever fundamentally change. But for many other gays—my guess, a majority—while they don't deny the importance of rebellion 20 years ago and are grateful for what was done, there's now the sense of a new opportunity. A need to rebel has quietly ceded to a desire to belong. To be gay and to be bourgeois no longer seems such an absurd proposition. Certainly since AIDS, to be gay and to be responsible has become a necessity.

Gay marriage squares several circles at the heart of the domestic partnership debate. Unlike domestic partnership, it allows for recognition of gay relationships, while casting no aspersions on traditional marriage. It merely asks that gays be allowed to join in. Unlike domestic partnership, it doesn't open up avenues for heterosexuals to get benefits without the responsibilities of marriage, or a nightmare of definitional litigation. And unlike domestic partnership, it harnesses to an already established social convention the yearnings for stability and acceptance among a fast-maturing gay community.

Gay marriage also places more responsibilities upon gays: it says for the first time that gay relationships are not better or worse than straight relationships, and that the same is expected of them. And it's clear and dignified. There's a legal benefit to a clear, common symbol of commitment. There's also a personal benefit. One of the ironies of domestic partnership is that it's not only more complicated than marriage, it's more demanding, requiring an elaborate statement of intent to qualify. It amounts to a substantial invasion of privacy. Why, after all, should gays be required to prove commitment before they get married in a way we would never dream of asking of straights?

Legalizing gay marriage would offer homosexuals the same deal society now offers heterosexuals: general social approval and specific legal advantages in exchange for a deeper and harder-to-extract-yourself-from commitment to another human being. Like straight marriage, it would foster social cohesion, emotional security, and economic prudence. Since there's no reason gays should not be allowed to adopt or be foster parents, it could also help nurture children. And its introduction would not be some sort of radical break with social custom. As it has become more acceptable for gay people to acknowledge their loves publicly, more and more have committed themselves to one another for life in full view of their families and their friends. A law institutionalizing gay marriage would merely reinforce a healthy social trend. It would also, in the wake of AIDS, qualify as a genuine public health measure. Those conservatives who deplore promiscuity among some homosexuals should be among the first to support it. Burke could have written a powerful case for it.

The argument that gay marriage would subtly undermine the unique legitimacy of straight marriage is based upon a fallacy. For heterosexuals, straight marriage would remain the most significant—and only legal—social bond. Gay marriage could only delegitimize straight marriage if it were a real alternative to it, and this is clearly not true. To put it bluntly, there's precious little evidence that straights could be persuaded by any law to have sex with—let alone marry—someone of their own sex. The only possible effect of this sort would be to persuade gay men and women who force themselves into heterosexual marriage (often at appalling cost to themselves and their families) to find a focus for their family instincts in a more personally positive environment. But this is clearly a plus, not a minus: gay marriage could both avoid a lot of tortured families and create the possibility for many happier ones. It is not, in short, a denial of family values. It's an extension of them.

Of course, some would claim that any legal recognition of homosexuality is a de facto attack upon heterosexuality. But even the most hardened conservatives recognize that gays are a permanent minority and aren't likely to go away. Since persecution is not an option in a civilized society, why not coax gays into traditional values rather than rail incoherently against them?

THERE'S A LESS ELABORATE ARGUMENT FOR gay marriage: it's good for gays. It provides role models for young gay people who, after the exhilaration of coming out, can easily lapse into short-term relationships and insecurity with no tangible goal in sight. My own guess is that most gays would embrace such a goal with as much (if not more) commitment as straights. Even in our society as it is, many lesbian relationships are virtual textbook cases of monogamous commitment. Legal gay marriage could also help bridge the gulf often found between gays and their parents. It could bring the essence of gay life—a gay couple—into the heart of the traditional straight family in a way the family can most understand and the gay offspring can most easily acknowledge. It could do as much to heal the gay-straight rift as any amount of gay rights legislation.

If these arguments sound socially conservative, that's no accident. It's one of the richest ironies of our society's blind spot toward gays that essentially conservative social goals should have the appearance of being so radical. But gay marriage is not a radical step. It avoids the mess of domestic partnership; it is humane; it is conservative in the best sense of the word. It's also practical. Given the fact that we already allow legal gay relationships, what possible social goal is advanced by framing the law to encourage those relationships to be unfaithful, undeveloped, and insecure?

NO

Paula L. Ettelbrick

SINCE WHEN IS MARRIAGE A PATH TO LIBERATION?

"Marriage is a great institution . . . if you like living in institutions," according to a bit of T-shirt philosophy I saw recently. Certainly, marriage is an institution. It is one of the most venerable, impenetrable institutions in modern society. Marriage provides the ultimate form of acceptance for personal intimate relationships in our society, and gives those who marry an insider status of the most powerful kind.

Steeped in a patriarchal system that looks to ownership, property, and dominance of men over women as its basis, the institution of marriage long has been the focus of radical feminist revulsion. Marriage defines certain relationships as more valid than all others. Lesbian and gay relationships, being neither legally sanctioned or commingled by blood, are always at the bottom of the heap of social acceptance and importance.

Given the imprimatur of social and personal approval which marriage provides, it is not surprising that some lesbians and gay men among us would look to legal marriage for self-affirmation. After all, those who marry can be instantaneously transformed from "outsiders" to "insiders," and we have a desperate need to become insiders.

It could make us feel OK about ourselves, perhaps even relieve some of the internalized homophobia that we all know so well. Society will then celebrate the birth of our children and mourn the death of our spouses. It would be easier to get health insurance for our spouses, family memberships to the local museum, and a right to inherit our spouse's cherished collection of lesbian mystery novels even if she failed to draft a will. Never again would we have to go to a family reunion and debate about the correct term for introducing our lover/partner/significant other to Aunt Flora. Everything would be quite easy and very nice.

So why does this unlikely event so deeply disturb me? For two major reasons. First, marriage will not liberate us as lesbians and gay men. In fact, it will constrain us, make us more invisible, force our assimilation into the mainstream, and undermine the goals of gay liberation. Second, attaining the right to marry will not transform our society from one that makes narrow, but dramatic, distinctions between those who are married and those who are not married to one that respects and encourages choice of relationships and family diversity. Marriage runs contrary to two of the primary goals of the lesbian and gay movement: the affirmation of gay identity and culture; and the validation of many forms of relationships.

When analyzed from the standpoint of civil rights, certainly lesbians and gay men should have a right to marry. But obtaining a right does not always result in justice. White male firefighters in Birmingham, Alabama have been fighting for their "rights" to retain their jobs by overturning the city's affirmative action guidelines. If their "rights" prevail, the courts will have failed in rendering justice. The "right" fought for by the white male firefighters, as well as those who advocate strongly for the "rights" to legal marriage for gay people, will result, at best, in limited or narrowed "justice" for those closest to power at the expense of those who have been historically marginalized.

The fight for justice has as its goal the realignment of power imbalances among individuals and classes of people in society. A pure "rights" analysis often fails to incorporate a broader understanding of the underlying inequities that operate to deny justice to a fuller range of people and groups. In setting our priorities as a community, we just combine the concept of both rights and justice. At this point in time, making legal marriage for lesbian and gay couples a priority would set an agenda of gaining rights for a few, but would do nothing to correct the power imbalances between those who are married (whether gay or straight) and those who are not. Thus, justice would not be gained.

JUSTICE FOR GAY MEN AND LESBIANS WILL be achieved only when we are accepted and supported in this society *despite* our differences from the dominant culture and the choices we make regarding our relationships. Being queer is more than setting up house, sleeping with a person of the same gender, and seeking state approval for doing so. It is an identity, a culture with many variations. It is a way of dealing with the world by diminishing the constraints of gender roles which have for so long kept women and gay people oppressed and invisible. Being queer means pushing the parameters of sex, sexuality, and family, and in the process transforming the very fabric of society. Gay liberation is inexorably linked to women's liberation. Each is essential to the other.

The moment we argue, as some among us insist on doing, that we should be treated as equals because we are really just like married couples and hold the same values to be true, we undermine the very purpose of our movement and begin the dangerous process of silencing our different voices. As a lesbian, I am fundamentally different from non-lesbian women. That's the point. Marriage, as it exists today, is antithetical to my liberation as a lesbian and as a woman because it mainstreams my life and voice. I do not want to be known as "Mrs. Attached-To-Somebody Else." Nor do I want to give the state the power to regulate my primary relationship.

Yet, the concept of equality in our legal system does not support differences, it only supports sameness. The very standard for equal protection is that people who are similarly situated must be treated equally. To make an argument for equal protection, we will be required to claim that gay and lesbian relationships are the same as straight relationships. To gain the right, we must compare ourselves to married couples. The law looks to the insiders as the norm, regardless of how flawed or unjust their institutions, and requires that those seeking the law's equal protection situate themselves in a similar posture to those who are already protected. In arguing for the right to legal marriage, lesbians and gay men would be forced to claim that we are just like heterosexual couples, have the same goals and purposes, and vow to structure our lives similarly. The law provides no room to argue that we are different, but are nonetheless entitled to equal protection.

The thought of emphasizing our sameness to married heterosexuals in order to obtain this "right" terrifies me. It rips away the very heart and soul of what I believe it is to be a lesbian in this world. It robs me of the opportunity to make a difference. We end up mimicking all that is bad about the institution of marriage in our effort to appear to be the same as straight couples.

By looking to our sameness and de-emphasizing our differences, we don't even place ourselves in a position of power that would allow us to transform marriage from an institution that emphasizes property and state regulation of relationships to an institution which recognizes one of many types of valid and respected relationships. Until the constitution is interpreted to respect and encourage differences, pursuing the legalization of same-sex marriage would be leading our movement into a trap; we would be demanding access to the very institution which, in its current form,

would undermine *our* movement to recognize many different kinds of relationships. We would be perpetuating the elevation of married relationships and of "couples" in general, and further eclipsing other relationships of choice.

Ironically, gay marriage, instead of liberating gay sex and sexuality, would further outlaw all gay and lesbian sex which is not performed in a marital context. Just as sexually active non-married women face stigma and double standards around sex and sexual activity, so too would non-married gay people. The only legitimate gay sex would be that which is cloaked in and regulated by marriage. Its legitimacy would stem not from an acceptance of gay sexuality, but because the Supreme Court and society in general fiercely protect the privacy of marital relationships. Lesbians and gay men who do not seek the state's stamp of approval would clearly face increased sexual oppression.

UNDOUBTEDLY, WHETHER WE ADMIT IT OR not, we all need to be accepted by the broader society. That motivation fuels our work to eliminate discrimination in the workplace and elsewhere, fight for custody of our children, create our own families, and so on. The growing discussion about the right to marry may be explained in part by this need for acceptance. Those closer to the norm or to power in this country are more likely to see marriage as a principle of freedom and equality. Those who are more acceptable to the mainstream because of race, gender, and economic status are more likely to want the right to marry. It is the final acceptance, the ultimate affirmation of identity.

On the other hand, more marginal members of the lesbian and gay community (women, people of color, working class and poor) are less likely to see marriage as having relevance to our struggles for survival. After all, what good is the affirmation of our relationships (that is, marital relationships) if we are rejected as women, black, or working class?

The path to acceptance is much more complicated for many of us. For instance, if we choose legal marriage, we may enjoy the right to add our spouse to our health insurance policy at work, since most employment policies are defined by one's marital status, not family relationship. However, that choice assumes that we have a job *and* that our employer provides us with health benefits. For women, particularly women of color who tend to occupy the low-paying jobs that do not provide healthcare benefits at all, it will not matter one bit if they are able to marry their woman partners. The opportunity to marry will neither get them health benefits nor transform them from outsider to insider.

Of course, a white man who marries another white man who has a full-time job with benefits will certainly be able to share in those benefits and overcome the only obstacle left to full societal assimilation—the goal of many in his class. In other words, gay marriage will not topple the system that allows only the privileged few to obtain decent health care. Nor will it close the privilege gap between those who are married and those who are not.

Marriage creates a two-tier system that allows the state to regulate relationships. It has become a facile mechanism for employers to dole out benefits, for businesses to provide special deals and incentives, and for the law to make distinctions in distributing meager public funds. None of these entities bothers to consider the relationship among people; the love, respect, and need to protect that exists among all kinds of family members. Rather, a simple certificate of the state, regardless of whether the spouses love, respect, or even see each other on a regular basis, dominates and is supported. None of this dynamic will change if gay men and lesbians are given the option of marriage.

Gay marriage will not help us address the systemic abuses inherent in a society that does not provide decent health care to all of its citizens, a right that should not depend on whether the individual 1) has sufficient resources to afford health care or health insurance, 2) is working and receives health insurance as part of compensation, or 3) is married to a partner who is working and has health coverage which is extended to spouses. It will not address the underlying unfairness that allows businesses to provide discounted services or goods to families and couples—who are defined to include straight, married people and their children, but not domestic partners.

Nor will it address the pain and anguish of the unmarried lesbian who receives word of her partner's accident, rushes to the hospital and is prohibited from entering the intensive care unit or obtaining information about her condition solely because she is not a spouse or family member. Likewise, marriage will not help the gay victim of domestic violence who, because he chose not to marry, finds no protection under the law to keep his violent lover away.

IF THE LAWS CHANGE TOMORROW AND LESbians and gay men were allowed to marry, where would we find the incentive to continue the progressive movement we have started that is pushing for societal and legal recognition of all kinds of family relationships? To create other options and alternatives? To find a place in the law for the elderly couple who, for companionship and economic reasons, live together but do not marry? To recognize the right of a long-time, but unmarried, gay partner to stay in his rent-controlled apartment after the death of his lover, the only named tenant on the lease? To recognize the family relationship of the lesbian couple and the two gay men who are jointly sharing child-raising responsibilities? To get the law to acknowledge that we may have more than one relationship worthy of legal protection?

Marriage for lesbians and gay men still will not provide a real choice unless we continue the work our community has begun to spread the privilege around to other relationships. We must first break the tradition of piling benefits and privileges on to those who are married, while ignoring the real life needs of those who are not. Only when we de-institutionalize marriage and bridge the economic and privilege gap between the married and the unmarried will each of us have a true choice. Otherwise, our choice not to marry will continue to lack legal protection and societal respect.

The lesbian and gay community has laid the groundwork for revolutionizing society's views of family. The domestic partnership movement has been an important part of this progress insofar as it validates non-marital relationships. Because it is not limited to sexual or romantic relationships, domestic partnership provides an important opportunity for many who are not related by blood or marriage to claim certain minimal protections.

It is crucial, though, that we avoid the pitfall of framing the push for legal recognition of domestic partners (those who share a primary residence and financial responsibility for each other) as a stepping stone to marriage. We must keep our eyes on the goals of providing true alternatives to marriage and of radically reordering society's view of family.

The goals of lesbian and gay liberation must simply be broader than the right to marry. Gay and lesbian marriages may minimally transform the institution of marriage by diluting its traditional patriarchal dynamic, but they will not transform society. They will not demolish the two-tier system of the "haves" and the "have nots." We must not fool ourselves into believing that marriage will make it acceptable to be gay or lesbian. We will be liberated only when we are respected and accepted for our differences and the diversity we provide to this society. Marriage is not a path to that liberation.

POSTSCRIPT

Should Gays and Lesbians Fight for the Right to Marry?

In the first federal lawsuit of its kind, a surviving lesbian partner filed charges of discrimination against a large American corporation because it refused to pay her the benefits normally paid to marital partners after the death of a spouse. She claims that the relationship she had with her partner was as much a marriage as any heterosexual union.

Tamar Lewin describes this situation and its implications in an article in *The New York Times* (September 21, 1990). She explains that more and more companies are finding their policies coming under attack as increasing numbers of homosexual couples live more openly in long-term relationships. Within the next five years domestic partnership laws are expected to resolve some of the legal situations in which these couples find themselves, although Lewin admits that there is currently no agreement on what constitutes a domestic partnership. Marriage offers clearly defined expectations and responsibilities; domestic partnerships do not.

According to Sullivan, legalizing marriage between gay and lesbian couples would facilitate social approval of homosexual relationships, foster emotional security among lesbian and gay partners, and enable better financial planning and economic well-being in such partnerships. Ettelbrick contends that extending the right to marry to lesbian and gay couples would grant them rights but would deny them social justice. She argues that marriage does not provide freedom from being discriminated against for being racially, economically, or sexually different from the mainstream.

What would society gain or lose from removing the legal barriers to gay and lesbian marriages? Would the definition of all marriages (heterosexual, homosexual, and interracial, for example) be changed if gay and lesbian marriages became legal?

SUGGESTED READINGS

R. M. Berger, "Men Together: Understanding the Gay Couple," *Journal of Homosexuality*, 19 (1990): 31–50.

J. Miranda and M. Stroms, "Psychological Adjustment of Lesbians and Gay Men," *Journal of Counseling and Development*, 68 (1989): 41–45.

J. Penelope, "The Lesbian Perspective," in J. Allen, ed., *Lesbian Philosophies and Cultures* (State University of New York Press, 1990).

L. A. Peplau and S. O. Cochran, "A Relationship Perspective on Homosexuality," in D. P. McWirther, S. A. Sanders, and J. M. Reinisch, eds., *Homosexuality/Heterosexuality* (Oxford University Press, 1990).

PART 3

Parenthood

People used to get married specifically in order to have children. Now that marriage is no longer considered a prerequisite to childbearing, nor is parenthood required of married couples, there are many personal choices for potential parents to consider. A couple must first decide whether or not having children would necessarily be good for their relationship. Then, if that couple is one of the many who cannot produce children, questions regarding alternative methods of acquiring children may be raised. For example, should the couple be offered the potentially legally and emotionally sticky alternative of surrogate mothering? Changing morals and attitudes magnify the conflicts in these issues and others, such as what course a teenage mother should take regarding the father of her child. Some of the problems associated with children and parenthood are debated in this section.

Is It Possible to Be Pro-Life and Pro-Choice?

Is Parenthood Necessary for a Good Marriage?

Should Surrogate Parenting Be Permitted for Infertile Couples?

Should Pregnant Teens Marry the Fathers of Their Babies?

ISSUE 6

Is It Possible to Be Pro-Life and Pro-Choice?

YES: Carl Sagan and Ann Druyan, from "Is It Possible to Be Pro-Life and Pro-Choice?" *Parade Magazine* (April 22, 1990)

NO: Orrin G. Hatch, from *The Value of Life* (National Committee for a Human Life Amendment, Inc., 1984)

ISSUE SUMMARY

YES: Carl Sagan, a professor of astronomy and space sciences, and writer Ann Druyan argue that the abortion issue is not a simple dichotomy, pro-life *or* pro-choice, but one that has many facets worth considering. They explore the reasons to uphold the view that it is possible to value life and support abortion.

NO: Senator Orrin G. Hatch, a supporter of a constitutional amendment to overturn the Supreme Court *Roe v. Wade* decision on abortion, argues that the pro-choice position is morally and legally without foundation and is incompatible with and goes against biblical injunctions. To be pro-choice is to support the freedom to kill a human being, which is inhuman and should therefore not even be considered as an option.

The current abortion controversy has its roots most specifically in the U.S. Supreme Court case *Roe v. Wade*, decided on January 23, 1973, in which the court ruled that the nineteenth-century Texas statutes against abortion were unconstitutional. The Court divided the normal pregnancy into three trimesters and ruled as follows:

> For the stage prior to approximately the end of the first trimester, the abortion decision and its effectuation must be left to the medical judgment of the pregnant woman's attending physician. For the stage subsequent to approximately the end of the first trimester, the State, in promoting its interest in the health of the mother, may, if it chooses, regulate the abortion procedure in ways that are reasonably related to maternal health. For the stages subsequent to viability, the State, in promoting its interest in the potentiality of human life, may, if it chooses, regulate, and even proscribe, abortion except where it is necessary, in appropriate medical judgment, for the preservation of the life or health of the mother. (410 U.S. 113, 93 S.Ct. 705 [1973])

During the twentieth century, prior to 1973, the mores and laws of local communities exerted control over who did or did not have an abortion. Faced with an unwanted pregnancy, women with access to wealth and power were generally able to pass the review of so-called tissue committees, which were established by hospitals to approve dilation and curettage procedures (D and C). The stated purpose of the D and C would be to help with menstrual or infertility problems, but in reality the procedure would be used to end the pregnancy. Some seeking abortions went outside the United States to countries where abortion laws were less restrictive. Others resorted to folk medicine or to "back alley" abortionists, who were sometimes trained physicians, nurses, or midwives but were often only those who had simply proclaimed themselves as qualified to perform abortions.

Approximately 1.5 million abortions are performed annually in the United States. Almost 90 percent of abortions are obtained within the first 12 weeks of gestation; 49.7 percent are performed at under 9 weeks; 26 percent are performed at 9 to 10 weeks; 12.5 percent are performed at 11 to 12 weeks. Of legal abortions performed, 57.6 percent of abortions are performed on women who have never previously had an abortion; 26.9 percent on those who have had one previous abortion; 9.5 percent on women who have had two previous abortions; and 6.0 percent on women who have had three or more. (National Center for Health Statistics, *Health, United States, 1990.*)

Abortion issues are not particularly contemporary. Abortion can be traced back historically at least 4,000 years to a Chinese text that describes the procedure, while the ancient Romans and Greeks dealt with abortion in relation to population control and sex selection.

The terms *pro-life* and *pro-choice* are often bandied about by the "two sides" of abortion debate, implying that the discussion is strictly a dichotomous one. Like most issues having complex moral or political implications, such dichotomies are useful primarily as means to begin debate. The selections that follow raise many moral, ethical, political, religious, and personal issues. Together, they represent varying viewpoints as to what abortion means. They also explore basic issues about what life is, how we define various life forms, and how life is valued across cultures. Questions of when life begins, how we define a life as human, why we value human life over other forms, and why some human lives are more valued than others are raised. The selections essentially move beyond the dichotomous argument stage and provide elaboration on several contemporary positions on the pro-life *v.* pro-choice issue. The husband-and-wife team Carl Sagan and Ann Druyan present a questioning, middle-of-the-road frame of reference. Orrin G. Hatch sets forth what may be referred to as a politically conservative, religiously fundamental position on abortion and its consequences. He suggests that it is inappropriate to question the values he sets forth because they are indisputable.

YES

Carl Sagan and
Ann Druyan

IS IT POSSIBLE TO BE PRO-LIFE
AND PRO-CHOICE?

ABORTION IN AMERICAN HISTORY

From colonial times to the 19th century, the choice was the woman's until "quickening" (when she is first able to feel the fetus stirring within her). An abortion in the first or even second trimester was at worst a misdemeanor. Convictions were rarely sought and almost impossible to obtain, because they depended entirely on the woman's own testimony of whether she had felt quickening, and because of the jury's distaste for prosecuting a woman for exercising her right to choose. In 1800 there was not, so far as is known, a single statute in the U.S. concerning abortion. Advertisements for drugs to induce abortion could be found in virtually every newspaper and even in many church publications—although the language used was suitably euphemistic, if widely understood.

But by 1900, abortion had been banned at *any* time in pregnancy by every state in the Union, except when necessary to save the woman's life. What happened to bring about so striking a reversal? Religion had little to do with it. Drastic economic and social changes were turning this country from an agrarian to an urban-industrial society. America was in the process of changing from having one of the highest birthrates in the world to one of the lowest. Abortion certainly played a role and stimulated forces to suppress it.

One of the most significant of these forces was the medical profession. Up to the mid-19th century, medicine was an uncertified, unsupervised business. Anyone could hang up a shingle and become a doctor. With the rise of a new, university-educated medical elite, anxious to enhance the status and influence of physicians, the American Medical Association was formed. In its first decade, the AMA began lobbying against abortions performed by anyone except licensed physicians. New knowledge of embryology, the physicians said, had shown the fetus to be human even before quickening.

Their assault on abortion was motivated not by concern for the health of the woman but, they claimed, for the welfare of the fetus. You had to be a physician to know when abortion was morally justified, because the question depended on scientific and medical facts understood only by physicians. At the same time, women were effectively excluded from the medical schools, where such arcane knowledge could be acquired. So, as things worked out, women had almost nothing to say about terminating their own pregnancies. It was also up to the physician to decide if the pregnancy posed a threat to the woman and was entirely at his discretion to determine what was and was not a threat. For a rich woman, it might be a threat to her emotional tranquillity or even to her lifestyle. The poor woman was often forced to resort to the back alley or the coat hanger.

This was the law until the 1960s, when a coalition of individuals and organizations, the AMA now among them, sought to overturn it and to reinstate the more traditional values that were to be embodied in *Roe v. Wade*.

THE ISSUE HAD BEEN DECIDED YEARS AGO. The court had chosen the middle ground. You'd think the fight was over. Instead, there are mass rallies, bombings and intimidation, arrests, intense lobbying, legislative drama, Congressional hearings, Supreme Court decisions and clerics threatening politicians with perdition. Partisans fling accusations of hypocrisy and murder. The intent of the Constitution and the will of God are equally invoked. Doubtful arguments are trotted out as certainties. The contending factions call on science to bolster their positions. Families are divided, husbands and wives agree not to discuss it, old friends are no longer speaking. Politicians check the latest polls to discover the dictates of their consciences. Amid all the shouting, it is hard for the adversaries to hear one another. Opinions are polarized. Minds are closed.

Is it wrong to abort a pregnancy? Always? Sometimes? Never? How do we decide? We wrote this article to understand better what the contending views are and to see if we ourselves could find a position that would satisfy us both. We had to weigh the arguments of both sides for consistency and to pose test cases, some of which are purely hypothetical. If in some of these tests we seem to go too far, we ask the reader to be patient with us—we're trying to stress the various positions to the breaking point to see their weaknesses and where they fail.

In contemplative moments, nearly everyone recognizes that the issue is not wholly one-sided. Many partisans of differing views, we find, feel some disquiet, some unease when confronting what's behind the opposing arguments. (This is partly why such confrontations are avoided.) And the issue surely touches on deep questions: What are our responsibilities to one another? Should we permit the state to intrude into the most intimate and personal aspects of our lives? Where are the boundaries of freedom? What does it mean to be human?

TESTING "FREEDOM OF CHOICE"

Of the many actual points of view, it is widely held—especially in the media, which rarely have the time or the inclination to make fine distinctions—that there are only two: "pro-choice" and "pro-life." This is what the two principal warring camps like to call themselves, and that's what we'll call them here. In the simplest characterization, a pro-choicer would hold that the decision to abort a pregnancy is to be made only by the woman; the state has no right to interfere. And a pro-lifer would hold that, from the moment of conception, the embryo or fetus is alive; that this life imposes on us a moral obligation to preserve it; and that abortion is tantamount to murder. Both names—pro-choice and pro-life—were picked with an eye toward influencing those whose minds are not yet made up: Few people wish to be counted as being against freedom of choice or as opposed to life. Indeed, freedom and life are two of our most cherished values, and here they seem to be in fundamental conflict.

Let's consider these two absolutist positions in turn. A newborn baby is surely the same being it was just before birth. There is good evidence that a late-term fetus responds to sound—including music, but especially its mother's voice. It can suck its thumb or do a somersault. Occasionally, it generates adult brain wave patterns. Some people say they remember being born, or even the uterine environment. Perhaps there is thought in the womb. It's hard to maintain that a transformation to full personhood happens abruptly at the moment of birth. Why, then, should it be murder to kill an infant the day after it was born but not the day before?

As a practical matter, this isn't very important: less than one percent of all tabulated abortions in the United States are listed in the last three months of pregnancy (and, on closer investigation, most such reports turn out to be due to miscarriage or miscalculation). But third-trimester abortions provide a test of the limits of the pro-choice point of view.

Does a woman's "innate right to control her own body" include the right to kill a near-term fetus who is, for all intents and purposes, identical to a newborn child?

We believe that many supporters of reproductive freedom are troubled at least occasionally by this question. But they are reluctant to raise it because it is the beginning of a slippery slope. If it is impermissible to abort a pregnancy in the ninth month, what about the eighth, seventh, sixth . . .? Once we acknowledge that the state can interfere at *any* time in the pregnancy, doesn't it follow that the state can interfere at all times?

This conjures up the specter of predominantly male, predominantly affluent legislators telling poor women they must bear and raise alone children they cannot afford to bring up; forcing teenagers to bear children they are not emotionally prepared to deal with; saying to women who wish for a career that they must give up their dreams, stay home and bring up babies; and, worst of all, condemning victims of rape and incest to carry and nurture the offspring of their assailants. Legislative prohibitions on abortion arouse the suspicion that their real intent is to control the independence and sexuality of women. Why should legislators have any right at all to tell women what to do with their bodies? To be deprived of reproductive freedom is demeaning. Women are fed up with being pushed around.

And yet, by consensus, all of us think it proper that there be prohibitions against, and penalties exacted for, murder. It would be a flimsy defense if the murderer pleads that this is just between him and his victim and none of the government's business. If killing a fetus is truly killing a human being, is it not the *duty* of the state to prevent it? Indeed, one of the chief functions of government is to protect the weak from the strong.

If we do not oppose abortion at *some* stage of pregnancy, is there not a danger of dismissing an entire category of human beings as unworthy of our protection and respect? And isn't that dismissal the hallmark of sexism, racism, nationalism and religious fanaticism? Shouldn't those dedicated to fighting such injustices be scrupulously careful not to embrace another?

TESTING THE "RIGHT TO LIFE"

There is no right to life in any society on Earth today, nor has there been at any former time (with a few rare exceptions, such as among the Jains of India): We raise farm animals for slaughter; destroy forests; pollute rivers and lakes until no fish can live there; kill deer and elk for sport, leopards for their pelts and whales for fertilizer; entrap dolphins, gasping and writhing, in great tuna nets; club seal pups to death; and render a species extinct every day. All these beasts and vegetables are as alive as we. What is (allegedly) protected is not life, but *human* life.

And even with that protection, casual murder is an urban commonplace, and we wage "conventional" wars with tolls so terrible that we are, most of us, afraid to consider them very deeply. (Tellingly, state-organized mass murders are often justified by redefining our opponents—by race, nationality, religion or ideology—as less than human.) That protection, that right to life, eluded the 40,000 children under 5 who died on our planet today—as every day—from preventable starvation, dehydration, disease and neglect.

Those who assert a "right to life" are for (at most) not just any kind of life, but for—particularly and uniquely—human life. So they too, like pro-choicers, must decide what distinguishes a human being from other animals and when, during gestation, the uniquely human qualities—whatever they are—emerge.

Despite many claims to the contrary, life does not begin at conception: It is an unbroken chain that stretches back nearly to the origin of the Earth, 4.6 billion years ago. Nor does *human* life begin at conception: It is an unbroken chain dating back to the origin of our species, tens or hundreds of thousands of years ago. Every human sperm and egg is, beyond the shadow of a doubt, alive. They are not human beings, of course. However, it could be argued that neither is a fertilized egg.

In some animals, an egg develops into a healthy adult without benefit of a sperm cell. But not, so far as we know, among humans. A sperm and an unfertilized egg jointly comprise the full genetic blueprint for a human being. Under certain circumstances, after fertilization, they can develop into a baby. But most fertilized eggs are spontaneously miscarried. Development into a baby is by no means guaranteed. Neither a sperm and egg separately, nor a fertilized egg, is more than a *potential* baby or a *potential* adult. So if a sperm and an egg are as human as the fertilized egg produced by their union, and if it is murder to destroy a fertilized egg—despite the fact that it's only *potentially* a baby—why isn't it murder to destroy a sperm or an egg?

Hundreds of millions of sperm cells (top speed with tails lashing: 5 inches per hour) are produced in an average human ejaculation. A healthy young man can produce in a week or two enough spermatozoa to double the human population of the Earth. So is masturbation mass murder? How about nocturnal emissions or just plain sex? When the unfertilized egg is expelled each month, has someone died? Some lower animals can be grown in the laboratory from a single body cell. If such cloning technology were ever developed for humans, would we be committing genocide by shedding a drop of blood?

All human sperm and eggs are genetic halves of "potential" human beings. Should heroic efforts be made to save and preserve all of them, everywhere, because of this "potential"? Is failure to do so immoral or criminal? Of course, there's a difference between taking a life and failing to save it. And there's a big difference between the probability of survival of a sperm cell and that of a fertilized egg. But the absurdity of a corps of high-minded semen-preservers moves us to wonder whether a fertilized egg's mere "potential" to become a baby really does make destroying it murder.

Opponents of abortion worry that, once abortion is permissible immediately after conception, no argument will restrict it at any later time in the pregnancy. Then, they fear, one day it will be permissible to murder a fetus that is unambiguously a human being. Both pro-choicers and pro-lifers (at least some of them) are pushed toward absolutist positions by parallel fears of the slippery slope.

Another slippery slope is reached by those pro-lifers who are willing to make an exception in the agonizing case of pregnancy resulting from rape or incest. But why should the right to live depend on the *circumstances* of conception? If the same child were to result, can the state ordain life for the offspring of a lawful union but death for one conceived by force or coercion? How can this be just?

And if exceptions are extended to such a fetus, why should they be withheld from any other fetus? This is part of the reason some pro-lifers adopt what many others consider the outrageous posture of opposing abortions under any and all circumstances—only excepting, perhaps, when the life of the mother is in danger.

By far the most common reason for abortion is birth-control. So shouldn't opponents of abortion be handing out contraceptives? That would be an effective way to reduce the number of abortions. Instead, the United States is far behind other nations in the development of safe and effective methods of birth control—and, in many cases, opposition to such research (and to sex education) has come from the same people who oppose abortions.

WHEN DO WE BECOME HUMAN?

The attempt to find an ethically sound and unambiguous judgment on when, if ever, abortion is permissible has deep historical roots. Often, especially in Christian traditions, such attempts were connected with the question of when the soul enters the body—a matter not readily amenable to scientific investigation and an issue of controversy even among learned theologians. Ensoulment has been asserted to occur in the sperm before conception, at conception, at the time of "quickening" (when the mother is first able to feel the fetus stirring within her) and at birth. Or even later.

Different religions have different teachings. Among hunter-gatherers, there are usually no prohibitions against abortion, and it was common in ancient Greece and Rome. The Assyrians impaled women on stakes for attempting abortions. The Jewish Talmud teaches that the fetus is not a person and has no rights. The Old and New Testaments—rich in detailed prohibitions on dress, diet and permissible words—contain not a word specifically prohibiting abortion. The only passage that's remotely relevant (*Exodus* 21:22) decrees that if there's a fight and a woman bystander should accidentally be injured and made to miscarry, the assailant must pay a fine. The Catholic Church's first and longstanding collection of canon law (according to the leading historian of the Church's teachings on abortion, John Connery, S. J.) held that abortion was homicide only after the fetus was already "formed"—roughly, the end of the first trimester. Surprisingly, it was not until 1869 that abortion at any time for any reason became grounds for excommunication.

If you deliberately kill a human being, it's called murder. If you deliberately kill a chimpanzee—biologically, our closest relative—whatever else it is, it's not murder. To date, murder uniquely applies to killing human beings. Therefore, the question of when personhood (or, if we like, ensoulment) arises is key to the abortion debate. When does the fetus become human? When do distinct and characteristic human qualities emerge?

We recognize that specifying a precise moment will overlook individual differences. Therefore, if we must draw a line, it ought to be drawn conservatively—that is, on the early side. There are people who object to having to set some numerical limit, and we share their disquiet; but if there is to be a law on this matter, and it is to effect some useful compromise between the two absolutist positions, it must specify, at least roughly, a time of transition to personhood.

Every one of us began from a dot. A fertilized egg is roughly the size of the period at the end of this sentence. The momentous meeting of sperm and egg generally occurs in one of the two fallopian tubes. One cell becomes two, two become four, and by the sixth day the fertilized egg has become a kind of hollow sphere wandering off to another realm: the womb. It destroys tissue in its path. It sucks blood from capillaries. It establishes itself as a kind of parasite on the walls of the uterus.

• By the third week, around the time of the first missed menstrual period, the forming embryo is about 2 millimeters long and is developing various body parts. But it looks a little like a segmented worm.

• By the end of the fourth week, it's about 5 millimeters (about 1/5 inch) long. It's recognizable as a vertebrate, its tube-shaped heart is beginning to beat, something like the gill arches of a fish or an amphibian become conspicuous, and there is a pronounced tail. It looks something like a newt or a tadpole. This is the end of the first month after conception.

• By the fifth week, the gross divisions of the brain can be distinguished. What will later develop into eyes is apparent, and little buds appear—on their way to becoming arms and legs.

• By the six week, the embryo is 13 millimeters (about 1/2 inch) long. The eyes are still on the side of the head, as in most animals, and the reptilian face has connected slits where the mouth and nose eventually will be.

• By the end of the seventh week, the tail is almost gone, and sexual characteristics can be discerned (although both sexes look female). The face is mammalian but somewhat piglike.

• By the end of the eighth week, the face resembles that of a primate but is still not quite human. Most of the human body parts are present in their essentials.

Some lower brain anatomy is well-developed. The fetus shows some reflex response to delicate stimulation.

• By the tenth week, the face has an unmistakably human cast. It is beginning to be possible to distinguish males from females. Nails and major bone structures are not apparent until the third month.

• By the fourth month, you can tell the face of one fetus from that of another. Quickening is most often first felt in the fifth month. The bronchioles of the lungs do not begin developing until approximately the sixth month, the alveoli still later. Recognizably human brain activity begins intermittently around the middle of the seventh month.

So, if only a person can be murdered, when does the fetus attain personhood? When its face becomes distinctly human, near the end of the first trimester? When the fetus becomes responsive to stimuli—again, at the end of the first trimester? When the fetus becomes active enough to be felt as quickening, typically in the middle of the second trimester? When the lungs have reached a stage of development sufficient that the fetus might, just conceivably, be able to breathe on its own in the outside air?

The trouble with such developmental milestones is not just that they're arbitrary. More troubling is the fact that none of them involves *uniquely human* characteristics—apart from the superficial matter of facial appearance. All animals respond to stimuli and move of their own volition. Large numbers are able to breathe. But that doesn't stop us from slaughtering them. Reflexes and motion and respiration are not what makes us human.

Other animals have advantages over us—in speed, strength, endurance, climbing or burrowing skills, camouflage, sight or smell or hearing, mastery of the air or water. Our one great advantage, the secret of our success, is thought—characteristically human thought. We are able to think things through, imagine events yet to occur, figure things out. That's how we invented agriculture and civilization. Thought is our blessing and our curse, and it makes us who we are.

Thinking occurs, of course, in the brain—principally in the top layers of the convoluted "gray matter" called the cerebral cortex. The roughly 100 billion neurons in the brain constitute the material basis of thought. The neurons are connected to each other, and their linkups play a major role in what we experience as thinking. But large-scale linking up of neurons doesn't begin until the 24th to 27th week of pregnancy—the sixth month.

By placing harmless electrodes on a subject's head, scientists can measure the electrical activity produced by the network of neurons inside the skull. Different kinds of mental activity show different kinds of brain waves. But brain waves with regular patterns typical of adult human brains do not appear in the fetus until about the 30th week of pregnancy—near the beginning of the third trimester. Fetuses younger than this—however alive and active they may be—lack the necessary brain architecture. They cannot yet think.

Acquiescing in the killing of any living creature, especially one that might later become a baby, is troublesome and painful. But we've rejected the extremes of "always" and "never," and this puts us—like it or not—on the slippery slope. If we are forced to choose a developmental criterion, then this is where we draw the line: when the beginning of characteristically human thinking becomes barely possible. It is, in fact, a very conservative definition: Regular brain waves are rarely found in fetuses. More research would help. If we wanted to make the criterion still more stringent, to allow for precocious fetal brain development, we might draw the line at six months. This, it so happens, is where the Supreme Court drew it in 1973—although for completely different reasons.

VIABILITY AND THE COURT

Its decision in the case of *Roe v. Wade* changed American law on abortion. It permits abortion at the request of the woman without restriction in the first trimester and, with some restrictions intended to protect her health, in the second trimester. It allows states to forbid abortion in the third trimester, except when there's a serious threat to the life or health of the woman. In a recent reassessment, the Supreme Court declined explicitly to overturn *Roe v. Wade* but in effect invited the 50 state legislatures to decide for themselves.

What was the reasoning in *Roe v. Wade*? There was no legal weight given to what happens to the children once they are born, or to the family. Instead, a woman's right to reproductive freedom is protected, the court ruled, by constitutional guarantees of privacy. But that right is not unqualified. The woman's guarantee of privacy and the fetus's right to life must be weighed—and when the court did the weighing, priority was given to privacy in the first trimester and to life in the third. The transition was decided not from any of the considerations we have been dealing with so far in this article—not when "ensoulment" occurs, not when the fetus takes on sufficient human

characteristics to be protected by laws against murder. Instead, the criterion adopted was whether the fetus could live outside the mother. This is called "viability" and depends in part on the ability to breathe. The lungs are simply not developed, and the fetus cannot breathe—no matter how advanced an artificial lung it might be placed in—until about the 24th week, near the start of the sixth month. This is why *Roe v. Wade* permits states to prohibit abortions in the last trimester. It's a very pragmatic criterion.

If the fetus at a certain stage of gestation would be viable outside the womb, the argument goes, then the right of the fetus to life overrides the right of the woman to privacy. But just what does "viable" mean? Even a full-term newborn is not viable without a great deal of care and love. There was a time before incubators, only a few decades ago, when babies in their seventh month were unlikely to be viable. Would aborting in the seventh month have been permissible then? After the invention of incubators, did aborting pregnancies in the seventh month suddenly become immoral? What happens if, in the future, a new technology develops so that an artificial womb can sustain a fetus even before the sixth month by delivering oxygen and nutrients through the blood—as the mother does through the placenta and into the fetal blood system? We grant that this technology is unlikely to be developed soon or become available to many. But *if* it were available, does it then become immoral to abort earlier than the sixth month, when previously it was moral? A morality that depends on, and changes with, technology is a fragile morality; for some, it is also an unacceptable morality.

And why, exactly, should breathing (or kidney function, or the ability to resist disease) justify legal protection? If a fetus can be shown to think and feel but not be able to breathe, would it be all right to kill it? Do we value breathing more than thinking and feeling? Viability arguments cannot, it seems to us, coherently determine when abortions are permissible. Some other criterion is needed. Again, we offer for consideration the earliest onset of human thinking as that criterion.

Since, on average, fetal thinking occurs even later than fetal lung development, we find *Roe v. Wade* to be a good and prudent decision addressing a complex and difficult issue. With prohibitions on abortion in the last trimester—except in cases of grave medical necessity—it strikes a fair balance between the conflicting claims of freedom and of life.

NO

Orrin G. Hatch

THE VALUE OF LIFE

[The Value of Life was written in 1984. While there are some references within the article that are no longer timely, Senator Hatch's eloquence in the defense of human life will never be out-of-date. Current statistics, information, and polling data can be obtained from the National Committee for a Human Life Amendment. —Note from the National Committee for a Human Life Amendment, Inc.]

Sooner or later everyone involved deeply in the abortion controversy, as I have been, comes to realize that in this area, above all, myths conflict with facts, slogans with truths. In what follows I propose to contrast some of the myths with the facts, to scrutinize the emptiness of pro-abortion slogans when exposed to the truth. Only in this way, I am convinced, can the carnage of abortion be halted and respect for all human life be restored to the status of a right protected under our Constitution.

In 1983, a constitutional amendment to overturn the controversial Supreme Court decision legalizing abortion on demand failed to secure the two-thirds majority necessary for Senate approval. Perhaps the major reason was public unawareness of the dimensions and implications of the brutal practice of abortion. Few realize that over 15 million children have been killed in the United States since abortion was legalized in 1973; that only one other country in the world—Communist China—has a more permissive abortion policy; that in our country two million unborn children a year fall prey to the tools of the abortionist's trade; that some of our nation's leading cities record more abortions than live births; or that at least 97% of these killings are performed solely for reasons of convenience. Furthermore, there are more than 50 million abortions worldwide each year. This is truly a calamity of catastrophic proportions.

FREEDOM OF CHOICE

Ironically, this dreadful carnage takes place under the misleading banner of a laudable principle: "freedom of choice." One day, while preparing for an

From *The Value of Life* by Senator Orrin Hatch of Utah. Reprinted by permission of the National Committee for a Human Life Amendment, Inc., Suite 335, 1511 K Street, NW, Washington, DC 20005.

important debate on the floor of the U.S. Senate, I learned that one of the Senate aides was pregnant. My immediate reaction was to enthusiastically congratulate her and to assure her of the joy of family life. As I told of the arrival of our first child and the joys Elaine and I had experienced as our family had grown to include six unique, challenging and rewarding children, my happy reminiscing was cut short by her uncharacteristically sullen demeanor. Stopping in mid-sentence, I asked if something was wrong. Indeed there was.

With an apology, she explained that she was considering the alluring option of abortion. Her career was just getting underway, and she felt that this interruption could disrupt her plans. Her hasty speech concluded with the most common justification for abortion: "After all, I must be able to choose, myself, what I will do with my body."

"The real question is not the freedom to choose," I replied, "but freedom to choose *what?*" We exercise freedom of choice when we elect to get out of bed, or play tennis, or eat lunch. Every deliberate action, good or bad, involves a choice. Mere freedom of choice does not justify any action, but only describes the process by which we weigh the pros and cons and arrive at decisions.

If freedom of choice were itself a justification for choice, then individuals could justify stealing, or pushing drugs, selling pornography, or even killing another human, on the basis that they were free to choose to do so. Anyone who drives a car, for instance, is free to exceed speed limits. Because of the threat to other drivers and innocent pedestrians, however, society has chosen wisely to protect itself against speeding by punishing that particular choice. Even tax laws favor

some choices over others. Every governmental action in some way influences individual choices.

Choices must be governed by a careful and thoughtful search for the right course of action. The real question for you is not whether you are free to terminate the life of your infant, but what the moral significance and the consequences of that choice will be for you, your family—including your unborn child—and for society as a whole. From that vantage point, freedom of choice may have some meaning.

Ask yourself who is protecting your unborn child's freedom of choice. If we value freedom of choice, shouldn't we respect the choice the unborn child would obviously make—the choice to live? What I am saying is that, once a life begins within a woman, she isn't the only one involved. Just where does she get the right to "choose" someone else's death? None of us has absolutely unrestricted rights. Our rights are limited by the rights of other persons—preeminently, by this right to live.

WORDS OF SCRIPTURE

Since then, I have often had occasion to reflect on the calamity of abortion. While presiding as chairman of the Senate's Constitution Subcommittee during nine lengthy hearings exploring every philosophical, legal, moral, medical, and social aspect of this crisis, I thought about the plain commands of scripture on this subject. Not that abortion is a sectarian or even uniquely "religious" issue; the public policy arguments against abortion are overwhelming. For a religious believer, however, religious considerations do add an extra dimension of concern.

If men strive, and hurt a woman with child, so that her fruit depart from her . . . he shall surely be punished. (Exodus 21:22)

Can a woman forget her sucking child, that she should not have compassion on the son of her womb? Yea, they may forget, yet will I not forget thee. Behold, I have graven thee upon the palms of my hands. (Isaiah 49:15-16)

He (John the Baptist) shall be filled with the Holy Ghost even from his mother's womb. (Luke 1:15)

The baby (John the Baptist) leaped in her womb (when Mary, bearing the Savior, came into the presence of Elizabeth). (Luke 1:41)

So God created man in his own image, in the image of God created he him; male and female created he them. And God blessed them and God said unto them, be fruitful and multiply and replenish the earth. (Genesis 1:27-28)

While listening to the testimony of over 80 witnesses, I reflected on how our Father has shaped human history through the common miracle of sending children into the world. With Israel in bondage, He sent Moses and Aaron (Exodus 6:20). With the birth of the Saviour approaching, He sent John the Baptist. With the entire family of Adam in inescapable spiritual and physical bondage, He sent His own Son (John 3:16). Indeed, my wife Elaine and I have often thought that our greatest mission in life is to provide a home for the six special spirits He has sent to us. The simple phrase concerning Ruth, through whose lineage came the Savior, captures for us the Lord's hand in the birth process: "The Lord gave her conceptions" (Ruth 4:12). The birth of each child is indeed a small means by which the Lord can bring about great miracles.

HISTORIC VIEW OF ABORTION

The hearing process also gave me an opportunity to recall that, even during the times when the fullness of the gospel did not light the world, enlightened men still understood the sanctity of unborn life. John Calvin wrote:

If it seems more disgraceful that a man be killed in his own home than in his field—since for every man his home is his sanctuary—how much more abominable is it to be considered to kill a fetus in the womb who has not yet been brought into the light. (John Calvin, Commentaries on Exodus, 21,22.)

Blackstone, the great eighteenth-century codifier of the common law, maintained that:

Life is the immediate gift of God, a right inherent by nature in every individual . . . (Abortion) was by the ancient law homicide or manslaughter. (1 W. Blackstone Commentaries, 129-130.)

Our own Declaration of Independence decreed without equivocation:

We hold these Truths to be self-evident, that all Men are created equal, *that they are endowed by the Creator with certain inalienable Rights, that among these are Life,* Liberty, and the Pursuit of Happiness. (emphasis added)

Most somber among my reflections, however, was that countless young women, like my friend, submit to abortion on the basis of a hollow "freedom of choice" without considering the consequences of that choice. Accordingly, I resolved to write this article to spotlight some of those consequences and, at the same time, to dispel some myths employed in the all too successful attempts to make abortion an acceptable choice.

The most tragic consequence of abortion, of course, is that more than 15 million children have been killed in the United States since the Supreme Court legalized abortion on demand. The war on the unborn has cost more than ten times the number of American lives lost in all our nation's other wars lumped together. Moreover, the death rate is still climbing. Over 1.5 million abortions a year are performed in America. Nearly one in every three pregnancies ends in abortion.

SUPREME COURT ERROR

These staggering totals have prompted many conscientious Americans to ask how abortion, banned for centuries by civilized cultures, could become legal. The sad truth is that on January 22, 1973, the Supreme Court declared that the Constitution includes a right to abortion. The effect was to overturn the prohibitions against abortion in each of the 50 states and substitute a more permissive policy than exists, or had ever existed, in any other nation except Communist China.

Indeed, this judge-created policy is so permissive that even during the last months of pregnancy, after the child is capable of surviving outside the womb, the mother may obtain an abortion by simply alleging any impediment to her "physical, emotional, or psychological . . . well-being," [Doe v. Bolton, 410 U.S. 179, 192 (1973).] In the words of professor John Noonan, a woman's determination to abort her viable late-term infant is only curbed by "the necessity of a physician's finding that she needs an abortion" for any of the above reasons. [J. Noonan, A Private Choice, 12 (1979).] As the Senate Judiciary Committee reported, "it would be a rare physician who would be incapable of defending an abortion on the grounds that in his best medical judgment the 'well-being' of the mother demanded it." [Senate Report 98–149, Senate Judiciary Committee 6, 98th Congress, 1st Session (1983).]

Leading constitutional scholars immediately began to attack the Supreme Court's opinion. Even some who, like Professor John Ely, favored abortion, conceded that the ruling was a "very bad decision. . . . It is bad because it is bad constitutional law, or rather because it is not constitutional law and gives almost no sense of an obligation to try to be." [Ely, "The Wages of Crying Wolf," 82 Yale L.R. 920 (1973).] Another proponent of abortion who nonetheless felt the Court's decision had no basis in the Constitution was Professor Archibald Cox:

> Neither historian, layman, nor lawyer will be persuaded that all the details prescribed in Roe v. Wade are part of either natural law or the Constitution. [A. Cox, The Role of the Supreme Court 114 (1976).]

The frankest assessment of the constitutional question relative to abortion was made by Professor Ely: "The Constitution simply says nothing, clear or fuzzy, about abortion." [Supra at 927.] Therefore, under the Constitution the people in the states should have retained the authority to regulate abortion as they had for nearly two centuries prior to 1973. This proper interpretation of the Constitution could have prevented the loss of countless lives.

PROTECTING THE MOTHER'S LIFE

In discussing the cost in terms of human life, I must reiterate my concern for all human life. When the life of the mother is endangered in pregnancy, she is entitled to medical treatment even at the terrible cost of the life of the infant. There are cases—fortunately, rare ones—where dreadful choices may be necessary. But, even then the decision must be made by the mother after prayerful consideration.

I know of mothers who were told by doctors that without abortion they would die. After praying about this momentous decision, they opted not to terminate pregnancy. Both the mothers and babies survived.

Every state prior to 1973 protected the life of the mother by law. Protecting the life of the mother has little or nothing to do with today's indulgent regime of abortion. Preserving the mother's life is hardly at stake when abortions are performed at the rate of nearly 5,000 per day. Nor is the mother's life at stake when in some American cities—notably both the nation's capital and its largest city—more children are aborted than are permitted to be born alive. The sky-rocketing increase in the number of abortions since 1973 dispels the myth that our current abortion regime is somehow related to preserving the life of the mother. Risks to maternal health are declining with the advance of medicine, yet the number of abortions is growing at an alarming rate.

THE CONVENIENCE FACTOR

The explanation for this dramatic increase is not related to maternal health. Only in extremely rare instances are abortions performed for health reasons. Indeed, even taking "health" in its broadest sense, an ardent advocate of abortion conceded that less than two percent of all abortions can be justified as medically expedient. [See hearings on Abortion, Subcommittee on the Constitution of the Senate Judiciary Committee, 97th Congress, 1st Session (1981) (Statement of Dr. Irving Cushner).] Raising this estimate by fifty percent would still mean that only three percent of all abortions were really necessary to prevent medical complications. Several qualified physicians testified before my Senate Subcommittee on the Constitution that they had never encountered a case where abortion was necessary to save the life of the mother. Beyond a few medically expedient abortions, all the rest—at least ninety-seven percent—are performed for what amounts to reasons of convenience.

This convenience factor takes various forms. Perhaps the birth of a child will mean a financial burden; perhaps tests have disclosed that the unborn child is not of the sex which the parents prefer; perhaps the pregnancy will interrupt an education; or perhaps, as with my friend, it will simply interfere with other plans. In such instances abortion is a tool of convenience, not a medical necessity.

HANDICAPS AND HARDSHIPS

Another myth used to justify the abortion ethic is that hardships, like poverty or the possibility of a handicap, make abortion necessary. The implications are tragic.

Consider the following case—a true one in its factual circumstances—of a mother weighing the consequences of her pregnancy. She announces to her physician that her husband is an alcoholic with a syphilitic infection; that one of her children was born dead; that another child is blind; and that another had tuberculosis. Finally, she confesses that she is living in abject poverty and that her family has a history of deafness. She is also past the normal child-bearing years. When this situation has been posed to classes of medical students, they have recommended abortion almost without exception.

The child described here is Ludwig von Beethoven. Yet this example does not just apply to Beethoven. Every child is unique and capable of making a contribution to family, community, and nation, which no other can make.

"Freedom of choice?" Where do we get the "freedom" to deny life to a potential Beethoven—or to any other human being?

LIBERTY OF LICENSE

Again, religious convictions add an extra dimension for believers. The Lord Himself said to Jeremiah, "Before thou camest forth out of the womb I sanctified thee, and I ordained thee a prophet unto the nations" (Jeremiah 1:5). Do we enjoy the "freedom" to deny life to a potential Jeremiah or to any other child the Lord may have sanctified before birth? Such liberty is a license to kill. A society that cannot protect its own most defenseless and helpless members has lost sight of the basic purpose of our War for Independence in 1776: "To preserve these rights (including the right to life), governments are instituted among men, deriving their just powers from the consent of the governed." No society will long remain free which abandons the most fundamental purpose of societal bonds.

UNWANTED CHILDREN?

There is yet another abortion myth—the myth that abortion is better than bringing an "unwanted child" into the world. Suppose Beethoven had been "unwanted"? What does "unwanted" really mean? In this context, it apparently means that whether one person "wants" another is sufficient to decide whether or not the other shall live. This is absurd. Each individual has his own inestimable worth, regardless of whether another person "wants" him or not.

Another question is—"unwanted by whom?" I know of several young couples who pray regularly that they might be permitted to adopt these supposedly "unwanted" children. Throughout the nation there are long waiting lists of couples who want to adopt children; in Utah there are nine couples who wish to adopt for every child available. As one adoptive parent stated the other day, "placing a child for adoption is a great act of love—both for the child and for the adoptive couple, who, without the child, would never have the joy of being parents." I find it unbelievably tragic that some individuals would justify the killing of their own unborn infant on the basis of their own fleeting wants.

CHOOSING TO TAKE A LIFE

Here, then, is the real problem for those who advocate abortion as a way to avoid the passing difficulties that another child might create. Pope John Paul II summarized the moral aspects of abortion in two concise comments:

Whoever attempts to destroy human life in the womb of the mother not only violates God's Law, but also attacks society by undermining respect for all human life.

Human life is the basis of human dignity and human rights. If it can be destroyed in the womb of the mother it will be difficult to establish compelling safeguards at other times and in other circumstances.

Our wisdom is inadequate for us to judge that our own inconveniences or difficulties are more important than the life of another human being. President Ronald Reagan restated this same principle in haunting terms:

Wholesale abortion has become a continuing prod to the conscience of the nation. . . . We cannot survive as a free nation when some men decide that others are not fit to live and should be abandoned to abortion or infanticide. . . . Americans do not want to play God with the value of human life. It is not for us to decide who is worthy to live and who is not. [*Human Life Review,* Spring 1983.]

INFANTICIDE

The President's characterization of the abortion crisis is not overstated. Our nation has regrettably witnessed hundreds of thousands of late-term abortions since 1973. Over 15,000 abortions a year are performed after the mother's 20th week of pregnancy—the margin of viability, when the child might be delivered and survive on its own. It is not uncommon to abort a child very late in the pregnancy, even into the 7th or 8th month. Abortions after this point are more accurately described as judicially legalized infanticides.

MEDICAL SCIENCE AND THE UNBORN

Let us be specific about what is being aborted. I was very deeply impressed by the powerful story told by an obstetrician, an atheist, who presided for years over the largest abortion clinic in New York City. Indeed, he was one of four founders of the National Abortion Rights Action League (NARAL), the nation's leading abortion advocacy organization. A skillful and able physician, he began to study an advancing new field of medicine: fetology, the study of the unborn human. He described in detail how he learned of the humanity of the unborn:

- At three weeks, the new life has already developed its own blood cells;
- At four weeks, a muscle may flex—this will become a beating heart in a few weeks, a heart which is fully audible at eight weeks;
- At six weeks, the child's skeletal system is complete;
- At seven weeks, electrical brain patterns are discernible;
- At twelve weeks, all organ systems are functioning—stomach, heart, liver, kidney, brain—in fact, some infants have already developed a thumb-sucking habit;
- At twenty weeks, the fetus is kicking, punching, swimming, and recognizes his mother's voice;
- At twenty-two weeks the child can survive outside the womb.

Facing these realities day after day, Dr. Bernard Nathanson, for medical reasons, stopped performing abortions and began actively campaigning to tell the nation about the scientific facts which show that *the fetus is a distinct, living human being.* In his own words, "I changed my mind because of advances in the field of fetology which have allowed us to understand the fetus much more completely and much more carefully than we ever did before. This has posed a very severe philosophical problem, in that you can't be operating on the fetus and giving it drugs to cure it, and at the same time be destroying it." (*Washington Times,* page 3C, January 17, 1983.)

FETAL PAIN

These scientific and medical facts refute the myth that the fetus is little more than a lump of tissue, without feeling, which can be extracted much like a bloated appendix. On the contrary, the unborn child is human, with human features, human behavior, human feelings. Medical experts now tell us that the neurological developments necessary for feeling pain are complete by the 13th week after conception and perhaps earlier. It is unbearable to contemplate the excruciating pain the unborn must feel as their lives are torn asunder. It is a wrenching nightmare to see in the mind's eye the delicate little hand of an unborn infant reaching out playfully to touch the very curette that is poised to rip him apart. We must ask again, "Freedom to choose what?" The answer is, "freedom to choose to exterminate a being whom science identifies as a unique, living person." The implications of that medical fact are frightening and far-reaching.

AMERICAN OPINION

Given the advances in fetology, it is easy to see why reliable opinion polls show that 80 to 90 percent of all Americans consider abortion at some stage as the destruction of a living person. As to when the fetus becomes a living being, there is a slight gender gap. Most women believe that life begins at conception. This gender gap is exactly the opposite of current stereotypes, which claim that most women view abortion tolerantly. That is another myth. Women who personally experience pregnancy have a much stronger conviction than men that life begins at conception. A similar result has been demonstrated in other surveys, where women are more likely than men to oppose indiscriminate abortion on demand.

Having drawn special attention to the woman's point of view, let us examine another myth. It maintains that only legalized abortion can protect women from the merciless knife of the back-alley abortionist. On the contrary, legalization of abortion on demand should receive little, if any, credit for saving women's lives. Since 1941, the major factors contributing to a drop in maternal abortion mortality have been medical advances: sulfa drugs, penicillin, and finally the widespread use of the safer suction curette instead of the sharp curette, a 1970 innovation. The regime of elective abortion seeks something far different from maternal safety. As noted earlier, every state already acknowledged and permitted abortions necessary to save the life of the mother prior to the 1973 Court decisions.

A particularly insidious myth about abortion is that the majority of Americans want practically unrestricted access to abortion at any stage of pregnancy. To the contrary, a majority would favor a constitutional amendment to protect the unborn. In reality, by a two-thirds margin, they are not only against abortion, but willing to adhere to those convictions should their 15-year-old daughters face an abortion decision.

Ironically, the Supreme Court stated . . . that fifteen-year-olds may have abortions without even consulting their parents. [*Akron v. Akron Center for Reproductive Health,* (June 15, 1983).] If choice is really at stake in the abortion controversy, here is where it is relevant. Every state in the Union recognizes that minors must be protected against the consequences of immature choices. Accordingly, parental consent is required by law for marrying, attending certain movies, and in some cases even having one's ears pierced. Yet abortions performed on minors are allowed without proper parental protection against immature or poorly-considered choices.

After examining many of these myths with the pregnant Senate aide, I encouraged her to ponder the consequences of her choice before making it. We also discussed the horror many women experience years after their abortions, when they come to realize that they have killed their babies.

Indeed, a new organization with the name of Women Exploited By Abortion (WEBA), which has a rapidly growing membership of over 10,000, is dedicated to helping women avoid the mental anguish, the sleepless nights, and the inescapable guilt of making the wrong choice. These women are still suffering years after their own hasty decisions to have abortions; they wish only to warn others of the emptiness that accompanies the realization that they will never be able to teach, love, hold, or cherish the child they killed.

I also discussed with my friend the feelings of her family and their role in this decision. We discussed, although in terms new to her, the eternal consequences of her decision. At length we parted.

I hope our discussion helped her. It certainly strengthened my resolve to make the consequences of abortion known. I still trust that when Americans know that over 15 million children have already died (more than ten times all our war dead), and as many as 2 million more will become victims of convenience each year this policy continues, they will put an end to the slaughter.

The chance to make that case again came sooner than I expected. One of my own assistants, a member of our church, had repeatedly stated that she was personally against abortion, but felt that every woman should have the freedom to choose whether to terminate the life of her unborn infant. After she had listened to two days of testimony, pro and con, and considered what abortion really entails—what the choice really is—she came to me to say that she had not only changed her mind, but was horrified that she had based her position on a hollow slogan instead of considering this most important issue in depth. One human being simply cannot determine the value of another's life. A human being cannot exercise the power which God has reserved to Himself—the power to determine when men and women shall be born and when they shall die, the "bounds of their habitation" (Acts 17:26).

Since then, I have had the opportunity to take a constitutional amendment to reverse the Supreme Court's erroneous abortion decision to the Senate floor and to appeal to the nation in terms similar to those that helped my assistant. Moreover I have had the opportunity to preside over Senate hearings which have disclosed a new threat to the unborn, namely the proposed Equal Rights Amendment (ERA). In its current form, ERA would likely invalidate any state or federal laws, such as the so-called Hyde Amendment, that restrict taxpayer funding of abortion, because these laws deny funding to a "medical procedure" performed only on females. In 1980, the Supreme Court held that these funding restrictions were constitutional by the barest margin of five to four. [*Harris v. McRae*, 448 U.S. 227 (1980).] Yet even that narrow victory was based on the Court's reasoning that the

Hyde Amendment does not disadvantage any "suspect class" of citizens who have been denied constitutional rights in the past. Both pro- and anti-ERA scholars agree that ERA will make sex-based classifications "suspect." Thus, using its former reasoning, the Court would be likely to strike down even modest limitations on abortion funding. Indeed a 1983 report by the Congressional Research Service concluded that "ERA would reach abortion and abortion funding situations," thus confirming the testimony of devoted pro-life advocates, like Congressman Henry Hyde and Professor John Noonan, that ERA could subject even more unborn children to jeopardy.

This last thin reason for denying the threat that the ERA poses to abortion restrictions disappeared, however, when the Commonwealth Court of Pennsylvania ruled on March 9 that two state laws restricting funding of elective abortions violated the state's ERA. That court stated that "[the ERA/abortion argument] is meritorious and sufficient in and of itself to invalidate the statutes before us in that those statutes do lawfully discriminate against women with respect to a physical condition unique to women." The warnings issued months earlier by numerous expert witnesses before my constitution subcommittee had been realized.

These advocates, as well as numerous dedicated pro-life Senators, have effectively and convincingly unmasked the moral and legal bankruptcy of a policy that allows the wholesale destruction of innocent human life. All of the insightful words from Senate debates on abortion, however, do not match the simple majesty of the Bible: "Thou shalt not kill."

POSTSCRIPT

Is It Possible to Be Pro-Life and Pro-Choice?

Much of the rhetoric surrounding the pro-life *v.* pro-choice debate attempts to point to one specific "answer": Yes or no, right or wrong, good or bad, moral or immoral, my way or your way. "It all depends" may be the necessary bridge to understanding what the many positions regarding life and, specifically, abortion are expressing.

Sagan and Druyan try to establish some historical perspective on abortion by briefly reviewing past practices regarding abortion in the United States. They indicate that abortions were banned near the beginning of the twentieth century because of social and economic changes in the United States that occurred as it moved from an agrarian to an industrial economy. Hatch presents important figures regarding the frequency of abortion on demand and raises serious moral and philosophical questions about issues of choice and freedom and about whose choices and freedoms are being protected. His view that Americans are indulgent and misusing abortion as a method of birth control in its fullest, darkest sense is shared by many people of varying cultural and religious backgrounds. Recent Supreme Court rulings and executive branch administrative decisions are somewhat supportive of his position, although opinion polls evidence diverse opinions among Americans on the subject.

SUGGESTED READINGS

J. Baskin, "Prenatal Testing for Tay-Sachs Disease in the Light of Jewish Views Regarding Abortion," *Issues of Health Care of Women*, 4 (1984): 41–56.

A. L. Clarke, "Moral Reform and the Anti-Abortion Movement," *Sociological Review*, 35 (1987): 123–149.

M. W. Gillespie, "Secular Trends in Abortion Attitudes: 1975–1980–1985," *Journal of Psychology*, 122 (1988): 323–341.

L. Leight, "When Abortion is a Blessing," *Women and Therapy*, 7 (1988): 145–157.

J. P. Lemkau, "Emotional Sequelae of Abortion: Implications for Clinical Practice," *Psychology of Women Quarterly*, 12 (1988): 461–472.

R. J. Lilford, "Surgical Abortion at 20 Weeks: Is Morality Determined Solely by the Outcome?" *Journal of Medical Ethics*, 15 (1989): 82–85.

A. L. McCutcheon, "Sexual Morality, Pro-Life Values and Attitudes Toward Abortion," *Sociological Methods and Research*, 16 (1987): 256–275.

A. C. Mehta, "Ethical Issues in Abortion, Amniocentesis and Sterilization," *The Journal of Family Welfare*, 34 (1987): 49–53.

B. Ryan, "When Married Women Have Abortions: Spousal Notification and Marital Interaction," *Journal of Marriage and the Family*, 51 (1989): 41–50.

ISSUE 7

Is Parenthood Necessary for a Good Marriage?

YES: Irving Sarnoff and Suzanne Sarnoff, from *Love-Centered Marriage in a Self-Centered World* (Hemisphere Publishing Corp., 1989)

NO: J. E. Veevers, from *Childless by Choice* (Butterworth & Co., 1980)

ISSUE SUMMARY

YES: Professor of psychology Irving Sarnoff and Suzanne Sarnoff, an adjunct lecturer in psychology, discuss their holistic model of love-centered marriage and argue that the satisfaction of love needs through marriage and parenthood is essential to human realization and fulfillment.

NO: Sociologist J. E. Veevers describes the stages that lead to childlessness and concludes that having children is no longer considered to be a solution for an unhappy marriage nor a necessity for a happy marriage.

Previous generations once assumed unquestioningly that marriage was for parenthood and that parenthood made for a good marriage. Parenthood epitomized what life was all about; it was what churches required of their members and what popular culture romanticized. But in the 1960s, 1970s, and 1980s, for a variety of reasons, people began to question the purposes of marriage, and marriages began to change accordingly. Divorce became more frequent, if not nearly normal, and single parenthood as a result of divorce, or even without marriage in the first place, became more common. People started to ask, "Why does a good marriage depend on having kids?" Couples could notice that Sally and Sam next door didn't have children but they had careers, travel, and other experiences not necessarily as available to couples with children. Sally and Sam also had what appeared to be a good marriage. Childlessness began to lose its negative connotations.

E. E. LeMasters, in his classic article "Parenthood as Crisis," *Marriage and Family Living* (vol. 19, no. 4, 1957), shocked the academic world by concluding that first parenthood was a crisis for a large proportion of couples who experienced it. This conclusion prompted a series of articles that redefined and refined what it was that researchers were talking about, and how well the measures used were gauging marital stress. The ensuing studies indicated that although measurable crisis was seen less often, stress over a period of time was probable but manageable. For example, researchers found that pressures from in-laws regarding how best to parent often became internalized, causing distress within the marriage and sparking arguments over such subjects as appropriate spousal behavior, money, or sex.

It has become apparent and acknowledged in the research literature and in the popular press (see E. Peck, *The Baby Trap* [Pinnacle Books, 1971]) that parenthood is a mixed bag. Parenthood goes better for some people at some times than for others. In a study that looked at the joys and sorrows experienced by couples who had been married 50 or more years, Sporak-owski and Hughston (1978) found that as couple members looked back over their marriages, they often said tasks of parenthood were some of their best times, but they also said they were some of the worst.

Decade review articles in *The Journal of Marriage and the Family* for the 1970s and 1980s, as well as recent issues of *The Inventory of Marriage and Family Literature*, indicate that studies of parenting stress continue to be frequently published. Even Ann Landers once reported that when people who were parents were asked, "If you had to do it over again, would you choose to become a parent?" 70 percent of those who responded said no. Many claimed they felt that they sacrificed a marriage for a family.

In the following selections, Irving Sarnoff and Suzanne Sarnoff maintain that children are an integral part of a loving, fulfilling marital union. J. E. Veevers, on the other hand, indicates that there are many styles of marriage. She argues that for some couples, remaining childless is probably the best option in terms of personal as well as couple growth and fulfillment.

YES

Irving Sarnoff and
Suzanne Sarnoff

REPRODUCING AND RETREATING

By coupling successfully mates demonstrated the power of their joint creativity. Together, they made their symbolic creation—their loving relationship—gratifying and robust. Now they yearn to transform this intangible offspring of their love into an actual child whose entire existence would personify, enlarge, and celebrate the fruitfulness of their union.

Thus, the second objective of love-centered marriage invites a husband and wife to decide to reproduce, to implement their decision, and to heighten the intensity of their love throughout the entire process of going from the "gleam in their eyes" to the arrival of their baby. Just *wishing* to attain this objective is a great boost to a couple's relational development. Never have they presumed to be so daring and responsible, to put so much faith in their ability to face the unknown. Indeed, they may have to overcome many difficulties in conceiving, in going through pregnancy and birth, or in the unfolding of genetic defects, all of which exceed their power to predict, control, or remedy.

By reproducing, therefore, spouses can improve their ability to coordinate the involuntary and voluntary aspects of loving. In reaching a decision to conceive, they must cease their procrastination and opt in favor of their inner promptings. While attempting to conceive, they must accept their inability to exert voluntary control over the outcome of their intercourse. Obviously, they cannot guarantee that conception will take place precisely when they want it to occur. They are obliged to wait until the wife becomes pregnant and, subsequently, until the baby arrives. Likewise, they cannot willfully determine the gender of the fetus, its intrauterine development, or the exact time and course of its birth.

However, mates *do* have the power to *choose how they will relate to each other* during those involuntary intervals of waiting. In keeping with the desirable objective of this stage, they can decide to intensify their romance by fulfilling all the promises of love in ways that pertain specifically to the periods of decision making, conception, pregnancy, and birth. Knowing they are

From Irving Sarnoff and Suzanne Sarnoff, *Love-Centered Marriage in a Self-Centered World* (Hemisphere Publishing, 1989). Copyright © 1989 by Irving Sarnoff and Suzanne Sarnoff. Reprinted by permission. Notes omitted.

courageous enough to accept the benefits and burdens of reproducing, spouses become stronger as individuals. They also increase their mutual respect, setting into motion a self-fulfilling prophecy about how loving they will be as parents.

Although they can fulfill the promises of love in special ways at each juncture in the reproductive process, mates are prey to the accompanying threats. Consequently, they defend themselves against their fear of loving by devising complicities in which they temporarily *retreat* from reproducing *and* from a concomitant increase in their intimacy. They may shy away from the decision to procreate. Even after making a decision, they may avoid putting it into effect. Then, once having conceived, they may withdraw excessively from one another.

DECIDING TO CONCEIVE

By meeting their past commitments, spouses validated their mutual trust and cemented their collective identity. They now are considering an irrevocable pledge of love and devotion not only to each other but also to any child they produce. Of course, they can revel in constructing new romantic images for their common dream by exchanging fantasies of how they will literally merge their separate beings by combining their genes, the biological core of each one's uniqueness, and they can anticipate how well their individual characteristics will be fused within their child. Regarding their imagined offspring as an embodiment of the archetypical wish to ensure their personal and relational continuity, they can also look forward to satisfying their existential longings for immortality as individuals and as a couple.

Still, the commitment to become parents is more sobering than any they have made since agreeing to marry. Now, they are contemplating an offer of unfailing dependability to a human being who will have to rely on the success of their unity and interdependence for many years after his or her birth.

The solemnity surrounding this decision encourages spouses to be fully accountable for telling the truth. They have the greatest possible incentive to say what they mean and to mean what they say. To guarantee the future of their marital well-being, each needs unequivocal reassurance of the other's motivation and aptitude for parenting. Both want to know that their desires for a child are equally intense and authentic, that one partner is not merely accommodating the other's stronger wish for a baby. Each needs to believe in the other's ability to be a source of emotional support *no matter what happens* after they decide to conceive. Certainly, neither mate can feel secure about opting for parenthood if he or she thinks the other will fold up under the pressure of any complications that might occur. Similarly, both need to feel they can count on each other, *without any reservations,* to cooperate in providing the patience, wisdom, and firmness for guiding their child's physical and emotional development.

Envisioning another person to feed, clothe, and shelter, a couple's financial arrangements for the future become linked with sheer survival. Despite their intention to share all their marital roles equally, pregnancy may interfere with a wife's earning power. It is thus highly appropriate for couples to ask themselves how reproducing could affect their family income. How long will the wife remain on her job during pregnancy?

How soon do they want her to return to work after their baby is born? What maternity benefits does she have? Does the husband have equivalent paternity benefits? Can they afford to have a child if she is required, for reasons of health, to stop working altogether? What about medical provisions? Do they have insurance to cover prenatal care, hospitalization, and other expenses they may incur after the baby is born? Or do they have enough money saved up for those purposes?

While spouses may answer these practical questions to their mutual reassurance, they remain vulnerable to the psychological threats connected with irrevocable increases in their interpersonal merger and interdependence. Therefore, although they have no rational reasons to delay reproduction, they may yield to those apprehensions by shrinking away from a definite decision to conceive.

Some mates feel particularly threatened by the thought of how thoroughly conception will overlap the boundaries of their individuality. Anticipating an irreversible loss of their personal identities, they worry about "losing out" to each other by having a child. So, they formulate complicities in which they forestall a decision to reproduce and retreat, instead, into intense occupational rivalry. Thus, they defensively strive to emphasize their separateness. . . .

For many . . . couples, the threat of increased interdependence motivates their vacillation. In one widespread complicity mates act as if the choice to have a child really is not theirs to make. These couples tacitly agree to take chances about conceiving. Forming a pact to avoid any discussion of what they are doing, both of them pretend they are not taking the risk of having an "accident." . . .

In many cases, however, an "accidental" conception may shock a couple into a new level of honesty. Burnt by reacting defensively to the threat of interdependence, spouses often wake up to the fact that they can readily turn it into a promise of love fulfilled; and, by pledging to be more reliable, they are able to deal with the conception as a unified team.

If they choose to have the baby, a couple is motivated to overcome the remnants of their ambivalence before its arrival. Taking full responsibility for *this* decision enables them to implement it by doing all the planning necessary to welcome their child into an emotionally warm and economically secure environment.

On the other hand, if they decide on an abortion, mates may approach it with a new mutuality of emotional support. Being considerate, kind, and tender, they minimize the inevitable suffering involved in this painful choice. And, when the abortion is over, they maintain the momentum of their deepening interdependence by using contraception faithfully until they reach a deliberate, well-considered, and unequivocal decision to have a child.

Exhilarated by talking about the possibility of conception, we too felt very threatened. True, we *thought* we were emotionally ready for this challenge. We were also doing everything possible to anticipate the economic demands of pregnancy and parenthood. Irv was earning a good salary as a psychotherapist at the University of Michigan Student Health Service and supplementing his income by teaching an undergraduate course. Sue was making just as much money as a psychiatric social worker at the State Mental Hospital. We planned on her working for at least a year so we could save most of her salary. In addition, we knew her Blue Cross policy required that she be insured for at least 6 months before becoming pregnant to qualify for hospitalization benefits during delivery. So we were very careful about accommodating those stipulations in our plans.

Still, could we *really* depend on each other to raise a child? What if we were still too immature? What if our relationship proved too fragile to withstand the constant presence and demands of a baby?

Of course, we regarded ourselves as much too dependable to play Russian Roulette with our decision to conceive. Instead, like some contemporary couples, we used the fearful state of world affairs to mask and rationalize our fear about taking on such a heavy responsibility. At that time, a "cold war" was raging on the symbolic "front" with the Soviet Union, and a shooting war in Korea seemed likely to erupt. Inflation was rampant without any end in sight. Food, housing, baby clothes, and diapers were soaring in price, and many of our friends who had recently become parents complained about their struggle to make ends meet.

Rather than admit the *inner* threat of becoming more interdependent, we attributed it entirely to the menace outside of us. Falsely, we wove those *external* dangers into the scenario of our complicity, pointing to those conditions as the source of our vacillation. Engaging in dismal discussions on the uncertainty of everyone's future, we lamented over how little we could depend upon the world to give us the reassurance we wanted before having a child. What if Irv was called back into service and shipped overseas? Could Sue cope with an infant on her own? Would Irv be strong enough to bear such a separation, knowing he was leaving Sue and our baby to risk his life in a war we believed was unnecessary?

After procrastinating in this way for several months, we realized that the more we tried to retreat from making a definite decision, the less we felt we could count on each other *or* society to give us the crucial push to "go over the line." Ultimately, our desire to become parents outweighed our concerns about international tensions and the national economy. Trusting ourselves to do the best we could to take care of business on our own "home front," we finally decided to have a child. By that time, Sue was sure of receiving the maternity benefits from her insurance. Allowing 9 months for gestation, we looked forward to a spring birth when the weather would be ideal for taking a newborn baby out-of-doors. Finally, in June of 1950 we threw away our crippling caution and began to make love more passionately than ever before.

MAKING LOVE TO MAKE A BABY

Once spouses decide to conceive, their sexual intercourse gives them a fresh appreciation for one another. They infuse their physical contact with increased tenderness and affection, and the specialness of this emotional exchange feeds into their erotic sensibilities. As a result, they discard many old compartments between their psychological affinity and their bodily reactions. By blending the affectionate and erotic components of their love more fully, they add tremendous energy to their romance.

Every time we went to bed, we were charged with elation. This could be *it!* This could be *the* moment when we would ring the great gong of conception! Of course, we never could be sure we had succeeded. But this uncertainty did not cause us any apprehension. Instead, it added to the excitement of our gamble with the uncontrollable forces of impregnation that would meld one of Irv's sperm with one of Sue's eggs into the evolving miracle of *our* child.

Repeatedly, we were awed by the fact that a new life could result from the same sexual coupling we had done so often in the past. There we were, doing nothing different at all, and yet now it could be *for real!* This marvelous drama affected us more powerfully than any aphrodisiac we could have taken. Feeling so turned on, we could hardly wait for the next chance to make love.

Mates also benefit, as we did, from freeing themselves of all the unpleasurable constrictions of contraception. For the first time in their marriage, neither one has to think about any form of birth control. Without any device or chemicals to trouble their minds or reduce their physical sensations, they can be completely spontaneous, making love in the most natural and holistic way. They don't have to mar the delights of foreplay by stopping to insert a diaphragm or don a condom, and they don't have to worry about the health hazards of the pill or an I.U.D. Rather, they amplify their excitement largely because they are *planfully* trying to achieve the very outcome they had just as carefully sought to prevent. Besides, since they joyfully *hope they will conceive* whenever they have intercourse, they are inclined to make love more frequently than ever before.

Both partners now have the greatest incentive to maximize the depth of their sexual interpenetration. The more deeply they "get into" each other emotionally, the more complete will be their erotic pleasure. But it is also highly functional for the husband to thrust his penis as far as possible into his wife's vagina as he approaches orgasm. This thrusting ensures the furthest reach of his ejaculate, which must deliver his sperm cells up through his wife's cervix, into her uterus, and then make contact with the egg cell that has been released into her fallopian tubes—where conception usually occurs.

Reciprocally, it is best for the wife to be as relaxed and lubricated as possible during intercourse. By yielding happily to her husband's thrusts and climactic ejaculation, she can receive his sperm with the greatest accessibility to her ovum. And when she enjoys sexual intercourse to orgasm, many of the physical reactions that accompany her climax may serve to facilitate conception.

Of course, it is not necessary for a woman to have an orgasm in order to become pregnant. However, Masters and Johnson have found that strong contractions in the "orgasmic platform"—the outer third of a woman's vagina—that occur during climax can help to force out all the semen from her husband's penis. Right after orgasm her uterus rapidly descends, dipping the mouth of the cervix into the seminal pool and making it easier for the sperm to move up into her uterus and fallopian tubes. Without orgasm this lowering of the uterus occurs more slowly.

Recent research has also found that uterine suction immediately follows orgasm, helping to draw up the sperm more effectively for fertilization. This suction may be due to the hormone oxytocin, released during orgasm, which stimulates muscular waves in the woman's vagina, uterus, and fallopian tubes from an *outer to an inner* direction.

Now, mates long to give up all self-control and stay forever in a mindless ocean of sensual pleasure. In fact, most authorities advise couples to engage in sexual intercourse every 2 to 3 days in order to maximize their chances for conception. Yet a husband and a wife can become very threatened by this prescription for immersion in erotic fulfillment, especially since they feel more tempted than ever before to forgo all their worldly responsibilities and do nothing else but make love. Of course, they know that abstinence is not conducive to reproducing. So, they do not renounce sexual relations. . . .

For a minority of couples, it may take only a month of trying for the wife to become pregnant. But most spouses go through a much longer period before conception takes place. Only one fourth of all couples conceive in the first month; on average, it takes 4 to 6 months. Some couples have to keep on trying for a whole year, even when they are in perfect health. Consequently, most doctors suggest waiting for that length of time before consulting them.

Sometimes, however, when a couple does not conceive for a year, both mates may begin to doubt their reproductive powers. Threatened by the need to increase their interdependence by confronting this problem, they defend themselves from facing the possibility that one or both of them might have some physical obstacle to conception. They devise a complicity in which they *pretend not to recognize* that they could be infertile, and they resist taking the responsibility of going *together* for a medical consultation. Instead, *each suspects the other* of having a secret malady, yet they do not voice what is on their minds.

The wife may wonder if her husband knew he was sterile before they got married. Maybe he had a bad case of the mumps, ruining his capacity to produce sperm. Or maybe he had something much more shameful—a sexually transmitted disease! *That* could certainly have wiped out his ability to reproduce. But even if he didn't have an illness, couldn't he be lowering his sperm count by exposing himself so often to the heat in the steam room at his gym?

Similarly, the husband privately condemns his wife. Could she possibly have had gonorrhea before he met her? Perhaps some scar tissue was left in her fallopian tubes that was preventing fertilization. Or maybe she had an abortion that was badly botched. Could her uterus be so messed up that it can't ever be fixed?

Stewing in the rancid juices of their suspicions, these mates get caught up in a vicious cycle of mutual misgivings. Each becomes more and more unreliable in the eyes of the other, and they actually begin to act less and less dependably. Yet they behave as if no problem exists; while they continue trying to conceive, their defensiveness widens the gulf of detachment between them. Through this mutual and unexpressed paranoia, a couple can sink quickly into a slough of relational stress and disharmony; by preventing themselves from taking any action to remedy what might be a *physical* problem, they reinforce their complicity.

By contrast, mates can relieve their tensions by talking about what they have been thinking. This communication permits them to let go of groundless suspicions about one another. Then they can consult a doctor to find out what malfunction is at the root of their infertility. Given this information, they can reaffirm their relational reliability by doing whatever is necessary to improve their reproductive ability. . . .

PREGNANCY

Whenever they do conceive, mates can exult in their good fortune, feeling blessed by their ability to fuse into one. Knowing it is possible for them to create a child, they are apt to feel deeply validated about their suitability for each other.

The expansion of the wife's abdomen is joyful evidence of their success in expanding the boundaries of their individuality. Later, when "quickening" begins, the couple can share the exhilaration of seeing *and* feeling movements made by the active fetus, and they can rightly regard the process of gestation as *their* pregnancy—not merely as the wife's.

Pregnancy provides spouses with an additional and external source for building their romance. Previously, they could anchor their loving interactions only in *mental* representations. But now they can regard the fetus as a tangible locus of their collective identity, and they can see themselves as united in love within the physical reality of a being who is actually growing as a fruition of their common dream.

Spouses magnify their romance by melding their individual talents and efforts in preparations for their infant's arrival. Some couples remodel an extra room they had been using for their individual hobbies into a nursery, gladly relinquishing their "personal space" for the cooperative project of raising their baby under optimal conditions. Others get involved happily in the challenge of finding and moving to a larger home where the literal expansion of their living quarters reflects the physical and psychological expansion they have already achieved through conception.

Nevertheless, pregnancy is also threatening proof of how completely the wife and husband have merged their individual beings, and both may become panicky at the thought of permanently losing their personal identity. No longer able to retreat from conception, spouses often defend themselves by *retreating from each other.* Impeding their closeness and cooperation, couples may establish a complicity based on controversies over whose preference will prevail in naming their baby. They argue vehemently about who should select the name or whose relatives the child should be named after. This scenario can be especially ghoulish if the parents or grandparents of both mates are already deceased. In such cases a couple may become embroiled in a tenacious struggle, each one greedily vying to coopt *their* child as a means for carrying on the identity of *his or her own family.*

Because this form of rivalry is so direct *and* so utterly absurd, spouses may be struck by their own folly before they do appreciable damage to their relationship. Then, after a hearty laugh at themselves, they can reduce their competitiveness sufficiently to agree on a name that gives neither of them a "one-up" advantage over the other. . . .

Mutual Accountability

Almost as if by "divine design," the shift in attitude required for conception—from the pursuit of personal aspirations to the attainment of an interpersonal goal—prepares mates for the degree of interdependence desirable for prospective parents. Relying upon one another, they can meet the vicissitudes of pregnancy; maintain their physical, mental, and economic well-being; and make all the preparations to welcome their child into an emotionally secure environment.

The more mates depend on each other, the more they reinforce their mutual trust and their romantic image of themselves as a trustworthy pair, building their confidence to be loving parents. Still, because of her physical vulnerability, a pregnant wife cannot deny that she might have to call on her husband to play the role of compassionate nurse in coping with unforeseen problems. Sometimes, when there is a possibility of miscarriage, a woman may have to stay in bed for weeks, and she might have to give up her job prior to giving birth. In such a situation, she would want to count on her husband to take care of her, to run their household, and to relate lovingly to her.

The husband also has to face these possibilities and be ready to sustain an income for both of them. However, he is just as dependent on his wife's willingness to be reliable in preserving her health and morale. If complications in pregnancy force her to leave her job, she is the one who is carrying *their* child. Thus, while he provides help for her, he is also dependent on her to do everything possible to remedy her condition and protect the fetus.

Because couples are required to increase their interdependence in these crucial ways, the actual reality of their pregnancy can be very threatening. With their baby soon to appear, husbands and wives often reexperience the old threat of being "stuck" with one another forever. Under these circumstances, they may want to retreat from the responsibilities they have assumed in conceiving, and they may form complicities by which they *reduce* their relational reliability.

In one widespread scenario, spouses turn away from each other in detachment and distrust, and they covertly agree to rely instead on their parents. Whenever the wife has any question regarding pregnancy, she telephones her mother for detailed instructions about what she should do. She may even ask her mother to accompany her on visits to the doctor. Other women routinely take their mothers along when shopping for the baby, relying totally on their mother's taste, and they put more credence in their father's opinions than in their husband's about how to remodel a room for their child.

Sometimes, the wife resumes a childlike dependency on her father. As a little girl, she often relied on "Daddy's" judgment on many important matters. Now feeling distrustful of her own husband, she consults "Dear Old Dad" for advice on managing her finances or on how to continue her career after she gives birth.

Resuming exactly the same kind of clinging with his own parents, the husband does not protest against the wife's behavior—just as she raises no objection to his. "After all," the husband reasons as he retreats in distrust from his wife, "didn't my mom understand my problems better than anyone else? And she *never* failed me." So *he* starts to call *his* mother whenever he is anxious about the pregnancy, questioning her on topics ranging from how to treat his wife's morning sickness to what kinds of furnishings are best for the baby. He might also arrange frequent visits to his parents' home, where he can be fed by his mother who happily slaves all day to prepare his favorite dishes.

At the same time, the husband begins to act like a naive boy in relating to his father. He airs his vocational dilemmas with him, instead of with his wife, and he gets "The Old Man" into lengthy conversations about how to invest savings for his family's future. . . .

Equality Within Diversity

Having proven the normalcy of their reproductive organs, spouses may feel they have finally attained "real" manhood and womanhood. Seeing each other as unquestionably equal in their contributions to conception, they reach a new plateau in their ability to appreciate and accept their intrinsic gender differences. Now they can marvel at nature's way of saying, "Vive la difference!" in the creation of human life.

However, mates can be very threatened by the opportunity that pregnancy offers for continuing to transcend their differences in gender. Both may balk at acknowledging the biological limitations of each one's gender in the process of gestation and birth. For example, a husband may feel very envious of his wife's capacity to carry their child within her for 9 months, to give birth to it, and to feed it from her own breasts. This is a formidable combination of powers that nature reserves exclusively for the female sex and that induces feelings of inadequacy and deprivation in men. Indeed, according to Karen Horney, even young boys have expressed "wishes to possess breasts or to have a child," and Benjamin Spock has also remarked on how much boys envy girls for their ability to bear children.

A wife can just as intensely covet the freedom her husband enjoys from the danger and pain of bearing and giving birth to children. Contemplating her exclusive assumption of these physical burdens, she may fret about "what we women have to go through." She may also regard the prospect of breast-feeding as a physically draining and emotionally coercive chore that will ruin the shape of her bosom, restrict her participation in other activities, and keep her tied to a stereotyped gender role.

Consequently, a husband may want to spite his wife because she *is* pregnant, while she wants to spite him because he is *not!* Together, they contrive complicities in which they express their spiteful feelings and "get back" at each other. Sometimes they can be downright vengeful, ostentatiously spurning each other's company to spend time in gender-typed pursuits, either alone or with members of their own sex. Naturally, mates are also spiting themselves in these sexist defense pacts that impede their ability to accept their gender differences and to progress in relational equality.

Appropriating the fetus as hers—and hers alone—the wife may blot out the husband's part in its creation. Like a queen bee, she considers him a mere drone. Quitting her job, she indulges her "feminine" whims by becoming excessively focused on her appearance. Constantly looking at herself in the mirror and checking her weight, she spends lavishly on chic maternity clothes without consulting her husband. Whenever she has any worries about her pregnancy, rather than discuss her concerns with him, she telephones a "girlfriend" for advice. Afraid of losing her sex appeal by exposing her husband to the nitty-gritty details of her physiological changes, she never suggests that he go with her to the obstetrician for her regular examinations. When shopping for the layette, she relies totally on the judgment of the saleswomen. At home she refuses to let her husband get into *her* act, rejecting his suggestions about what they should buy for the baby.

Meanwhile, the husband adopts a pose of "masculine" perfection in an effort to become the "top man" in his field. Of course, he may rationalize this preoccupation with his work on the grounds of preparing to meet the economic demands of parenthood. But he goes far beyond the "call of duty" and spends inordinate amounts of time with his male colleagues, staying late at the office and going out with them after work to bowl or play cards.

Further exaggerating his stereotyped gender role, the husband projects his "masculine" prowess into the future, visualizing himself in a brilliant career while "keeping" his "little woman" and a child in an ever improving style of comfort. At the same time he spitefully avoids discussing the physical aspects of his wife's pregnancy, and he never offers to accompany her to the doctor or become better informed about the birthing process.

Of course, the developing fetus literally is part of the wife's body, and her husband can only empathize vicariously with her unique experience. Still, cognizant of the desirability of promoting their relational equality, mates can share as many aspects of pregnancy and birth as possible.

Visiting *their* obstetrician together, a couple can become equally aware of any special precautions the wife may be advised to take in preventing physical complications, and the husband can help her to follow whatever regimen the doctor prescribes. Similarly, they can agree on a particular type of birthing procedure. Mates can also participate, *as a couple,* in classes on prenatal care and preparations for birth. Sitting side by side in these classes, they acquire a commonality of roles as expectant parents. Like the wife, the husband can learn about the physiology of her changes. With this knowledge

he can help her to stay in good condition and, later, to deliver the baby. By assisting her and sharing her experience, he can express the soft, tender side of his nature that he may have suppressed previously.

The wife can foster the couple's relational equality by enthusiastically welcoming her husband's involvement in every aspect of her prenatal care and delivery. If he is resistant to such participation, she can prod him into it, and her prodding may evoke productive discussions of the gender-role stereotypes they are still reluctant to relinquish. If she has a job she can continue working, unless the doctor advises her to stop, and she can remain at work until she is almost ready to give birth. Thus, she can avoid becoming overly self-absorbed, develop her occupational skills and interests, and responsibly contribute to the family income.

BIRTH

When the wife goes into labor, the couple can apply everything they were taught for the climactic episode of birth. Comforting and encouraging his wife, the husband can help her with the breathing and pushing exercises they had practiced. Even if unexpected complications, such as a weak fetal heartbeat or a breech position, require the wife to undergo a caesarean section, these egalitarian mates are optimally prepared to tolerate the attendant shock and to deal with their common disappointment at being unable to go through with the natural delivery they had planned.

With the husband present when the baby is born, *both* parents can usher it into life, and the infant can immediately form the same kind of loving bond with its father as it does with its mother. Spouses also add new strength to the loving bond between them. In fact, Lorna and Philip Sarrel regard the physiology of labor and delivery as a very sexual event. After all, birth " . . . is the culmination of an act of intercourse, the product of male-female union, and unless there is heavy sedation or a caesarean delivery, it is a moment of surrender to natural body rhythms and processes." Women actually have described the birth of a baby as similar to an orgasmic response, both physically and psychologically. Thus, when delivery is shared by a husband and a wife, it can be one of their most intimate experiences. Indeed, they can attain lasting emotional benefits for themselves and the baby—advantages that show up in many aspects of their postnatal contacts with their child and each other.

Richard, a former student of ours, told us how much it helped his marriage for him to assist in the birth of his first child. Since he and his wife, Sharon, were living in a remote section of Oregon, they had no access to courses on preparation for childbirth. Still, they prepared themselves by reading everything they could find on various methods of natural birthing. When Sharon went into labor, Richard took off from work and remained at her bedside, where they could implement everything they had learned.

Their doctor had agreed to let them do their own thing. But he remained "on call," coming in periodically to check on Sharon's progress while the couple got into their breathing exercises. Carefully, they timed the length of every contraction and the intervals between them. Every time Sharon felt a pain coming on, she grabbed Richard's hand and held it tight while he soothed her head and gently rubbed her belly, telling her how much he loved her. Soon, they were functioning like an obstetrical team.

Within a few hours, however, the rhythm and strength of the contractions declined. Eventually, they ceased completely, leaving Sharon and Richard emotionally deflated. Still, something *had* happened. But the doctor said there was nothing they—or anyone else—could do, either to predict when her labor would begin again or to spur it on.

Sharon remained in intermittent labor for over 24 hours. During this long span she had a number of very severe contractions, but her cervix was not dilating much, and she grew increasingly anxious and exhausted. But Richard's warm and constant presence helped to relieve her torment and sustain her morale. As their harrowing ordeal continued, they felt like lovers grappling with a life-and-death danger in which everything they valued was on the line. With Richard's efforts synchronized with Sharon's, they were united in the same lifesaving mission, and they cherished each other more than ever before.

Suddenly, *it* happened again! Yes, again and again! Much stronger and more quickly. One stab of pain after another. Harder and harder, lasting longer and longer. Sharon could barely ride out one wave of cramping spasms before another began. Curling her legs up against her huge belly for comfort, she urged Richard to ring for the nurse.

Yes, the nurse announced, the baby was on its way. Quickly, she called for the doctor. But there had been an unexpected rush of births and he was still busy with another patient. While they waited for him the nurse summoned an orderly to take Sharon into the delivery room. Before they started to move her, the baby decided to come into the world, and Richard was right there beside the nurse to catch it! After the cord was cut, he put the lovely little girl on Sharon's chest. Drunk with the ecstasy of knowing their baby was alive and well, they were awed by her angelic beauty: the halo of fuzz around her luminous head, the symmetry of her full lips, the velvet folds of her tiny neck, and the exquisite shape of her little hands and feet. Yes, she was certainly worth waiting for. She made everything they had just suffered—and everything they had ever gone through in their marriage—meaningful and worthwhile. Sharon and Richard experienced a sense of communion that went beyond their fondest imaginings of spiritual transcendence, and the human commonality they felt could not be diminished by any of their differences in gender, either intrinsic or learned. Later, they discovered that they had permanently improved not only their ability to communicate as husband and wife but also their ability to make passionate love.

Inspired by the arrival of a newborn infant, mates uncork all the reserves of love they had been storing up for it. In every glance and touch, they communicate their adoration. Feeling their love, which is as essential as food to its well-being, the baby reciprocates in its own infantile way. Snuggling and sleeping in their embrace, an infant's utter contentment satisfies the need its mother and father have to be loved by their own offspring. Reveling in the validation of the infant's response to them, they intensify their love for one another and feel mutually grateful for having produced this miracle of their joint creativity.

Building on this wonderful reciprocity of feeling, mates can meet the triple ob-jective for this stage: developing their own relationship for the better while raising a loving child and making a living sufficient for the increased size of their family. However, this complex challenge can throw them into a chaos of disorientation and a whirl of cross-purposes. Now, with another life entirely in their hands, a husband and wife must make extremely rapid adjustments in behavior and mental set, altering their previous routines of eating, sleeping, working, making love, and relating to other people. In fact, following the birth of their first child, spouses, may feel *really married* for the first time. Looking back, we recall our childless years as very lighthearted and carefree, indeed, as if we had only been "shacking up," as cohabitation was referred to in those days. But once we had a baby to raise into adulthood, we *knew* how "heavy" the very fruitfulness of marriage could be. . . .

NURTURING AS A MIRROR OF MARITAL DEVELOPMENT

In the process of helping their children to grow as loving persons, spouses fulfill all the promises of their marital love in new ways. For example, in showing children how to be considerate and honest, parents increase their own ability to cooperate, make compromises, and communicate honestly, thereby expanding the boundaries of their individuality and the strength of their unity. By being economically and emotionally reliable in parenting, mates intensify their own interdependence and motivate their children to become trusting and trustworthy. By sharing the diverse tasks of rearing in a nonsexist manner, husband and wife progress in transcending their own differences in gender and foster similarly egalitarian behavior in their children. Finally, while teaching children to integrate the erotic and affectionate components of their needs for love, mates can advance in the same integration and become more fully immersed in the pleasure of lovemaking.

Yet couples cannot attain the fulfillments of childrearing without succumbing, in varying degrees, to the inherent threats of love. As in every stage of marriage, they form complicities that contain pockets of alienation between them. Now, however, they can include the children in their pacts, often weaving disagreements about parenting into their scenarios. They may also use their children—rather than their *own* inner feelings of threat—as an excuse for their defensiveness. Thus, they expose a son or daughter to their own fear of loving, to the negative emotions into which they have transformed that fear, and to their methods of fighting and fleeing.

As a defense against the threat of expanding the boundaries of their individuality, mates may covertly agree to compete for a child's allegiance. By this dramatization of their own rivalry, they encourage the child to employ the same egocentric and divisive tactics in relating to them and others. Similarly, when feeling threatened by the increase in interdependence required for parenting, spouses enact their distrust and detachment, becoming mutually unreliable in meeting their responsibilities; as they let themselves "off the hook," they disregard a child's inclination to be undependable. Defending against the threat of transcending their gender differences, mates may stop accepting each other's intrinsic characteristics and feel dissatisfied with a child's particular gender. Locking themselves into stereotypical roles, they revert back to a sexist type of parenting, which limits the child's acceptance of its own gender and makes it more difficult for him or her to reject gender-role stereotypes. Lastly, in reacting against the threat of immersion in the pleasure of lovemaking, mates reduce their own erotic enjoyment and become more repressive toward a child's sexual feelings and behavior, thereby inhibiting his or her ability to integrate the sexual and affectionate components of love.

Thus, all couples frequently stand before their children as examples of how to be unloving, of how thoroughly mates can upset one another, and of how miserable they can feel about their relationship. Indeed, from the perspective of evolving the ability to love, spouses cannot fail to induce their offspring to develop for the *worse*, even as they motivate them to develop for the *better*. In this respect the impact mates exert on every child's personal development mirrors the dialectic of their own relational development: while parenting they are nurturing *and* negating not only their own potentials for loving but also their children's.

The simultaneity of this nurturance and negation produces both joy and anguish for spouses. This mixture of feelings may account for the contradictory findings that have been reported on the relationship between parenting and marital satisfaction. In some retrospective studies, a majority of spouses viewed their years of childrearing as the unhappiest in their marriage. By contrast, in other research most of the mates said they were satisfied with their children and their roles as parents. Likewise, a large national survey conducted by Yankelovich and his associates found that 90% of the couples would have children again.

Reacting to these discrepant results, Frank Cox, author of a leading text on marriage, concludes that emotional ambivalence is intrinsic to parenting: " . . . the 'lows' and 'highs' are so extreme that you want to cry at one moment and laugh at the next." Of course, even love-centered mates swing between these polarities in reacting to uncontrollable strokes of misfortune and good luck in a child's development. However, they can keep the balance of their "homemade" ambivalence consistently on the "high" side by promptly breaking the complic-ities in which they have implicated their children. By this parental diligence, mates further the constructive development of their relationship and free their children to go on actualizing their own capacity for love.

Seeing themselves as partners in parenting as well as in marriage, spouses permanently enlarge their collective identity. They also transform a major element of their common dream into a living reality; this transformation gives them a tremendous uplift in personal and relational potency.

NO

J. E. Veevers

PERMANENT POSTPONEMENT: CHILDLESSNESS AS A WAITING GAME

ABSTRACT: *By interviewing married couples who are childless by choice, Veevers found there were definite stages in becoming permanently childless: (1) postponement for a definite (specific) time; (2) postponement for an indefinite time; (3) deliberating the pros and cons; and (4) accepting permanent childlessness. Factors that accelerated commitment to permanent childlessness were pregnancy scares, aging and the possibility of adoption, and ambivalence toward achievement.*

More than two-thirds of the couples interviewed remained childless as a result of a series of decisions to postpone having children until some future time, a time which never came. Rather than explicitly rejecting parenthood prior to marriage, they repeatedly deferred procreation until a more convenient time. These temporary postponements provided time during which the evaluations of parenthood were reassessed relative to other goals and possibilities. At the time of their marriages, most couples who became postponers had devoted little serious thought to the question of having children, and had no strong feelings either for or against parenthood. Typically, they simply made the conventional assumption that, like everybody else, they would probably have one or two children eventually.

The transition from wanting to not wanting children typically evolves through four separate stages, which will be described in some detail. Although it is convenient to discuss each stage separately, it must be realized that in reality the stages are not discrete and discontinuous categories, but represent overlapping foci of the marriage at various times. Movement from one stage to the next is facilitated, or in some instances retarded, by various career contingencies which will be outlined and illustrated.

Postponement for a Definite Time
The first stage in the postponement route to childlessness involves deferring childbearing for a definite period of time. At this stage, the voluntarily childless are difficult to distinguish from the conventional and conforming

couples who will eventually become parents. In most groups, it is not necessarily desirable for the bride to conceive during her honeymoon. It is considered understandable that, before starting a family, a couple might want to achieve certain goals, such as graduating from school, travelling, buying a house, saving a nest egg, or simply getting adjusted to one another. The reasons for waiting vary, but there remains a clear commitment to have children as soon as conditions are right. For example, one wife had formulated very definite fertility plans very early in her marriage. It was her intention to work until her husband completed graduate school. His graduation was scheduled for a specific date, to be followed, if all went well, by a satisfactory job offer. When these two conditions had been met, her intentions were to conceive as soon as possible, to quit her job sometime in the middle of her pregnancy, and thereafter to devote herself full time to raising children.

During Stage One, childless couples practice birth control conscientiously and continuously. If the couple manage to postpone pregnancy deliberately for even a few months, they have established a necessary but not a sufficient condition to voluntary childlessness, namely the habit of effective birth control within marriage. Once this has occurred, habit and inertia tend to make them continue in the same behavior. The couple must now decide whether or not they wish to stop using birth control so as to have a child. Although for the first few months of marriage the postponement of pregnancy is widely accepted, even at this stage the permanently childless are somewhat different from their preparental counterparts. Many conventional couples, even those who approve of birth control and have access to it, do not seriously try to control their own fertility until they have had at least one child.

Postponement for an Indefinite Time

The second stage of the postponement route involves a shift from postponement for a definite period of time to an indefinite one. The couple often cannot recall exactly when they shifted into this second stage. They continue to remain committed to being parents, but become increasingly vague about when the blessed event is going to take place. It may be when they can "afford it" or when "things are going better" or when they "feel more ready." For example, one immigrant couple had recently experienced a rapid series of changes in country of residence, in cities within Canada, and in occupations, some of which were terminated involuntarily and some of which were terminated because they were unsatisfactory. They had very limited savings and felt that, without any family in Canada, there was no one on whom they could rely in an emergency. After nearly five years of marriage, they still wanted to remain childless until they felt financially and occupationally secure.

A more conventional couple postponed parenthood until they were "ready" and had "had some fun" in their adult, married lifestyle. The husband summed up their situation during this stage as follows:

> We were very happy and satisfied the way things were—our jobs, friends, new house, vacation trips—and we didn't want to change it just then. Our ambivalence about kids began to grow during this time, but we still assumed that someday we'd be parents just like everybody else.

Some couples postpone parenthood until they feel that they can give children all the things they think children should have. Under these circumstances, Stage Two of the postponement process closely parallels the reticence felt by many parents who do not want children too soon. A common concern is not having children until one is living in a "large enough" space, which might be defined as a two-bedroom apartment or as a three-bedroom house. Often, couples are concerned with being able to spend enough time with their children, a condition which may depend upon the woman's readiness to quit work, and/or the couple's readiness to manage on one salary. These kinds of reasons are generally relatively acceptable, in that they are attempts to maximize the advantages available to children, rather than to minimize the disadvantages that accrue to parents. A common consequence of such reasoning, however, is that the standards to be achieved before one is truly "ready" to have a child can escalate indefinitely, resulting in a series of successive "temporary" postponements.

Deliberating the Pros and Cons of Parenthood

Stage Three involves a qualitative change in the thinking of childless couples, in that for the first time there is an open acknowledgement of the possibility that, in the end, the couple may remain permanently childless. In this phase of the career, the only definite decision is to postpone deciding until some vague and unspecified time in the future. For example, a nurse reported a typical progression from Stage One to Stage Three:

When we were first married, we had long discussions about children. He wanted four and I only wanted two at the most, but it was no problem be-

cause it was still at the intellectual level because we were still discussing whether we wanted children and if we did, how many we would have. But we didn't want them then, we wanted to enjoy each other. Later on, we were trying to save to buy a house, the down-payment anyway, and we did, not this one but another we have sold since. Then my husband decided to go back to school, and he talked me into going back too. So that meant no kids for several years. We had been married I guess about three years when we really started to think that maybe we wouldn't have kids at all. We still haven't definitely decided never-never; it is a very hard decision to make, really. But a pregnancy now would just disrupt our whole way of life. Maybe later. He is thinking of a vasectomy, has been for a year or so. Maybe later; or maybe we might adopt or—I just don't know yet.

. . . [H]usbands are often less articulate about their rationale for avoiding parenthood because they have tended to think about it considerably less than have their wives. Since wives most often raise the issue of the advantages of a childfree lifestyle, the husband often ends up in the role of the devil's advocate, articulating the advantages of children in order to encourage his mate to consider both sides of the issue. One husband reported:

It really became silly for a while there. She would give the routine that kids would tie us down, that they would be a big pain in the ass, etc. Then I chime in with all the "howevers" and "buts," supporting the notion of being parents and the joys of watching our own kid grow. I wasn't all that hip about the idea, but wanted to be sure she was seeing both sides of the issue. . . .

Most couples who follow the normal moral career of parenthood cope with these questions [of the disadvantages of having children], in part by keeping them below the level of awareness. They do not have to decide to become parents because they have never questioned the inevitability of parenthood, or if they have questioned it, they have remained committed to the idealized and romanticized notions of what it will be like. A significant step in the moral career of childlessness is simply questioning the inevitability of parenthood and considering negative as well as positive aspects.

Acceptance of Permanent Childlessness

The fourth stage involves the definite conclusion that childlessness is a permanent rather than a transitory state. For most couples, there is never a direct decision made to avoid having children. Rather, after a number of years of postponing pregnancy until some future date, they become aware that an implicit decision has been made to forego parenthood. One wife reported a typical sequence:

Our decision not to have children was a very gradual thing. When we first got married, we decided we were going to do a little bit of travelling before we had a family. We went to England first of all for a holiday. We decided we definitely wanted to do that before we settled down. And then when we came back from England, we decided we couldn't stand not having a car any longer; we wanted to be able to go out for drives and so on, so we figured we could wait another year and buy a car instead. And it kept getting postponed and the more we postponed, the less I really wanted to have children. Actually, I

don't know that I ever really did want to have children; it was sort of a matter of this is what you do. I was never really wild about the idea. It was always going to be two at the most, and then it went down to one. We decided we would have one and if it was a girl, we would adopt a boy, and if it was a boy, we would adopt a girl. And then after that it went down to none and maybe adopt one. Or maybe just adopt one and we went to see the agency, like I told you. And then we just dropped it altogether.

The process is one of recognizing an event which has already occurred, rather than of posing a question and then searching or negotiating for an answer. At first, it was "obvious" that "of course" the couple would eventually have children; later it became equally "obvious" that "of course" they would not.

Every couple of years we'd discuss whether to have a child or not, not because we really wanted children, but because the time seemed to be right. And then we'd look at the bank balance and put it off for another two years. After five years, we sort of stopped discussing it. We just decided let's let it ride, we're really not that keen on it anymore. If he really wanted to have a family, I'd go along with it wholeheartedly. Of the two of us, I'm the wishy-washy one. I would do it just because it wouldn't destroy any preconceived ideas I had about being married; you know, you get married and have children—that was already set. This is more of an unfamiliar terrain at this point, to say you are not going to. He was the one who made the decision. I never really disputed the preconceived notion that married people have children. I never even thought about it much one way or the other.

Two years later, at the age of thirty-six, the husband decided to get a vasectomy and the wife agreed it was a good decision. . . .

COMMITMENT TO CHILDLESSNESS

The degree of certainty attached to the acceptance of permanent childlessness varied among the respondents interviewed. All of the persons who were early articulators, and who had demanded a childlessness clause in their marriage contracts, felt that not wanting children was an immutable characteristic of themselves. Together with some persons who were involved in the postponement process, they felt that "becoming a parent is not the right thing for me." Such persons are "independents" (Cooper et al., 1978) in that they make their decision to parent or not independently of the attitudes of their spouse. In discussing the extent to which childless persons were committed to childlessness, and the extent to which that commitment did or did not relate to their current marriage, respondents were asked: "What would you do if you (or if your wife) got pregnant?" Most immediately protested that such a thing could not happen accidentally, but were then persuaded to consider the consequences if, hypothetically, the "impossible" did occur. As an illustration of the extent to which some persons are committed to childlessness as an immutable personal attribute, rather than merely as a decision reflecting their current circumstances, one young husband replied concisely:

Well, in that case, my wife could have three choices. One, she could have an abortion. I hope she would do that, but I guess I couldn't make her do it. If not, two, she could have the baby and place it for adoption. Or three, she could have a divorce. . . .

In contrast to persons who characterize themselves as irrevocably childless by choice, more than half of our respondents related their decision not to have children to their present marriages. They acknowledge that, if they happened to marry someone else, they might well have decided to have a child. Moreover, they often speculate that, if in the future they were to be married to someone who did want children, they might very well be persuaded to change their minds. Such persons feel that not wanting children reflects not their own nature per se so much as the situation in which they find themselves. After a period of negotiation, they and their mates came to agree that "becoming parents is not the right thing for us" or more likely "becoming parents is not the right thing for us right now." This does not imply a lack of consensus or a lack of satisfaction, but it does imply an openness to the potential for sometime living differently. One husband, who resisted the idea of sterilization, explained:

Right now, I'm totally happy. We have a good marriage, we don't need kids. But who knows? Suppose we got a divorce. Suppose she got killed? I'd remarry, I know I would, and if my next wife wanted a baby, I would not automatically be opposed to it. That would be a different marriage, I'd be a different kind of husband married to a different kind of wife. If she wanted to be a mother, I'd be a father, I suppose. But now, here, for us? No way!

MOVING FROM STAGE TO STAGE: SOME FACTORS ACCELERATING COMMITMENT

Couples who know before they marry that they will never have children are not troubled by decisions, other than by choosing how they will avoid pregnancy. However, couples who remain childless through continued postponement, and who in doing so progress through four rather distinct phases, tend to have considerable variation in the ease and speed with which they move from one step to the next. Some circumstances tend to push couples rapidly on to the next stage; others tend to provide ample opportunity for continued delay.

Pregnancy Scares

One traumatic event which may serve to accelerate a couple's movement from one state of postponement to the next is a pregnancy scare. When the wife's menstrual period is late, or even worse, when a period is missed entirely, the possibility of pregnancy may serve to crystallize hitherto vague and unrecognized feelings about parenthood. Irregular periods, or even amenorrhea, may have many causes other than conception, but for sexually active women pregnancy is the explanation which comes most readily to mind. The abstract idea of a child is quite different in its psychological impact from the concrete idea of a child's forming and growing day by day. For example, in response to the question of when she first knew she did not want children, one woman replied very emphatically and precisely: "The first moment I knew, and I was absolutely certain about it, was the first moment I knew I was pregnant." In fact, although she "knew" she was pregnant, her menstrual period was simply delayed and started spontaneously ten days later. During that time, she had been involved in an intense search for a competent abortionist, a search which she described as discouraging and humiliating. She was greatly relieved to discover that she was not pregnant after all, but by that time, the decision had been crystallized, and she and her husband were weighing the relative advantages of vasectomy versus tubal ligation.

The husband of another couple in a similar position stated:

> When we thought she was pregnant we found ourselves desperately trying to look on the positive side of it—that it will be fun being parents—but we weren't fooling ourselves, though we *thought* we were being nice guys and fooling each other. When her period came, we knew we'd made our decision never to risk pregnancy again.

Aging and the Decline of Fecundity: The Adoption Alternative

One of the problems of opting for the postponement model is the biological fact that childbirth cannot be postponed indefinitely. . . . Three interrelated problems are involved. In the first place, fecundity is known to decline with advancing age. Although it is theoretically possible for a woman to bear a child until her menopause is completed, in actuality her fecundity tends to decline with each year, as to a lesser extent does her husband's. Couples who could have had a child in their twenties but who chose to wait until their thirties may find that their fecundity has declined, or has been lost, during the intervening decade and that conception is no longer possible. In the second place, many childless couples perceive that once the wife is in her late thirties or early forties, the chances of having a defective child are much increased and that it therefore would be dangerous to do so at that late date.* Third, it must be realized that a larger part of the definition of how old is "too old" to having children is social, rather than biological in origin (Rindfuss and Bumpass, 1976). When the mother's age is too advanced, it is believed that her tolerance of young children is reduced and that the family situation would not be "good" for the child. Moreover, since couples tend to associate with persons their own age, a late birth would place them in the unusual situation of coping with toddlers while their friends were coping with teenagers.

As a consequence of these three factors, as the age of the wife approaches thirty, the decision to postpone deciding whether or not to have a child becomes less comfortable. In order to avoid the stress of having to make an imminent decision, one strategy is to redefine the maximum age at which reproduction would still be safe and desirable. Interestingly, this age seems to recede in time, depending upon the age of the woman, with a tendency to leave a margin of about two years. Thus, women of twenty-

eight report they feel they must make a decision by the time they are thirty; women of thirty-four say they must do so by thirty-six; and women of thirty-eight vow to make up their minds by forty. Although such stalling defers immediate pressure, it is inevitably a temporary solution. When a forced choice appears imminent, a more practical solution is to include the vague possibility of adoption as a satisfactory "out" should one be needed. One wife makes a typical comment when she trails off her discussion of children by concluding: "If we've left having children too late, we might adopt one." An ex-nurse of twenty-nine, who believes that if you are going to have children, you should have them before you are thirty, suggests that: "If at fifty we decide we did miss something after all, we will adopt an Indian kid, or maybe a homeless teenager."

When we examined our childless couples closely on this subject of future adoption, however, it became clear that, in most instances, talk about adoption is unlikely to be a precursor of actually becoming adoptive parents. Although many of the childless couples referred at least once to the possibility of someday adopting a child, their discussions of this eventuality were exceedingly vague. They had apparently given no thought to the kind of child they might like to adopt, not even in terms of such obviously important traits as sex, age, or race. They had no information regarding the conditions under which adoption would be possible or what steps it would entail. It is noteworthy that it apparently never occurred to any of the couples who discussed adoption that, if they wanted to adopt, a suitable child might not be available. Nor did it occur to them that, if a child were available, he or she might not

*The increased medical risks associated with late pregnancies are more important relative to other women at younger ages than they are in absolute terms. For example, Down's syndrome is a congenital malformation which clearly increases in risk with advancing maternal age, especially after the age of forty. However, among births to women aged forty to forty-four, the incidence of Down's syndrome is less than one per cent (Nortman, 1974:7). In other words, a childless woman of this age has a better than 99 per cent chance of not having a Mongolian idiot. "Clearly, in the absence of a personal history to the contrary, older women run only a small risk of producing a congenitally malformed child, although their risk is much higher than that faced by younger women" (Nortman, 1974:7).

be placed with them. Although adoption is seldom a pragmatic option for voluntarily childless couples, it does have considerable symbolic importance in that it allows postponers to remain indefinitely at the third stage of debating endlessly the pros and cons of parenthood.

Ambivalence Toward Achievement

Couples in the first stage of postponement, who hold out other goals as "excuses" for not starting a family, may find themselves feeling quite ambivalent when they do finally achieve their goals. Such achievement is intrinsically desirable and presumably satisfying, but at the same time, it removes one of the most readily acceptable reasons for avoiding parenthood. Thus, one can be happy about graduating from college or about getting a good job, and at the same time be apprehensive about the attendant responsibilities that may come with it. For example, one husband reflected:

> I remember we were out celebrating the fact that we would both be finished with school and would graduate from college a full semester sooner, but when it dawned on us that now we didn't have any excuses left to postpone a family, we got a sinking feeling inside. Neither of us wanted that now. We found ourselves agreeing that it wouldn't be a good idea to have kids yet. We still acted the same way, but after that, it was a lot harder to explain. It was like our days of grace had run out, like on a mortgage or something.

Similarly, if couples have postponed having children until they are "out of debt" or until they can "afford to buy a house," their achievement of these goals necessitates a re-evaluation of their parenthood aspirations. Thus, removing the once-perceived obstacles to "being ready" for parenthood accelerates the couples more quickly toward a resolution of their dilemma and their inevitable entrance into either parenthood or a childfree lifestyle. . . .

Insecurity About the Marriage

A final factor in moving couples through the stages of postponement related to grave doubts about the future of their present marriage. This dimension was not frequently mentioned by our respondents, but it did surface in the course of some interviews. Marital insecurity often leads to a more immediate decision about having children, but does not necessarily mean that either parenthood or childlessness is the automatic choice. Folklore suggests, for example, that a child may be an effective solution to some kinds of marital problems. Family-life specialists have suggested that, although the effectiveness of this "solution" is at best questionable, the motivation of improving marital relationships may be a significant factor in fertility planning. It is possible that unhappily-married childless wives reject this solution for one of two reasons; either they do not accept its probable efficacy, or they do not want their "problem" to be solved. Simmel notes that there is a tendency for "cold, intrinsically alienated, unhappy spouses" not to want children, a phenomenon he attributes to the fact that:

> it might unify them; and this unifying function would contrast the more effectively, but the less desirably with the parent's overwhelming estrangement. . . . They instinctively feel that the child would close the circle within which they would be nearer one another, not only externally but also in their deeper psychological layers, than they are inclined to be (Simmel, 1950: 146).

While this may well be so, it is difficult to elaborate in terms of the present research, since only a few of the couples interviewed reported markedly unsatisfactory and conflict-ridden marriages. In interpreting this fact, it must be remembered that a criterion for inclusion in the sample was a marriage duration of at least five years. For some, marital unhappiness may have been a major factor in both the decision to remain childless and the decision to get a divorce.

REFERENCES

Cooper, Pamela E., Barbara Cumber, and Robin Hartner, 1978. "Decision-making patterns and postdecision adjustment of childfree husbands and wives." *Alternative Lifestyles,* 1 (February): 71–94.

Nortman, Dorothy, 1974. "Parental age as a factor in pregnancy outcome and child development." *Reports on Population/Family Planning,* 16 (August):1–51.

Rindfuss, Ronald R., and Larry L. Bumpass, 1976. "How old is too old? Age and the sociology of fertility," *Family Planning Perspectives,* 8 (September/October):226–230.

Simmel, George, 1950. *The Sociology of George Simmel.* (Translated by Kurt H. Wolff). New York: The Free Press.

POSTSCRIPT

Is Parenthood Necessary for a Good Marriage?

In a recent issue of Lynn Johnston's popular comic strip, *For Better or for Worse*, the father is pictured thinking to himself what a wonderful thing parenthood is, how sweet the baby is, how joyous caring for children is, how well his wife has taken care of the house and children. He wonders, "What words can describe the intense and special feeling a mother has after being at home with her baby all day?" At that point he is confronted by his wife, Ellie, who grabs him by the shirt and yells, "GET ME OUT OF HERE!!"

Can the need to be a parent be misinterpreted? Does the need to relate to, to nurture, or to aid in growth and development of another human being have to be met through parenthood? Also to what extent does the need to be a parent arise when a couple or individual feels pressure from family, friends, or society to become a parent? Postponing parenthood may be the most useful decision for couples who may be unsure of their desires or readiness.

Whether or not to become a parent and how that choice will affect marital happiness are not easily answered questions. The Sarnoffs present some of the more positive, altruistic views about why parenthood is good for marriage. Veevers presents another option, permanent postponement, and why it is a viable choice. The literature on parenthood indicates that the decision not to have children evokes a variety of social and personal reactions. The literature also tells us that parents' reactions to parenthood can be expected to vary with time and experience.

SUGGESTED READINGS

J. Belsky, L. Youngblade, M. Rovine, and B. Volling, "Patterns of Marital Change and Parent-Child Interaction," *Journal of Marriage and the Family,* **53** (1991): 487–498.

V. J. Callan, "Perceptions of Parents, the Voluntary and Involuntary Childless: A Multidimensional Scaling Analysis," *Journal of Marriage and the Family,* **47** (1985): 1045–1050.

S. L. Nock, "The Symbolic Meaning of Childbearing," *Journal of Family Issues,* **8** (1987): 373–393.

K. Secombe, "Assessing the Costs and Benefits of Children: Gender Comparisons Among Childfree Husbands and Wives," *Journal of Marriage and the Family,* **53** (1991): 191–202.

M. J. Sporakowski and G. A. Hughston, "Prescriptions for Happy Marriage: Adjustments and Satisfactions of Couples Married for 50 or More Years," *The Family Coordinator,* **27** (4), (1978): 321–327.

ISSUE 8

Should Surrogate Parenting Be Permitted for Infertile Couples?

YES: John A. Robertson, from "Surrogate Mothers: Not So Novel After All,"
Hastings Center Report (October 1983)

NO: Herbert T. Krimmel, from "The Case Against Surrogate Parenting,"
Hastings Center Report (October 1983)

ISSUE SUMMARY

YES: Professor of law John A. Robertson argues that the legal and ethical
problems associated with surrogate motherhood are not significantly different from those that already exist with artificial insemination by a donor and
adoption.

NO: Professor of law Herbert T. Krimmel questions the morality of bearing
children for the purpose of giving them up, especially for payment, and
asserts that society's shared moral values will suffer additional stress if the
practice is allowed to continue.

Approximately 10 to 15 percent of married couples in the United States who
want to have children find that they are not able to bear children due to
infertility problems attributable to one couple member or both. These
problems can be the result of any of a number of conditions, such as a low
sperm count, or irreparably damaged fallopian tubes, or developmental
anomalies. When infertility is discovered, there are options to be explored,
choices to be made, and questions to be contemplated: Is marriage only for
having children? What role would children play in our lives as married
people? How important is it to us as individuals, as a couple, as members of
extended families, and as members of a larger community to be parents? Can
we adopt? Are infants available who are somewhat like us? Is artificial
insemination a legitimate, moral, or religious option? Who would act as
donor? How vital is it to carry on the family name? Should we consider
adopting a "hard to place" or "unwanted" child? Are foreign-born children
available for adoption? Can we afford the expenses? How will the extra
efforts put into becoming parents affect our marriage?

Depending on the circumstances, surrogate parenting is one possible
option for couples facing infertility. But it does pose dilemmas not easily
resolved for the couple, the potential surrogate, and the larger social order.

The idea of collaborative reproduction may have positive outcomes for the marital couple concerned: parenting needs may be met, sex-linked illnesses may not have to be passed on to the couple's children, and marital needs based on the expectation to bear and raise children may be satisfied. All of which could contribute to a potentially better marriage. However, issues related to the separation of the decisions to create and to raise children may spark moral or ethical dilemmas for the individuals involved, their extended families, and the larger community.

In the following selections, John A. Robertson sees the issues as similar to those that are already inherent to blended families, adoption, or artificial insemination, practices that he feels are entirely accepted by society. He views surrogate motherhood as a viable alternative to adoption and maintains that it can benefit all parties involved. Herbert T. Krimmel feels that it is unethical to create human life for the purpose of giving it up. He raises issues pertaining to the value and sanctity of human life as well as specific doubts about surrogate parenting.

YES

John A. Robertson

SURROGATE MOTHERS:
NOT SO NOVEL AFTER ALL

All reproduction is collaborative, for no man or woman reproduces alone. Yet the provision of sperm, egg, or uterus through artificial insemination, embryo transfer, and surrogate mothers makes reproduction collaborative in another way. A third person provides a genetic or gestational factor not present in ordinary paired reproduction. As these practices grow, we must confront the ethical issues raised and their implications for public policy.

Collaborative reproduction allows some persons who otherwise might remain childless to produce healthy children. However, its deliberate separation of genetic, gestational, and social parentage is troublesome. The offspring and participants may be harmed, and there is a risk of confusing family lineage and personal identity. In addition, the techniques intentionally manipulate a natural process that many persons want free of technical intervention. Yet many well-accepted practices, including adoption, artificial insemination by donor (AID), and blended families (families where children of different marriages are raised together) intentionally separate biologic and social parenting, and have become an accepted thread in the social fabric. Should all collaborative techniques be similarly treated? When, if ever, are they ethical? Should the law prohibit, encourage, or regulate them, or should the practice be left to private actors? Surrogate motherhood—the controversial practice by which a woman agrees to bear a child conceived by artificial insemination and to relinquish it at birth to others for rearing—illustrates the legal and ethical issues arising in collaborative reproduction generally.

AN ALTERNATIVE TO AGENCY ADOPTIONS

Infertile couples who are seeking surrogates hire attorneys and sign contracts with women recruited through newspaper ads. The practice at present probably involves at most a few hundred persons. But repeated attention on *Sixty Minutes* and the *Phil Donahue Show,* and in the popular press is likely to engender more demand, for thousands of infertile couples might find surrogate mothers the answer to their reproductive needs. What began as an enterprise involving a few lawyers and doctors in Michigan, Kentucky, and California is now a national phenomenon. There are surrogate mother centers in Maryland, Arizona, and several other states, and even a surrogate mother newsletter.

Surrogate mother arrangements occur within a tradition of family law that gives the gestational mother (and her spouse, if one exists) rearing rights and obligations. (However, the presumption that the husband is the father can be challenged, and a husband's obligations to his wife's child by AID will usually require his consent.)[1] Although no state has legislation directly on the subject of surrogate motherhood, independently arranged adoptions are lawful in most states. It is no crime to agree to bear a child for another, and then relinquish it for adoption. However, paying the mother a fee for adoption beyond medical expenses is a crime in some states, and in others will prevent the adoption.[2] Whether termination and transfer of parenting rights will be legally recognized depends on the state. Some states, like Hawaii and Florida, ask few questions and approve independent adoptions very quickly. Others, like Michigan and Kentucky, won't allow surrogate mothers to terminate and assign rearing rights to another if a fee has been paid, or even allow a paternity determination in favor of the sperm donor. The enforcibility of surrogate contracts has also not been tested, and it is safe to assume that some jurisdictions will not enforce them. Legislation clarifying many of these questions has been proposed in several states, but has not yet been enacted.

Even this brief discussion highlights an important fact about surrogate motherhood and other collaborative reproductive techniques. They operate as an alternative to the non-market, agency system of allocating children for adoption, which has contributed to long queues for distributing healthy white babies. This form of independent adoption is controlled by the parties and planned before conception, and enables both the father and mother of the adopted child to be selected in advance.

Understood in these terms, the term "surrogate mother," which means substitute mother, is a misnomer. The natural mother, who contributes egg and uterus, is not so much a substitute mother as a substitute spouse who carries a child for a man whose wife is infertile. Indeed, it is the adoptive mother who is the surrogate mother for the child, since she parents a child borne by another. What, if anything, is wrong with this arrangement? Let us look more closely at its benefits and harms before discussing public policy.

ALL THE PARTIES CAN BENEFIT

Reproduction through surrogate mothering is a deviation from our cultural norms of reproduction, and to many persons it seems immoral or wrong. But surrogate mothering may be good for the parties involved.

Surrogate contracts meet the desire of a husband and wife to rear a healthy child, and more particularly, a child with one partner's genes. The need could arise because the wife has an autosomal dominant or sex-linked genetic disorder, such as hemophilia. More likely, she is infertile and the couple feels a strong need to have children. For many infertile couples the inability to conceive is a major personal problem causing marital conflict and filling both partners with anguish and self-doubt. It may also involve multiple medical work-ups and possibly even surgery. If the husband and wife have sought to adopt a child, they may have been told either that they do not qualify or to join the queue of couples waiting several years for agency adoptions (the wait has grown longer due to birth control, abortion, and the greater willingness of illegitimate mothers to keep their children[3]). For couples exhausted and frustrated by these efforts, the surrogate arrangement seems a Godsend. While the intense desire to have a child often appears selfish, we must not lose sight of the deep-seated psychosocial and biological roots of the desire to generate children.[4]

The arrangement may also benefit the surrogate. Usually women undergo pregnancy and childbirth because they want to rear children. But some women want to have the experience of bearing and birthing a child without the obligation to rear. Phillip Parker, a Michigan psychiatrist who has interviewed over 275 surrogate applicants, finds that the decision to be a surrogate springs from several motives.[5] Most women willing to be surrogates have already had children, and many are married. They choose the surrogate role primarily because the fee provides a better economic opportunity than alternative occupations, but also because they enjoy being pregnant and the respect and attention it draws. The surrogate experience may also be a way to master, through reliving, guilt they feel from past pregnancies that ended in abortion or adoption. Some surrogates may also feel pleased or satisfied, as organ donors do, that they have given the "gift of life" to another couple.[6]

The child born of a surrogate arrangement also benefits. Indeed, but for the surrogate contract, this child would not have been born at all. Unlike the ordinary agency or independent adoption, where a child is already conceived or brought to term, the conception of this child occurs solely as a result of the surrogate agreement. Thus even if the child does suffer identity problems, as adopted children often do, because they are not able to know their mother, this child has benefited, or at least has not been wronged, for without the surrogate arrangement, she would not have been born at all.[7]

BUT PROBLEMS EXIST TOO

Surrogate mothering is also troublesome. Many people think that it is wrong for a woman to conceive and bear a child that she does not intend to raise, particularly if she receives a fee for her services. There are potential costs to the surrogate and her family, the adoptive couple, the child, and even society at large from satisfying the generative needs of infertile couples in this way.

The couple must be willing to spend about $20,000–25,000, depending on lawyers' fees and the supply of and demand for surrogate mothers. (While this price tag makes the surrogate contract a consumption item for the middle classes, it is not unjust to poor couples, for it does not leave them worse off than they were.) The couple must also be prepared to experience, along with the adjustment and demands of becoming parents, the stress and anxiety of participating in a novel social relationship that many still consider immoral or deviant. What do they tell their friends or family? What do they tell the child? Will the child have contact with the mother? What is the couple's relationship with the surrogate and her family during the pregnancy and after? Without established patterns for handling these questions, the parties may experience confusion, frustration, and embarrassment.

A major source of uncertainty and stress is likely to be the surrogate herself. In most cases she will be a stranger, and may never even meet the couple. The lack of a preexisting relation between the couple and surrogate and the possibility that they live far apart enhance the possibility of mistrust. Is the surrogate taking care of herself? Is she having sex with others during her fertile period? Will she contact the child afterwards? What if she demands more money to relinquish the child? To allay these anxieties, the couple could try to establish a relationship of trust with the surrogate, yet such a relationship creates reciprocal rights and duties and might create demands for an undesired relationship after the birth. Even good lawyering that specifies every contingency in the contract is unlikely to allay uncertainty and anxiety about the surrogate's trustworthiness.

The surrogate may also find the experience less satisfying than she envisioned. Conceiving the child may require insemination efforts over several months at inconvenient locations. The pregnancy and birth may entail more pain, unpleasant side effects, and disruption than she expected. The couple may be more intrusive or more aloof than she wishes. As the pregnancy advances and the birth nears, the surrogate may find it increasingly difficult to remain detached by thinking of the child as "theirs" rather than "hers." Relinquishing the baby after birth may be considerably more disheartening and disappointing than she anticipated. Even if informed of this possibility in advance, she may be distressed for several weeks with feelings of loss, depression, and sleep disturbance.[8] She may feel angry at the couple for cutting off all contact with her once the baby is delivered, and guilty at giving up her child. Finally, she will have to face the loss of all contact with "her" child. As the reality of her situation dawns, she may regret not having bargained harder for access to "her baby."

As with the couple, the surrogate's experience will vary with the expectations, needs, and personalities of the parties, the course of the pregnancy, and an advance understanding of the problems that can arise. The surrogate should have a lawyer to protect her interests. Often, however, the couple's lawyer will end up advising the surrogate. Although he has recruited the surrogate, he is paid by and represents the couple. By disclosing his conflicting interest, he satisfies legal ethics, but he may not serve the interests of the surrogate as well as independent counsel.

HARMS TO THE CHILD

Unlike embryo transfer, gene therapy, and other manipulative techniques (some of which are collaborative), surrogate arrangements do not pose the risk of physical harm to the offspring. But there is the risk of psychosocial harm. Surrogate mothering, like adoption and artificial insemination by donor (AID), deliberately separates genetic and gestational from social parentage. The mother who begets, bears, and births does not parent. This separation can pose a problem for the child who discovers it. Like adopted and AID children, the child may be strongly motivated to learn the absent parent's identity and to establish a relationship, in this case with the mother and her family. Inability to make that connection, especially inability to learn who the mother is, may affect the child's self-esteem, create feelings of rootlessness, and leave the child thinking she had been rejected due to some personal fault.[9] While this is a serious concern, the situation is tolerated when it arises with AID and adoptive children. Intentional conception for adoption—the essence of surrogate mothering—poses no different issue.

The child can also be harmed if the adoptive couple are not fit parents. After all, a willingness to spend substantial money to fulfill a desire to rear children is no guarantee of good parenting. But then neither is reproduction by paired mates who wish intensely to have a child. The nonbiologic parent may resent or reject the child, but the same possibility exists with adoption, AID, or ordinary reproduction.

There is also the fear, articulated by such commentators as Leon Kass and Paul Ramsey,[10] that collaborative reproduction confuses the lineage of children and destroys the meaning of family as we know it. In surrogate mothering, as with sperm or ovum or womb donors, the genetic and gestational mother does not rear the child, though the biologic father does. What implications does this hold for the family and the child's lineage?

The separation of the child from the genetic or biologic parent in surrogate mothering is hardly unique. It arises with adoption, but surrogate arrangements are more closely akin to AID or blended families, where at least one parent has a bloodtie to the child and the child will know at least one genetic parent. He may, as adopted children often do, have intense desires to learn his biologic mother's identity and seek contact with her and her family. Failure to connect with biologic roots may cause suffering. But the fact that adoption through surrogate mother contracts is planned before conception does not increase the chance of identity confusion, lowered self-esteem, or the blurring of lineage that occurs with adoption or AID.

The greatest chance of confusing family lines arises if the child and couple establish relations with the surrogate and the surrogate's family. If that unlikely event occurs, questions about the child's relations with the surrogate's spouse, parents, and other children can arise. But these issues are not unique. Indeed, they are increasingly common with the growth of blended families. Surrogate mothering in a few instances may lead to a new variation on blended families, but its threat to the family is trivial compared to the rapid changes in family structure now occurring for social, economic, and demographic reasons.

In many cases surrogate motherhood and other forms of collaborative reproduction may shore up, rather than undermine, the traditional family by enabling couples who would otherwise be childless to have children. The practice of employing others to assist in child rearing—including wet-nurses, neonatal ICU nurses, day-care workers, and babysitters—is widely accepted. We also tolerate assistance in the form of sperm sales and donation of egg and gestation (adoption). Surrogate mothering is another method of assisting people to undertake childrearing, and thus serves the purposes of the marital union. It is hard to see how its planned nature obstructs that contribution.

USING BIRTH FOR SELFISH ENDS

A basic fear about the new reproductive technologies is that they manipulate a natural physiologic process involved in the creation of human life. When one considers the potential power that resides in our ability to manipulate the genes of embryos, the charges of playing God or arrogantly tampering with nature, and the dark Huxleyian vision of genetically engineered babies decanted from bottles are not surprising. While *Brave New World* is the standard text for this fear, the 1982 film *Bladerunner* also evokes it. Trycorp, a genetic engineering corporation, manufactures "replicants," who resemble human beings in most respects, including their ability to remember their childhoods, but who are programmed to die in four years. In portraying the replicants' struggle for a long life and full human status, the film raises a host of ethical issues relevant to the issue of gene manipulation, from the meaning of personhood to the duties we have in "fabricating" people to make them as whole and healthy as possible.

Such fears, however, are not a sufficient reason to stop splicing genes or relieving infertility through external fertilization.[11] In any event they have no application to surrogate mothering, which does not alter genes or even manipulate the embryo. The only technological aid is a syringe to inseminate and a thermometer to determine when ovulation occurs. Although embryo manipulation would occur if the surrogate received the fertilized egg of another woman, the qualms about surrogate mothering stem less from its potential for technical manipulation, and more from the attitude that it reflects toward the body and mother-child relations. Mothers bear and give up

children for adoption rather frequently when the conception is unplanned. But here the mother conceives the child for that purpose, deliberately using her body for a fee to serve the needs of others. It is the cold willingness to use her body as a baby-making machine and deny the mother-child gestational bonds that bothers. (Ironically, the natural bond may turn out to be deeper and stronger than the surrogate imagined.)

Since the transfer of rearing duties from the natural gestational mother to others is widely accepted, the unwillingness of the surrogate mother to rear her child cannot in itself be wrong. As long as she transfers rearing responsibility to capable parents, she is not acting irresponsibly. Still, some persons take a deontological position that it is wrong to use the reproductive process for ends other than the good of the child.[12] But the mere presence of selfish motives does not render reproduction immoral, as long as it is carried out in a way that respects the child's interests. Otherwise most pregnancies and births would be immoral, for people have children to serve individual ends as well as the good of the child. In terms of instrumentalism, surrogate mothering cannot be distinguished from most other reproductive situations, whether AID, adoption, or simply planning a child to experience the pleasures of parenthood.

In this vein the problems that can arise when a defective child is born are cited as proof of the immorality of surrogate mothering. The fear is that neither the contracting couple nor the surrogate will want the defective child. In one recent case (*New York Times*, January 28, 1983, p. 18) a dispute arose when none of the parties wanted to take a child born with microcephaly, a condition related to mental retardation. The contracting man claimed on the basis of blood typing that the baby was not his, and thus was not obligated under the contract to take it, or to pay the surrogate's fee. It turned out that the surrogate had borne her husband's child, for she had unwittingly become pregnant by him before being artificially inseminated by the contracting man. The surrogate and her husband eventually assumed responsibility for the child.

An excessively instrumental and callous approach to reproduction when a less than perfect baby is born is not unique to surrogate mothering. Similar reactions can occur whenever married couples have a defective child, as the Baby Doe controversy, which involved the passive euthanasia of a child with Down's syndrome, indicates. All surrogate mothering is not wrong because in some instances a defective newborn will be rejected. Nor is it clear that this reaction is more likely in surrogate mothering than in conventional births for it reflects common attitudes toward handicapped newborns more than alienation inherent in the surrogate arrangement.

As with most situations, "how" something is done is more important than the mere fact of doing it. The morality of surrogate mothering thus depends on how the duties and responsibilities of the role are carried out, rather than on the mere fact that a couple produces a child with the aid of a collaborator.

NOTES

The author gratefully acknowledges the comments of Rebecca Dresser, Mark Frankel, Inga Markovits, Phillip Parker, Bruce Russell, John Sampson, and Ted Schneyer on earlier drafts.

1. People v. Sorenson, 68 Cal. 2d 280, 437 P.2d 495; Walter Wadlington. "Artificial Insemination: The Dangers of a Poorly Kept Secret," Northwestern Law Review 64 (1970), 777.

2. See, for example, Michigan Statutes Annotated, 27.3178 (555.54)(555.69).

3. William Landes and Eleanor Posner, "The Economics of the Baby Shortage," Journal of Legal Studies 7 (1978), 323.

4. See Erik Erikson, The Life Cycle Completed (New York: Norton, 1980), pp. 122–124.

5. Phillip Parker, "Surrogate Mother's Motivations: Initial Findings," American Journal of Psychiatry 140:1 (January 1983), 117–118; Phillip Parker, "The Psychology of Surrogate Motherhood: A Preliminary Report of a Longitudinal Pilot Study" (unpublished). See also Dava Sobel, "Surrogate Mothers: Why Women Volunteer," New York Times, June 25, 1981, p. 18.

6. Mark Frankel, "Surrogate Motherhood: An Ethical Perspective," pp. 1–2. (Paper presented at Wayne State Symposium on Surrogate Motherhood, Nov. 20, 1982.)

7. See John Robertson, "In Vitro Conception and Harm to the Unborn," 8 Hastings Center Report 8 (October 1978), 13–14; Michael Bayles, "Harm to the Unconceived," Philosophy and Public Affairs 5 (1976), 295.

8. A small, uncontrolled study found these effects to last some 4–6 weeks. Statement of Nancy Reame, R.N. at Wayne State University, Symposium on Surrogate Motherhood, Nov. 20, 1982.

9. Betty Jane Lifton, Twice Born: Memoirs of an Adopted Daughter (New York: Penguin, 1977); L. Dusky, "Brave New Babies," Newsweek, Dec. 6, 1982, p. 30.

10. Leon Kass, "Making Babies—the New Biology and the Old Morality," The Public Interest 26 (1972), 18; "Making Babies Revisited," The Public Interest 54 (1979), 32; Paul Ramsey, Fabricated Man: The Ethics of Genetic Control (New Haven: Yale University Press, 1970).

11. The President's Commission for the Study of Ethical Problems in Medicine and Biomedical and Behavioral Research, Splicing Life: The Social and Ethical Issues of Genetic Engineering with Human Beings (Washington, D.C., 1982), pp. 53–60.

12. Herbert Krimmel, Testimony before California Assembly Committee on Judiciary, Surrogate Parenting Contracts (November 14, 1982), pp. 89–96.

NO

Herbert T. Krimmel

THE CASE AGAINST SURROGATE PARENTING

Is it ethical for someone to create a human life with the intention of giving it up? This seems to be the primary question for both surrogate mother arrangements and artificial insemination by donor (AID), since in both situations a person who is providing germinal material does so only upon the assurance that someone else will assume full responsibility for the child he or she helps to create.

THE ETHICAL ISSUE

In analyzing the ethics of surrogate mother arrangements, it is helpful to begin by examining the roles the surrogate mother performs. First, she acts as a procreator in providing an ovum to be fertilized. Second, after her ovum has been fertilized by the sperm of the man who wishes to parent the child, she acts as host to the fetus, providing nurture and protection while the newly conceived individual develops.

I see no insurmountable moral objections to the functions the mother performs in this second role as host. Her actions are analogous to those of a foster mother or of a wet-nurse who cares for a child when the natural mother cannot or does not do so. Using a surrogate mother as a host for the fetus when the biological mother cannot bear the child is no more morally objectionable than employing others to help educate, train, or otherwise care for a child. Except in extremes, where the parent relinquishes or delegates responsibilities for a child for trivial reasons, the practice would not seem to raise a serious moral issue.

I would argue, however, that the first role that the surrogate mother performs—providing germinal material to be fertilized—does pose a major ethical problem. The surrogate mother provides her ovum, and enters into a surrogate mother arrangement, with the clear understanding that she is to avoid responsibility for the life she creates. Surrogate mother arrangements are designed to separate in the mind of the surrogate mother the decision to create a child from the decision to have and raise that child. The cause of this dissociation is some other benefit she will receive, most often money.[1] In other words, her desire to create a child is born of some motive other than the desire to be a parent. This separation of the decision to create a child from the decision to parent it is ethically suspect. The child is conceived not because he is wanted by his biological mother, but because he can be useful to someone else. He is conceived in order to be given away.

At their deepest level, surrogate mother arrangements involve a change in motive for creating children: from a desire to have them for their own sake, to a desire to have them because they can provide some other benefit. The surrogate mother creates a child with the intention to abdicate parental responsibilities. Can we view this as ethical? My answer is no. I will explain why by analyzing various situations in which surrogate mother arrangements might be used.

WHY MOTIVE MATTERS

Let's begin with the single parent. A single woman might use AID, or a single man might use a surrogate mother arrangement, if she or he wanted a child but did not want to be burdened with a spouse.[2] Either practice would intentionally deprive the child of a mother or a father. This, I assert, is fundamentally unfair to the child.

Those who disagree might point to divorce or to the death of a parent as situations in which a child is deprived of one parent and must rely solely or primarily upon the other. The comparison, however, is inapt. After divorce or the death of a parent, a child may find herself with a single parent due to circumstances that were unfortunate, unintended, and undesired. But when surrogate mother arrangements are used by a single parent, depriving the child of a second parent is one of the intended and desired effects. It is one thing to ask how to make the best of a bad situation when it is thrust upon a person. It is different altogether to ask whether one may intentionally set out to achieve the same result. The morality of identical results (for example, killings) will oftentimes differ depending upon whether the situation is invited by, or involuntarily thrust upon, the actor. Legal distinctions following and based upon this ethical distinction are abundant. The law of self-defense provides a notable example.[3]

Since a woman can get pregnant if she wishes whether or not she is married, and since there is little that society can do to prevent women from creating children even if their intention is to deprive the children of a father, why should we be so concerned about single men using surrogate mother arrangements if they too want a child but not a spouse? To say that women can intentionally plan to be unwed mothers is not to condone the practice. Besides, society will hold the father liable in a paternity action if he can be found and identified, which indicates some social concern that people should not be able to abdicate the responsibilities that they incur in generating children. Otherwise, why do we condemn the proverbial sailor with a pregnant girlfriend in every port?

In many surrogate mother arrangements, or course, the surrogate mother will not be transferring custody of the child to a single man, but to a couple: the child's biological father and a stepmother, his wife. What are the ethics of surrogate mother arrangements when the child is taken into a two-parent family? Again, surrogate mother arrangements and AID pose similar ethical questions: The surrogate mother transfers her parental responsibilities to the wife of the biological father, while with AID the sperm donor relinquishes his interest in the child to the husband of the biological mother. In both cases the child is created with the intention of transferring the responsibility for its care to a new set of parents. The surrogate mother situation is more dramatic than AID since the transfer occurs after the child is born, while in the case of AID the transfer takes place at the time of the insemination. Nevertheless, the ethical point is the same: creating children for the purpose of transferring them. For a surrogate mother the question remains: Is it ethical to create a child for the purpose of transferring it to the wife of the biological father?

At first blush this looks to be little different from the typical adoption, for what is an adoption other than a transfer of responsibility from one set of parents to another? The analogy is misleading, however, for two reasons. First, it is difficult to imagine anyone conceiving children for the purpose of putting them up for adoption. And, if such a bizarre event were to occur, I doubt that we would look upon it with moral approval. Most adoptions arise either because an undesired conception is brought to term, or because the parents wanted to have the child, but find that they are unable to provide for it because of some unfortunate circumstances that develop after conception.

Second, even if surrogate mother arrangements were to be classified as a type of adoption, not all offerings of children for adoption are necessarily moral. For example, would it be moral for parents to offer their three-year-old for adoption because they are bored with the child? Would it be moral for a couple to offer for adoption their newborn female baby because they wanted a boy?

Therefore, even though surrogate mother arrangements may in some superficial ways be likened to adoption, one must still ask whether it is ethical to separate the decision to create children from the desire to have them. I would answer no. The procreator should desire the child for its own sake, and not as a means to attaining some other end. Even though one of the ends may be stated altruistically as an attempt to bring happiness to an infertile couple, the child is still being used by the surrogate. She creates it not because she desires it, but because she desires something from it.

To sanction the use and treatment of human beings as means to the achievement of other goals instead of as ends in themselves is to accept an ethic with a tragic past, and to establish a precedent with a dangerous future. Already the press has reported the decision of one couple to conceive a child for the purpose of using it as a bone marrow donor for its sibling (*Los Angeles Times*, April 17, 1979, p. I-2). And the bioethics literature contains articles seriously considering whether we should clone human beings to serve as an inventory of spare parts for organ transplants[4] and articles that foresee the use of comatose human beings as self-replenishing blood banks and manufacturing plants for human hormones.[5] How far our society is willing to proceed down this road is uncertain, but it is clear that the first step to all these practices is the acceptance of the same principle that the Nazis attempted to use to justify their medical experiments at the Nuremberg War Crimes Trials: that human beings may be used as means to the achievement of other goals, and need not be treated as ends in themselves.[6]

But why, it might be asked, is it so terrible if the surrogate mother does not desire the child for its own sake, when under the proposed surrogate mother arrangements there will be a couple eagerly desiring to have the child and to be its parents? That this argument may not be entirely accurate will be illustrated in the following section, but the basic reply is that creating a child without desiring it fundamentally changes the way we look at children—instead of viewing them as unique individual personalities to be desired in their own right, we may come to view them as commodities or items of manufacture to be desired because of their utility. A recent newspaper account describes the business of an agency that matches surrogate mothers with barren couples as follows:

> Its first product is due for delivery today. Twelve others are on the way and an additional 20 have been ordered. The "company" is Surrogate Mothering Ltd. and the "product" is babies.[7]

The dangers of this view are best illustrated by examining what might go wrong in a surrogate mother arrangement, and most important, by viewing how the various parties to the contract may react to the disappointment.

WHAT MIGHT GO WRONG

Ninety-nine percent of the surrogate mother arrangements may work out just fine; the child will be born normal, and the adopting parents (that is, the biological father and his wife) will want it. But, what happens when, unforeseeably, the child is born deformed? Since many defects cannot be discovered prenatally by amniocentesis or other means, the situation is bound to arise.[8] Similarly, consider what would happen if the biological father were to die before the birth of the child. Or if the "child" turns out to be twins or triplets. Each of these instances poses an inevitable situation where the adopting parents may be unhappy with the prospect of getting the child or children. Although legislation can mandate that the adopting parents take the child or children in whatever condition they come or whatever the situation, provided the surrogate mother has abided by all the contractual provisions of the surrogate mother arrangement, the important point for our discussion is the attitude that the surrogate mother or the adopting parent might have. Consider the example of the deformed child.

When I participated in the Surrogate Parent Foundation's inaugural symposium in November 1981, I was struck by the attitude of both the surrogate mothers and the adopting parents to these problems. The adopting parents worried, "Do we have to take such a child?" and the surrogate mothers said in response, "Well, we don't want to be stuck with it." Clearly, both groups were anxious not be responsible for the "undesirable child" born of the surrogate mother arrangement. What does this portend?

It is human nature that when one pays money, one expects value. Things that one pays for have a way of being seen as commodities. Unavoidable in surrogate mother arrangements are questions such as: "Did I get a good one?" We see similar behavior with respect to the adoption of children: comparatively speaking, there is no shortage of black, Mexican-

American, mentally retarded, or older children seeking homes; the shortage is in attractive, intelligent-looking Caucasian babies.[9] Similarly, surrogate mother arrangements involve more than just the desire to have a child. The desire is for a certain type of child.

But, it may be objected, don't all parents voice these same concerns in the normal course of having children? Not exactly. No one doubts or minimizes the pain and disappointment parents feel when they learn that their child is born with some genetic or congenital birth defect. But this is different from the surrogate mother situation, where neither the surrogate mother nor the adopting parents may feel responsible, and both sides may feel that they have a legitimate excuse not to assume responsibility for the child. The surrogate mother might blame the biological father for having "defective sperm," as the adopting parents might blame the surrogate mother for a "defective ovum" or for improper care of the fetus during pregnancy. The adopting parents desire a normal child, not *this* child in any condition, and the surrogate mother doesn't want it in any event. So both sides will feel threatened by the birth of an "undesirable child." Like bruised fruit in the produce bin of a supermarket, this child is likely to become an object of avoidance.

Certainly, in the natural course of having children a mother may doubt whether she wants a child if the father has died before its birth; parents may shy away from a defective infant, or be distressed at the thought of multiple births. Nevertheless, I believe they are more likely to accept these contingencies as a matter of fate. I do not think this is the case with surrogate mother arrangements. After all, in the surrogate mother arrangement the adopting parents can blame someone outside the marital relationship. The surrogate mother has been hosting this child all along, and she is delivering it. It certainly *looks* far more like a commodity than the child that arrives in the natural course within the family unit.

A DANGEROUS AGENDA

Another social problem, which arises out of the first, is the fear that surrogate mother arrangements will fall prey to eugenic concerns.[10] Surrogate mother contracts typically have clauses requiring genetic tests of the fetus and stating that the surrogate mother must have an abortion (or keep the child herself) if the child does not pass these tests.[11]

In the last decade we have witnessed a renaissance of interest in eugenics. This, coupled with advances in biomedical technology, has created a host of abuses and new moral problems. For example, genetic counseling clinics now face a dilemma: amniocentesis, the same procedure that identifies whether a fetus suffers from certain genetic defects, also discloses the sex of a fetus. Genetic counseling clinics have reported that even when the fetus is normal, a disproportionate number of mothers abort female children.[12] Aborting normal fetuses simply because the prospective parents desire children of a certain sex is one result of viewing children as commodities. The recent scandal at the Repository for Germinal Choice, the so-called "Nobel Sperm Bank," provides another chilling example. Their first "customer" was, unbeknownst to the staff, a woman who "had lost custody of two other children because they were abused in an effort to 'make them smart.'"[13] Of course, these and similar evils may occur whether or not surrogate mother arrangements are allowed by law. But to the extent that they promote the view of children as commodities, these arrangements contribute to these problems. There is nothing wrong with striving for betterment, as long as it does not result in intolerance to that which is not perfect. But I fear that the latter attitude will become prevalent.

Sanctioning surrogate mother arrangements can also exert pressures upon the family structure. First, as was noted earlier, there is nothing technically to prevent the use of surrogate mother arrangements by single males desiring to become parents. Indeed, single females can already do this with AID or even without it. But even if legislation were to limit the use of the surrogate mother arrangement to infertile couples, other pressures would occur: namely the intrusion of a third adult into the marital community.[14] I do not think that society is ready to accept either single parenting or quasi-adulterous arrangements as normal.

Another stress on the family structure arises within the family of the surrogate mother. When the child is surrendered to the adopting parents it is removed not only from the surrogate mother, but also from her family. They too have interests to be considered. Do not the siblings of that child have an interest in the fact that their little baby brother has been "given" away?[15] One woman, the mother of a medical student who had often donated sperm for artificial insemination, expressed her feelings to me eloquently. She asked, "I wonder how many grandchildren I have that I have never seen and never been able to hold or cuddle." Intrafamily tensions can also be expected to result in the family of the adopting parents due to the asymmetry of relationship the adopting parents will have toward the child. The adopting mother has no biological relationship to the child, whereas the adopting father is also the child's biological father. Won't this unequal biological claim on the child be used as a wedge in child-rearing arguments? Can't we imagine the father saying, "Well, he is my son, not yours"? What if the couple eventually gets divorced? Should custody in a subsequent divorce between the adopting mother and the biological father be treated simply as a normal child custody dispute? Or should the biological relationship between father and child weigh more heavily? These questions do not arise in typical adoption situations since both parents are equally unrelated biologically to the child. Indeed, in adoption there is symmetry. The surrogate mother situation is more analogous to second marriages, where the children of one party by a prior marriage are adopted by the new spouse. Since asymmetry in second marriage situations causes problems, we can anticipate similar difficulties arising from surrogate mother arrangements.

There is also the worry that the offspring of a surrogate mother arrangement will be deprived of important information about his or her heritage. This also happens with adopted children or children conceived by AID,[16] who lack information about their biological parents, which could be important to them medically. Another less popularly recognized problem is the danger of half-sibling marriages,[17] where the child of the surrogate mother unwittingly falls in love with a half sister or brother. The only way to avoid these problems is to dispense with the confidentiality of parental records; however, the natural parents may not always want their identity disclosed.

The legalization of surrogate mother arrangements may also put undue pressure upon poor women to use their bodies in this way to support themselves and their families. Analogous problems have arisen in the past with the use of paid blood donors.[18] And occasionally the press reports someone desperate enough to offer to sell an eye or some other organ.[19] I believe that certain things should be viewed as too important to be sold as commodities, and I hope that we have advanced from the time when parents raised children for profitable labor, or found themselves forced to sell their children.

While many of the social dilemmas I have outlined here have their analogies in other present-day occurrences such as divorced families or in adoption, every addition is hurtful. Legalizing surrogate mother arrangements will increase the frequency of these problems, and put more stress on our society's shared moral values.[20]

A TALE FOR OUR TIME

An infertile couple might prefer to raise a child with a biological relationship to the husband, rather than to raise an adopted child who has no biological relationship to either the husband or the wife. But does the marginal increase in joy that they might therefore experience outweigh the potential pain that they, or the child conceived in such arrangements, or others might suffer? Does their preference outweigh the social costs and problems that the legalization of surrogate mothering might well engender? I honestly do not know. I don't even know on what hypothetical scale such interests could be weighed and balanced. But even if we could weigh such interests, and even if personal preference outweighed the costs, I still would not be able to say that we could justify achieving those ends by these means; that ethically it would be permissible for a person to create a child, not because she desired it, but because it could be useful to her.

REFERENCES

1. See Philip J. Parker, "Motivation of Surrogate Mothers: Initial Findings," *American Journal of Psychiatry* 140:1 (January 1983), 117–18; see also Doe v. Kelley, Circuit Court of Wayne County, Michigan (1980) reported in 1980 Rep. on Human Reproduction and Law II-A-1.
2. See, e.g., C.M. v. C.C., 152 N.J. Supp. 160, 377 A.2d 821 (1977); "Why She Went to 'Nobel Sperm Bank' for Child," *Los Angeles Herald Examiner*, Aug. 6, 1982, p. A9; "Womb for Rent," *Los Angeles Herald Examiner*, Sept. 21, 1981, p. A3.
3. See also Richard McCormick, "Reproductive Technologies: Ethical Issues" in *Encyclopedia of Bioethics*, edited by Walter Reich, Vol. 4 (New York: The Free Press, 1978) pp. 1454, 1459; Robert Snowden and G. D. Mitchell, *The Artificial Family* (London: George Allen & Unwin, 1981), p. 71.
4. See, e.g., Alexander Peters, "The Brave New World: Can the Law Bring Order Within Traditional Concepts of Due Process?" *Suffolk Law Review* 4 (1970), 894, 901–02; Roderic Gorney, "The New Biology and the Future of Man," *UCLA Law Review* 15 (1968), 273, 302; J. G. Castel, "Legal Implications of Biomedical Science and Technology in the Twenty-First Century," *Canadian Bar Review* 51 (1973), 119, 127.
5. See Harry Nelson, "Maintaining Dead to Serve as Blood Makers Proposed: Logical, Sociologist Says," *Los Angeles Times*, February 26, 1974, p. II-1; Hans Jonas, "Against the Stream: Comments on the Definition and Redefinition of Death," in *Philosophical Essays: From Ancient Creed to Technological Man* (Chicago: University of Chicago Press, 1974), pp. 132–40.
6. See Leo Alexander, "Medical Science under Dictatorship," *New England Journal of Medicine* 241:2 (1949), 39; United States v. Brandt, Trial of the Major War Criminals, International Military Tribunal: Nuremberg, 14 November 1945–1 October 1946.

7. Bob Dvorchak, "Surrogate Mothers: Pregnant Idea Now a Pregnant Business," *Los Angeles Herald Examiner*, December 27, 1983, p. A1.

8. "Surrogate's Baby Born with Deformities Rejected by All," *Los Angeles Times*, January 22, 1983, p. I-17; "Man Who Hired Surrogate Did Not Father Ailing Baby," *Los Angeles Herald Examiner*, February 3, 1983, p. A-6.

9. See, e.g., Adoption in America, Hearing before the Subcommittee on Aging, Family and Human Services of the Senate Committee on Labor and Human Resources, 97th Congress. 1st Session (1981), p. 3 (comments of Senator Jeremiah Denton) and pp. 16–17 (statement of Warren Master, Acting Commissioner of Administration for Children, Youth and Families, HHS).

10. Cf. "Discussion: Moral, Social and Ethical Issues," in *Law and Ethics of A.I.D. and Embryo Transfer* (1973) (comments of Himmelweit); reprinted in Michael Shapiro and Roy Spece, *Bioethics and Law* (St. Paul: West Publishing Company, 1981), p. 548.

11. See, e.g., Lane (Newsday), "Womb for Rent," *Tucson Citizen* (Weekender), June 7, 1980, p. 3; Susan Lewis, "Baby Bartering? Surrogate Mothers Pose Issues for Lawyers, Courts," *The Los Angeles Daily Journal*, April 20, 1981; see also Elaine Markoutsas, "Women Who Have Babies for Other Women," *Good Housekeeping* 96 (April 1981), 104.

12. See Morton A. Stenchever, "An Abuse of Prenatal Diagnosis," *Journal of the American Medical Association* 221 (1972), 408; Charles Westoff and Ronald R. Rindfus, "Sex Preselection in the United States: Some Implications," *Science* 184 (1974), 633, 636; see also Phyllis Battelle, "Is It a Boy or a Girl"? *Los Angeles Herald Examiner*, Oct. 8, 1981, p. A17.

13. "2 Children Taken from Sperm Bank Mother," *Los Angeles Times*, July 14, 1982; p. I-3; "The Sperm-Bank Scandal," *Newsweek* 24 (July 26, 1982).

14. See Helmut Thielicke, *The Ethics of Sex*, John W. Doberstein, trans. (New York: Harper & Row, 1964).

15. According to one newspaper account, when a surrogate mother informed her nine-year-old daughter that the new baby would be given away, the daughter replied: "Oh, good. If it's a girl we can keep it and give Jeffrey [her two-year-old half brother] away." "Womb for Rent," *Los Angeles Herald Examiner*, Sept. 21, 1981, p. A3.

16. See, e.g., Lorraine Dusky, "Brave New Babies"? *Newsweek* 30 (December 6, 1982). Also testimony of Suzanne Rubin before the California Assembly Committee on Judiciary, Surrogate Parenting Contracts, Assembly Publication No. 962, pp. 72–75 (November 19, 1982).

17. This has posed an increasing problem for children conceived through AID. See, e.g., Martin Curie-Cohen, et al., "Current Practice of Artificial Insemination by Donor in the United States," *New England Journal of Medicine* 300 (1979), 585–89.

18. See e.g., Richard M. Titmuss, *The Gift Relationship: From Human Blood to Social Policy* (New York: Random House, 1971).

19. See, e.g., "Man Desperate for Funds: Eye for Sale at $35,000," *Los Angeles Times*, February 1, 1975, p. II-1; "100 Answer Man's Ad for New Kidney," *Los Angeles Times*, September 12, 1974, p. I-4.

20. See generally Guido Calabresi, "Reflections on Medical Experimentation in Humans," *Daedalus* 98 (1969), 387–93; also see Michael Shapiro and Roy Spece, "On Being 'Unprincipled on Principle': The Limits of Decision Making 'On the Merits,' " in *Bioethics and Law*, pp. 67–71.

POSTSCRIPT

Should Surrogate Parenting Be Permitted for Infertile Couples?

The legal, ethical, religious, and moral questions raised by the surrogate parenting issue are profound for both modern American culture and the people directly concerned. The issue of a legal contract may be moot in some jurisdictions if the natural mother protests the surrender of "her" child. To some the issue might seem to be only a legal matter, but emotions and personal attachment often surface after a child is born to a surrogate mother.

We rarely hear about surrogate cases where the biological mother does not fight to keep the child. This may reflect the strength of maternal attachments, but it may also indicate that legal custody battles are subject to more media coverage than are successfully completed surrogate contracts.

What are the marital dynamics behind the need to contract for someone outside the marriage to bear the child? Perhaps having children is so strongly desired that the marriage would break up if reproduction does not occur. Do a husband and wife require a certain level of commitment to each other to be able to psychologically endure the surrogate parenting process, especially if there is the possibility for a custody battle after the child is born?

Should the importance of having children be discussed and resolved in premarital counseling or couple-member discussions before a marriage takes place? And if a prospective marriage that is potentially childless is too painful, is it more prudent to terminate the relationship or to seek counseling or medical assistance in dealing with the issues?

SUGGESTED READINGS

L. Andrews, *Between Strangers: Surrogate Mothers, Expectant Fathers and Brave New Babies* (Harper & Row, 1988).

G. J. Annas, "Baby M: Babies (and Justice) for Sale," *Hastings Center Report,* **17** (1987): 13–15.

S. R. Lieblum, "Intimacy and the New Reproductive Options," *Women and Therapy,* **7** (1988): 131–143.

M. B. Morris, "Reproductive Technology and Restraints," *Society,* **25** (March 1988).

R. J. Neuhaus, "Renting Women, Buying Babies and Class Struggles," *Society,* **25** (March 1988).

P. Singer and D. Wells, *Making Babies: The New Science and Ethics of Conception* (Scribner's, 1985).

W. Wadlington, "United States: The Continuing Debate About Surrogate Parenthood," *Journal of Family Law,* **27** (1988–1989): 321–328.

ISSUE 9

Should Pregnant Teens Marry the Fathers of Their Babies?

YES: P. Lindsay Chase-Lansdale and Maris A. Vinovskis, from "Should We Discourage Teenage Marriage?" *The Public Interest* (Spring 1987)

NO: Naomi Farber, from "The Significance of Race and Class in Marital Decisions Among Unmarried Adolescent Mothers," *Social Problems* (February 1990)

ISSUE SUMMARY

YES: P. Lindsay Chase-Lansdale, a fellow of developmental and family research at the Chapin Hall Center for Children, and professor of history Maris A. Vinovskis accuse public policy proponents of overlooking any benefits of marriage for adolescents and their children. They call for a reexamination of research findings and current policies that cast doubt on the benefits of having adolescent mothers and fathers rear their own children.

NO: Human services educator and family researcher Naomi Farber replies that, although adolescent mothers—regardless of race or class—value marriage, they express legitimate concerns about rushing into marriage simply because they are pregnant or have given birth.

Adolescent pregnancy is a topic that has periodically aroused the public interest over the last two decades. Though the number of births among teenagers has decreased since the 1970s, enough adolescent women become pregnant each year that there is great concern for the economic and social costs of teenage parenthood.

In *Family Relations* (1989), Gina Adams, Sharon Adams-Taylor, and Karen Pittman explain that one aspect of teenage pregnancy that has remained relatively constant is the statistical profile of adolescent mothers. The great majority of adolescent births is to white mothers; however, black teens, who make up 15 percent of the adolescent population, now give birth to at least 30 percent of the babies. Close to 70 percent of teen births are to nonpoor families and about the same percentage of births occurs to teens who live outside of urban areas. So the common belief that adolescent parenthood is primarily a minority problem among poor youth who live in large cities is a myth.

Despite persistent negative stereotypes, some recent research also shows that the young fathers of these children do not always victimize the mothers. Some fathers do provide various types of monetary and emotional support for the mothers and their children, but such support typically comes through informal means rather than through marriage and the establishment of legal paternity.

One reason why people are so concerned about teenage pregnancy is that children in young single-mother families are at greater risk of being poor. Even though most births are to nonpoor adolescents, all single teenage mothers and their children are more likely to have financial difficulties and end up in poverty. High numbers of adolescent mothers drop out of school and are then unable to find well-paying jobs. As a result, they are less able to provide adequate support for their babies.

In past generations, young men more often married the adolescent mothers of their babies. Today, the marriage rate of this population has dropped to less than 30 percent. P. Lindsay Chase-Lansdale and Maris A. Vinovskis contend that this trend is due to current beliefs that marriage between people so young decreases the likelihood that the affected adolescents will finish their schooling, and that most of these early marriages will eventually end in divorce. They propose that there is no real evidence that such beliefs are true. They then discuss recent research studies that suggest that there are potential benefits to having young fathers marry the adolescent mothers of their children, and question prevailing opinions that these children are more disadvantaged if their young parents marry.

Naomi Farber contends that to understand more fully adolescent pregnancy it is necessary to look at differences by race and class. She argues that it is imperative to ask the young mothers why they do not want to marry the fathers. Farber reports that, upon interviewing various adolescent mothers, many legitimate reasons for not marrying the fathers came to light, including family influences, unreadiness for marriage, and low regard for the fathers themselves.

YES

P. Lindsay Chase-Lansdale
and Maris A. Vinovskis

SHOULD WE DISCOURAGE TEENAGE MARRIAGE?

Adolescent sexual activity, pregnancy, and childbearing have received an extraordinary amount of public and scholarly attention during the past decade. The enormous interest in the topic stems from concern about the negative consequences to the mother, to her children, and to society as a whole. Public concern has been further galvanized by the dramatic increase in the number of out-of-wedlock births. Indeed, it is estimated that half of the federal expenditures for Aid to Families with Dependent Children (AFDC) in 1975 went to families where the woman had had her first child as a teenager. Many observers, however, seem to accept the irreversibility of the growing tendency for teen mothers not to marry. Indeed, some would even discourage pregnant teenagers from marrying because they believe that an early marriage would curtail the adolescent's education and lead to an early divorce. Although there seems to be a near-consensus among social scientists that teenage marriages are impermanent and disadvantageous to the mother and her child, no one has recently reviewed the scientific basis for these ideas nor analyzed the implications for past and future policy when we discourage teenagers from marrying.

PROLONGED MAIDENHOOD

Any discussion of policy toward teenagers must begin by acknowledging that adolescent behavior has undergone a great deal of change over the last two decades. The life course of adolescents is, of course, much affected by general trends in American society. The age at which men and women first marry is one example. Americans in the decade after World War II married at much earlier ages than ever before in the twentieth century. But recently, this trend toward early first marriage has been reversed. . . .

As it happens, this new marriage pattern is really a return to the more traditional marriage pattern dating back to the nineteenth century. But if the

From P. Lindsay Chase-Lansdale and Maris A. Vinovskis, "Should We Discourage Teenage Marriage?" *The Public Interest*, no. 87 (Spring 1987), pp. 23–37. Copyright © 1987 by National Affairs, Inc. Reprinted by permission of *The Public Interest* and the author.

timing of marriages among today's youth resembles that of their counterparts in the nineteenth century, the current pattern of sexual activity is quite different. While there have been considerable fluctuations in premarital sexual activity in our nation's past, the extent of sexual activity among contemporary teenagers seems unprecedented. . . . American teenagers during the 1970s were increasingly apt to engage in premarital sexual activity at the same time that they postponed marriage until their early or mid-twenties. Beatrice and John Whiting, in their book *Adolescents in a Changing World*, refer to this phenomenon as "prolonged maidenhood."

These changes in adolescent sexual behavior have been accompanied by a greater use of contraception among teens. Some maintain that the increased availability of contraception to teens beginning in the 1970s has failed to reduce the number of adolescent pregnancies, both because few teens are likely to use contraception effectively, and because the very availability of contraception has actually legitimized premarital sexual relations. On the contrary, although contraceptive availability may have contributed to a more permissive sexual climate in the past decade, there is little direct evidence that it alone has played a major role in promoting early sexual activity.

Furthermore, contraceptive use among unmarried sexually active female adolescents has increased steadily during the 1970s and 1980s. . . . Nevertheless, a sizable proportion of sexually active teens still do not use any contraceptives, use them intermittently, or rely upon ineffective methods. This fact may account for why many commentators speak of an ongoing unprecedented "epidemic" of adolescent childbearing. In actuality, the adolescent birth rate peaked in the late 1950s. . . . [B]y the time they turn twenty years old, 19 percent of white females and 41 percent of black females have become mothers. Although the proportion of childbearing for blacks is twice that of whites, the absolute numbers of white teen births is more than double that of blacks: 320,953 versus 134,392.

While the number of actual births to teens is high, the number of pregnancies is significantly higher. . . . This recent increase in teenage pregnancies, however, has *not* led to a sizable increase in adolescent childbearing because of the greater use of legal abortions to terminate pregnancies. . . .

One might conclude that since the rate of adolescent childbearing has decreased as well as the total number of children born to teenagers, public concern and interest in this issue would diminish. But in fact concern has grown, in part because the proportion of out-of-wedlock births among all teen births has increased dramatically, from 15.4 percent in 1960 to 56.3 percent in 1984. . . . In other words, more than four out of ten births to white teenagers and nearly nine out of ten births to black teenagers are out-of-wedlock. One could conclude from these statistics that attitudes toward teenage sexual behavior have indeed been changing.

ATTITUDES TOWARD MARRIAGE

But perhaps what has undergone an even greater change has been the general attitude toward marriage. Even as Americans in the past postponed marrying until their twenties, few questioned the importance and centrality of marriage as an institution. The family was considered by our ancestors as the cornerstone of society both in theory and practice. Although attitudes toward premarital sex varied over time, there was, until recently, a general consensus among Americans that out-of-wedlock child-bearing was immoral and a serious threat to the economic well-being of the community. There was great social and legal pressure for the father of the child to marry the mother. As a result, the practice of marrying after conception was widely accepted and played a key role in keeping the number of out-of-wedlock births to a minimum. In 1955, for example, only 14.9 percent of births to adolescent girls were out-of-wedlock (6.6 percent for whites and 41.9 percent for nonwhites). In addition, pregnant adolescents comprised 25 percent of first marriages. What, then, happened to the notion of teen marriage in the intervening years?

To begin with, the moral stigma attached to out-of-wedlock births seemed to diminish considerably during the 1960s and 1970s. Unwed adolescent mothers were no longer forced to drop out of public schools and the term "illegitimate birth" was gradually replaced by the more neutral designation of "out-of-wedlock birth." At the same time, the expansion of federal, state, and local assistance to unwed mothers and their children made it more feasible economically for single mothers to raise children. While the increase in welfare assistance does not appear to have caused adolescents to initiate sexual activity earlier, it may have helped those who became pregnant to raise their children by themselves rather than marrying the father, having an abortion, or putting the child up for adoption. In addition, the growing recognition that young mothers needed to finish their own education in order to be self-supporting weakened the attractive-ness of an early marriage where the teen mother would drop out of school in order to care for her child and husband. Furthermore, the growing unemployment among young men, especially among young blacks, meant that the financial ability of the father to support the adolescent mother and her child appeared greatly diminished, making marriage seem a less feasible life-course option. These patterns may have been reinforced as the emphasis, during the 1960s and 1970s, shifted from the responsibilities of individuals for their actions to their rights to choose and pursue freely their own particular life styles.

Despite these changes, almost fifteen years passed before the federal government reacted to them. When federal action finally came in the 1970s, it was fueled by a combination of increased media attention, vociferous and organized advocates, emerging scholarly findings on the negative consequences to the teen mother's educational and occupational attainment, growing concern regarding the heightened levels of teen sexual activity, the changing proportion of out-of-wedlock births, the increase in teens choosing to keep their babies rather than give them up for adoption, and the rising cost of existing federal assistance programs. The primary focus of the congressional hearings, the proposed and enacted programs, and the scholarly testimony in the 1970s was not the numbers of unmarried adolescent parents, but rather the plight of the teenage mother herself and to a lesser extent, her children. Surprisingly little effort was made to consider the role of the father or the advantages and disadvantages of having pregnant adolescents marry.

The few scholars who considered the role of fathers downplayed their importance to the economic or emotional well-being of the young mother and her child. . . .

Throughout the extensive congressional hearings on adolescent pregnancy and childbearing in the 1970s and 1980s, virtually all of the participating members of Congress and social scientists accepted the trend in out-of-wedlock births and were more concerned with the stigma associated with out-of-wedlock births and the practices of schools in previous years of requiring pregnant teens to drop out. They did not challenge the view that pregnant adolescents should be discouraged from marrying. . . . While the discouragement of early marriages by social scientists was not a primary cause of the rise in out-of-wedlock births, it contributed to an atmosphere which minimized the responsibility of the father.

A ROLE FOR THE FATHER

. . . The change in administrations in 1981 brought greater interest in adolescent pregnancy and childbearing from a broader family perspective and a renewed focus on out-of-wedlock births. In 1984, the Office of Adolescent Pregnancy Programs under the Reagan administration solicited social science research on "The Characteristics and Family Involvement of Fathers of Adolescent Premaritally Conceived Births." This request sought information about the fathers, their interactions with the mother and young child, and the "social, economic, health and developmental consequences of the fathers' involvement in the lives of their partners and their out-of-wedlock children." The Reagan administration . . . also called for research to analyze both the negative and positive impacts of adolescent mar-

riages on the teenage mother, her partner, and young child. It remains to be seen, however, how the current administration will incorporate this research into policies that pursue the issue of teenage marriage and out-of-wedlock births.

SURPRISING STABILITY

This new interest in teenage marriage for the parents of out-of-wedlock children marks an important change in policy emphasis. Although the recommendations of social scientists to policymakers in the 1970s regarding teen marriage were based on scientific studies at the time, we would argue that there has been too much emphasis on the inevitability of divorce. Even though the rate of marital stability is lower among teens than among older women, the *stability* of teenage marriage should be underscored. Those who argue against early marriages point to the likelihood of these unions to dissolve. Yet the rates of marital disruption are very high today for all couples, but few would suggest that we abandon marriage as an institution altogether. What is needed, though, is a closer look at the characteristics of those teens who do marry and those teen marriages that do survive.

In his classic study of low-income black teens in Baltimore, Frank Furstenberg concluded that the chances of the successful continuation of the marriages occurring in the years following the birth of a child were "minuscule." Yet half of the marriages of adolescent mothers in the Baltimore sample were intact after four years. In a follow-up study by Furstenberg and Brooks-Gunn of the teen mothers seventeen years later, almost one-third of all first marriages had survived. Similarly, Sheppard Kellam and his associates in their 1982 study found that approximately 35 percent of married teen mothers in Woodlawn, a Chicago community, remained married over a ten year period. While the Baltimore and Woodlawn studies do illustrate higher rates of marital instability among low-income black teen mothers than their older counterparts, it is important to recognize the stability that does exist and to examine more closely the reasons for this.

Two new studies based on national data also provide evidence that teen marriages are more durable than previously believed. Using data from the Current Population Surveys of the Census Bureau in 1980 and 1982, Martin O'Connell and Carolyn Rogers of the Population Division of the Bureau of the Census found that although teenage marriages were twice as likely as adult marriages to be disrupted within the first five years, 76 percent of women who married between ages 15-17 and 85 percent of women who married between ages 18-19 were still married five years later. . . .

In sum, although the sexual activity, pregnancy, and childbearing of adolescents have received an extraordinary amount of public and scholarly attention, teen marriages—especially those precipitated by pregnancy or childbirth—have been understudied by researchers and neglected by policymakers. Recent studies, it is true, have supported the perspective of scientists and policymakers in the 1970s—namely that rates of marital dissolution are higher among teen marriages than those of their older peers. But what has been ignored is that these same studies also reveal the resiliency of some teen marriages in the face of difficult circumstances.

THE BENEFITS OF MARRIAGE

But even if some teen marriages have endured, what advantages or disadvantages have they provided for the individuals and their children? The negative impact of early childbearing on the educational attainment of the young mother is well documented. Although some female adolescents already had dropped out of school prior to their pregnancy or probably would have done so anyway, the additional stress and responsibility associated with early parenting reduces the likelihood of remaining in school. Young black mothers are more likely to continue their education than their white counterparts as their educational careers seem to be relatively less affected by an unintended birth.

The disruption of schooling is a serious problem since it is likely to place limits upon the job opportunities for a young woman throughout her lifetime. It also makes her a more probable candidate for welfare assistance and thereby increases the societal costs of early childbearing. Yet if there is general agreement upon the negative consequences of early childbearing on the educational and economic development of the young mother, there is still considerable uncertainty about the effects of early marriage on her educational and economic success. Again, most social scientists have argued that pregnant adolescents are better advised not to marry the putative father since this so often results in the termination of the young mother's education. Instead, they argue, the pregnant teenager should continue to live with her own parents, who will provide child care and economic support, thereby enabling the teen to complete her education and enhance her future economic well-being.

Few studies have looked specifically at the question of whether marriage helps or hinders a pregnant teenager's ability to continue her education and improve her long-term economic situation. . . . [A] study by [Steven] McLaughlin and his associates [at the Battelle Human Affairs Research Center] . . . found that early marriage had negative effects on black mothers, but not on white mothers. Overall, the high school enrollment rate of black teen mothers, whether married or not, was higher than that of white teen mothers. For black mothers, a marriage either before or after the birth had a significant adverse impact on school enrollment. For white mothers marriage had only a minor impact compared to that of parenthood.

These findings reinforce the growing impression that early marriages following an adolescent pregnancy may damage the teenage mother's educational prospects. Yet this conclusion needs to be tempered by new research that finds that the long-term economic prospects for the young mother may be *adversely* affected by staying with her own parents rather than marrying the father. Furstenberg and Brooks-Gunn found in their seventeen-year follow-up of the Baltimore study that while staying with one's parents for the first year or two promoted school attendance, those teens who remained with their parents for three or more years seemed to become too dependent and were *the least likely* to be economically self-sufficient as thirty-five-year-old adults. In addition, those women who were married at the time of the five-year follow-up were much more likely to have succeeded economically, presumably because of their husbands' income, than those who had never married. Indeed, the small proportion of teens in the Bal-

timore study who remained married for twenty years were in families most likely to achieve middle-class status. What these statistics tell us is that although a stable marriage for pregnant adolescents is difficult to attain, it offers tangible economic benefits for those who are able to achieve it.

In promoting a policy that argues that pregnant teens should stay with their own parents rather than marry, one must also question the effects of such a strategy upon the family of origin itself. Since teenage pregnancy and childbearing are disproportionately concentrated among low-income families, does the added financial responsibility upon grandparents in helping to raise their new grandchildren bring additional hardship to the household? Moreover, given the increasing proportion of women of all ages in the labor force, is it realistic to expect that many grandmothers will be available during the day to teen mothers and their babies? . . .

WHAT ABOUT THE CHILDREN?

Missing in this discussion so far is an emphasis on the children of teen mothers. The predominant viewpoint has been that the advantages for children of teen marriages are few because the putative fathers are poor providers, prone to divorce, and uninterested and incompetent in parenting. Marriage, this argument continues, would fail to alleviate economic disadvantage, would promote husband-wife conflict, and expose the child to inept fathering, all of which are related to poor cognitive and emotional development in children.

In light of the virtual absence of research on the economic potential and parenting abilities of young fathers and on the quality of teen marriages, we believe that these three concerns remain open questions. Moreover, while some studies have documented demographic characteristics of teen marriages, e.g., rates of stability and divorce, virtually no one has examined the ways in which teen mothers and their spouses interact, nor the impact of the quality of their relationship on their children's well-being. We know from a substantial body of psychological research on older families that in good marriages, a father's emotional support to his wife and vice versa and a father's involvement with his children are important to healthy child development. Why, then, when so little is actually known about the psychological strengths and weaknesses of young families, do social scientists and politicians persist in discouraging teen marriages?

Similarly, remarkably little research has been devoted to the parenting abilities of teen mothers, and only one study, by Michael Lamb and Arthur Elster of the University of Utah, has actually observed the parenting behaviors of young fathers (young fathers are typically not teens themselves; the majority are in their twenties). Lamb and Elster's results tentatively suggest that these men behave toward their six-month-old infants in ways that are typical of older fathers. When we turn to how the children of teen marriages fare, studies suggest that they do indeed benefit from their parents' marriage. According to Furstenburg's study, children whose teen mothers had married the father performed better at age five on assessments of cognitive and social development. Kellam's study found that these children were rated higher in school adjustment by their first grade teachers than those children whose teen mothers lived alone. Furstenberg also

found high cognitive performance for preschool children who had regular contact with their absent fathers. In his follow-up study with Brooks-Gunn, those mothers who were economically independent by age thirty-five due to employment or marriage (to the child's father or someone else) had adolescents who performed better in school and reported lower rates of deviance.

While we do not have sufficient research to disentangle the relative importance of economic advantage, emotional assistance from adults, and the unique impact of the father, the effects of economic well-being seem clear. The Baltimore study suggests that within groups of teenage mothers, those who are the most economically disadvantaged have children who do the least well. Although some Baltimore teen mothers successfully lifted themselves out of poverty in later adulthood, as a group their children, in their own adolescence, showed much higher rates of school drop-out, grade retention, and behavior problems than adolescents of older parents. The question emerges: Why must the majority of teen mothers in this country struggle to improve their economic status without financial assistance from the fathers?

Young fathers are believed to be incapable of providing financial support to their families. In fact, little is known about the eventual earning power of young fathers, and work in progress by Robert Lerman of Brandeis University on data from the 1979–1982 National Longitudinal Survey of Labor Force Behavior suggests that young fathers have greater economic potential than previously believed. . . .

Furstenberg . . . found a low rate of child support payment by never or previously married fathers; not surprisingly, at the five-year follow-up, married fathers were continuing to support their children.

Thus, while it is clear that the vast majority of young absent never-married fathers are not contributing to their children's financial security, we cannot conclude at this time that most young fathers are potentially or even currently incapable of economic assistance. In the context of the poor economic standing of many teen mothers, any level of assistance would be helpful. And what is being required by the federal government as current court-ordered child support is not exorbitant. . . .

Although child-support enforcement has received considerable attention lately, the focus of recent reform has been on middle-class fathers, the vast majority of whom have not come under the system's purview. While this represents an important shift in child-support policy, an equally indifferent group—absent young fathers—has not received enough attention . . .

A CALL FOR REEXAMINATION

In the 1970s teenage pregnancy and childbearing became a matter of pressing concern to policymakers and social scientists. As out-of-wedlock births were beginning to soar, lawmakers and experts chose to focus on the teen mother herself, the stigma of adolescent pregnancy, and the detrimental impact of early childbearing on educational and occupational advancement. Marriage as a life course option for adolescent mothers was actively discouraged and consideration of the role of the father was practically nonexistent.

In the 1980s, as out-of-wedlock births have reached unprecedented levels, it is necessary to reexamine policies and research related to adolescent parenthood and marriage. New research findings indicate that some teen marriages are more resilient than previously believed. Recommendations that adolescent mothers remain with their own parents in order to maximize educational attainment are being brought into question by recent evidence suggesting adverse long-term outcomes of such an arrangement. Policies that promote single parenthood for teen mothers seem to prevail in the face of very little systematic information about the young fathers and their potential as providers, husbands, or parents. Government policies should be redirected toward helping young couples stay together rather than focusing almost exclusively on the young mother and her child. Furthermore, in a society that claims that children are the future, one must question why a young man's financial responsibility toward his children is open to debate. These and many other issues need to be raised and addressed before we conclude that pregnant teenagers should be discouraged from marrying.

NO

Naomi Farber

THE SIGNIFICANCE OF RACE AND CLASS IN MARITAL DECISIONS AMONG UNMARRIED ADOLESCENT MOTHERS

Overall fertility rates among American adolescents have decreased since 1970. Yet researchers, policy-developers, service providers, and members of the American public alike continue to express deep concern over adolescent childbearing. This concern arises partly from the fact that, while teen birth rates have declined, the proportion of births to teenagers who are unmarried is rising steadily. . . . Young unmarried mothers and their offspring are at high risk of experiencing long-term poverty and associated disadvantages (Garfinkel and McLanahan 1986).

While marriage has declined sharply among all teens, differences in rates of out of wedlock births by race remain sizeable. In 1985, 45 percent of births to white teens were out of wedlock in contrast to about 90 percent of births to black teens (Hayes 1987). Black adolescents also have a higher rate of childbearing. In 1985 the adolescent birthrates were 42.8 births per 1000 white adolescents aged 15-19, compared to 97.4 births per 1000 black adolescents (Pittman and Adams 1988). Therefore, although black teenagers do not account numerically for the majority of illegitimate births to adolescents, they are much more likely than white teens to become young single mothers.

These differences in rates of illegitimate childbearing by race, coupled with the association between race and class in American society, set up the complex question of how race and class influence out of wedlock births. . . .

In 1985-86 I conducted in-depth interviews with 28 unmarried adolescent mothers aged 15-20 years in the Chicago area. The sample included six subgroups including black and white teenagers from middle-, working-, and lower-class families. Participants' race was self-defined as either black or white. . . .

Young mothers were classified as middle-class if their parent(s) had steadily held white-collar/managerial or highly skilled work. The working-class subgroup was composed of teens whose parent(s) worked at semi-

From Naomi Farber, "The Significance of Race and Class in Marital Decisions Among Unmarried Adolescent Mothers," *Social Problems*, vol. 37, no. 1 (February 1990), pp. 51–63. Copyright © 1990 by the Society for the Study of Social Problems. Reprinted by permission. Notes omitted.

skilled or clerical jobs. The lower-class group includes those whose parent(s) had been significantly unemployed or worked at low-skill or unskilled labor. . . .

I asked the young mothers questions that elicited descriptions of their attitudes toward men in general and as potential partners and husbands, the hopes and expectations regarding marriage and single motherhood that they remembered having as children, the hopes that they held at present and for the future, the history of their relationship with their baby's father and subsequent boyfriends, and their perceptions of their families' attitudes toward marriage and single motherhood. . . .

THE VALUE OF MARRIAGE AS AN IDEAL

Nearly all of the teens, regardless of their class or race, view marriage and marital childbearing as an ideal type of family. . . .

Most teens expressed . . . attitudes suggesting that, for them, being a single mother does not reflect changed values about how families should be formed. This ideal is also evident in their childhood memories of how they imagined their adult lives would be. . . .

Like the middle-class and working-class teens, the black lower-class mothers had childhood dreams of living in the ideal American family. . . .

The young mothers from all backgrounds described ideal visions that are congruent with traditional values about family formation. These childhood reflections suggest that their present judgments about the undesirability of out of wedlock childbearing are not simply responses to the stress of single motherhood. Most of these teen mothers grew up valuing a way of life from which they have deviated. They were unable to or chose not to act in accordance with these ideals. In the balance of the paper I discuss the factors these young mothers cited in their decisions to deviate from their stated ideals about marriage and remain single.

WHY TEENS DID NOT MARRY: VARIATIONS BY CLASS AND RACE

The young mothers expressed a variety of reasons for remaining unmarried. No teen stated only one specific factor that she believed was responsible for her remaining unmarried. Each teen offered a scenario that usually included the influence of her family, the baby's father, subsequent boyfriends, and her own beliefs, goals, and desires that led to her not marrying to legitimize the birth. Similarities in reasons given among black and white teens from middle-class and working-class backgrounds stand in contrast to the reasons given by lower-class mothers. . . .

Postponing Marriage: Perceptions of Middle- and Working-Class Mothers
Fathers unwilling or not ready. Whether a young woman, pregnant or not, marries depends partly upon the existence of concrete opportunities for marriage. The decision obviously is not hers alone. Among the twenty black and white middle-class and working-class teen mothers, only four of their babies' fathers offered to marry the young women when the women became pregnant.

Those teens whose babies' fathers were not willing to marry them described many kinds of involvement by those young men in their lives. These range from the white middle-class mother whose baby's father not only offered no help to her, but threatened to trip her going downstairs to induce a miscarriage, and eventually threw a volleyball hard at her stomach during a gym class at school, to those few young men who now spend time with and/or money on their children on a regular basis. Typically the young father did not want the young woman to carry the pregnancy to term or to keep the child. They told the pregnant girls that they felt unprepared for fatherhood in all respects.

Patterns of father involvement are an important issue in the study of adolescent parenthood. However, in terms of decisions about marriage, what is especially significant here is that, as far as the young women know, beyond the young men's own personal desires for involvement, the fathers did not receive any pressure from adults—parents or others—or peers to assume parental responsibility, let alone to marry the pregnant girl. In fact, there is little evidence that any young woman, except for one white middle-class teen whose family sent her to a home for unwed mothers, felt the weight of familial or community expectations to marry to legitimize the child's birth. In addition, in only one instance did the parents of a young man intervene by promising the pregnant girl that he would help pay for her medical expenses and provide child support. This is the only teen mother who now receives any regular financial support from the baby's father.

Mothers themselves not ready for marriage. Regardless of the young fathers' intentions, only one black teen from a working-class family expressed disappointment over not marrying her baby's father. While several young mothers wished the father had at least taken some paternal responsibility, they did not regret not having married the father. The decision not to marry in most instances was described by the girls as being mutual. Certainly one must consider the possibility that this expression of mutuality is a rationalization of rejection by the young fathers. However, nearly all non-poor teens have had subsequent boyfriends, most of whom have proposed marriage, but no teen has yet chosen to marry, suggesting that, for the girls, opportunity alone is not sufficient reason to marry.

A consistent theme expressed by the black and white middle-class and working-class teen mothers is that both they and their families believed that regardless of an unplanned—and nearly universally unwanted—pregnancy, the girls were too young to become wives as well as mothers. That is, both the teenagers and their parents believed that marriage was not appropriate for teenagers, even in the face of their impending motherhood. As one white working-class teen's mother remarked, marriage for her 16-year-old daughter would only be "adding one mistake on top of another."

Some teens and their families believed that in principle a "shotgun" marriage was ill-advised especially among adolescents. One 16-year-old black middle-class mother described her mother's, her grandmother's, and her own views about marriage to legitimize her unplanned pregnancy:

> My mother feels that you shouldn't marry because of a baby. It doesn't work, it creates hatred. Basically, that's how I felt, because when my grandmother found out I was pregnant, she was like, "Make him marry her, make him marry her." I'm like, "I don't want to marry him." And my mother was like, "No, she's 16. Seriously, what's she going to do married?"

Other families were in complete agreement in their opposition to early marriage, as described by this 15-year-old black working-class teen:

My father wouldn't let me get married because he doesn't think I'm old enough. He thinks you have to be mature—physical, mental, and financial ways to have a family. . . . They [parents] want us to be sure that's the person we love, because they're against divorce.

One 18-year-old white working-class mother was forbidden by her parents to marry the father of her child. She and her parents agreed on this matter, though for different reasons: "My parents don't think marriage is the answer for being pregnant . . . [and] I was young and wanted space. I seen all my girlfriends were still going out and new boyfriends every month, and I wanted to go out." Indeed, this young white mother has a new boyfriend who wants to marry her and has offered to support her until then, but she still feels too young to give up her remaining freedom. Some middle-class and working-class teens and their families, then, did not consider an unplanned pregnancy to be an adequate basis for marriage among teenagers.

For others marriage was a poor choice because it might interfere with the teen's education and career preparations. The desire to finish their education before marriage was mentioned frequently by black and white middle-class and working-class mothers as a major concern. One 17-year-old black middle-class teen stated:

I told [my boyfriend] I didn't want to marry him until after I got out of school because marriage is just an excuse for going to bed with somebody and . . . I don't need another kid. I told him that even after we get married, I'm going to stay on the pill for at least a year, if I haven't gotten my career together already.

A 15-year-old black working-class mother expressed her and her mother's concerns: "I would like to be married, but then again I wouldn't because I'm so young. . . . My mother's like, "You better go to school and get your education—thinking about marriage!" Another black working-class teen, aged 16, said: "I won't get engaged until I get established, get out of high school and figure everything out."

Thus, some parents considered early marriage to be a potential threat to the young woman's future educational and employment achievement. Implicit in this concern is the assumption expressed by all non-poor teens without exception that they plan to be economically self-supporting through employment. Whether this is a preference or necessity is unclear, but the expectation that they will work is evident in the teens' continuing participation in education and job training during and after the pregnancy. Even those young mothers who receive public assistance (nine out of 20) work and/or attend school full time.

These young women do not look to men and marriage to support them and their children. The absence of this expectation is reinforced by the fact that many teens are involved with young men who are not able to support them. Fifteen of the 20 non-poor mothers, in agreement with their parents, judged their baby's father and their current boyfriend as not being an acceptable marriage partner at present because the young men were poor risks financially and/or emotionally, regardless of their desire to marry. Consider the remarks of one 17-year-old black middle-class mother: "My mother thinks my daughter's father is a low-life, he's not good for anything. So she let him go about his way." . . . Two 19-year-old white working-class mothers and their parents had similar reservations about the fathers of their babies. One said,

> My mom thinks, well, they're not real happy with my boyfriend. He doesn't work or anything. I'd like to get married, have my baby have a father. We talked about it. . . . It would be a flop. Well, you know, he can't work since he hurt his back. So I would be the one working. And he would be sitting around drinking beers with his friends . . . trying to take care of the baby, which I don't think he would do.

Another said: "My parents would not allow me to get married. . . . They didn't want me to marry [my baby's father] because I was so young, one reason. And because he had never had a job and they looked at him as a real loser." These young women and their families have specific expectations regarding a husband's role as provider for his family. All of the non-poor teens expressed an intention to work even when they married in the future. However, they also expected a husband to be employed and take at least equal financial and emotional responsibility for his family. They preferred single motherhood to marriage to an unsuitable partner.

Family support. Whether the teen and her family were most concerned about the inappropriateness of marriage among teenagers or the prospects of the young man in her life, all teen mothers in this study reported that their families counseled them against marrying precipitously. The teen mothers further described how their families provided considerable material and/or emotional support to help them survive as single mothers while completing their education. Even when parents were angry about the pregnancy and expressed disapproval through refusing to pay for a grandchild's expenses, all parents at least offered a home to the young mother and her child.

Although all non-poor teens received significant aid from their families, there is an interesting difference between black and white teens in the significance they attached to this familial support and the meaning of single motherhood in their families. The white non-poor teens commonly described their parents' help as their rising to the occasion of a family crisis, often to the young women's surprise. Their experiences are typified by one 16-year-old white middle-class teen who was terrified of her parents' reaction to her pregnancy and feared they would ask her to leave home. Instead, she reported: "When I got pregnant all my parents told me about raising Joshua myself was that they were willing to help me as much as they possibly can to do whatever they can until I can do it on my own. Nobody said I need to get married." In all instances, the white teen was the first in her family to bear a child as an adolescent and outside of marriage. . . . Among these white middle-class and working-class teens, only one has a mother who was herself a single mother for any length of time, following a divorce, while another's mother was unmarried briefly between a divorce and remarriage. This stands in sharp contrast to the non-poor black teens, most of whom grew up with a single mother for much of their childhood. Several black middle-class and working-class teens described family traditions of women raising families alone, or at least without husbands. This is typified by the experience of one 17-year-old black middle-class mother: "The women in my family, we've had to support ourselves. And thank God I'm getting all this help [from mother and grandmother]. I couldn't stand it without it." This tradition of black women supporting their families seems to be expressed in these adolescents' belief that although marriage is preferable, single motherhood is an acceptable option when necessary. A 19-year-old black middle-class mother who is engaged expressed this view:

> The way I see it is that you don't necessarily have to have the father [of the baby] around all the time . . . I keep telling everybody—you can make it as long as you got your family with you. You can make it. You don't need him at all. It's not really the father a baby depends on. . . .

[O]ne indication of the complexity of the relationship between the teens' and their own mothers' marital experiences is that, though they grew up with a single mother, the non-poor black teens generally expect that they will marry in the future, as do their white counterparts. Both white and black non-poor teens perceive single motherhood to be a temporary situation until they find the "right" man or until, like the young woman quoted previously, they "figure everything out."

All but two black and white middle-class and working-class teen mothers now have steady boyfriends, either the father of their baby or, more often, a subsequent partner. Five of the teens are presently engaged to be married but want to wait to get married until they graduate from high school or college or until they have a steady job. Significantly, the young men to whom the teens are engaged are all steadily employed and considered by the young women to be stable and mature. . . . Even those young women who have not yet found a prospective husband believe that marriage is a normal and realistic goal that they expect to achieve.

"Mama's Baby, Papa's Maybe": Single Motherhood among Lower-Class Mothers

Like the working-class and middle-class teens, the black and white lower-class mothers value marriage as an ideal. Even so, unlike the more affluent young women, they are not as confident that they will actually marry. There are also differences by race among the lower-class teens in terms of their attitudes toward men and marriage, as well as how realistic they perceive the possibility of marriage to be.

Compromised ideals. Like the non-poor teens, the black and white lower-class teen mothers have specific expectations about what a husband and father should be. In accordance with mainstream values and norms, both black and white lower-class teens expect a husband to be able to provide emotional and financial support to his family. One 16-year-old black lower-class teen stated,

> I'm like, if I can't find [a man] that got a job or that can help me in some way, I don't want him. . . . I'm very choosy. Because like, I was walking home from school with one of my friends, and she was like, "Why don't you go and talk to that guy?" I said, "He got a job? Do he keep money?" She said, "No." I said, " 'Bye."

Yet their childhood dreams of ideal family life as described above have been compromised as they witness how family life around them diverges from that ideal. Another 16-year-old black lower-class mother remarked,

> I don't know, we all figured if you got pregnant, whoever you were with, he would help you. We never looked at it like, "Oh, he's not going to be there and I'm going to have to do this for myself." Being young we all had dreams or fantasies that he'd be there.

These teens have grown up and outgrown their "fantasies" at a very young age. Even this young woman's earlier hope of her baby's father "being there" has proved to be unrealistic. Experience has tempered their expectations, for the men in their lives often prove to be unreliable, or worse. . . .

Only one black and all three white teen mothers are still involved with their babies' fathers. Three of the four couples have discussed the possibility of marriage, but two of the young women feel they have been abused in the course of their relationships and see marriage to these men as a poor risk. . . .

A perception that is more common and explicit among the black lower-class teens is that marriage as actually experienced by the people they know offers no real advantage over single motherhood. A 16-year-old black lower-class mother said:

> Marriage doesn't make any difference. 'Cause my sister, you know, when she had her first child she was alone. Her second child, she was married . . . but it still was like she was on her own. Because no one can really help as much as yourself.

Cynicism about men. The black lower-class teen mothers seem to be more cynical than the whites about what it means to be involved with men. They seem almost to expect men not to be responsible for their families. The young black women convey a sense of self-protection about involvement with men. They want men to be more committed to them but anticipate that their hopes will not be fulfilled and so prepare themselves emotionally for disappointment. They learn this attitude of self-defense from their own experience and also from other women in their family. . . . A 15-year-old black lower-class teen was abandoned by the father of her baby, an experience that confirmed her mother's views about men:

> My mother just told me to be independent, not to depend on anybody. If your boyfriend backs out, you can go your own way, and I'll always be there to help. She used to say, "You can go hanging around those boys all you want, but when you end up pregnant, don't expect him to stay around. They by saying, "Mama's baby, papa's maybe." My ma said if you get married you're a fool. . . . First he's all right. But then he turns into—well, you'll be doing all the giving. She said you're better off if you just have a man to associate with and don't get married. . . . I suppose it's okay to wait 'till you get married to have a baby. Or if you don't, catch as catch can.

An underlying theme expressed by the black lower-class teens is a disjunction in both attitude and behavior between child-bearing and marriage. The conceptual separation between marriage and child-bearing, reinforced by their mothers' warning about the pitfalls of marriage, is associated with a deep distrust of men as marriage partners. A 16-year-old black lower-class mother who had dreamed of marriage and her "own house" doubts she will marry:

> Well, I don't think I will get married, but I'll just have a boyfriend or something, but I just wouldn't get mar-

ried. . . . No, most boys don't stick around. All they be doing is talking. I guess most of the boys think that it makes them feel like a man. "Hey, I've got a son" and all this stuff, and one coming and all. Just make them look stupid if they ain't taking care of it. All they doing is talking.

These young mothers think that most men have limited willingness and ability to support a family. . . .

The more typical experience of the young women is expressed by a 16-year-old black lower-class mother: "You know, he's not working now, so, I can't expect too much from him." She expresses the common perception that there is no point in expecting the young men with whom they are involved to offer much help because they cannot provide adequately for themselves.

The number of white lower-class teens interviewed is too small to offer a genuine racial comparison. However, it is interesting to note that all of the three white teens maintain ongoing relationships with the fathers of their babies. Two white lower-class teens have more than one child by their long-term boyfriends. These boyfriends have expressed willingness to marry if the women so desire. Even so, these young white women are rather vague and unsure about their present expectations regarding marriage to these young men. One 17-year-old white lower-class mother of three children expresses this sense of being unsure of her plans and how marriage fits into her future:

I want to get married—I told Tony I want to stay with him. [But] I can't imagine what I'm going to be doing ten years from now . . . 'cause I know that people change and stuff and I'm only seventeen. I may want to do something

else. At the moment I'm really not sure about marriage—maybe after I finish school and everything. I don't know, I think that if I finish school maybe I won't get pregnant no more. And I believe I'll get a job or something. And maybe I'll probably get married by then.

It is significant that of all the lower-class teens, only this white young woman mentioned that her hopes for an education or work might influence marriage or childbearing.

These white lower-class girls and their babies' fathers do suggest a possible difference between them and the black lower-class mothers. The poor white teens' boyfriends are objectively no more attractive than the poor black young men as marriage partners (one is married, one has abused the young woman, and the third cannot make a living wage as a sometime, part-time short-order cook), and these qualities may well largely account for not marrying. Still, the white young women perceive marriage as at least being possible in their future, depending upon how things go with their boyfriends. . . .

Two of their own mothers were single mothers for some time (the third teen became a ward of the state of Illinois and lived in group homes), but unlike their black counterparts, these mothers have not given the younger women messages that denigrate the value of marriage in principle. The white lower-class teens' social environment may not offer many opportunities to meet more eligible men, but that does not seem to be reflected in cynicism about men in general. The white lower-class teens differ significantly from the white middle-class and working-class teens in having fewer opportunities to achieve their marital goals and in not investing their energies in preparation for self-support. But, at the same time, their attitudes do not indicate the degree of hopelessness about marriage that the black lower-class teens display.

DISCUSSION

. . . Even though they retain traditional conceptions of the ideal family, these young women feel less pressure to conform to that ideal than did women—and men—in past generations. Significantly, this diminution of pressure to marry, both in general and to legitimize a birth, is supported by the young women's families. Moreover, beyond societal changes in norms such as reduced stigma toward single motherhood and "greater freedoms" for women (Burgess 1954), the young women's experiences with men and marriage are associated with their class background and race.

Typically, the black and white middle-class and working-class teens neither hoped nor expected to become single or adolescent mothers. They acted on contemporary norms permitting the separation of sex and marriage, but they still regard childbearing as properly a marital event. Yet, once pregnant and committed to bearing and keeping the child, the young women and their families did not then or subsequently judge that it was either necessary or in their best interests to marry *in order to legitimize the birth*. . . .

In contrast to the middle- and working-class teens, lower-class mothers perceived their prospects for marriage to be less promising. They saw the men in their lives were not acceptable as husbands, and they gave no indication that they expected to meet more eligible men in the future. . . . Certainly some poor black women maintain stable relationships with men, but the young women interviewed here display an unmistakable doubt about their own chances for a satisfactory and mutual relationship with a man.

The black lower-class teens are distinguished from the other young women in this study by their not even expecting childbirth to occur within the context of marriage. . . . As economic circumstances and the social environment have deteriorated for many poor urban blacks in the past two decades, adolescent girls in these communities have grown up surrounded by failed marriages and single mothers. They have been raised by women whose own difficult marital and non-marital relationships served as models to be avoided, while their personal experiences with young men provided no reason to believe their own chances for marital stability would be any better than those of their mothers. The poor black teens in this study expressed mainstream, traditional aspirations for marriage (cf. Anderson 1989). However, their opportunities to achieve their aspirations are severely limited. . . .

Until we know more specifically what differences and similarities exist in socio-familial dynamics among poor and non-poor whites as well as non-poor blacks in a variety of urban and rural community contexts, it will not be possible to specify with any confidence the true significance of race or class in the women's and men's decisions about forming families.

REFERENCES

Anderson, Elijah. 1989. "Sex codes and family life among poor inner-city youths." The Annals of the American Academy of Political and Social Science 501: 59–78.

Burgess, Ernest. 1954. On Community, Family and Delinquency. Chicago: University of Chicago Press.

Garfinkel, Irwin, and Sarah McLanahan. 1986. Single Mothers and their Children: A New American Dilemma. Washington, D.C.: The Urban Institute Press.

Hayes, Cheryl, ed. 1987. Risking the Future: Adolescent Sexuality, Pregnancy, and Child-bearing. Washington, D.C.: National Academy Press.

Pittman, Karen, and Gina Adams. 1988. Teenage Pregnancy: An Advocate's Guide to the Numbers. Washington, D.C.: The Children's Defense Fund.

POSTSCRIPT

Should Pregnant Teens Marry the Fathers of Their Babies?

Why don't more adolescent mothers marry the fathers of their children? Many people believe that society has moved beyond the "shotgun wedding" mentality and disapproves of forcing fathers and mothers to marry even when they are adolescents. Chase-Lansdale and Vinovskis, however, argue that this modern social norm is of questionable merit for all concerned and use recent studies to support their contention. They also ask how the decision not to marry serves the larger community. For example, if a mother lives with and is supported by her parents and becomes overattached and dependent upon them, consequently never learning economic self-sufficiency, even by midlife, how does this serve the family, the child, or society? Chase-Lansdale and Vinovskis discuss the need for additional research on families where the father and adolescent mother do marry, especially regarding how the children fare in such unions.

Farber, after interviewing adolescent mothers, concludes that race and class need to be considered before the marital patterns of adolescent mothers can be adequately understood. Though the mothers she interviewed believe in marriage, they provide very convincing arguments against marrying the fathers of their babies. Their attitudes seem to be based on the realities of their particular life situations.

Why don't adolescent mothers (even poor ones) seek legal action against the fathers of their children for the provision of financial support? Frank F. Furstenberg, in "As the Pendulum Swings: Teenage Childbearing and Social Concern," *Family Relations*, 40 (1991): 127–138, relates that the typical father of an adolescent's child, a young adult over age 20, usually lives with the mother and child only briefly or not at all. Furstenberg believes that the involvement of such fathers in the lives of their children has been exaggerated by clinicians who base their conclusions on the small number of these fathers they see in private practice and by researchers who rely on responses of small, nonrepresentative samples of such men. "Only a small minority of these children," he contends, "see their fathers regularly by the time they reach adolescence. Fewer still receive substantial financial support from them."

There could be several explanations for not using legal action to gain support: The father may be providing some type of support already; the mother and her family may not consider the father a good role model for the child and thus may try to distance themselves from him; legal action can work two ways—the father may be required to pay support, but the mother could then be required to give him partial custody; the mother may not know how the legal system operates or even that she has certain legal rights to support; to win support the mother must prove that he really is the father—an expensive, time-consuming, and emotionally wrenching experience; and the father may be unemployed or underemployed.

Other questions to be considered with regard to this issue are: Does government have a role in this issue? Has the current emphasis of government on "just say no to sex" proven effective in resolving the issue of adolescent pregnancy? Are there other government programs in place that are effective? What are the consequences to children of growing up in an out-of-wedlock family situation? How does that compare to family situations in which parents marry because of a pregnancy, but divorce after a few years? Has the cultural norm for marrying someone "for the sake of the child" and "to preserve the character and well-being of the mother," which prevailed through much of this century, been replaced by another norm? If so, what is that norm?

SUGGESTED READINGS

E. Anderson, "Sex Codes and Family Life Among Poor Inner-City Youths," *Annuals of the American Academy of Political and Social Science,* 501 (1989): 59–78.

L. M. Burton, "Teenage Childbearing as an Alternative Life-Course Strategy in Multigenerational Black Families," *Human Nature,* 1 (1990): 123–143.

K. Christmon, "Parental Responsibility and Self-Image of African-American Fathers," *Families in Society,* 71 (1990): 562–567.

L. Dash, *When Children Want Children: The Urban Crisis in Teenage Childbearing* (William Morrow, 1989).

D. J. Eggebeen, L. J. Crockett, and A. J. Hawkins, "Patterns of Adult Male Coresidence Among Young Children of Adolescent Mothers," *Family Planning Perspectives,* 22 (1990): 219–223.

F. F. Furstenberg, J. Brooks-Gunn, and P. L. Chase-Lansdale, "Teenage Pregnancy and Childbearing," *American Psychologist,* 44 (1989): 313–320.

B. C. Miller and K. A. Moore, "Adolescent Sexual Behavior, Pregnancy, and Parenting," *Journal of Marriage and the Family,* 52 (1990): 1025–1044.

M. N. Wilson, "Child Development in the Context of the Black Extended Family," *American Psychologist,* 44 (1989): 380–391.

PART 4

Stress in the Family

Present divorce rates indicate that marriage alone is difficult to manage. But additional negative factors in a marriage, if not handled properly, can destroy a family. As society changes, so do the factors affecting family life and, hence, family needs. The percentage of mothers in the work force, for example, has increased to a point at which new corporate policies to aid these women may be necessary. Black families may also be candidates for aid. Domestic violence is a common source of stress in the family, and battered husbands may be the latest victims of spouse abuse. And extramarital relationships, which may be occurring more frequently, also create stressful family situations. These issues invariably affect all of society, so they need to be addressed by society.

Does Arrest Reduce Domestic Violence?

_____

Would a "Mommy Track" Benefit Employed Women?

_____

Should the Government Establish Special Programs and Policies for Black Youths and Their Families?

_____

Husband Battering: Is It a Social Problem?

_____

Are Extramarital Relationships Becoming More Frequent?

Pamela Carley Petersen/DPG

177

ISSUE 10

Does Arrest Reduce Domestic Violence?

YES: Joan Meier, from "Battered Justice," *The Washington Monthly* (May 1987)

NO: Franklyn W. Dunford, David Huizinga, and Delbert S. Elliott, from "The Role of Arrest in Domestic Assault: The Omaha Police Experiment," *Criminology* (May 1990)

ISSUE SUMMARY

YES: Attorney Joan Meier, after reviewing several reports on domestic violence, maintains that arrest is the most effective deterrent to continued assault and that perpetrators of domestic violence must be forced to take responsibility for their crimes.

NO: Criminologists Franklyn W. Dunford, David Huizinga, and Delbert S. Elliott argue that there is no clear-cut best approach to minimizing the continuation of wife abuse, based on their study of policy intervention in domestic violence cases in the Omaha, Nebraska, area.

Family relationships are rarely as positive as they are sometimes portrayed to be. The Cosbys on television are entertaining, but they do not always parallel the next-door neighbors. Domestic violence in the form of husband, wife, child, and grandparent abuse is not new to the twentieth century. Historical accounts of the problems of family life and violent conflict resolution have been documented in many ways, including eyewitness accounts, fiction, and even nursery rhymes. Work by Gelles, Steinmetz, and Straus, among others, has provided a sense of the enormity of the problem, as well as possible explanations for why it continues to be as significant as it is. Although some published works have presented possible methods of intervening and preventing domestic abuse, few studies have been attempted to explore why and how specific modes of intervention work or what verifiable success rates might be.

The case accounts that Joan Meier reviews tell of major assaults on human dignity—rape, virtual imprisonment, debasement of character, beatings, and even murder. Are these accounts of what specific women have endured perhaps symptomatic of larger cultural issues relating to men, women, and power. Many people can sympathize with the suffering of abused women and be outraged at the callousness of the community and larger social order that sometimes seems to prevail toward them. However, few seem interested in closely examining the cultural structures or individual thought processes that lead to abuse.

The findings of Franklyn W. Dunford, David Huizinga, and Delbert S. Elliott gravitate toward the conclusion that how abusers and their victims are treated all depends on who is in power, how power is exercised, and what recourse and support exists in the community for victims. A combination of interventions, including arrest, separation, and mediation (and maybe some less direct treatment plans like individual, couple, or family therapy help with job or housing arrangements or counseling that focuses on self-worth), may prove to have better success in reducing recurrent as well as first-time wife abuse. Perhaps violence needs to be examined in its societal context, and changes in political, educational, or legal spheres of influence need to be implemented.

The following selections raise a number of questions about how to deal effectively with domestic violence. They also explore why it exists, what in human social behavior condones it, and to what ends. If arrest is shown not to be the answer, what alternatives are left? If a number of interventions all have seemingly equal outcomes, which method should be utilized?

YES

Joan Meier

BATTERED JUSTICE

Last August in Somerville, Massachusetts, Pamela Nigro-Dunn was coming home from work and got off the bus at the stop where her mother met her each day. A man drove up and insisted Nigro-Dunn get into his car. When she and her mother resisted, he threw mace into her mother's face. Then he shot Pamela, who was five months pregnant, in the abdomen and dragged her into the car. Her body was found in a garbage dump nine hours later. She had been shot, strangled, and stabbed. The murderer was arrested three months later in Florida. He was her husband.

Roughly 1,350 women were killed by their spouses, ex-spouses, or boy-friends in 1985. They were the victims of the most extreme form of wife battering but represent only a fraction of those who have suffered from what appears to be an epidemic of violence within marriages. National surveys have suggested that as many as one out of four married couples endure at least one act of serious violence during their marriage.

This domestic violence is one-sided: 85-95 percent of assault victims and two-thirds of domestic murder victims are women. And it usually is not an isolated event but part of a pattern of escalating violence. Where there has been murder, there has usually been a history of beating. Consequently, many killings were predictable and could have been stopped. In most cases, the victims had brought their abusers' earlier assaults to the attention of the police, prosecutors, or courts. Pamela Nigro-Dunn had been to court four times trying to stop her husband's attacks before she was murdered. She received a restraining order, but the judge refused to give her police protection. Similarly, the murder of Leedonyell Williams in Washington, D.C. . . . was committed the day after charges against her attacker were dropped. One Minneapolis study found that in 85 percent of spousal murder cases there had been prior contact with the police; in 50 percent they had been called at least five times in the preceding two years.

Many people are aware that wife-beating is a problem. But few are aware of the shocking way that violence is ignored by the criminal justice system. When called for help, police rarely make arrests. When they do, prosecutors

From Joan Meier, "Battered Justice," *The Washington Monthly*, vol. 19, no. 4 (May 1987). Copyright © 1987 by The Washington Monthly Company, 1611 Connecticut Avenue, NW, Washington, DC 20009; (202) 462-0128. Reprinted by permission of *The Washington Monthly*.

rarely bring charges. And when cases are brought to court, judges too often have the attitude of Paul Heffernan, the Massachusetts judge who was sitting on the bench when Pamela Nigro-Dunn requested help.

In the first affidavit Pamela filed, just six weeks after her wedding, she stated, "I'm a prisoner in my apartment. He locks me in and takes the phone cord out. He choked me and threatened to kill me if I try to leave. He made me work only where he works. . . . My life is in danger so long as he is around."

Pamela asked Heffernan to order Paul Dunn out of the apartment, but the judge refused and then asked her, "Did he demonstrate this type of behavior before you married him?" presumably reasoning that, if the husband had hit her before they were married, she was not entitled to police protection if she was beaten—however badly—after she was married. Pamela moved out.

Five days later, she returned to court to obtain a police escort so she could return to the apartment for her clothes. "I don't think it's the role of this Court to decide down to each piece of underwear who owns what," Heffernan said. "This is pretty trivial. . . . This court has a lot more serious matters to contend with. We're doing a terrible disservice to the taxpayers here." Heffernan then turned to her husband and said, "You want to gnaw on her and she on you fine, but let's not do it at the taxpayers' expense."

Pamela moved in with her parents, but after pressure from Paul to return and promises that he'd reform, she reconciled with him for several weeks. The abuse resumed. She didn't go back to court to seek further protection. Why would she? She moved back to her parents', and her mother began accompanying her to and

from the bus stop because they had seen Paul circling in his car. Shortly thereafter he murdered her.

It is appalling that so many women suffer as Pamela did at the hands of their spouses. But it is perhaps even more appalling that so many are further abused by the criminal justice system. Although in recent years several cities have moved toward reform, domestic violence remains at best a low priority. There are many reasons for the reluctance of police, prosecutors, and judges to handle these cases, but at the root is the belief that wife-beating is simply not criminal behavior.

POLICE WHO WON'T ARREST

The passivity of police in dealing with domestic assaults was made clear in a landmark case in New York City in 1976. Twelve battered wives sued the city police department and family court for failing to arrest and prosecute men who attacked their wives—simply because the victim and assailant were married. The out-of-court settlement required the police department to change its policies and was hailed as a turning point in the country's police and court treatment of domestic violence cases.

But in the four years I have represented battered women in Chicago and Washington, D.C., it has become clear that little has changed since the New York case. Catherine Klein, who has worked with about five hundred women over the past five years, cannot recall a single arrest that happened without her intervention. . . . [F]or example, the D.C. police were called by nurses at a hospital where Dawn Ronan,* who was five months pregnant, had gone for treat-

*Some of the victims' names have been changed.

ment after being kicked in the back by Jimmy Smith, her boyfriend and the father of her child. The police refused to arrest Jimmy because they hadn't seen the assault. "It's a domestic problem. We really don't get involved," they explained to the nurse.

Fearing what might happen if she continued to live with Jimmy, Dawn moved in with his sister. About two weeks after the baby was born he found her there and attacked her in her bed, splitting her cheek open with a belt buckle, and cutting her eye with the heavy ring he wore. When his sister tried to stop him, he threw her against a dresser. The police, called in from the street by the sister, again refused to arrest because they had not "seen" the assault, even though there was a witness. Instead, they simply advised Dawn to go to the hospital for her bleeding cheek and eye.

Similarly, in December 1985, D.C. police were called to the home of Barbara Nelson after her husband, who no longer lived there, broke into the house, brandishing a razor and yelling, "I'm going to kill you . . . in the basement." There was no other man in the house. When Nelson asked the police to arrest him, they refused. When later asked why, one officer responded that Barbara had seemed more excited and hysterical than her husband.

This reluctance to arrest is corroborated by studies conducted in the late seventies in Colorado and California that showed only 5 to 6 percent of domestic violence complaints to the police resulted in arrest.

Why don't police arrest these abusers? Some states have historically prohibited arrests on misdemeanor—though not felony—charges unless the police have witnessed the crime. Many states, however, have changed the law so police can make misdemeanor arrests in domestic violence cases without having seen the assault if there is sufficient evidence of probable cause. In D.C., police concede they have always been authorized to make arrests for misdemeanors they didn't witness. They simply don't—sometimes not even when they can see blood streaming down a woman's face.

The legal excuses often give way to the real reasons for not arresting. "They always said they couldn't do anything because he was my husband," recalls Jean Cook, whose husband had, on various occasions, thrown a brick through her window, broken a beer bottle over her head, threatened to kill her, and lurked with a gun around the shelter where she was staying. Barbara Nelson was advised by a supportive police officer to tell the dispatcher there was "a man with a knife" when she called for help, rather than say "my husband has a knife." . . . [A]nother D.C. woman was on the floor being kicked by her boyfriend when the police arrived. The police told the man that if the couple had lived together at least six months, making them common law husband and wife, they couldn't do anything. The police then asked how long the two had lived together. The man said six months; she denies they had ever lived together. The police left. Yet another recent D.C. victim, who had been held hostage all of one night and hit repeatedly in the head with a hammer, was told by the police, "he'd have to kill you or damn near kill you" for them to take any action.

The hands-off approach that still operates in most police departments gained theoretical justification in the early seventies when social work alternatives to punishment were popular for a number of offenses, including drug use and prostitution. In 1970, Morton Bard, a clinical psychologist, set up a demonstration project to teach police special counseling skills for intervening in family disputes. Even though the project did not show a reduction in violence, it was hailed as a success. Other well-intended psychologists followed suit. By 1977, a national survey of the larger police departments found that more than 70 percent had implemented some kind of family crisis intervention training program.

At best, such policies help the victim. Police should usually be applauded for their efforts to be more human, but it is curious, given their occupational bias toward punishing offenders, that they eagerly embrace a soft approach towards domestic violence. Unfortunately, experts in domestic violence now agree that mediation as a substitute for arrest is the wrong answer when there is violence.

D.C. police officers typically say they are reluctant to arrest wife-beaters because these "fights"—a term reflecting a belief that spousal violence is minor and mutual—"are much more dangerous for police." They also reason that, as one said, "when people are in a relationship, I assume she could leave and avoid the man if she wanted to."

Both reasons contain a kernel of truth. That police fear domestic violence cases is understandable, although it contrasts strikingly with their notion that such cases are trivial and not very dangerous for the women. When police respond to a domestic call, tempers are usually still hot, and often get hotter at the sight of a cop. One 1983 study by the D.C. Metropolitan Police Department stated that "nationally, more police officers were injured while responding to disturbance calls than in any other type of call for service." But recent FBI Uniform Crime Reports show that police fears are overstated and that a domestic call is one of the least likely of all calls to lead to assaults on officers or to their deaths. Similarly, Don Pfouts, a detective with the Baltimore City Police Department who has been reviewing his department's records, confirms that domestic calls are "not that dangerous."

NOWHERE TO HIDE

Underlying police reluctance to arrest is the feeling that domestic violence is not a real crime. The perception, shared by many people, is that women in some way consent to the violence by being in a relationship with the man. To put it crudely: "If she doesn't take it seriously enough to stay away, why should society take it seriously enough to arrest the man?"

But the assumption that women have control over the situation is mistaken. It can be almost impossible for a woman to relocate, especially when she has children to care for or when she has no independent income. More important, many women don't leave their spouses for fear that the violence will get worse. Angela Browne, a social psychologist at the University of New Hampshire, says, "Some women who have left an abusive partner have been followed and harrassed for months and even years; some have been killed." Jean Cook left her husband only to begin seven months of moving from shelter to shelter in an attempt to hide from him. He always found her. From restaurant to shelter, from shelter to work, to and from church, wherever she went, he tracked and harrassed her. Twice, when she sought court protection he assaulted her the next day. Cook was not truly free of her husband's terrorizing until he was finally put in jail and she left the state.

In her many attempts to get away from her abuser, Dawn Ronan went to her parents', a shelter with a supposedly secret address, and the house of a shelter counselor. Jimmy Smith tracked her down each time. On the last occasion, he forced her into the car, held a knife to her neck, then thrust her head out the car window and choked her.

The legal system also makes it impossible for women to avoid their batterers when it enforces the man's "rights." Even if Dawn could somehow escape Jimmy, she would still have to be in contact with him by order of the court since he has been awarded visitation rights with their baby. Many judges appear to share the opinion of Massachusetts Judge Tempone, who said, in refusing a woman's plea to deny her batterer visitation rights, "Even Dillinger could have made a good father. . . . How about Manson?"

While misperceptions about women's ability to end the violence may make the reluctance of police to arrest more understandable, their behavior in many instances indicates something far worse: an identification with the male attacker and a lack of sympathy for the woman. In the landmark New York case, a policeman who had been called to a scene where a man had stabbed his wife with a knife, said to the husband, "Maybe if I beat my wife, she'd act right too."

Police sympathies can be more subtly expressed. Jimmy Smith broke into the shelter where Dawn Ronan was staying and attacked several of those who lived there. After three calls, a policeman came but stood outside at least ten minutes before coming in. When he got inside, a shelter worker was holding Jimmy down, but the officer, smiling, addressed Jimmy: "What's up Jimmy, what are you doing in here?" He then asked Jimmy, but not the women, if he was hurt. Then the officer escorted him out of the house and proceeded to smoke a cigarette with him, both of them talking and laughing. The officer stood silent when Jimmy said to Dawn, "I'm going to kill you, if that's the last thing I do." Only when Dawn got angry did the officer finally take action: He insisted that she go inside. He then escorted Jimmy to the hospital, though he had no noticeable injuries.

There was no subtlety, however, in the response to Tracy Thurmon, who later won a suit against the Torrington, Connecticut, police department. She had successfully prosecuted her husband in 1982 for repeatedly beating her and threatening her and their child's life. Despite a probation order barring him from further harassment, he assaulted her twice and repeatedly threatened and harassed her. The police consistently refused to respond to her calls. In June 1983, Thurman called the police again when her husband came to her house. By the time they arrived, he had already stabbed her in front of the house. While the police watched, her husband dropped the bloody knife, kicked her in the head, went into the house, came back out, dropped her child on her, kicked her in the head again, and walked around the crowd that had gathered to watch. Not until he approached Thurman a third time, as she lay on a stretcher, did the police arrest him. Thurman said the police frequented the restaurant where her husband worked and that he had boasted to them that he intended to kill her. . . .

VIOLENCE IS VIOLENCE

Slowly, things are changing. . . . [P]olice departments, including D.C.'s, are beginning to adopt policies that favor arrests or require that domestic violence cases be treated no differently from other assault cases. When Denver recently adopted a pro-arrest policy, arrests jumped 60 percent one year and 46 percent the next.

Recently, the Attorney General's Task Force on Domestic Violence, the Bureau of Justice Statistics, and the National Institute of Justice produced reports urging that domestic violence be treated as a serious crime. Justice Department funding, although far lower than in the past, now supports eight demonstration projects to develop new policies and procedures for police and prosecutors.

A firm criminal justice response works. After Duluth, Minnesota, instituted a mandatory arrest program, 70 of a group of 86 women reported at the end of two years that the combined assistance of police, courts, and shelters was helpful in ending their abusers' violence. According to Dr. Anne Ganley, a psychologist and counselor for batterers, "Perpetrators tend to minimize and deny the violence and place the blame on others." Therefore, she says, it is crucial that batterers be held responsible for their violence. As one former abuser said in the National Institute of Justice report: "It was such an extreme experience having actually been arrested and dealt with rather harshly . . . that I sought help." Advocates frequently comment that even the slightest acknowledgment from an official that women do not deserve to be beaten can give victims an enormous boost of strength and energy to take action to end the abuse. Even if the couple stays together, outside disapproval can make both aware that the man does not have "the right to beat" the woman. Barbara Nelson's husband, who was finally arrested and jailed after ten years of violence now says, "There's nothing I want to do enough to go back there. . . . You don't have to be afraid of me; it's not worth it to go back."

If the message is clear, the actual punishment is less important. A study of the Minneapolis Police Department by the Police Foundation concluded that when the officer "advised" the suspect and did not lock him up, violence recurred within the next six months in 37 percent of the cases; when the suspect was arrested, even if he wasn't prosecuted later, violence recurred in only 19 percent of the cases. In Jean Cook's case, a mere warning letter from her attorney to her abuser brought a sudden halt to seven months of almost daily harassment.

Even if the evidence weren't as clear as it is that criminal justice intervention reduces domestic violence, it would still be called for. Society punishes behavior it finds morally opprobrious. The refusal of the police and courts to insist that domestic violence is a crime allows people to go on believing it's not so bad. It's time to teach a different set of lessons.

NO

Franklyn W. Dunford, David Huizinga, and Delbert S. Elliott

THE ROLE OF ARREST IN DOMESTIC ASSAULT: THE OMAHA POLICE EXPERIMENT

In what has come to be known as a landmark study, the Minneapolis Domestic Violence Experiment (Sherman and Berk, 1984a, 1984b) assessed the effects of different police responses on the future violence of individuals apprehended for domestic assault. The authors . . . reported that

> arrest was the most effective of three standard methods police use to reduce domestic violence. The other police methods—attempting to counsel both parties or sending assailants away—were found to be considerably less effective in deterring future violence in the cases examined.

Sherman and Berk specified arrest and initial incarceration, "alone," as deterring continued domestic assault and recommended that the police adopt arrest as the favored response to domestic assault *on the basis* of its deterrent power. These findings and recommendations came at a time when advocacy for increased sensitivity to women's rights was strong and pressure was mounting to change the social service approach to domestic violence that had dominated law enforcement and court policy over the preceding two decades. . . . Sherman and Berk's recommendations were uniquely appealing for the times and were received by many women's advocates and law enforcement administrators as justification for change (Cohn and Sherman, 1987, Sherman and Cohn, 1989).

The overwhelming reaction of the research community to the Minneapolis experiment, with its recommendation for presumptory arrests in cases of misdemeanor domestic assault, was a call for additional studies to corroborate its conclusions. . . . The Omaha Domestic Violence Police Experiment, funded by the National Institute of Justice, was conceived and designed to determine if the findings reported for the Minneapolis experiment could be replicated elsewhere.

From Franklyn W. Dunford, David Huizinga, and Delbert S. Elliott, "The Role of Arrest in Domestic Assault: The Omaha Police Experiment," *Criminology,* vol. 28, no. 2 (1990). Reprinted by permission. Some notes omitted.

THE OMAHA RESEARCH DESIGN

Omaha is a city of approximately 400,000 inhabitants, 10% of whom are black and 2% of Hispanic origin (U.S. Department of Commerce, 1983). The city is split into three sectors (south, west, north) for police purposes. In concert with Chief Robert Wadman of the Omaha Police Division and after surveying 911 dispatch records, it was determined that approximately 60% of all disturbance calls were reported during the hours of "C" shift (4 p.m. to midnight). On this basis, the decision was made to limit the replication experiment in Omaha to eligible domestic assaults coming to the attention of the police throughout the city (all three sectors) during the hours of "C" shift. In this way, no segment of the city (e.g., socioeconomic status [SES] or ethnic group) would be excluded from participation in the experiment by the research design, and the majority of domestic violence calls would be included in the study.

Following the design of the Minneapolis experiment, police calls for domestic violence found to be eligible for the study were randomly assigned to "arrest," "separation," or "mediation" for all instances in which both victims and suspects were present when the police arrived. A case was eligible for the experiment if (1) probable cause for an arrest for misdemeanor assault existed, (2) the case involved a clearly identifiable victim and suspect, (3) both parties to the assault were of age (18 or older), (4) both parties had lived together sometime during the year preceding the assault, and (5) neither party to the offense had an arrest warrant on file. Cases for which the police had no legal authority to make an arrest (i.e., no probable cause to

believe that an assault had occurred) were excluded from the experiment, as were more serious cases (i.e., felony cases). . . .

DESCRIPTION OF THE EXPERIMENT

In February 1986 all of the command and patrol officers assigned to "C" (and "D") shift were trained during a succession of three-day training sessions. Training focused on the rationale, content, and mechanics of the experiment. At each shift change thereafter, officers new to "C" shift were similarly trained. A total of 194 officers were ultimately assigned to the participating shifts and received training on the methods and procedures of the experiment. Of that number, 31 (16%) did not refer any cases to the study, and 61 (31%) accounted for approximately 75% of the referrals.

One of the greatest challenges faced when implementing random assignment in field settings is monitoring and identifying all violations of randomized outcomes. Although researchers may not be able to prevent violations of randomly designated treatments (e.g., arresting when treatment is randomized to mediating), they should be able to ensure that such violations do not go undetected when they occur. . . . Some of the discrepancies between Treatment as Assigned and Treatment as Immediately Delivered appear to have involved differences in perceptions of what happened rather than any real differences, while others were clear misdeliveries of treatment.[1] . . .

As a check on the misapplication of treatment, the disparities between Treatments as Assigned and Treatments as Delivered were examined. As presented in Table 1, 95% of the cases assigned to an arrest received an arrest, 92% of those assigned to be separated were separated, and 89% of the mediation cases were mediated; overall, 92% of the treatments were delivered as assigned. . . .

Table 1

Assigned and Delivered Treatments

Assigned		As Delivered	
Disposition	Mediate	Separate	Arrest
Mediate			
N	102	8	2
%	89	7	2
Separate			
N	5	98	3
%	5	92	3
Arrest			
N	3	2	104
%	3	2	95

DISCUSSION

Conclusions based on the results of the research conducted in Omaha must be considered together with the outcomes of the five other research efforts currently funded by the National Institute of Justice to replicate the Minneapolis experiment. Since the results from all of these studies are not yet available, what follows must be considered tentative. It must also be remembered that the results of the Omaha experiment cannot be generalized beyond Omaha. . . .

Given the strength of the experimental design used in Omaha and the absence of any evidence that the design was manipulated in any significant way, the inability to replicate findings associated with the Minneapolis experiment calls into question any generalization of the Minneapolis findings to other sites. First, arrest in Omaha, by itself, did not appear to deter subsequent domestic conflict any more than did separating or mediating those in conflict. Arrest, and the immediate period of custody associated with arrest, was not the deterrent to continued domestic conflict that was expected. If the Omaha findings should be replicated in the other five sites conducting experiments on this issue, policy based on the presumptory arrest recommendation coming out of the Minneapolis experiment may have to be reconsidered. Second, although arrest, by itself, did not act as a deterrent to continued domestic conflict for the misdemeanor domestic assault cases coming to the attention of the Omaha police, neither did it increase continued domestic conflict between parties to an arrest for assault. That is, victim-reported measures of repeated conflict, which are measures of behavior (as opposed to arrest and complaint data, which are measures of official police reaction to known violations of the law), clearly did not indicate that victims whose partners were arrested were at greater risk of subsequent conflict than were those whose partners were handled informally (mediated or separated) by the police. Arrest did not appear to place victims in greater danger of increased conflict than did separation or mediation. It would appear that what the police did in Omaha after responding to cases of misdemeanor domestic assault (arrest, separate, mediate), neither helped nor hurt victims in terms of subsequent conflict.

The failure to replicate the Minneapolis findings will undoubtedly cast some doubt on the deterrent power of a mandatory or even a presumptory arrest policy for cases of misdemeanor domestic assault. At this point, researchers and policymakers are in the awkward position of having conflicting results from two experiments and no clear, unambiguous direction from the research on this issue. Nevertheless, the data from the Omaha police experiment clearly suggest that the adoption of an arrest policy for cases of misdemeanor domestic assault may not, by itself, have any impact on the likelihood of repeated violent acts. From those who are directly involved in responding to domestic assaults, it might be profitable to begin thinking about new or additional strategies for dealing with this problem.

NOTES

1. Victims were not always sure of what happened as a result of police interventions. Some of their confusion was to be expected. The police, for example, would mediate a dispute, after which the suspect would leave, but at the time of the interview the victim would report a separation as the intervention. Or, after the police left, one of the parties to a separation treatment would return and the event would be recalled as a mediation. This kind of confusion is even more understandable given that (by responding officer estimates) over 30% of the victims had been drinking at the time of the police intervention, which may have affected what victims remembered as happening during those time periods. Further, many victims were clearly traumatized by the presenting assault, which also may have affected their recall.

REFERENCES

Sherman, Lawrence W. and Richard A. Berk 1984a The Minneapolis Domestic Violence Experiment. Police Foundation Reports. Washington, D.C.: Police Foundation. 1984b The specified deterrent effects of arrest for domestic assault. American Sociological Review 49(2):261–272.

Cohn, Ellen G. and Lawrence W. Sherman 1987 Police policy on domestic violence. Paper presented at the annual meeting of the Academy of Criminal Justice Sciences, St. Louis. Sherman, Lawrence W. and Ellen G. Cohn 1989 The impact of research on legal policy: The Minneapolis domestic violence experiment. Law and Society Review 23(1):117–144.

POSTSCRIPT

Does Arrest Reduce Domestic Violence?

Certainly the immediate separation of spouses can be an effective crisis intervention technique for stopping abuse as it is occurring. The questions that must be addressed beyond stopping the violence concern basic issues of human behavior and interaction. Often the first question asked is "Who is to blame?" This assumes that *one* person is to blame and that if such blame is correctly attributed, the situation can be remedied. Such an assumption is dangerously simplistic and ignores the dynamics of marital and societal relationships. The position that arrest will inhibit or prohibit abusive behavior is functional only to the point that arrest may lead to permanent incarceration and separation. At the time the abuser is released, in many cases, the likelihood of the behavior recurring takes a leap forward. Nothing has occurred beyond temporary and immediate stress alleviation.

On the other hand, if there is some doubt as to why the behavior occurs, the questions might be: Is there some interpersonal or interactional basis for its occurrence? Is there something that can be done to reduce or eliminate the chances of the specific act recurring? Or can attempts be made to help all the individuals involved to gain better control of the situation? Such issues might involve taking personal initiative to control anger, receive counseling to enhance self-image, obtain employment or better employment, discuss expectations and negotiate something that is acceptable to all concerned people, work toward extended family relationships that are productive and relatively nonstressful, and (especially for the victim) gain knowledge of the law, how to effectively use it, and where informational, financial, social, and protective services might be available in case of repeated abuse.

Domestic violence can be a complex topic. In the United States, the earliest attention was paid to the topic of child abuse and neglect. Henry Kempe and his coworkers made a significant impact upon the country's awareness of the problem with their 1962 article "The Battered Child Syndrome." C. H. Kempe and R. E. Helfer's *The Battered Child* (University of Chicago Press, 1974) and D. Bakan's *Slaughter of the Innocents: A Study of the Battered Child Phenomenon* (Jossey-Bass, 1971) did much not only to focus awareness but also to bring about programs aimed at the problem and its causes. Later, domestic violence became more broadly conceived, as *The Abusing Family*, by R. Justice and B. Justice (Human Science Press, 1976); *The Cycle of Violence: Assertive, Aggressive, and Abusive Family Interaction*, by S. K. Steinmetz (Praeger, 1977); *The Battered Woman*, by L. Walker (Harper & Row, 1979); and *Behind Closed Doors: Violence in the American Family*, by M. Straus and R. J. Gelles (Doubleday, 1980) were published. Even more recently, issues of dating violence and female-initiated violence have introduced many people to the widespread outcomes and implications of violence. In addition, the literature has moved beyond simply presenting the clinical gore and documentation of these significant problems to a point where programs of intervention, remediation and education, and the evaluation of such programs have been proposed, presented, and implemented.

Even though Meier believes that spouse attackers should be dealt with punitively, it appears that there is little indisputable evidence that such an approach would necessarily reduce the incidence of wife abuse. The conclusions of Dunford, Huizinga, and Elliott promote caution when viewing possible solutions to abuse. Such solutions should contain elements ensuring immediate safety for those victimized, education and treatment for those requiring it, and long-term plans for reducing the need for violence between family members or people in general.

SUGGESTED READINGS

R. A. Berk, P. Newton, and S. F. Berk, "What a Difference a Day Makes: An Empirical Study of the Impact of Shelters for Battered Women," *Journal of Marriage and the Family*, **48** (1986): 481–490.

D. G. Dutton, "The Outcome of Court-Mandated Treatment for Wife Assault: A Quasi-Experimental Evaluation," *Violence and Victims*, **1** (1986): 163–176.

B. Egeland, D. Jacobvitz, and L. A. Sroufe, "Breaking the Cycle of Abuse," *Child Development*, **59** (1988): 1080–1088.

R. E. Emery, "Family Violence," *American Psychologist*, **44** (1989): 321–328.

C. P. Flynn, "Relationship Violence by Women: Issues and Implications," *Family Relations*, **39** (1990): 194–198.

R. J. Gelles and J. W. Harrop, "Violence, Battering, and Psychological Distress Among Women," *Journal of Interpersonal Violence*, **4** (1989): 400–420.

E. W. Gondolf, "Evaluating Progress for Men Who Batter: Problems and Prospects," *Journal of Family Violence*, **2** (1987): 95–108.

D. Kalmuss and J. A. Seltzer, "Continuity of Marital Behavior in Remarriage: The Case of Spouse Abuse," *Journal of Marriage and the Family*, **48** (1986): 113–120.

W. A. Lo and M. J. Sporakowski, "The Continuation of Violent Dating Relationships Among College Students," *Journal of College Student Development*, **30** (1989): 432–439.

R. L. McNeely and G. Robinson-Simpson, "The Truth About Domestic Violence: A Falsely Framed Issue," *Social Work*, **32** (1987): 485–490.

M. A. Pirog-Good and J. Stets, "Programs for Abusers: Who Drops Out and What Can Be Done," *Response*, **9** (1986): 17–19.

M. A. Pirog-Good and J. Stets, eds., *Violence in Dating Relationships: Emerging Social Issues* (Praeger, 1989).

ISSUE 11

Would a "Mommy Track" Benefit Employed Women?

YES: Felice N. Schwartz, from "Management Women and the New Facts of Life," *Harvard Business Review* (January–February 1989)

NO: Barbara Ehrenreich and Deirdre English, from "Blowing the Whistle on the 'Mommy Track,' " *Ms.* (July–August 1989)

ISSUE SUMMARY

YES: Felice N. Schwartz, president and founder of Catalyst, an organization that consults with corporations on the career and leadership development of women, argues that it is in the best interests of corporations to retain valued managerial women by creating two career paths within the organization, one for "career-primary" women and the other for "career-and-family" women.
NO: Journalists Barbara Ehrenreich and Deirdre English maintain that the "mommy track" notion is based on stereotypical assumptions about women and ignores the real issue of why corporations continue to promote work policies that are incompatible with family life.

The composition of the work force is changing, with women comprising an ever-increasing percentage of new workplace entrants. Many of these women have college degrees and seek management positions. As they advance in rank and status, the majority of managerial women marry, and most continue to work after having children, taking only a limited amount of time off for maternity leave. Upon returning to work after leave, women are usually expected to retain primary responsibility for family roles and at the same time pursue active careers.

Such expectations create problems for women with children because traditional work schedules require excessive work hours. The workday generally begins very early or ends very late or both, which prevents employed women from spending time with their family members. In addition, work scheduling typically does not mesh well with child care arrangements. Finding reliable child care is, women say, among the most problematic and worrisome concerns for parents. Providing care for children when they are too ill to go to day care is particularly difficult. The result is that career mothers with small children often feel overloaded, anxious, and guilty.

Corporations typically respond to women's concerns by initiating seminars on stress management and advising women to focus on finding new ways to balance career goals and parenthood. Such programs are inexpensive to initiate and maintain and spare organizations the financial costs of instituting other, more comprehensive but more costly programs. These stopgap measures, currently used by many organizations, are not very beneficial for either women or corporations, and they have not been proven effective in reducing the absenteeism, tardiness, and employee turnover associated with child care issues.

Another reason why corporations seem hesitant to implement policies that are friendlier to family concerns is that many supervisors in the managerial hierarchy made their career advances during a time when women were primarily homemakers and family caregivers. The career paths of these supervisors are characterized by the primacy of career goals over family roles. When new work patterns are proposed to ease the burden of work responsibilities on family life, such supervisors often view them as alien to what seems appropriate and normative from their own personal perspectives and experiences.

Despite these barriers, some employers, aware of the changing demographics of the work force, worried about losing productive female employees, and conscious of the need to attract talented women for future positions, have begun to listen more intently to women's concerns and to develop and implement policies that are targeted to family needs, such as maternity leave, flexible work hours, and part-time employment. Women are increasingly voicing unhappiness about being employed in positions where job expectations are incompatible with family life. Men with young children are also becoming more aware of work and family issues. Since women today are likely to be employed, their husbands are under greater pressure than in the past to assume more of the child-rearing responsibilities and household tasks. Men and women together are becoming more vocal in supporting corporate policies that help combine work and family roles.

The authors of the following selections believe that corporations must adjust work policies to attract and keep talented women. Felice N. Schwartz believes that corporations should develop two career paths for women. One path would be for those who intend to pursue careers as their primary life goal, and the other path would be for women who want to combine career and family roles by temporarily working part-time after having children. Barbara Ehrenreich and Deirdre English maintain that Schwartz's "mommy track" would perpetuate gender role stereotypes. They also claim that the "mommy track" would be difficult to administer fairly and would continue to promote work policies that are incompatible with contemporary family life.

YES
Felice N. Schwartz

MANAGEMENT WOMEN AND THE NEW FACTS OF LIFE

A new study by one multinational corporation shows that the rate of turnover in management positions is 2¹/₂ times higher among top-performing women than it is among men. A large producer of consumer goods reports that one half of the women who take maternity leave return to their jobs late or not at all. And we know that women also have a greater tendency to plateau or to interrupt their careers in ways that limit their growth and development. . . .

Career interruptions, plateauing, and turnover are expensive. The money corporations invest in recruitment, training, and development is less likely to produce top executives among women than among men, and the invaluable company experience that developing executives acquire at every level as they move up through management ranks is more often lost. . . .

It is terribly important that employers draw the right conclusions from the studies now being done. The studies will be useless—or worse, harmful—if all they teach us is that women are expensive to employ. What we need to learn is how to reduce that expense, how to stop throwing away the investments we make in talented women, how to become more responsive to the needs of the women that corporations *must* employ if they are to have the best and the brightest of all those now entering the work force. . . .

THE ONE IMMUTABLE, ENDURING DIFFERENCE BETWEEN MEN AND WOMEN IS maternity. Maternity is not simply childbirth but a continuum that begins with an awareness of the ticking of the biological clock, proceeds to the anticipation of motherhood, includes pregnancy, childbirth, physical recuperation, psychological adjustment, and continues on to nursing, bonding, and child rearing. Not all women choose to become mothers, of course, and among those who do, the process varies from case to case depending on the health of the mother and baby, the values of the parents, and the availability, cost, and quality of child care.

In past centuries, the biological fact of maternity shaped the traditional roles of the sexes. Women performed the home-centered functions that related to the bearing and nurturing of children. Men did the work that required great physical strength. Over time, however, family size contracted, the community assumed greater responsibility for the care and education of children, packaged foods and household technology reduced the work load in the home, and technology eliminated much of the need for muscle power at the workplace. Today, in the developed world, the only role still uniquely gender related is childbearing. Yet men and women are still socialized to perform their traditional roles. . . .

In the decades ahead, as the socialization of boys and girls and the experience and expectations of young men and women grow steadily more androgynous, the differences in workplace behavior will continue to fade. At the moment, however, we are still plagued by disparities in perception and behavior that make the integration of men and women in the workplace unnecessarily difficult and expensive.

Let me illustrate with a few broadbrush generalizations. Of course, these are only stereotypes, but I think they help to exemplify the kinds of preconceptions that can muddy the corporate waters.

Men continue to perceive women as the rearers of their children, so they find it understandable, indeed appropriate, that women should renounce their careers to raise families. Edmund Pratt, CEO of Pfizer, once asked me in all sincerity, "Why would any woman choose to be a chief financial officer rather than a full-time mother?" By condoning and taking pleasure in women's traditional behavior, men reinforce it. Not only do they see parenting as fundamentally female, they see a career as fundamentally male—either an unbroken series of promotions and advancements toward CEOdom or stagnation and disappointment. This attitude serves to legitimize a woman's choice to extend maternity leave and even, for those who can afford it, to leave employment altogether for several years. By the same token, men who might want to take a leave after the birth of a child know that management will see such behavior as a lack of career commitment, even when company policy permits parental leave for men.

Women also bring counterproductive expectations and perceptions to the workplace. Ironically, although the feminist movement was an expression of women's quest for freedom from their homebased lives, most women were remarkably free already. They had many responsibilities, but they were autonomous and could be entrepreneurial in how and when they carried them out. And once their children grew up and left home, they were essentially free to do what they wanted with their lives. Women's traditional role also included freedom from responsibility for the financial support of their families. Many of us were socialized from girlhood to expect our husbands to take care of us, while our brothers were socialized from an equally early age to complete their educations, pursue careers, climb the ladder of success, and provide dependable financial support for their families. To the extent that this tradition of freedom lingers subliminally, women tend to bring to their employment a sense that they can choose to change jobs or careers at will, take time off, or reduce their hours.

Finally, women's traditional role encouraged particular attention to the quality and substance of what they did, specifically to the physical, psychological, and intellectual development of their children. This traditional focus may explain women's continuing tendency to search for more than monetary reward—intrinsic significance, social importance, meaning—in what they do. This too makes them more likely than men to leave the corporation in search of other values.

The misleading metaphor of the glass ceiling suggests an invisible barrier constructed by corporate leaders to impede the upward mobility of women beyond the middle levels. A more appropriate metaphor, I believe, is the kind of cross-sectional diagram used in geology. The barriers to women's leadership occur when potentially counterproductive layers of influence on women—maternity, tradition, socialization—meet management strata pervaded by the largely unconscious preconceptions, stereotypes, and expectations of men. Such interfaces do not exist for men and tend to be impermeable for women.

One result of these gender differences has been to convince some executives that women are simply not suited to top management. Other executives feel helpless. If they see even a few of their valued female employees fail to return to work from maternity leave on schedule or see one of their most promising women plateau in her career after the birth of a child, they begin to fear there is nothing they can do to infuse women with new energy and enthusiasm and persuade them to stay. At the same time, they know there is nothing they can do to stem the tide of women into management ranks.

Another result is to place every working woman on a continuum that runs from total dedication to career at one end to a balance between career and family at the other. What women discover is that the male corporate culture sees both extremes as unacceptable. Women who want the flexibility to balance their families and their careers are not adequately committed to the organization. Women who perform as aggressively and competitively as men are abrasive and unfeminine. But the fact is, business needs all the talented women it can get. Moreover, as I will explain, the women I call career-primary and those I call career-and-family each have particular value to the corporation.

WOMEN IN THE CORPORATION ARE ABOUT to move from a buyer's to a seller's market. The sudden, startling recognition that 80% of new entrants in the work force over the next decade will be women, minorities, and immigrants has stimulated a mushrooming incentive to "value diversity."

Women are no longer simply an enticing pool of occasional creative talent, a thorn in the side of the EEO officer, or a source of frustration to corporate leaders truly puzzled by the slowness of their upward trickle into executive positions. A real demographic change is taking place. The era of sudden population growth of the 1950s and 1960s is over. The birth rate has dropped about 40%, from a high of 25.3 live births per 1,000 population in 1957, at the peak of the baby boom, to a stable low of a little more than 15 per 1,000 over the last 16 years, and there is no indication of a return to a higher rate. The tidal wave of baby boomers that swelled the recruitment pool to overflowing seems to have been a one-time phenomenon. For 20 years, employers had the pick of a very large crop and were able to choose males almost exclusively for the executive track. But if future population remains fairly stable while the economy continues to expand, and if the new information society simultaneously creates a greater need for creative, educated managers, then the gap between supply and demand will grow dramatically and, with it, the competition for managerial talent.

The decrease in numbers has even greater implications if we look at the traditional source of corporate recruitment for leadership positions—white males from the top 10% of the country's best universities. Over the past decade, the increase in the number of women graduating from leading universities has been much greater than the increase in the total number of graduates, and these women are well represented in the top 10% of their classes.

The trend extends into business and professional programs as well. In the old days, virtually all MBAs were male. I remember addressing a meeting at the Harvard Business School as recently as the mid-1970s and looking out at a sea of exclusively male faces. Today, about 25% of that audience would be women. The pool of male MBAs from which corporations have traditionally drawn their leaders has shrunk significantly. . . .

UNDER THESE CIRCUMSTANCES, THERE IS no question that the management ranks of business will include increasing numbers of women. There remains, however, the question of how these women will succeed—how long they will stay, how high they will climb, how completely they will fulfill their promise and potential, and what kind of return the corporation will realize on its investment in their training and development.

There is ample business reason for finding ways to make sure that as many of these women as possible will succeed.

The first step in this process is to recognize that women are not all alike. Like men, they are individuals with differing talents, priorities, and motivations. For the sake of simplicity, let me focus on the two women I referred to earlier, on what I call the career-primary woman and the career-family woman.

Like many men, some women put their careers first. They are ready to make the same trade-offs traditionally made by the men who seek leadership positions. They make a career decision to put in extra hours, to make sacrifices in their personal lives, to make the most of every opportunity for professional development. . . .

The secret to dealing with such women is to recognize them early, accept them, and clear artificial barriers from their path to the top. After all, the best of these women are among the best managerial talent you will ever see. And career-primary women have another important value to the company that men and other women lack. They can act as role models and mentors to younger women who put their careers first. Since upwardly mobile career-primary women still have few role models to motivate and inspire them, a company with women in its top echelon has a significant advantage in the competition for executive talent. . . .

Clearing a path to the top for career-primary women has four requirements:

1. Identify them early.

2. Give them the same opportunity you give to talented men to grow and develop and contribute to company profitability. Give them client and customer responsibility. Expect them to travel and relocate, to make the same commitment to the company as men aspiring to leadership positions.

3. Accept them as valued members of your management team. Include them in

every kind of communication. Listen to them.

4. Recognize that the business environment is more difficult and stressful for them than for their male peers. They are always a minority, often the only woman. The male perception of talented, ambitious women is at best ambivalent, a mixture of admiration, resentment, confusion, competitiveness, attraction, skepticism, anxiety, pride, and animosity. . . .

Stereotypical language and sexist day-to-day behavior do take their toll on women's career development. . . . With notable exceptions, men are still generally more comfortable with other men, and as a result women miss many of the career and business opportunities that arise over lunch, on the golf course, or in the locker room.

THE MAJORITY OF WOMEN, HOWEVER, ARE what I call career-and-family women, women who want to pursue serious careers while participating actively in the rearing of children. These women are a precious resource that has yet to be mined. Many of them are talented and creative. Most of them are willing to trade some career growth and compensation for freedom from the constant pressure to work long hours and weekends.

Most companies today are ambivalent at best about the career-and-family women in their management ranks. They would prefer that all employees were willing to give their all to the company. They believe it is in their best interests for all managers to compete for the top positions so the company will have the largest possible pool from which to draw its leaders. . . .

These companies lose on two counts. First, they fail to amortize the investment they made in the early training and experience of management women who find themselves committed to family as well as to career. Second, they fail to recognize what these women could do for their middle management.

The ranks of middle managers are filled with people on their way up and people who have stalled. Many of them have simply reached their limits, achieved career growth commensurate with or exceeding their capabilities, and they cause problems because their performance is mediocre but they still want to move ahead. The career-and-family woman is willing to trade off the pressures and demands that go with promotion for the freedom to spend more time with her children. She's very smart, she's talented, she's committed to her career, and she's satisfied to stay at the middle level, at least during the early child-rearing years. . . .

Consider a typical example, a woman who decides in college on a business career and enters management at age 22. For nine years, the company invests in her career as she gains experience and skills and steadily improves her performance. But at 31, just as the investment begins to pay off in earnest, she decides to have a baby. Can the company afford to let her go home, take another job, or go into business for herself? The common perception now is yes, the corporation can afford to lose her unless, after six or eight weeks or even three months of disability and maternity leave, she returns to work on a full-time schedule with the same vigor, commitment, and ambition that she showed before.

But what if she doesn't? What if she wants or needs to go on leave for six months or a year or, heaven forbid, five years? In this worst-case scenario, she works full-time from age 22 to 31 and from 36 to 65—a total of 38 years as opposed to the typical male's 43 years. That's not a huge difference. Moreover, my typical example is willing to work part-time while her children are young, if only her employer will give her the opportunity. There are two rewards for companies responsive to this need: higher retention of their best people and greatly improved performance and satisfaction in their middle management.

The high-performing career-and-family woman can be a major player in your company. She can give you a significant business advantage as the competition for able people escalates. Sometimes, too, if you can hold on to her, she will switch gears in mid-life and re-enter the competition for the top. The price you must pay to retain these women is threefold: you must plan for and manage maternity, you must provide the flexibility that will allow them to be maximally productive, and you must take an active role in helping to make family supports and high-quality, affordable child care available to all women. . . .

TIME SPENT IN THE OFFICE INCREASES PRODuctivity if it is time well spent, but the fact that most women continue to take the primary responsibility for child care is a cause of distraction, diversion, anxiety, and absenteeism—to say nothing of the persistent guilt experienced by all working mothers. A great many women, perhaps most of all women who have always performed at the highest levels, are also frustrated by a sense that while their children are babies they cannot function at their best either at home or at work.

In its simplest form, flexibility is the freedom to take time off—a couple of hours, a day, a week—or to do some work at home and some at the office, an arrangement that communication technology makes increasingly feasible. At the complex end of the spectrum are alternative work schedules that permit the woman to work less than full-time and her employer to reap the benefits of her experience and, with careful planning, the top level of her abilities.

Part-time employment is the single greatest inducement to getting women back on the job expeditiously and the provision women themselves most desire. A part-time return to work enables them to maintain responsibility for critical aspects of their jobs, keeps them in touch with the changes constantly occurring at the workplace and in the job itself, reduces stress and fatigue, often eliminates the need for paid maternity leave by permitting a return to the office as soon as disability leave is over, and, not least, can greatly enhance company loyalty. The part-time solution works particularly well when a work load can be reduced for one individual in a department or when a full-time job can be broken down by skill levels and apportioned to two individuals at different levels of skill and pay.

I believe, however, that shared employment is the most promising and will be the most widespread form of flexible scheduling in the future. It is feasible at every level of the corporation except at the pinnacle, for both the short and the long term. It involves two people taking responsibility for one job. . . .

Flexibility is costly in numerous ways. It requires more supervisory time to coordinate and manage, more office space, and somewhat greater benefits costs (though these can be contained with flexible benefits plans, prorated benefits, and, in two-paycheck families, elimination of duplicate benefits). But the advantages of reduced turnover and the greater productivity that results from higher energy levels and greater focus can outweigh the costs.

A few hints:

• Provide flexibility selectively. I'm not suggesting private arrangements subject to the suspicion of favoritism but rather a policy that makes flexible work schedules available only to high performers.

• Make it clear that in most instances (but not all) the rates of advancement and pay will be appropriately lower for those who take time off or who work part-time than for those who work full-time. Most career-and-family women are entirely willing to make that trade-off.

• Discuss costs as well as benefits. Be willing to risk accusations of bias. Insist, for example, that half time is half of whatever time it takes to do the job, not merely half of 35 or 40 hours. . . .

FAMILY SUPPORTS—IN ADDITION TO MATERNITY leave and flexibility—include the provision of parental leave for men, support for two-career and single-parent families during relocation, and flexible benefits. But the primary ingredient is child care. The capacity of working mothers to function effectively and without interruption depends on the availability of good, affordable child care. Now that women make up almost half the work force and the growing percentage of managers, the decision to become involved in the personal lives of employees is no longer a philosophical question but a practical one. To make matters worse, the quality of child care has almost no relation to technology, inventiveness, or profitability but is more or less a pure function of the quality of child

care personnel and the ratio of adults to children. These costs are irreducible. Only by joining hands with government and the public sector can corporations hope to create the vast quantity and variety of child care that their employees need.

Until quite recently, the response of corporations to women has been largely symbolic and cosmetic, motivated in large part by the will to avoid litigation and legal penalties. In some cases, companies were also moved by a genuine sense of fairness and a vague discomfort and frustration at the absence of women above the middle of the corporate pyramid. The actions they took were mostly quick, easy, and highly visible—child care information services, a three-month parental leave available to men as well as women, a woman appointed to the board of directors. . . .

Now that interest is replacing indifference, there are four steps every company can take to examine its own experience with women:

1. Gather quantitative data on the company's experience with management-level women regarding turnover rates, occurrence of and return from maternity leave, and organizational level attained in relation to tenure and performance.

2. Correlate this data with factors such as age, marital status, and presence and age of children, and attempt to identify and analyze why women respond the way they do.

3. Gather qualitative data on the experience of women in your company and on how women are perceived by both sexes.

4. Conduct a cost-benefit analysis of the return on your investment in high-performing women. Factor in the cost to the company of women's negative reactions to negative experience, as well as

the probable cost of corrective measures and policies. If women's value to your company is greater than the cost to recruit, train, and develop them—and of course I believe it will be—then you will want to do everything you can to retain them.

WE HAVE COME A TREMENDOUS DISTANCE since the days when the prevailing male wisdom saw women as lacking the kind of intelligence that would allow them to succeed in business. For decades, even women themselves have harbored an unspoken belief that they couldn't make it because they couldn't be just like men, and nothing else would do. But now that women have shown themselves the equal of men in every area of organizational activity, now that they have demonstrated they can be stars in every field of endeavor, now we can all venture to examine the fact that women and men are different.

NO
Barbara Ehrenreich and Deirdre English

BLOWING THE WHISTLE ON THE "MOMMY TRACK"

When a feminist has something bad to say about women, the media listen. Three years ago it was Sylvia Hewlett, announcing in her book *A Lesser Life* that feminism had sold women out by neglecting to win child-care and maternity leaves. This year it's Felice Schwartz, the New York–based consultant who argues that women—or at least the mothers among us—have become a corporate liability. They cost too much to employ, she argues, and the solution is to put them on a special lower-paid, low-pressure career track—the now-notorious "mommy track."

The "mommy track" story rated prominent coverage in the New York *Times* and *USA Today*, a cover story in *Business Week*, and airtime on dozens of talk shows. Schwartz, after all, seemed perfectly legitimate. She is the president of Catalyst, an organization that has been advising corporations on women's careers since 1962. She had published her controversial claims in no less a spot than the *Harvard Business Review* ("Management Women and the New Facts of Life," January-February 1989). And her intentions, as she put it in a later op-ed piece, seemed thoroughly benign: "to urge employers to create policies that help mothers balance career and family responsibilities."

Moreover, Schwartz's argument seemed to confirm what everybody already knew. Women haven't been climbing up the corporate ladder as fast as might once have been expected, and women with children are still, on average, groping around the bottom rungs. Only about 40 percent of top female executives have children, compared to 95 percent of their male peers. There have been dozens of articles about female dropouts: women who slink off the fast track, at age 30-something, to bear a strategically timed baby or two. In fact, the "mommy track"—meaning a lower-pressure, flexible, or part-time approach to work—was neither a term Schwartz used nor her invention. It was already, in an anecdotal sort of way, a well-worn issue.

Most of the controversy focused on Schwartz's wildly anachronistic "solution." Corporate employers, she advised, should distinguish between two

From Barbara Ehrenreich and Deirdre English, "Blowing the Whistle on the 'Mommy Track,' " *Ms.*, vol. 18, no. 1 & 2 (July/August 1989). Copyright © 1989 by *Ms.* magazine. Reprinted by permission.

categories of women: "career-primary" women, who won't interrupt their careers for children and hence belong on the fast track with the men, and "career-and-family" women, who should be shunted directly to the mommy track. Schwartz had no answers for the obvious questions: how is the employer supposed to sort the potential "breeders" from the strivers? Would such distinction even be legal? What about *fathers*? But in a sense, the damage had already been done. A respected feminist, writing in a respected journal, had made a case that most women can't pull their weight in the corporate world, and should be paid accordingly.

Few people, though, actually read Schwartz's article. The first surprise is that it contains *no* evidence to support her principal claim, that "the cost of employing women in management is greater than the cost of employing men." Schwartz offers no data, no documentation at all—except for two unpublished studies by two *anonymous* corporations. Do these studies really support her claim? Were they methodologically sound? Do they even exist? There is no way to know.

Few media reports of the "mommy track" article bothered to mention the peculiar nature of Schwartz's "evidence." We, however, were moved to call the *Harvard Business Review* and inquire whether the article was representative of its normal editorial standard. Timothy Blodgett, the executive editor, defended the article as "an expression of opinion and judgment." When we suggested that such potentially damaging "opinions" might need a bit of bolstering, he responded by defending Schwartz: "She speaks with a tone of authority. That comes through."

(The conversation went downhill from there, with Blodgett stating sarcastically, "I'm sure your article in *Ms.* will be *very* objective." Couldn't fall much lower than the *Harvard Business Review*, we assured him.)

Are managerial women more costly to employ than men? As far as we could determine—with the help of the Business and Professional Women's Foundation and Women's Equity Action League—there is no *published* data on this point. A 1987 government study did show female managerial employees spending less time with each employer than males (5 years compared to 6.8 years), but there is no way of knowing what causes this turnover or what costs it incurs. And despite pregnancy, and despite women's generally greater responsibility for child-raising, they use up on the average only 5.1 sick days per year, compared to 4.9 for men.

The second surprise, given Schwartz's feminist credentials, is that the article is riddled with ancient sexist assumptions—for example, about the possibility of a more androgynous approach to child-raising *and* work. She starts with the unobjectionable statement that "maternity is biological rather than cultural." The same thing, after all, could be said of paternity. But a moment later, we find her defining maternity as " . . . a continuum that begins with an awareness of the ticking of the biological clock, proceeds to the anticipation of motherhood, includes pregnancy, childbirth, physical recuperation, psychological adjustment, and continues on to nursing, bonding, and child-rearing."

Now, pregnancy, childbirth, and nursing do qualify as biological processes. But slipping child-rearing into the list, as if changing diapers and picking up socks were hormonally programmed activities, is an old masculinist trick. Child-raising is a *social* undertaking, which may involve nannies, aunts, grandparents, day-care workers, or, of course, *fathers*.

Equally strange for a "feminist" article is Schwartz's implicit assumption that employment, in the case of married women, is strictly optional, or at least that *mothers* don't need to be top-flight earners. The "career-and-family woman," she tells us, is "willing" and "satisfied" to forgo promotions and "stay at the middle level." What about the single mother, or the wife of a low-paid male? But Schwartz's out-of-date—and class-bound—assumption that every woman is supported by a male breadwinner fits in with her apparent nostalgia for the era of the feminine mystique. "Ironically," she writes, "although the feminist movement was an expression of women's quest for freedom from their home-based lives, *most women were remarkably free already* [emphasis added]."

But perhaps the oddest thing about the "mommy track" article—even as an "expression of opinion and judgment"—is that it is full of what we might charitably call ambivalence or, more bluntly, self-contradictions. Take the matter of the "glass ceiling," which symbolized all the barriers, both subtle and overt, that corporate women keep banging their heads against. At the outset, Schwartz dismisses the glass ceiling as a "misleading metaphor." Sexism, in short, is not the problem.

Nevertheless, within a few pages, she is describing the glass ceiling (not by that phrase, of course) like a veteran. "Male corporate culture," she tells us, sees both the career-primary and the career-and-family woman as "unacceptable." The woman with family responsibilities is likely to be seen as lacking commitment to the organization, while the woman who *is* fully committed to the organiza-tion is likely to be seen as "abrasive and unfeminine." She goes on to cite the corporate male's "confusion, competitive-ness," and his "stereotypical language and sexist . . . behavior," concluding that "with notable exceptions, men are still more comfortable with other men."

And we're supposed to blame *women* for their lack of progress in the corporate world?

Even on her premier point, that women are more costly to employ, Schwartz loops around and rebuts herself. Near the end of her article, she urges corporations to conduct their own studies of the costs of employing women—the two anonymous studies were apparently not definitive after all—and asserts confidently ("of course I believe") that the benefits will end up outweighing the costs. In a more recent New York *Times* article, she puts it even more baldly: "The costs of employ-ing women pale beside the payoffs."

Could it be that Felice Schwartz and the editors of the *Harvard Business Review* are ignorant of that most basic financial management concept, the cost-benefit analysis? If the "payoffs" outweigh the costs of employing women—runny noses and maternity leaves included—then the net cost may indeed be *lower* than the cost of employing men.

In sum, the notorious "mommy track" article is a tortured muddle of feminist perceptions and sexist assumptions, good intentions and dangerous sugges-tions—unsupported by any acceptable evidence at all. It should never have been taken seriously, not by the media and not by the nation's most prestigious aca-demic business publication. The fact that it was suggests that something serious *is* afoot: a backlash against America's high-status, better paid women, and poten-tially against all women workers.

We should have seen it coming. For the past 15 years upwardly mobile, managerial women have done everything possible to fit into an often hostile corporate world. They dressed up as non-threatening corporate clones. They put in 70-hour workweeks; and of course, they postponed childbearing. Thanks in part to their commitment to the work world, the birthrate dropped by 16 percent since 1970. But now many of these women are ready to start families. This should hardly be surprising; after all, 90 percent of American women do become mothers.

But while corporate women were busily making adjustments and concessions, the larger corporate world was not. The "fast track," with its macho camaraderie and toxic work load, remains the only track to success. As a result, success is indeed usually incompatible with motherhood—as well as with any engaged and active form of fatherhood. The corporate culture strongly discourages *men* from taking parental leave even if offered. And how many families can afford to have both earners on the mommy track?

Today there's an additional factor on the scene—the corporate women who *have* made it. Many of them are reliable advocates for the supports that working parents need. But you don't have to hang out with the skirted-suit crowd for long to discover that others of them are impatient with, and sometimes even actively resentful of, younger women who are trying to combine career and family. Recall that 60 percent of top female executives are themselves childless. Others are of the "if I did it, so can you" school of thought. Felice Schwartz may herself belong in this unsisterly category. In a telling anecdote in her original article, she describes her own problems with an executive employee seeking maternity leave, and the "somewhat awkward conversations" that ensued.

SOONER OR LATER, CORPORATIONS WILL have to yield to the pressure for paid parental leave, flextime, and child care, if only because they've become dependent on female talent. The danger is that employers—no doubt quoting Felice Schwartz for legitimization—will insist that the price for such options be reduced pay and withheld promotions, i.e., consignment to the mommy track. Such a policy would place a penalty on parenthood, and the ultimate victims—especially if the policy trickles down to the already low-paid female majority—will of course be children.

Bumping women—or just fertile women, or married women, or whomever—off the fast track may sound smart to cost-conscious CEOs, but eventually it is the corporate culture itself that needs to slow down to a human pace. No one, male or female, works at peak productivity for 70 hours a week, year after year, without sabbaticals or leaves. Think of it this way. If the price of success were exposure to a toxic chemical, would we argue that only women should be protected? Work loads that are incompatible with family life are themselves a kind of toxin—to men as well as women, and ultimately to businesses as well as families.

POSTSCRIPT

Would a "Mommy Track" Benefit Employed Women?

There is little question that corporations need to address the unique problems that employed mothers face in the workplace. Some women eagerly resume their career activities at the end of their maternity leaves; others feel less committed but must continue to work because of family financial responsibilities. Still other career women with children opt to take additional time off and prefer to work part-time for some months or years before returning to full-time employment.

Given that women do not always share the same needs, expectations, and motivations, what kinds of corporate policies should be implemented to help them successfully balance career and family roles? Schwartz believes that identifying "career- primary" women early in their careers and investing more heavily in their training as compared to "career-and-family" women is the best corporate response to this problem. Ehrenreich and English reply that policies that support stereotypical images and roles for women and relegate them to less powerful positions with lower pay and fewer company benefits early in their careers would not result in recruiting and retaining the most talented and productive women. They argue for acknowledging women's and men's changing roles in both family and work situations and challenge organizations to provide flexible options that better reflect the diversity of today's families.

In "A Mother's Dilemma," in the July–August 1989 issue of *Ms.* magazine, Kim Triedman discusses the middle-class mother who wants both a career and children. She describes the struggle of balancing these needs without much support from anyone. From her own experiences she writes, "Our fathers and mothers (who underwrote our higher education) remind us that 'our careers won't wait forever' and we 'didn't go to college for nothing.' Our employers give us explicit policy on maternity leave—and subtler shows of our bosses' displeasure. Our husbands let us know that the mortgage is due and our bank balances are dropping. And sadly, some of our career-oriented, childless female friends see us as total and unredeemable idiots."

Is a "mommy track" the answer? In what other ways might parents, friends, and employers be more supportive of career mothers? Some social commentators have suggested that corporations should also implement a "daddy track." At least having both a "mommy track" and a "daddy track" would make balancing financial responsibilities and childrearing a *parental* concern rather than solely a *woman's* concern. Are fathers at least partially responsible for the evolution of the "mommy track" idea? If fathers were more involved parents, would there be less need for a "mommy track"?

Would this issue be less controversial if more women were corporate heads? What workplace policies might alleviate the pressure for a "mommy track"? Does corporate America have any obligation to be more supportive of parents in the workplace? Will businesses that continue to ignore or postpone support for parents suffer?

SUGGESTED READINGS

E. Ehrlich, "The Mommy Track: Juggling Kids and Careers In Corporate America Takes a Controversial Turn," *Business Week* (March 20, 1989): 126–134.

J. Fierman, "Why Women Still Don't Hit the Top," *Fortune*, 122 (1990): 40–58.

E. Hopkins, "Who Is Felice Schwartz and Why Is She Saying Those Terrible Things About Us?" *Working Woman* (October 1990): 116–120, 148.

G. W. Loveman, "The Case of the Part-Time Partner," *Harvard Business Review*, 68 (1990): 12–29.

K. O'Neill and A. Tocco, "Are Child Care Assistance Programs a Crucial Investment?" *Financial Executive*, 6 (1990): 19–23.

C. R. Stoner and R. I. Hartman, "Family Responsibilities and Career Progress: The Good, the Bad, and the Ugly," *Business Horizons*, 33 (1990): 7–14.

ISSUE 12

Should the Government Establish Special Programs and Policies for Black Youths and Their Families?

YES: Ronald L. Taylor, from "Black Youth: The Endangered Generation," *Youth and Society* (September 1990)

NO: Jean M. Granger, from "African American Family Policy or National Family Policy: Are They Different?" *Urban League Review* (Summer/Winter 1989–1990)

ISSUE SUMMARY

YES: Sociology professor Ronald L. Taylor argues that black youths and their families are disproportionately affected by poverty, crime, and unemployment and should therefore be targeted for federal and state support.
NO: Jean M. Granger, a professor in the Department of Social Work at California State University, asserts that the needs of black families should not be separated and distinguished from the needs of all American families. Singling out black families would only perpetuate negative myths concerning the black family.

According to Z. Lois Bryant and Marilyn Coleman, in "The Black Family as Portrayed in Introductory Marriage and Family Textbooks," *Family Relations* (1988), when black families are written about or discussed, one of three perspectives is usually taken—cultural deviant, cultural equivalent, or cultural variant. The first two approaches are used more often than the latter. Sociologists using the cultural deviant perspective compare black families to white middle-class families, which they take as the norm, and discuss any differences from that norm as pathological or dysfunctional. Under the cultural equivalent perspective, black families are compared to white middle-class families; however, differences are discussed in terms of membership in a particular social class. This perspective does not focus on dysfunction or label black families as pathological, but it usually considers black families as being low-income and lower-class. Scholars using this perspective hold the view that social and economic discrimination is the primary cause of problems in black families. The least-used perspective, cultural variant, does not rely on comparing black families to white families but rather considers the black family within the context of its own social, economic, and political heritage.

Black families comprise about 12 percent of the total population in the United States. Although recently much attention has been focused on the black American family, most of that attention has been on how certain social problems, such as female-headed households, adolescent pregnancy, poverty and dependency on social programs, and youth gang violence, affect black families. The fact that over one-third of black families earn annual incomes of between $25,000 and $50,000 and that 40 percent are middle-class has received little, if any, attention. The point here is that black families do not make up a homogeneous group. Like other family groups, they are a diverse population that differs by income, education, and social status. Most black families are, however, united by a common historical and cultural heritage.

One of the main strengths common to black families is the way family members and friends come together to support one another during stressful times and family crises. Among the distinguishing features of the black family that differentiate it from other American families are that young children are present in most black households and that a growing percentage of black families are headed by single mothers. Reasons for these characteristics of black families vary, but most scholars agree that such patterns reflect the adaptation of black families to their particular life circumstances. Some suggest that these characteristics may also be a reflection of certain child-centered values.

In the following selections, Ronald L. Taylor discusses what he terms "the plight of black youths." Taylor argues that black youths and their families have suffered inordinate hardships over the last 20 years because society has ignored their needs. He considers black youths to be at an extreme disadvantage as compared to their white counterparts and feels that federal resources should be allocated to address the problems evidenced in the black community. Jean M. Granger agrees that the black family appears to be in trouble despite its strengths, but the solution is not to single out the black community for special programs that are inevitably weakly funded and short-lived. Special programs, according to Granger, would further stereotype the black family as dysfunctional. She maintains that the problems discussed by Taylor affect not only black families but many other American families as well. Consequently, a national family policy that would serve the needs of all American families should be adopted.

YES

Ronald L. Taylor

BLACK YOUTH: THE ENDANGERED GENERATION

After more than a decade of public neglect, the plight of Black youths, particularly poor youths concentrated in the inner cities of the nation's major metropolitan areas, has resurfaced as a topic of intense national interest and concern. In contrast to the 1960s when family disorganization, welfare dependency, poverty, and other social ills plaguing Black communities were attacked by a plethora of new legislation, social programs, and vastly expanded resources at the federal and state levels, the mid-1970s and early 1980s were marked by the rise of political conservatism, economic retrenchment, and growing public skepticism regarding government's role and effectiveness involving many of the nation's most pressing social problems. With the ascendancy of these trends, together with the emergence of a new scholarship emphasizing the more positive and adaptive features of behavior and social life in the urban ghettos, adverse social and economic conditions affecting an ever-increasing number of Black children and youth receded from public view. These ominous trends were further obscured by the growing reluctance among liberal social scientists to address such problems as teen pregnancy, crime, drug abuse, school failure, and unemployment in race-specific terms, in an effort, as Wilson (1984) notes, to protect themselves and their work from the charge of racism or "blaming the victim." In consequence, those social problems that affected Black youths disproportionately failed to receive the serious and systematic attention they clearly deserved.

As data from the 1980 census and other sources made clear, the level and quality of life among some segments of the Black youth population declined precipitously over the past two decades. Indeed, by almost any measure of socioeconomic well-being, Black youths fared considerably worse than their White counterparts since the mid-1960s. In 1987, almost half (45.1%) of all Black children under 18 lived in households with incomes below the poverty level, a rate higher than at any time since 1967 (Edelman, 1989). By contrast, in 1987, only 15% of White children lived in poverty. Thus Black children and

From Ronald L. Taylor, "Black Youth: The Endangered Generation," *Youth and Society*, vol. 22, no. 1 (September 1990). Copyright © 1990 by Sage Publications. Reprinted by permission.

youth are three times more likely than their White counterparts to live in poverty (U.S. Bureau of the Census, 1987). Moreover, according to a recent congressional report: "The average black child can expect to spend more than five years of his childhood in poverty, the average white child 10 months" (quoted in Norton, 1985, p. 44). The labor market position and employment prospects of Black youth also grew worse during the past two decades, reaching what some analysts describe as "catastrophic" proportions in the 1980s (Freeman & Holzer, 1986). In 1986, the ratio of jobless Black youths to White youths was 2.4:1, compared to a ratio of 1.86:1 in 1965 (Wetzel, 1987). Black youth unemployment is particularly severe in the inner cities where, by some estimates, the jobless rate approaches 60% (Larson, 1988). Such high rates of joblessness and poverty among black youths are identified as major contributing factors to dramatic increases in the level of crime and delinquency in Black communities in recent years (Duster, 1987; Freeman & Holzer, 1986; Wilson, 1984). Although Blacks constituted approximately 14% of all youths aged 15–19 in 1984, more than half of all arrests for violent crimes, and a quarter of all property crimes reported in that year, involved Black youths. In fact, the rate of delinquency and crime among Black youths increased from 19.6% in 1960 to 23.2% in 1985 (Federal Bureau of Investigation, 1986). The major victims of such crimes are Black females, adult Black males, and the youths themselves (Gibbs, 1988).

Although pregnancy and childbearing among unwed teenagers are not exclusively Black problems, they do affect Black youths disproportionately. Out-of-wedlock birthrates among Black teens actually declined (from 96.9 to 86.4 per 1,000 unmarried women, age 15–19 between 1970 and 1983) but increased among White teens (from 10.9 to 18.5 per 1,000) during this period (Children's Defense Fund, 1986). Despite declining birthrates, Black teenagers are more than three times more likely than White teens to have children out-of-wedlock (U.S. Department of Education, 1988). To a large extent, "the higher birthrate for Black teenagers can be accounted for by the earlier initiation of sexual intercourse (on average 2 years earlier than Whites); less use of contraception; less likelihood of abortion; and almost universal decision to keep and rear children who are born, rather than offering them for adoption" (National Research Council, 1989, p. 412). Whatever the cause, childbearing among unwed teenagers has become a problem of epidemic proportion in the Black community, where nearly 9 of 10 babies born to Black teens are out-of-wedlock (Children's Defense Fund, 1986).

To be sure, some of the problems plaguing Black youths are a function of changes in the age structure and other recent demographic trends in Black communities. Although the Black youth population has grown only moderately during the 1980s, the period 1960–1980 saw a dramatic increase in the percentage of Black youths in central cities. During the decade of the 1960s alone, Black youths, ages 16–19, increased by nearly 75% in central cities compared to a 14% increase among White youths in this age group (U.S. Department of Labor, 1972). By 1980, more than half (56%) of Blacks under 25 years of age were located in central cities, twice the percentage for Whites in these age groups (U.S. Bureau of the Census, 1982). It is likely, as J. Q. Wilson (1983) has argued, that such a dramatic increase in the size and concentration of Black youths in central cities had "an exponential effect on the rate of certain social problems" (p. 24). That is, abrupt and large increases in the number of Black youths created a critical mass in central cities that, in turn, triggered a self-sustaining chain reaction, resulting in "an explosive increase in the amount of crime, addiction, welfare dependency" (J. Q. Wilson, 1983, p. 24), and other social problems. Because their proportion in the total youth population is expected to rise over the next decade (to 15.2% in 1996, from 13.7% in 1980), Black youth are likely to continue to contribute disproportionately to such social problems as teen pregnancy, crime, unemployment, and poverty (Hill, 1989).

Yet changes in the age structure alone are not sufficient to account for the precipitous rise in social problems among Black youths in central cities. The major sources of their difficulties are rooted in fundamental changes in the structure of local economies and in the processes of social and economic marginalization or "hyperghettoization" that have occurred in the inner cities during the past two decades (Harris & Wilkins, 1988; Taylor, 1991; Wacquant & Wilson, 1989). Industrial decentralization, combined with structural shifts in city economies from centers of goods-producing or manufacturing activities to higher-order service-providing industries, has severely affected the employment opportunities of inner-city Blacks, especially the job prospects of poorly educated Black youths. More specifically, as Kasarda (1989) has noted, such structural changes have substantially reduced the number of unskilled and semiskilled jobs in those industries that have traditionally attracted and economically upgraded previous generations of urban Blacks: "Loss of these

employment opportunities, in turn, had devastating effects on black families, which further exacerbated the problems of the economically displaced" (p. 27). The results have been widespread joblessness, intractably high levels of urban poverty, and accelerating physical decay (Kasarda, 1985; W. J. Wilson, 1987).

Indeed, a substantial segment of urban Blacks is far more isolated and concentrated in extreme poverty areas within central cities today than two decades ago. The proportion of all poor Blacks residing in extreme-poverty areas (i.e., census tracts with a population of at least 40% or more), as Wacquant and Wilson (1989) have shown, grew substantially during the 1970s, so that by 1980, "fully 38 percent of all poor blacks in the 10 largest American cities lived in extreme-poverty tracts, contrasted with 22 percent a decade before, and with only 6 percent of poor non-Hispanic whites" (p. 10). The growing spatial and socioeconomic segregation of the Black urban poor has been accelerated by the exodus of working-class and middle-income Black families in record numbers from the inner cities to other neighborhoods in the metropolitan area and the suburbs (Nelson, 1979; Taylor, 1991; W. J. Wilson, 1987). These developments, in turn, have exacerbated the problems of Black youths by depriving them of those role models, social networks, and facilitative institutions that have heretofore been critical to success and mobility in the larger society.

Thus, in the face of a deteriorating local economy, disintegrating community institutions, socioeconomic segregation, and spatial concentration, a *subculture of disengagement* (Taylor, 1989) has apparently emerged among some segments of the Black youth population in the inner cities, as evidenced by the rise of teenage gangs and violent behavior (Hagedorn, 1988); the spread of drugs and alcohol abuse; high rates of homicide, suicide, and other self-destructive behaviors; and growing participation in crime and other illicit activities (Gibbs, 1988). Though this subculture has little in common with the so-called culture of poverty described by some scholars, it has its origins in the limited opportunities and widespread disarray in the institutional contexts experienced by Black youths. In such a context, poor Black youths are free to establish their own norms, to select their own means of survival in a hostile and dangerous environment (Ianni, 1989).

In sum, the problems of Black youths are qualitatively and quantitatively different from what they were two decades ago, when their social and economic circumstances were more tractable. Yet federal and state support for policies and programs designed to address these problems has been slow in coming and remains gravely insufficient given the magnitude of the problem. With initiative and support from major national civil and philanthropic organizations and the media, the plight of Black youths is once again in public view and may yet attract the federal resources it rightly deserves.

REFERENCES

Children's Defense Fund. (1986). *Welfare and teen pregnancy: What do we know? What do we do?* Washington, DC: Author.

Duster, T. (1987). Crime, youth unemployment, and the Black urban underclass. *Crime and Delinquency, 33,* 300–316.

Edelman, M. (1989). Black children in America. In J. Dewart (Ed.), *The state of Black America, 1989* (pp. 63–76). New York: National Urban League.

Federal Bureau of Investigation. (1986). Crime in the U.S., 1985. *Uniform Crime Reports.* Washington, DC: U.S. Government Printing Office.

Freeman, R. B., & Holzer, H. J. (Eds.). (1986). *The black youth employment crisis.* Chicago: University of Chicago Press.

Gibbs, J. T. (Ed.). (1988). *Young, Black, and male in America: An endangered species.* Dover, MA: Auburn House.

Hagedorn, J. M. (1988). *People and folks: Gangs, crime and the underclass in a Rustbelt city.* Chicago: Lake View Press.

Harris, F. R., & Wilkins, R. W. (Eds.). (1988). *Quiet riots: Race and poverty in the United States.* New York: Pantheon.

Hill, R. (1989). Critical issues for Black families by the year 2000. In J. Dewart (Ed.), *The state of Black America, 1989* (pp. 41–61). New York: National Urban League.

Ianni, F. A. J. (1989). *The search for structure: American youth today.* New York: Free Press.

Kasarda, J. D. (1985). Urban change and minority opportunities. In P. Peterson (Ed.). *The new urban reality* (pp. 33–67). Washington, DC: Brookings Institution.

Kasarda, J. D. (1989). Urban industrial transition and the underclass. *Annals of the American Academy of Political and Social Science, 501,* 26–47.

Larson, T. E. (1988). Employment and unemployment of young Black males. In J. T. Gibbs (Ed.), *Young, Black, and male in America* (pp. 97–128). Dover, MA: Auburn House.

National Research Council. (1989). *A common destiny: Blacks and American society.* Washington, DC: National Academy Press.

Nelson, K. P. (1979). *Recent suburbanization of Blacks: How much, who, and where.* Washington, DC: U.S. Government Printing Office.

Norton, E. H. (1985, June 2). Restoring the traditional Black family. *New York Times Magazine,* p. 43.

Taylor, R. L. (1989). African-American inner city youth and the subculture of disengagement. *Urban League Review, 12,* 15–24.

Taylor, R. L. (1991). Improving the plight of Black inner-city youths: Whose responsibility. In F. W. Smith & J. Swift (Eds.), *Dream and reality: The modern Black struggle for freedom and equality.* Westport, CT: Greenwood.

U.S. Bureau of the Census. (1982). *Characteristics of American children and youth.* Washington, DC: U.S. Government Printing Office.

U.S. Bureau of the Census. (1987). *Current population reports* (Series P-60, No. 161). Washington, DC: U.S. Government Printing Office.

U.S. Department of Education. (1988). *Youth indicators: 1988.* Washington, DC: U.S. Government Printing Office.

U.S. Department of Labor. (1972). *Employment and training report of the president.* Washington, DC: U.S. Government Printing Office.

Wacquant, L. J., & Wilson, W. J. (1989). The cost of racial and class exclusion in the inner city. *Annals of the American Academy of Political and Social Science, 501*, 8–25.

Wetzel, J. R. (1987). *American youth: A statistical snapshot.* New York: W. T. Grant Foundation.

Wilson, J. Q. (1983). *Thinking about crime.* New York: Vintage.

Wilson, W. J. (1984). The urban underclass. In L. W. Dunbar (Ed.), *Minority report* (pp. 75–117). New York: Pantheon.

Wilson, W. J. (1987). *The truly disadvantaged: The inner city, the underclass and public policy.* Chicago: University of Chicago Press.

NO

Jean M. Granger

AFRICAN AMERICAN FAMILY POLICY OR NATIONAL FAMILY POLICY: ARE THEY DIFFERENT?

The African American family appears to be in trouble, but it remains a strong institution providing nurturance and maintenance for family members. Several centuries of perpetuation of negative myths concerning African Americans and their families have served to provide the rest of American society with a rationale for oppression of and discrimination against African Americans. Oppression and lack of opportunity have contributed to African American poverty and family breakdown. African American and white professionals and publications frequently refer to statistics concerning the increasing rate of African American adolescent pregnancies, suicide and homicide, unemployment, family problems, and children being raised in poverty. Clearly it is important for us to continue to seek solutions for these problems.

Justifiably, there is also tremendous concern for the number of African American children who have lost, or who are at risk of losing, their families because of poverty and other societal ills impacting upon families. This situation has been exacerbated by racism, or at the least, by a lack of recognition, understanding, and acceptance of cultural differences and a variety of types of family structures, both in society generally and, more specifically, by agency workers in child welfare, family services, and public assistance. We must continue to confront these issues and concentrate on maintaining and reuniting children with their families, wherever possible.

But we are faced with unfortunate complications. Extensive evidence exists concerning these problems, with documentation of societal contributions to the causation and perpetuation of the problems. Solutions have been suggested and many have been tested and found to work. Careful analysis of publications about these issues demonstrates that most of the researchers, authors, and other persons involved are African American. Special conferences are arranged, and primary attendance is by African Americans.

Federal and other funding is made available sporadically for projects, but invariably, such funding is insufficient and/or does not continue long enough. Similar issues exist with other ethnic-minority groups. However, other members of society use statistics in their publications in a way that increases negative attitudes toward African Americans. The result is national, state, and local recommendations and actions that are basically punitive and hostile to African Americans, other ethnic minorities, and poor persons.

Rarely is it indicated that, in spite of all of the societal obstacles, the largest percentage of African American families—whether low, middle, or upper income, whether single-parent, nuclear, or extended in structure—continue to function and furnish productive members of this society. Moreover, when suggestions are made for an African American family policy, too often the idea that certain services should be made available to all African Americans (as needed) due to societal conditions is ignored in favor of focusing on assisting African American families who have already developed problems.

Is it possible that singling out African American family problems and suggesting an African American family policy are counterproductive? By emphasizing our concerns over the problems noted above, are we adding our voices to forces in the larger society that use the available information to suggest that African American families are increasingly "pathological," and that provision of services is a "waste" of funds? Is the information we are furnishing achieving the purpose of making the rest of society empathetic toward the African American experience? Or are we providing more ammunition to those controlling societal forces that

shape policies and practices that are destructive to African Americans (and other ethnic minorities and families)? Do we need to develop a larger perspective in working for societal change, by reminding others that many of these problems are shared by all American groups, while at the same time not losing our concern for African American families and those matters of particular importance to us?

This article addresses these issues and suggests some other avenues of approach. With the end of the Reagan era, renewed interests in family policy could produce support for ways to resolve some of the dilemmas faced by African American families.

FAMILY POLICY ISSUES

In our concern about African American families, we have tended to lose sight of a major point: the growing problems and concerns listed in the preceding section do not apply only to African American families. Disproportionately more African American families, considering our overall population numbers, are involved because of poverty, oppression, and discrimination. However, these problems are part of a national malaise affecting American families. It is more appropriate to say that the American family is still strong, but in trouble. Programs for African American families will be affected by societal attitudes toward American families, in general, as well as by the attitudes toward African Americans, in particular.

Highly industrialized, complex societies increasingly have acknowledged that all governmental (and private) policies impact on families, frequently in negative ways. Therefore, decisions have been made that nationally mandated family policies and programs are necessary to fortify and sustain families as well as to prevent problems that can lead to family breakdown.

The United States remains one of the few industrialized countries that does not have a national family policy. Many recommendations were made between the late 1960s and early 1980s for an American national family policy that would contain specific goals for strengthening families and for implementing policies and programs to achieve these goals. A national family policy could consist of multiple goals, policies, and programs in all major areas affecting the daily lives of families (for example, child care, personal social services, guaranteed family income, housing, health, education, reformation of social security, employment). Or a national family policy could address one of these areas as a major family priority and focus on policies and programs to achieve the stated goals of that priority.

One of the major reasons that the United States has not implemented a national family policy, in spite of recommendations in this regard, is our country's historical bias against governmental involvement in the personal welfare of citizens. This bias has resulted in a lack of cohesive national policies and programs for families and residual, poorly planned, and inadequately funded services at the local, state, and federal levels.

Another reason for the lack of national family policy is the fragmented, residual nature of social policy in this country, which exists because of three major considerations that take precedence in any social policy decisions and actions. These are the desires of powerful interest groups that represent their members' attitudes and beliefs; economic factors; and the prevention of major alteration of the societal structure. Thus, despite demographic data, research outcomes, and social realities that indicate great family need, social and political forces, serving the perspectives of special-interest groups, conspire against an effective family policy.

The situation is further complicated by attitudes about family structures, the needs of American families, and the role of government with regard to families that often divide along the liberal-conservative continuum. Conservatives' proposals are focused on returning families to the "traditional nuclear family" and reducing the role of government in families. Liberals' proposals accept the plurality of family forms and recommend federally mandated, cohesive family policy and preventive programs that anticipate family needs.

Biases, attitudes, and special interests are also impacted by the actual outcomes of empirical data, and affect the interpretations of those outcomes, concerning programs with the potential for becoming part of a national family policy. Because of the abundance of studies and information in these areas, only three examples will be given.

Provision of child care is affected by beliefs that maternal employment outside the home is "bad for children" or partially responsible for the breakdown of family life. Consequently, with the increase of (white) maternal employment, much research attention has focused on its effects and/or the effects of child care by paid providers outside the home on the social and emotional development of children. But analysis of this research finds conflicting outcomes: maternal employment has positive and negative effects upon children; and child care contributes to positive and negative social growth and development in children.

In the guaranteed-minimum-income experiments, negative results were reported that contributed to the decisions not to reform the public welfare system to a national policy of guaranteed incomes for families. It was reported that guaranteed incomes led to decreased work on the part of family members and increased rates of marital breakups. What was not publicized was that when work decreased it was among young wives and adolescents, who concentrated on increasing their parenting and coping skills and pursuing additional education to increase employment skills. Breakups of marriages were lower where income supports were higher, serving to support the many studies reporting relationships between family stability and income or employment stability.

The study indicating that Headstart and other preschool programs for children from disadvantaged backgrounds had no lasting results was much publicized and used as one of the reasons to cut back such programs. However, other studies, some of which were longitudinal in nature, found that compared to control groups, Headstart children scored higher on achievement tests and had higher rates of high school and college completion and employment.

Clearly, any national family policy proposals are likely to be affected by controversies such as those surrounding the three areas of child care, education, and a guaranteed family income. It is important to note that the latter two examples—that is, studies concerning guaranteed income and preschool programs—contained numbers of ethnic-minority participants. Moreover, previous federally mandated child care plans that did not come to fruition were perceived as furnishing assistance to large numbers of ethnic-minority children. The current child care policies under discussion are, in large part, the results of pressures from a number of white interest groups. It is possible that the more positive societal responses are related to perceptions that whites, as well as other racial groups, will benefit.

Given the complexity of the issues involved in any area of potential family policy, policymakers, family policy and child welfare experts, and members of the public have strong attitudes about governmental family policy. Since these attitudes will significantly shape the nature of family policy in the years to come, it is important to know what evidence exists concerning attitudes toward governmental provision of family programs.

ATTITUDES TOWARD FAMILY POLICY

In spite of the importance of attitudes, little empirical evidence exists concerning the attitudes among comparative societal groups toward an explicit governmental family policy. Two studies concerning attitudes toward family policy have been identified.

Zimmerman, Matessich, and Leik surveyed Minnesota state legislators about their attitudes toward family policy. These legislators were generally favorable toward the idea of family policy, but viewed such policy as helping families with problems (for example, child abuse). Of 12 goals for family policy, they ranked assisting families with young children as 12th in appropriateness, and helping all families as 11th. They felt that government should confine itself to helping families, financially and otherwise, only when absolutely necessary. Legislators' age, education, income, family experience, marital status, and political party affiliation significantly influenced their attitudes toward family policy. For example, Republicans were less likely than Democrats to perceive helping all families as an appropriate goal of family policy, and were more likely to restrict government help only to families with problems.

Granger compared attitudes among national family policy experts, California career professionals in family services, and members of the general public (other citizens) toward three suggested components of a national family policy. These components were supportive services for families: a guaranteed minimum income, personal social services, and child care. Respondents were asked if they supported universal provision of these services for all families, as needed. Although favorableness toward these measures generally was exhibited in the expected rank order of experts, career professionals, and other citizens, all three groups were found to be favorable toward the universal provision of personal social services and, even more so, of child care (for working parents and parents having difficulty coping) as preventive and interventive measures for family problems. They were also favorable toward tax credits and tax changes as methods for guaranteeing that families would have an income no less than the governmental poverty level.

Responses were affected by the possibility of tax increases to implement the programs and the respondents' degree of liberalism-conservatism and educational levels. When income taxes were required to implement these programs, experts remained favorable, career professionals became uncertain, and members of the general public became slightly unfavorable toward these programs. Liberals and persons with higher educational levels were more favorable toward the measures than were conservatives and persons with lower educational levels, regardless of whether implementation required increases in personal income taxes. These outcomes were similar to those found in the survey by Zimmerman, Mattesich, and Leik and other surveys concerning social welfare expenditures discussed below.

In the Granger study, even though support for social services decreased when income tax increases were required to fund programs, the fact that members of the public became only slightly unfavorable was encouraging. The majority (86%) of the respondents were white and had older children. (Demographic data for white and ethnic-minority respondents were very similar.) Thirty-six percent of the other citizens and 56 percent of the career professionals lived in a very fiscally and politically conservative county, and 100 percent of the career professionals worked in such a county. Moreover, both of the counties primarily involved have large and growing ethnic-minority populations.

There is significantly more empirical evidence available, including the results of national public opinion surveys, on attitudes toward present social welfare expenditures. These attitudes could also be expected to impact upon the development of a national family policy. They have impacted upon services for members of ethnic minorities and poor persons for many years.

Studies of the public's attitudes toward social and public welfare expenditures indicate ambivalence and inconsistency in these attitudes. American citizens support, in varying degrees, social welfare programs, but tend to be more favorable toward programs such as Social Security and health care programs for the elderly and disabled than they are toward programs viewed as serving "less deserving" groups (for example, single parents or ethnic minorities). Many respondents were found to believe, erroneously, that most poor persons and public assistance recipients were members of ethnic-minority groups.

Americans also have been found, generally, to be positive toward social welfare programs, but reluctant to fund them if they require additional personal income taxes. Persons with higher educational levels have been more likely than have others to have positive attitudes about funding social welfare services.

Liberalism or conservatism has also affected attitudes toward the provision of social welfare programs. Liberal respondents (usually Democrats) have been more likely to be favorable toward social welfare expenditures; conservative respondents (usually Republicans) have been more likely to be unfavorable toward such expenditures.

IMPLICATIONS FOR AFRICAN AMERICAN FAMILIES AND NATIONAL FAMILY POLICY

. . . In spite of ambivalent attitudes toward governmental assistance to families, tremendous pressures have increasingly been brought to bear upon the larger society, by white Americans, to furnish supportive and fortifying services for families.

The outcomes of studies of attitudes suggest two opposite but related attitudes. First, if Americans believe that policy and programs will benefit only certain types of families (for example, ethnic-minority families), they will be less willing, or unwilling, to fund or pursue such programs. Second, if they are convinced that policies and programs furnish benefits for all families, as needed, American citizens will be more likely to support such programs. . . .

It would seem, then, that, as African Americans, our public focus should be directed toward the needs and problems of all American families, not just African American families. A national family policy would be primarily preventive (rather than residual), and holistic (focusing on the entire family constellation). Family policy, properly implemented, would take into account differences in culture and family structures. . . . [E]mphasizing the needs of ethnic minorities makes it more likely that such issues will be ignored or will result in punitive measures and cutbacks in services, such as those carried out during the Reagan years. A national family policy that addresses one or several of the areas of recommendation (for example, child care, personal social services, guaranteed family income, housing, health, education, reformation of social security, and employment) for all families, as needed, will automatically benefit African American families. Our concentration could then be directed toward the types of policies needing development and the manner in which these policies are implemented so that the impact upon African American families is appropriate and positive.

Perhaps we also must form coalitions with other ethnic-minority groups and white women. For example, the most recent national focus and funding for research and discussion have been upon working families, child care, and the impact of both upon families and children.

Although these issues have been important to African Americans for decades, it is only since the majority of white mothers have entered the workforce and the numbers of white single parents have grown that these concerns have become a matter for public pressure. For the first time, white researchers are acknowledging that, not only is systematic research lacking in these areas, but African American families have coped, usually successfully, with work and child care for years, and should be studied for their coping skills. These issues might be a good starting point for coalitions and family policy proposals, particularly those concerning child care and full employment. The child care proposals presently under discussion in the 101st Congress represent only a beginning attempt to address child care needs. . . .

Ultimately, the implementation of a comprehensive national family policy would address many of the needs and problems of African American families. More specifically, a national family policy would permit African American social workers, researchers, and other interested persons to focus their efforts and funding on problems in the African American community that remained insufficiently resolved by the national family policy.

POSTSCRIPT

Should the Government Establish Special Programs and Policies for Black Youths and Their Families?

Even though there is a general belief in the United States that the government should stay out of the personal and family matters of its citizens, public support is growing for the provision of needed services to families. Granger points out that Americans are less willing to approve funding for policies and programs that only benefit certain segments of the population, such as black families. She maintains that publishing the facts and forcing people to face the realities of how black families are disadvantaged in America only serves to increase negative attitudes and stereotypical thinking about such families. In the past this strategy has resulted in punitive measures and cutbacks in existing programs. Granger advocates focusing on *all* American families in need of support services and adopting a national family policy, a strategy she believes would be more likely to succeed.

Taylor, on the other hand, wants all Americans to know of the current plight of black youths and their families. He believes that publicizing the adverse living conditions of black families, especially in America's central cities and urban areas, would increase support for needed policies and programs targeted to these families. According to Taylor, media attention to the enormous problems in black communities increases the likelihood of attracting state and federal resources.

In August 1991, the *Washington Post* and *Los Angeles Times* both ran stories titled "Black Americans' Gains Dividing Them," based on a newly released research report published by the Population Reference Bureau. This report describes the widening gap between affluent middle-class black Americans and low-income black Americans (about one-third of blacks live in poverty). In the report, the black population is portrayed as no longer being represented by a unified sense of racial solidarity. Black Americans are instead described as increasingly divided in their ideology along class lines—middle versus lower.

If this trend is stable, then Granger's argument gathers strength, because even among blacks there is no longer one unified voice addressing common critical needs. Needs have become more diverse because black life experiences have become more diverse. But Taylor's concerns also continue to seem relevant. If, as the report concludes, one-third of blacks live in poverty and have made little economic progress since the 1960s, then this information needs to be brought to the attention of all Americans in a dramatic way if the situation is to improve for this segment of the black population, according to Taylor.

Is there is a position of compromise between what Granger and Taylor suggest? Can these authors' approaches be brought together? Does the same argument raised by Granger and Taylor apply to other racial or ethnic groups? If government policies are implemented, should programs take the form of economic help, educational directives, social aid, or some other form? What kinds of support would be most beneficial to poor black families? To black communities?

SUGGESTED READINGS

L. Bennett, "The 10 Biggest Myths About the Black Family," *Ebony*, 46 (1990): 166–171.

J. Dewart, ed., *The State of Black America, 1989* (National Urban League, 1989).

J. T. Gibbs, ed., *Young, Black, and Male in America: An Endangered Species* (Auburn House, 1988).

S. S. Gray and L. M. Nybell, "Issues in African-American Family Preservation," *Child Welfare* (November/December 1990): 513–524.

K. S. Jewell, *Survival of the Black Family* (Praeger, 1978).

H. P. McAdoo, *Black Families* (Sage Publications, 1988).

National Research Council, *A Common Destiny: Blacks and American Equality* (National Academy Press, 1989).

P. Schroeder, "Toward a National Family Policy," *American Psychologist*, 44 (1989): 1410–1413.

F. S. Smith and J. Smith, eds., *Dream and Reality: The Modern Black Struggle for Freedom and Equality* (Greenwood, 1991).

ISSUE 13

Husband Battering: Is It a Social Problem?

YES: Suzanne K. Steinmetz and Joseph A. Lucca, from "Husband Battering," in Vincent B. Van Hasselt et al., eds., *Handbook of Family Violence* (Plenum, 1988)

NO: R. Emerson Dobash and Russell P. Dobash, from "Research as Social Action: The Struggle for Battered Women," in Kersti Yllö and Michele Bograd, eds., *Feminist Perspectives on Wife Abuse* (Sage Publications, 1988)

ISSUE SUMMARY

YES: Professor of sociology Suzanne K. Steinmetz and professor of physical therapy Joseph A. Lucca contend that the detrimental consequences of husband battering are real but are being ignored because wives' violence against husbands is not considered a serious social problem.
NO: R. Emerson Dobash and Russell P. Dobash, professors at the University of Stirling in Scotland, argue that husband battering is not a real social problem because women do not typically evidence patterns of severe, persistent, and intimidating violence against their husbands. They assert that the rare acts of violence women do direct toward their husbands are almost exclusively in self-defense.

When a woman fights back during marital violence that is initiated by her husband, should it be considered husband battering, mutual battering, or self-defense? Though we know a lot about the statistics of marital violence—when and where it usually happens, the approximate number of marriages affected, and the cyclical nature of its occurrence—we know much less about the context within which couples use violence and the motives behind it.

Some researchers, family life educators, and counselors strongly believe that husband battering should not even be acknowledged as a problem. They cite studies to show that men are responsible for an overwhelming majority of marital violence and that violence by men is more likely to result in serious physical damage than violence by women. Men more often repeat violent acts and use objects and weapons during abusive episodes. Women, because they often have young children and are likely to be economically dependent on their abusive husbands, are less able to leave violent marital situations. Women, in contrast to men, are more often seriously injured during marital violence, and they more frequently seek medical help after being battered. Men are usually referred to legal and psychological counseling services following violent episodes. Battered women, on the other hand, generally need shelter, clothing, and job counseling, as well as financial, legal, and psychological counseling.

Only rarely do women report that they initiate violence in their marital relationships, and men are equally reluctant to admit that their wives physically abuse them. Women and men both admit that women sometimes fight back during episodes of marital violence. Some researchers label such reciprocal aggression as "mutual combat," while others strongly object to this terminology, arguing that the motive is self-defense rather than any kind of "blow-for-blow" fighting. Available research shows that, when women fight back to protect themselves, men typically escalate the violence, making matters worse.

Many people believe that women often kill their violent mates, but that is not true. On the rare occasion that a woman *does* kill her abusive marital partner, however, the reasons center around the husband's behavior. Husbands who are murdered are generally among the most frequent and severely abusive of men. Incidents of forced sexual intercourse, threats to kill the wife or the children, and untreated alcoholism are usually present in marriages where wives, after years of abuse, do resort to homicide.

Since husband battering is rare and usually occurs in instances where wives are trying to protect themselves, and since it does not typically lead to severe injury, can it be considered a serious social problem? Suzanne K. Steinmetz and Joseph A. Lucca believe that because such violence can have physical and psychological consequences for the victims, because it can lead to regular and more severe violence over time, because it can be used as a reason for the husband to retaliate, and because it can profoundly affect the children who witness it, husband battering should be categorized as a social problem. They reason that any violence between spouses, regardless of who initiates it, should never be considered inconsequential. Accepting some types of violence as "right" and other types of violence as "wrong" supports the negative cultural stereotype that violence is sometimes an acceptable way to resolve conflict or to gain control of a person or a situation.

R. Emerson Dobash and Russell P. Dobash maintain that husband battering does not exist as a serious social problem that requires public policy or social action. They assert that its existence is based on faulty research methodology and that promoting its worth as a social concern diminishes the significance of the real needs of battered women. Because so-called husband battering mostly consists of comparatively less extreme forms of violence, which almost always occur in instances where a wife tries to protect herself from a husband's initial violence, research directed at understanding marital aggression must necessarily focus on men's battering of women. According to the Dobashes, the needs of battered wives and their children are much more critical than are those of husbands.

YES

Suzanne K. Steinmetz and
Joseph A. Lucca

HUSBAND BATTERING

Research on victimization resulting from discrimination has focused on racial minorities (e.g., Blacks, Hispanics, and Indians) and on women. Thus, it is not surprising that research on spouse violence has tended to focus almost exclusively on wife abuse. Although studies of infanticide (Radbill, 1968) and homicide (Wolfgang, 1958) clearly indicate that women have the potential to be violent, their use of physical violence on their husbands has carefully been avoided.

Unfortunately, to ignore the phenomena of the battered husband not only denies the existence of this type of violence, but assumes that the consequences in terms of the physical injury to the victim and the psychological damage to both the victim and the children that witness these attacks are inconsequential. Considerable data on the power of social modeling and social learning suggest that his behavior will have profound effects on the children. . . .

IGNORING THE BATTERED HUSBAND PHENOMENON

Abuse of men, as a topic of investigation, has received very little attention. There are two possible reasons for this. Men will go to great lengths to avoid reporting that they are abused, because such an admission would stigmatize them in the eyes of others. As a result, men tend to report only the most extreme abuse, and would not dream of reporting lesser abuse—such as slapping or kicking—which women routinely report. In other words, a greater percentage of women are likely to report less severe injuries, and as a result, the highly visible evidence would suggest that women are abused more often than men, whereas this actually is not the case. A second factor is that men often have greater resources (money, credit, status, power) that allows them to utilize private sources of help and avoid reporting their victimization.

There also are a relative lack of empirical data on the topic. The selective inattention of the media and researchers, the greater severity of physical damage to women, which makes their victimization more visible, and the reluctance of men to acknowledge abuse at the hand of women, makes it more apparent why the battered husband has received so little attention.

The discussion of the husband-abuse data . . . suggests that husband beating constitutes a sizable proportion of marital violence. . . . 3% of the husbands in Levinger's study considered their wives' physically abusive treatment of them to be grounds for divorce. This percentage might have been larger had the following factors not been present.

First, Levinger's study, conducted before no-fault divorce, showed that women had nearly twice the number of total complaints as men. Therefore, unless one assumes that it is always the husband's fault when a marriage fails, it appears that women might be more comfortable voicing their complaints.

A second factor to be examined is the time frame during which Levinger's study was conducted. At that time, considerable fault had to be established in order for a divorce to be granted. The traditional role of a husband in a divorce action at that time was to take the blame for the failure. Thus, even if the husband desired the divorce, etiquette demanded that he allow his wife to initiate the action. During a conciliatory interview it is reasonable, then, to expect the husband to be less ready to expose his wife's faults. Some support is provided for this position by examining the types of complaints commonly made by husbands (i.e., sexual incompatibility and in-laws, both traditionally accepted male-oriented complaints).

Finally, the male in our society is under pressure to maintain a dominant position over a female (Balswick & Peek, 1971;

Steinmetz, 1974). The psychological stress of recognizing the wife's physical dominance makes it unlikely that many men would be willing to admit their physical weakness to a third party.

The stigma attached to this topic, which is embarrassing for beaten wives, is doubly so for beaten husbands. The patriarchal concept of the husband's right to chastise his wife with a whip or rattan no bigger than his thumb is embedded in ancient law and was upheld by a Mississippi court in 1824, "in case of great emergency and with salutary constraints" (Bradley v. State, Walker, 158, Miss., 182–184). This idea has provided some legal and social understanding for the woman who has suffered because her husband has gone beyond permissible bounds. Because there is no recognition of the woman's right to chastise her husband, there is little likelihood that society will recognize that the wife may go beyond that which is permissible.

As one respondent who had been terrorized by a knife-wielding spouse and has gone to work with deep fingernail gashes on his face related: "I never took the fights outside, I didn't want anyone to know. I told the guys at work that the kids did it with a toy."

This fear of stigma also affects the official statistics collected on husband-wife violence. Curtis (1974) reported that whereas violence by men against women was responsible for about 27% of the assaults and 17.5% of the homicides, violence by women against men accounted for 9% of the assaults and 16.4% of the homicides in his study. Thus, although women commit only about one third as many assaults against men as men commit against women, the number of cross-sex homicides committed by the two groups are nearly identical.

Wilt and Bannon (1976) warned that caution should be applied when interpreting the Curtis finding. They note that

nonfatal violence committed by women against men is less likely to be reported to the police than is violence by men against women; thus, women assaulters who come to the attention of the police are likely to be those who have produced a fatal result. (p. 20)

Also helping to camouflage the existence of husband beating is the terminology used to describe it. This can be illustrated by referring to Gelles's monograph *The Violent Home* (1974). An examination of the entries in the subject index shows that, although there is one page each devoted to "wife-to-husband" and "husband-to-wife" violence, seven pages under the heading "wife beating," two under "battered wife," yet no corresponding listing can be found for "husband beating." However, Gelles's data provide ample evidence that many wives do in fact beat their husbands. In addition to the data from Gelles's study, . . . many quotes from his respondents support this. For example, one respondent noted, "He would just yell and yell—not really yell, just talk loudly, and I couldn't say anything because he kept talking, so I'd swing" (Gelles, 1974, p. 80).

Even though Gelles reports that one respondent, a retired cook, was often verbally and physically attacked by his jealous wife, and quotes another as saying, "My wife is very violent. It's a miracle that I didn't go out because she really put a hell of a dent in my head," these are not labeled as husband beatings. Thus, although Gelles readily acknowledges that men are physically victimized by their wives, he does not provide a discussion of this phenomenon as a distinct parallel to wife beating. Because Gelles's study was the first study ever systematically to examine spouse abuse, and the term *wife-abuse* was fairly new, it is easy to understand his choice of terms. What is even more puzzling, however, is the denial of this phenomenon in Walker's (1984) book on wife battering.

This cyclical aspect of family violence is demonstrated by her study of over 400 battered women. She reported that 67% of the women were battered as children (41% by their mothers, 44% by their fathers); about 20% had brothers and sisters who were also battered; 44% of their fathers battered their mothers; and 29% of their mothers battered their fathers. Furthermore, 28% of these battered women reported that they battered their own children and 5% attributed this behavior to being angry at their husband.

She further reported that 15% of these battered women used violence against their spouse (either in retaliation or self-defense) when in a battering relationship, and five had continued this violent behavior after they left the first relationship and had entered into a nonbattering relationship. Her conclusion that these date "refute the 'mutual combat' or 'battered man' problem as being a large one" (1984, p. 150) is indeed puzzling.

Even if one were willing to assume that 5% of these new relationships characterized by husband battering were relatively inconsequential, the nondirect, next-generation effects noted by Walker (the 41% of children battered by their mothers, the 29% of mothers who battered the father, the 5% of women who batter the child because they are angry at the husband) surely must be considered significant. Given the data from nationally representative samples, these women may differ only in the degree of violence experienced and perpetrated from non-shelter-based samples.

These findings are especially disturbing in light of three factors, which popular culture has suggested should mitigate against women using violence against their husbands. First, as a result of their socialization, women are taught better impulse control—they stop aggressive behavior before any danger occurs. Second, women are more verbal than men, and therefore men resort more readily to physical means to support their dominant position. A third explanation focuses on the superior physical strength of men and their greater capability of causing more physical damage to their spouses than wives are capable of doing to their husbands.

In reality, the contention that women are socialized for greater impulse controls appears to have little support, at least as far as marital fights are concerned. . . . [I]nsights gained from the in-depth interviews suggest that women are as likely to select physical violence to resolve marital conflicts as are men.

Furthermore, child abusers are more likely to be women. Throughout history women have been the prime perpetrators of infanticide (Straus, Gelles, & Steinmetz, 1980). Although it is recognized that women spend more time with children and are usually the parent in a single-parent home (which makes them prone to stress and strains resulting in child abuse) and that fathers in similar situations might abuse their children more severely, some findings do indicate that women have the potential to commit acts of violence and that under certain circumstances they do carry out these acts.

Wolfgang (1958), in an investigation of homicides occurring between 1948 and 1952, found that spouses accounted for 18% of the incidents and that there were virtually no differences between the percentage of husbands or wives who were offenders. According to FBI statistics, 15% of the homicides in 1975 were between husband and wife. In 7% of the cases the husbands were victims, whereas in 8% of the cases the victims were wives (U.S. Bureau of the Census, *Vital Statistics Reports*, 1976). In 1984 there were about 1700 spousal homicides, 43% of the victims were husbands (*Uniform Crime Reports*, 1985).

The second point is also questionable. Although the myth of the verbally abusing, nagging woman is perpetuated in the media, mainly in comic form, the data do not support this myth. There appeared to be small random differences in the use of verbal violence in the families studied. Furthermore, Levinger (1976), in his study of divorce applicants, found that wives were three times more likely to complain of verbal abuse than their husbands.

It appears that the last reason is more plausible. The data reported suggest that at least the intention of men and women to use physical violence in marital conflicts is equal. Identical percentages of men and women reported hitting or hitting with an object. Furthermore, data on homicide between spouses suggest that an almost equal number of wives kill their husbands as husbands kill their wives (Wolfgang, 1958). Thus it appears that men and women might have equal potential for violent marital interaction; initiate similar acts of violence; and when differences of physical strength are equalized by weapons, commit similar amounts of spousal homicide.

The major difference appears to be the males' ability to do more physical damage during nonhomicidal marital physical fights. When the wife slaps her husband, her lack of physical strength plus his ability to restrain her reduce the physical damage to a minimum,. When the husband slaps his wife, however, his strength plus her inability to restrain him result in considerably more damage. . . .

WHY DO HUSBANDS STAY?

In answer to the question, "Why would a woman who has been physically abused by her husband remain with him?" Gelles (1974, p. 650) suggested that there are three major factors influencing wives' decision to leave. The less severe and the less frequent the violence, the more the wife experienced violence as a child, and the fewer the resources and power the wife has, the more likely she is to stay with [her] husband.

These three factors were also found to influence the husbands' decision to stay. Lower levels of violence were not likely to be considered a major concern. Only when the violence appeared to be affecting the children, rather than affecting the husband's physical safety, did the husband consider leaving. The background of violent wives is often characterized by violence and trauma. One violent wife, as a child, witnessed her own father force her mother, who was in the last stages of pregnancy, to walk home in deep snow carrying bags of groceries. The father drove behind his wife in a car bumping her with the car to keep her moving and beating her when she stopped or stumbled. Another wife felt responsible for her father's suicide, which occurred when she was 10. Still another wife as a teenager slept with weapons under her pillows and lived in constant fear of brutal beatings from her alcoholic father (Steinmetz, 1977–78).

The perceived availability of resources also affects the man's decision to leave. According to most studies (as well as popular knowledge), women remain because they feel that the children will be worse off if they leave. Not only does the wife often lack the economic resources to provide adequately for the children, but she feels that separating will have a more harmful effect on the children than would remaining with her abusive husband. It is always assumed that the husband's greater economic resources could allow him to leave more easily a disruptive marital situation. Not only do men tend to have jobs that provide them with an adequate income, but they have greater access to credit and are not tied to the home because of the children. This perspective rests on erroneous sexist assumptions.

Although males, as a group, have considerably more economic security, if the husband leaves the family, he is still responsible for a certain amount of economic support of the family in addition to the cost of a separate residence for himself. Thus, the loss in standard of living is certainly a consideration for any husband who is considering a separation. Furthermore, it is assumed that because wives are "tied to their homes," they would be the ones who would most likely regret it if they moved. Until recently, custody was almost always awarded to mothers, thus the mother remained in the family home while father sought a new residence. Interviews with abused men suggest that leaving the family means leaving many hours of home improvements, family rooms, dens, workshops, in other words the comfortable and familiar, that which is not likely to be reconstructed in a small apartment.

Probably the most erroneous assumption, however, is that the husband's decision to leave would not be influenced by concern over the children. Often the husband becomes the victim when he steps in to protect the children and becomes the target of abuse. Those men are afraid to leave for fear that further violence would be directed toward the children. Recognizing that men are not likely to receive custody of the children, even in times of increased recognition of their ability to care for them, men feel that by staying they are providing some protection for their children. These men also express the idea that keeping the family together at all costs is best for the children. Another man, who lived in fear for 2 years and did not know when his wife would attack him with knives and other objects, an almost daily occurrence, remained because as an orphan, he knew what it was like to be without a father. Also, he considered his wife to be attractive, personable, a good housekeeper and mother and, except for her violent attacks, a good wife. The wife, however, was insecure, dissatisfied with herself, had low self-esteem, and was uncomfortable with her low position as a secretary, and with a paycheck that was smaller than her husband's. She wanted a career and to be the economically dominant partner (Steinmetz, 1977–78).

Why, then do these husbands not protect themselves? Several reasons evolve. The first, based on chivalry, considers any man who would stoop to hit a woman to be a bully. The second, usually based on experience, is a recognition of the severe damage that a man could do to a woman. In fact, several men expressed the fear that if they ever lost control, they could easily kill their wives. One husband noted that he hit his wife only once, "in retaliation with hands and fist, and smacked her in the mouth. She went flying across the room." Because he realized how badly he could hurt his wife, he continued to take the physical abuse. He noted, with hindsight, that probably she continued her abuse because she knew she should get away with it.

A final reason expressed by the beaten men is perhaps a self-serving one. The combination of crying out in pain during the beating and having the wife see the injuries, which often take several weeks to heal, raises the wife's level of guilt, which the husbands consider to be a form of punishment (Steinmetz, 1977–78). . . .

SUMMARY

The critics of research on battered husbands have labeled women's violence against their husbands as "usually insignificant physical attacks" (Field & Kirchner, 1978). However, we contend that physical violence between spouses is never insignificant. Although an initial attack may be mild, it is often a precursor to more violent attacks, and may serve as a later justification for a husband's violence toward his wife.

In an earlier article, "The Battered Husband Syndrome," it was concluded:

> Although the data discussed do not represent, for the most part, a systematic investigation of representative samples of battered husbands, it is important to understand husband beating because of the implications for social policies to help resolve the more global problem of family violence. (Steinmetz, 1977–78, p. 507)

When the focus remains on the battered wife, the remedies often suggested revolve around support groups, crisis lines, and shelters for the woman and her child. This stance overlooks a basic condition of violence between spouses—a society that glorifies violence if done for the "right reasons," the good of society, or that of one's own family. It is critical to shift at least some of the blame from individual family members to basic sociocultural conditions so that more resources will become available to help families and a greater emphasis will be placed on changing the attitudes and values of society (Steinmetz, 1977–78).

Almost 10 years have passed since the first article on battered husbands appeared. Knowledge in this area has expanded and professionals in the field realize more than ever the importance of reducing all forms of domestic violence.

REFERENCES

Balswick, J. O., & C. Peek (1971). The inexpressive male: A tragedy of American society. *Family Coordinator, 20*(4), 363–368.

Curtis, L. A. (1974). *Criminal violence: National patterns and behavior.* Lexington, MA: Lexington Books.

Field, M., & Kirchner, R. M. (1978). Services to battered women. *Victimology, 3*(1-2), 216–222.

Gelles, R. J. (1974). *The violent home: A study of physical aggression between husbands and wives.* Beverly Hills, CA: Sage.

Levinger, C. (1976). Sources of marital dissatisfaction among applicants for divorce. *American Journal of Orthopsychiatry, 36*(5), 803–807.

Radbill, S. X. (1968). A history of child abuse and infanticide. In R. E. Helfer & C. H. Rempe (Eds.), *The battered child* (1st ed., pp. 3–21). Chicago, IL: University of Chicago Press.

Steinmetz, S. K. (1977a). *The cycle of violence: Assertive, aggressive and abusive family interaction.* New York, NY: Praeger Press.

Steinmetz, S. K. (1974). Male liberation—Destroying the stereotypes. In E. Powers & M. Lee (Eds.), *The Process of Relationships* (pp. 55–67). Minneapolis: West Publishing Co.

Steinmetz, S. K. (1977b). Secondary analysis of data from "The use of force for resolving family conflict. The training ground for abuse." *Family Coordinator,* Vol. 33(4), 19–26.

Straus, M. A., Gelles, R. J., & Steinmetz, S. K. (1980). *Behind closed doors: Violence in the American family.* New York, NY: Doubleday.

U.S. Bureau of the Census (1976). *Vital statistics reports: Annual summary for the United States.* Vol. 24, No. 13. Washington, DC: National Center for Health Statistics.

U.S. Department of Justice (1985). *F.B.I. uniform crime reports.* Washington, DC: U.S. Government Printing Office.

Walker, L. (1984). *The battered woman syndrome.* New York: Springer.

Wilt, G. M. & Bannon, J. D. (1976). *Violence and the police: Homicides, assaults and disturbances.* Washington, DC: The Police Foundation.

Wolfgang, M. (1958). *Patterns in criminal homicide.* New York, NY: Wiley.

NO

R. Emerson Dobash and
Russell P. Dobash

RESEARCH AS SOCIAL ACTION: THE STRUGGLE FOR BATTERED WOMEN

The question of the relationship between science and social action is relevant to every investigation undertaken, but it is particularly important when the phenomenon under study is a social problem. The facile response to the question is that there is no relationship between science and social action and that there should be none. We argue that a relationship between research, beliefs, values, and social action is inevitable; however, the nature of that relationship is not a straightforward one. When focused on a social problem, this relationship usually involves, at the very least, the evidence, ideas, explanations, and actions of social scientists as well as those of powerful institutions and struggling grass roots groups. They are intertwined in a dynamic and fluid process that will usually result in some form of development, that will, in turn, move either toward fundamental social change or to the maintenance of the status quo. While this is a general approach that may apply to any social issue from race relations to drug abuse, the present work has been particularly informed by critical and feminist perspectives.

In this chapter, we consider some of the specific issues and problems relating to the relationship between social science and social action as they have developed in the context of our research on violence against wives. . . .

WOMEN'S AID AND VIOLENCE AGAINST WOMEN

The social problem of wife abuse first came to the attention of the British public in 1972 after being "discovered" by a small group of women working to put the principles of the women's movement into practice. In 1971, this group set up a community meeting and advice center for women in a small derelict house in Chiswick, a London borough. The problem of assaults on women soon became apparent as women began talking about brutal and habitual attacks by their husbands or cohabitants. Although the house was meant to be used during office hours, the women obviously needed a 24-hour refuge where they and their children might escape from violence and the center quickly became a refuge for battered women. This inauspicious beginning was soon to explode into a social movement of national and, later, international proportions with the accompanying struggles for recognition, splits, alliances, and metamorphoses that characterize all dynamic social movements (Charlton, 1972; Pizzey, 1974; Rose, 1978; Sutton, 1977). . . .

The plight of battered women is now generally recognized as a significant social problem and there have been changes [in Britain] in housing, social services, and legal reforms (Coote, Gill, & Richardson, 1977; Delamont & Ellis, 1979; Pahl, 1985; Parliamentary Select Committee on Violence in Marriage, 1975; Wasoff, Dobash, & Dobash, 1979).

As can be seen from this brief account, both the social movement and the social problem upon which it is focused are dynamic and complex. The social scientists who would do action research enter the arenas of other researchers, grass roots activists, legislators, policy makers, and agency practitioners. To study the social problem and provide a contribution to the changes necessary to develop meaningful proposals for solutions necessitates the entrance of the social scientists into the political world of ongoing social change. Despite all protestation to the contrary, social research and political issues are inevitably related. Yet, social science is largely lacking in models of how to develop scientific work within this context, how to analyze the social and political consequences of the messages inherent in research, and how to participate with community groups and social agencies in the collective creation of social change. . . .

ACTION RESEARCH: THE SIGNIFICANCE OF METHODOLOGY

It is often assumed that good intentions are enough to ensure the importance and utility of research. This is, of course, a naive stance, because research methods and epistemological assumptions are very important in the type of evidence presented, and in the manner in which the research enters the public and political debates regarding a particular social problem and the proposed solutions to it. . . .

Historical and concrete analysis is a necessary aspect of our efforts to explain and understand recurrent social patterns such as violence against wives. Historical analysis must, however, be coupled with a concrete investigation of the everyday context of violence and the meanings and interpretations that women and men attach to these events. In pursuing these general methodological principles we employed various research strategies, including analysis of in-depth interviews with 109 battered women, 34,724 police and court records, historical documents, and media coverage, as well as informal interviews with representatives of social agencies.

In order to learn about the violence in a concrete, meaningful, and sensitive manner we employed a reflexive and contextual form of interviewing (Dobash & Dobash, 1979, 1983). Naturalistic and ethnographic researchers have employed this method in various research arenas and found it to provide a more thorough description and understanding of the area under study than can be achieved through survey analysis. . . . In deciding to use this approach, we explicitly rejected the use of survey methods employing large probability samples that must invariably use superficial questionnaires and interviews based on abstract categories relating to preconceived and, in our view, irrelevant issues. Instead, we developed a technique that enabled us to learn a great deal about the violence itself and about the context in which it occurs. This was achieved by focusing on specific violent events experienced by the women and encouraging them to provide elaborate and detailed accounts of the physical attack, the interaction relating to it, the meanings attached to it, and the immediate and long-term actions of both the woman and the man. We do not, however, see this interpretative approach as a complete methodology, and consider it necessary to locate individual perceptions in the context of a wider cultural and institutional analysis.

Through the use of this methodology and allied research techniques, we were able to gather a wealth of historical and contemporary evidence that pointed to the significance of male dominance in the etiology of violence. . . . On an interactional level, we discovered that it is through taking on the position of wife that women are most likely to become the victims of systematic and severe violence. [I]t is in the family where men's "right" and privileges are given the most free reign. Once married, women are seen as rightly subject to the control and direction of men who use various methods to achieve these ends, including intimidation, coercion, and violence. Men learn these violent techniques, and the appropriate contexts for their use, through a male culture that condones and encourages violence. In the violent events experienced by the women we studied, violence was used by the men they lived with to silence them, to "win" arguments, to express dissatisfaction, to deter future behavior and to merely demonstrate dominance (Dobash & Dobash, 1979, 1984). . . .

Women feel guilty and trapped in these relationships. Guilty, because cultural prescriptions make family problems into women's problems regardless of the source. Trapped, because it is considered disloyal to betray patriarchal privacy by seeking help from outsiders and thus expose husbands and the family to potential scrutiny. Women are also trapped by the difficulties associated with living an independent life free from men. Gender stratification keeps women in low paid positions with little possibility of gaining employment that would enable them to live on their own with children.

Women are also faced with the negative responses of the wider society. Our contextual analysis led us to consider the role of outsiders' responses in the perpetuation of violence. We found that relatives and friends often provided support and sometimes material assistance, especially through a supportive female culture. However, women also experienced dismissive responses, and even the helpful ones were usually short-lived. The responses of state agencies were often even less effective. A legacy of patriarchal justice and psychiatric assumptions about women often resulted in less than meaningful responses from the police and social services. The overall effect of these patterns of response leaves women more isolated than they are before they seek help. They also strengthen the position of the husband who gains support for his belief that his behavior is either justified or not truly serious, and who is also strengthened by the certain knowledge that others will not intervene so as to challenge this violent behavior or protect his victim.

In contrast, other researchers studying violence in the home . . .[attempted] to isolate and abstract the violence out of its wider historical and social contexts. Using the social survey in an attempt to approximate the controls of the experimental method within natural settings, they have tried to isolate the problem under study by using probability sampling, abstract measurement, and statistical manipulation. . . . While this is a powerful technique when used in the investigation of certain issues, it has inherent limitations when applied to the study of complex phenomena such as violence. Although the method can be used to obtain information pertaining to relatively straightforward sociodemographic characteristics of respondents, it can provide little explanatory information regarding the processes associated with a sensitive problem such as wife beating. These criticisms do not constitute a rejection of the social survey in toto—indeed, we believe it can be employed in feministic-inspired forms of analysis (Yllö, 1983)—but rather an objection to its application to complex problems and to an unflinching reliance on it as a sure route to knowledge.

The research program of Murray Straus and his colleagues Richard Gelles and Suzanne Steinmetz (Straus, Gelles, & Steinmetz, 1980) provides an example of such an approach and illustrates the problems arising from its use on a complex problem such as violence in the home. Their major study was based on a probability sample of over 2,000 families,

which revealed fewer than 200 cases of violence, and formed the basis of most of the analysis. The approach is based on simple correlations and ad hoc explanations. As such, many of the findings and conclusions are contradictory, inconsistent, and unwarranted (Dobash & Dobash, 1983; Pagelow, 1986; Pleck, Pleck, & Bart, 1977). The most obvious and contentious example of this comes from the "finding" that there is near "equality between the sexes" in the use of violence between spouses (Straus, 1980, p. 681), that is, "husband beating" and a "battered husband syndrome" are as prevalent as wife beating and battered wives (Steinmetz, 1977; Straus, 1977, p. 447). Furthermore, a 10-year follow-up survey, using the same approach to the measurement of violence, has "found" the same equality between the sexes in the use of violence (Straus & Gelles, 1986).

In fact, such claims cannot be justified given the nature of the research conducted and the results achieved. One of the primary problems with this research is a failure to consider the context of violence and an over-emphasis on abstract measurement such as the Conflict Tactics Scale (CTS) (Straus, 1979). Although abstract scales are not particularly useful in attempts to explain and understand social problems, this is especially the case when they are poorly conceived and constructed. The CTS, for example, suffers from numerous internal faults that call into question many of the results achieved through its use.

Briefly, the scale includes poorly conceived categories of violence (combining threatened, attempted, and actual violence) that are not mutually exclusive (e.g., separate categories of "Kicked, bit, or hit with a fist" and "Beat up the other one," (Straus, 1979, p. 88). These inadequacies are compounded in the construction of a Violence Score for each respondent. Having failed to collect any information about injuries actually sustained, the researchers assume that certain acts "carry a high risk of injury" while others do not. Included in the "high-risk" category is "trying to hit with something" and excluded from it is "slapping." Yet, our own research, which does examine injuries sustained from particular attacks, demonstrates that a slap can result in anything from a temporary red mark to a broken nose, tooth, or jaw, and that trying to hit with something never results in an injury unless the blow is actually landed.

These defects, plus the additional failure to develop an overall analysis of specific violent events considered over time, led to fundamental problems in the use of terms such as *wife beating* and *husband beating*. For example, it is possible, and indeed very likely, that a man may have "kicked, hit with a fist" and "beaten up" his wife on numerous occasions injuring her on each, while she may have responded to these attacks by "trying to hit [him] with something" or "threatening [him] with a knife" in order to try to stop him from beating her, but without ever actually hitting or injuring him. By employing the aggregating and dichotomizing techniques used to produce the Violence Scores, it appears that these researchers would describe both husband and wife as "beaten" (Straus, 1979, pp. 77, 80, 88). Given such inadequacies, Straus, Gelles, and Steinmetz have no empirical warrant to employ the terms *battered* or *beaten*, and their results cannot be construed as indicating the existence of "battered husbands" or even "battered wives."

Certainly, there is a vast body of evidence confirming the existence of persistent, systematic, severe, and intimidating force men use against their wives (Dobash & Dobash, 1979; Gaquin, 1978; Martin, 1976; Pagelow, 1981; Parliamentary Select Committee on Violence in Marriage, 1975; U.S. Commission on Civil Rights, 1979). This evidence does warrant the use of terms such as *wife beating* or *battered women*, but there is no systematic evidence showing a pattern of severe, persistent, and intimidating violence against husbands that would warrant the use of terms such as *beaten* or *battered*. As such, the results of the research of Straus and his colleagues may tell us more about the response of women to their husband's violence (and about the problems of abstract measurement and scaling) than they do about any persistent or severe pattern of husband beating. Indeed, our research and that of virtually everyone else who has actually studied violent events and/or their patterning in a concrete and detailed fashion reveal that when women do use violence against their spouses or cohabitants, it is primarily in self-defense or retaliation, often during an attack by their husbands. On occasions, women may initiate an incident after years of being attacked, but it is extraordinarily rare for women to persistently initiate severe attacks. Although there is no doubt that women do slap and shove their husbands on occasion or throw things at them, one must question any statistical manipulation that defines this, or violence used in self-defense, as husband beating.

Debates about research methods may appear to be purely academic—unrelated to social and political issues. However, this is not the case. For example, the claims made about "battered husbands," although derived from inadequate research, had significant consequences for community groups. After the publication of this research, and its apparent promulgation by the mass media, women's groups in the United States reported greater difficulty in obtaining support for establishing shelters and crisis centers. Some authorities argued that because of the "findings" about battered husbands, battered women did not suffer from a unique problem and as such did not need special resources and assistance (Crowe, 1980; Pagelow, 1986; Pleck et al., 1977). Such misleading findings were easily incorporated within a dominant belief system in which problems of women are either denied, diminished, or blamed on the female victim. The interplay between research findings, whatever their scientific merit, public policy, and popular beliefs and/or prejudice, is all too familiar to grass roots activists and action researchers. . . .

THE ALTERNATIVE MESSAGE AND SOCIAL CHANGE

Inherent in every piece of social research are messages about the nature of the phenomenon and the individuals under study. Some of these messages reiterate and support the status quo while others challenge it and offer alternatives constituting fundamental change. Mathiesen (1974) has argued that social scientists interested in producing research oriented to social action, directed at social change, should offer alternatives, or messages, that not only *contradict* the status quo, but are also taken seriously and therefore *compete* with other proposals for consideration. In order to contradict, the message must differ from the existing ideology. . . .

NONCOMPETING AGREEMENT

The type of message that does not contradict the status quo or compete for consideration, the Noncompeting Agreement, brings nothing new and is simply a restatement of the existing order. There are many such messages concerning wife abuse, and a few examples will suffice here. There are the traditional notions that this is strictly an individual problem, relating simply to personalities, upbringing, or biology (as opposed to being a complex individual, social, institutional, and cultural problem); that the problem can be solved solely through individual therapeutic means; and that patriarchal relations (often disguised by the label "the traditional family") should be maintained in any proposals advanced. The usual messages regarding wife beating have focused primarily on the traits of the victim and sometimes on those of the offender, but rarely on wider social issues. This has largely taken the form of blaming the victim, excusing the violence, and setting limits on when violence is "legitimate" by concentrating on ideas such as female masochism, provocation, nagging, and insubordination.

Such messages fit well with the existing patriarchal system. They require no change and advance no challenges to it. It is not surprising that such arguments appear in some of the early statements on wife beating . . . and that they have been popularized by the press and entertained by some government bodies. A report in *The Guardian* (1974) illustrated these types of arguments. It quoted two psychiatrists who proclaimed that the perpetrators of such assaults are usually "badly brought up, heavy drinkers, spoilt as a child, and incapable of looking after themselves." A third psychiatrist reported that drink was "a very potent cause of unhappiness" and invoked a strong British prejudice by stating that "a disproportionate number of the women had Irish husbands." In the United States, people of color might be substituted, but the nature of the argument remains the same. Minority groups, deviants and/or the inadequate, are violent. Thus the logic of difference separates them from "us." But the most comforting explanation, for the complacent public and statutory bodies, has been that "wife often puts herself in a violent situation." Messages of this nature do not compete with the existing views of the problem because the proposals are fully integrated into the established order and reiterate what everyone intuits as the "cause" of the problem. That is, the woman somehow "causes" the man to be violent and is therefore also responsible for the solution to her problem.

Another example of the type of message and action that support the status quo involves the use of the highly dubious idea of the "battered husband" (Steinmetz, 1977; Straus et al., 1980). In its most simple form, the supposed existence of a population of battered husbands has been used to diminish the significance of the very real existence of a population of battered wives. A more convoluted form of reasoning takes place, however, when the violent behavior of one population (i.e., men known to beat their wives persistently and severely) is implicitly compared with an entirely different population (i.e., women who supposedly beat their husbands in the same fashion), and the behavior of each is seen to cancel out that of the other. Since each group of individuals are "equally" culpable, the usual victim, the woman, is guilty and not worthy of support and sympathy. Even more basic is the fact that there is little or no public, governmental, or scientific demand, as there was with wife beating, that we know in great detail the nature, extent, persistence, and injuries involved in this so-called husband battering before it is considered serious. Instead, it has been satisfactory for many simply to accept that those women who have ever hit their husbands or thrown something at them or threatened to hit them have "battered their husbands" (a definition that would never be allowed if the woman were the victim).

REFERENCES

Charlton, C. (1972). The first cow on Chiswick High Road. *Spare Rib, 24,* 24–25.

Coote, A., & Gill, T., with Richardson, J. (1977). *Battered women and the new law.* London: National Council for Civil Liberties.

Crowe, M. (1980, June 8). Research—Behind closed doors. *Equal Times,* pp. 11–13.

Delamont, S., & Ellis, R. (1979). *Statutory and voluntary responses to domestic violence in Wales: A pilot project.* Domestic Violence Project (SRU Working Paper No. 6). Cardiff, Wales: Department of Health and Social Security/Welsh Office.

Dobash, R. E., & Dobash, R. P. (1979). *Violence against wives: A case against the patriarchy.* New York: Free Press.

Dobash, R. E., & Dobash, R. P. (1983). The context specific approach to researching violence against wives. In D. Finkelhor, R. Gelles, G. Hotaling, & M. A. Straus (Eds.), *The dark side of families* (pp. 261–176). Newbury Park, Ca: Sage.

Dobash, R. E., & Dobash, R. P. (1984). The nature and antecedent of violent events. *British Journal of Criminology 24*(3), 269–288.

Gaquin, D. A. (1978). Spouse abuse: Data from the national crime survey. *Victimology, 2,* 632–643.

Martin, D. (1976). *Battered wives.* San Francisco: Glide.

Mathiesen, T. (1974). *The politics of abolition.* London: Martin Robertson.

Pagelow, M. (1981). *Woman battering.* Newbury Park, CA: Sage.

Pagelow, M. (1986). The battered husband syndrome. Social problem or much ado about nothing. In N. Johnson (Ed.), *Marital violence* (pp. 172–194). Boston: Routledge & Kegan Paul.

Pahl, J. (1985). *Private violence and public policy.* Boston: Routledge & Kegan Paul.

Parliamentary Select Committee on Violence in Marriage (1975). *Report from the Select Committee on violence in marriage together with the proceedings of the committee: Vol. 2. Report, minutes of evidence and appendices, session 1974–75* (HC 553-4). London: Her Majesty's Stationery Office.

Pizzey, E. (1974). *Scream quietly or the neighbours will hear you.* Harmondsworth, England: Penguin.

Pleck, E., Pleck, J., & Bart, P. (1977). The battered data syndrome: A reply to Steinmetz. *Victimology, 2,* 680–683.

Rose, H. (1978). In practice supported, in theory denied: An account of an invisible urban movement. *International Journal of Urban and Regional Research, 2,* 521–537.

Steinmetz, S. K. (1977). The battered husband syndrome. *Victimology, 2,* 499–509.

Storr, A. (1974). *Human aggression.* Harmondsworth, England: Penguin.

Straus, M. A. (1977). Wife beating: How common and why? *Victimology,* 443–458.

Straus, M. A. (1979). Measuring conflict and violence: The conflict tactics (CT) scales. *Journal of Marriage and the Family,* 40(1), 75–88.

Straus, M. A. (1980). Victims and aggressors in marital violence. *American Behavioral Scientist, 23,* 681–704.

Straus, M. A., & Gelles, R. (1986). Societal change and change in family violence from 1975 to 1985 as revealed by two national surveys. *Journal of Marriage and the Family, 48,* 465–479.

Straus, M., Gelles, R., & Steinmetz, S. (1980). *Behind closed doors.* New York: Doubleday.

Sutton, J. (1977). The growth of the British movement for battered women. *Victimology, 2,* 576–584.

U.S. Commission on Civil Rights (1979). *Battered women: Issues of public policy.* Washington, DC: U.S. Government Printing Office.

Wasoff, F., Dobash, R. E., & Dobash, R. P. (1979). The current evidence and legal remedies regarding battered women. *Journal of the Law Society of Scotland,* 14(5), 178–183.

Yllö, K. (1983). Using a feminist approach in quantitative research: A case study. In D. Finkelhor, R. J. Gelles, G. T. Hotaling, & M. A. Straus (Eds.), *The dark side of families* (pp. 227–288). Newbury Park, CA: Sage.

POSTSCRIPT

Husband Battering: Is It a Social Problem?

Steinmetz and Lucca insist that wives can be violent; that some husbands are physically and psychologically injured by abusive wives; and that husbands, like wives, may stay in violent relationships to protect their children. They contend that if society continues to ignore husband battering, men will continue to suffer physical and emotional damage and children will continue to be exposed to negative parental modeling.

Dobash and Dobash reply that research studies that report husband battering typically rely on the Conflict Tactics Scale (CTS), which distorts and misrepresents women's acts of physical violence and mislabels such acts as husband battering. They claim that the CTS does not take into account that most of the reported violence by women is self-protective in nature. Dobash and Dobash also argue that most data generated from the CTS fails to consider the context within which marital violence occurs, such as the motivation for the violence, what is said and done during and immediately after violent episodes, and what emotions are stirred throughout each incident.

Does husband battering exist as a social problem? Is *husband battering* the correct term for what violence wives inflict on husbands? Does it deserve to be treated as a serious social problem that requires publicity, research funding, public policy attention, and intervention programs equal to those recommended for battered women? Or should it be downplayed as a social problem because it is a rare and usually self-defensive action taken by women whose husbands attack them first? Will publicity about husband battering divert attention from abused wives who, some think, are in greater need? Would ignoring husband battering put husbands and their children at risk?

SUGGESTED READINGS

B. Andrews and C. R. Brewin, "Attributions of Blame for Marital Violence: A Study of Antecedents and Consequences," *Journal of Marriage and the Family*, 52 (1990): 757–768.

A. Browne, *When Battered Women Kill* (Free Press, 1987).

D. G. Dutton and J. J. Browning, "Power Struggles and Intimacy Anxieties as Causative Factors of Wife Assault," in G. W. Russell, ed., *Violence in Intimate Relationships* (PMA, 1988).

C. P. Flynn, "Relationship Violence by Women: Issues and Implications," *Family Relations*, 39 (1990): 194–198.

R. J. Gelles, *Family Violence* (Sage Publications, 1987).

ISSUE 14

Are Extramarital Relationships Becoming More Frequent?

YES: Lynn Atwater, from *The Extramarital Connection: Sex, Intimacy, and Identity* (Irvington Publishers, 1982)

NO: Andrew M. Greeley, Robert T. Michael, and Tom W. Smith, from "Americans and Their Sexual Partners," *Society* (July/August 1990)

ISSUE SUMMARY

YES: Associate professor of sociology Lynn Atwater argues that the incidence of extramarital involvement has been increasing over the past half-century in the United States.

NO: Sociologist Andrew M. Greeley, economist Robert T. Michael, and survey researcher Tom W. Smith critique research purporting an increased frequency of extramarital affairs and provide data indicating that extramarital liaisons are at a relatively low level.

People involve themselves in extramarital sexual relationships for a variety of reasons: for experimentation; out of boredom; because they are thrill-seekers; to bolster self-esteem; because a partner has become ill or handicapped; they "fall in love"; for sexual variety; because they feel alienated from their spouses; because they are apart from their spouses for extended periods of time, to name a few. But how is accurate information compiled, interpreted, and disseminated about a topic as intimate as extramarital sexual relationships?

Alfred C. Kinsey (1884–1956) was a noted American sex researcher whose work had a significant impact on legitimizing sex research as a subject for scientific pursuit. In 1948 and 1953 he and his associates published two studies that detailed the results of their interviews regarding the sex lives of more than 16,000 people—*Sexual Behavior in the Human Male; Sexual Behavior in the Human Female*. Kinsey and his associates reported that approximately 26 percent of the women interviewed and 50 percent of the men had had extramarital sexual contacts.

The literature of the 1960s and 1970s is filled with research and commentary about the extramarital sexual activities of women and men in Western cultures. Robert Rimmer's *The Harrad Experiment* (Sherbourne Press, 1966) and George and Nena O'Neill's *Open Marriage* (M. Evans & Co., 1972) are two early treatises on sexually nonexclusive relationships. Gerhard Neubeck edited an influential book of readings entitled *Extramarital Relations* (Prentice Hall, 1969), which included cross-cultural and religious perspectives, views on extramaritality as an extension of the normalcy, and healthy and disturbed reasons for having extramarital relations.

Other studies, including a work on "swinging" by Brian Gilmartin entitled *The Gilmartin Report* (The Citadel Press, 1976), Gilbert Bartell's *Group Sex: A Scientist's Eyewitness Report on the American Way of Swinging* (Peter Wyden, 1970), and Morton Hunt's *Sexual Behavior in the 1970s* (Dell, 1974) have provided further insights on extramarital sexual behavior. (Swinging, however, implies no deception about sexual relationships outside of the marital bond; whereas in a traditional affair, one or both of the spouses has a sexual relationship outside the marriage without the partner's knowledge.) More recently, Shere Hite, *Women and Love: A Cultural Revolution in Progress* (Knopf, 1987), has indicated that the gender discrepancy in extramarital sexual activity has narrowed. For women married five or more years who responded to her survey, the incidence of extramarital relationships was 70 percent.

As we enter the 1990s, how clear a picture do we have on extramarital sexual behavior and how contemporary behavior compares to past practices? In the following selections, Lynn Atwater reviews various reports on extramarital relationships and argues that the rate of extramarital sexual expression is increasing, especially among females. She sees the concept of greater equality in sexual behavioral expression between the sexes as being in line with other changes in contemporary human behavior. Not all researchers share her conclusions, however. Using a "during-the-last-12 months" survey approach, Andrew M. Greeley, Robert T. Michael and Tom W. Smith question the existence of a sexual revolution. They argue that the extent to which society continues to value monogamy is underrepresented in favor of more sensational-sounding findings.

YES

Lynn Atwater

EXTRAMARITAL RELATIONSHIPS

Sandra, a twenty-six year old social worker, is getting ready to go out for dinner with a friend. Before leaving, she stops to put the frosting on a cake she baked that afternoon for her husband's birthday. He'll be home later that night from a business trip, and she wants to surprise him with it. Satisfied with her efforts, she goes off to meet her friend Steve, a young law student. She plans to be home about the same time as her husband.

In another part of town, Alex is kissing his wife goodbye as he heads for an early evening meeting with some friends to wrap up a business deal. He hopes the meeting will be short, because afterward he's looking forward to stopping by to see his friend Ann. Ann is divorced and has her own apartment.

Both Sandra and Alex are involved in extramarital relationships. They are like most Americans who are, or will be, involved extramaritally at some point in their married lives. They are also like most Americans, who, when asked, say they disapprove of extramarital sex. In the latest available survey, 87% said that extramarital relations were "always wrong" or "almost always wrong."[1] But attitudes about extramarital relations tell only half the story. The other half of the story is what people do, not what they say.[2]

When Dr. Alfred Kinsey and his associates published their groundbreaking study of American male sexual behavior in 1948, they documented that half of all married men had extramarital relations at some point in their married lives. This figure of one in two men with extramarital experience was confirmed by surveys published in 1977 and 1979. Although the number of involved married men has remained steady over the years, these surveys indicate that the frequency with which men participate has apparently increased.[3] Moreover, younger men report they are more likely to engage in extramarital sex than older men. Seventy percent of all men under the age of 40 said they could see themselves getting involved in an extramarital situation, compared with 53% of men over 55.[4]

Women are also changing their rate of extramarital behavior. Extramarital relations are not the object of equal opportunity laws, federal suits, or demonstrations against discrimination. Nevertheless, women are quietly but steadily finding increased opportunities for sexual expression outside of their marriages. In 1953, Kinsey reported that 26% of married women had extramarital experience by age 40. In 1975, a generation later, the figure had risen to 38%. The most dramatic increase has been among the youngest married women, under age 25, where the rate has risen from one in ten to one in four.[5] As these young married women move through the life cycle, it is projected that one in two will have an extramarital experience.[6]

The evidence suggests that we are sexual schizophrenics. We say one thing and do another. We are still emotionally attached to traditional beliefs of sexual exclusivity, while we live with the needs and desires provoked by contemporary values which hold sexual expression to be a new social frontier. We have inherited a repressive set of legal, moral, and religious codes that we still use to guide our attitudes, yet these codes were never designed to meet the problems of modern intimacy that confront us today.

How did this chasm between our beliefs and our practices come to be? Part of the answer lies in the strength of our inherited attitudes. The proscription of extramarital sex is one of the most ancient and stringent cultural rules regulating family life. In Western civilization, it can be traced back at least to early Hebraic society.[7] This prohibition did not develop because of concern about sexuality as such, but because of the threat extramarital intercourse represented "to the stability of society; most specifically, male property rights."[8] The rule against extramarital sex originated in the concern of powerful males to preserve the economic system of private property,

and it forbade extramarital relations absolutely for women and relatively for men. This double standard required premarital abstinence and postmarital fidelity for women while leaving men free to pursue sexual variety with female slaves and prostitutes. By bequeathing property only to the sons of their wives, men could be certain they were passing on their inheritance to their legitimate heirs. An economic system built on the concept of private property required sexual faithfulness within marriage for its survival.

Although prohibition of extramarital sex originally functioned for economic reasons, it was incorporated into religion, law, and public attitudes of morality. Christianity, and particularly Puritanism in the United States, was markedly repressive of sexuality. Strict efforts were made to control premarital, marital, and extramarital behavior. These restrictions served to protect the institution of marriage as it then existed. In an earlier, primarily agricultural era, marriage was the principal way men and women joined with each other for mutual physical survival, as well as for whatever sexual expression was approved. Later, laws were passed reflecting Puritanism's anti-sexual attitudes and, over time, morality became largely synonymous with sexual behavior. Today, adultery is still illegal in many states.

Modern American society is dramatically different from the eras in which marriage was institutionalized. Marriage is no longer primarily for the creation of legal heirs, nor is it intrinsically linked to physical survival and well-being. For many, the primary purpose of marriage is the care and meeting of emotional needs. Deviations from sexual exclusivity no longer endanger our economic system, nor do they threaten our physical well-being. Consequently, public punishment has largely disappeared, and people are no longer branded with a scarlet 'A' nor prosecuted for adultery. Yet old attitudes still remain, largely intact.

In addition to the reduced social need for monogamy, many societal changes have occurred which tend to encourage non-exclusive behavior. In an urbanized and industrialized society, men and women come into contact with many more people each day than when America was rural. An individual can often meet hundreds of potential sexual partners in the course of a normal day's activities. This mobility, as well as population density in urban areas, contributes to a social anonymity, which makes it possible for unapproved behavior to remain unobserved as it never could in small town America. Furthermore, our increased longevity means that marriages have the potential for lasting longer, lengthening the period of susceptibility to others. A century ago, death broke up as many marriages as divorce does today.[9]

With the relaxation of control over exclusivity and increased opportunities for many more sexual outlets has come a predictable increase in extramarital behavior. What has not come is any appreciable increase in our approval of what we are doing extramaritally. We have made a hypocrisy of our belief in fidelity. We continue to cling to the ideal, because we believe it to be the best way to meet all of our personal needs in an intimate relationship. We have transformed what once was an economic necessity into an emotional one. We blindly believe that if only our love partners are faithful, all of our emotional needs will be satisfied.

There are several myths that contribute to our unrealistic faith in sexual exclusivity. They include the following:

Myth: One person can and will supply all of another's emotional, social, and sexual needs.

Reality: This may well be our most unrealistic expectation. It is never possible for one person to meet all of another's needs, for each human being's needs are complex and are also constantly changing. We have also raised our expectations for satisfaction in marriage to extremely high levels. As Americans, we now feel *entitled* to a happy marriage. If our first one is not happy, we feel further entitled to divorce in order to continue our pursuit.

Myth: People grow to love each other more as years go by.

Reality: The rate of divorce and research studies on happiness in marriage indicate otherwise.

Myth: Sexual exclusivity comes easily and naturally.

Reality: There is no evidence to indicate that human beings are "naturally" sexually exclusive. Exclusivity is not easy, as any married person (or any person who has promised exclusivity to another) can testify. It is likely that maintaining exclusivity will be even more difficult in marriages of the future because of the social trends already discussed.[10]

The extent of extramarital relations suggests that sexually exclusive marriage fails to meet the intimate needs and capabilities of many married people. Clearly, we have seduced ourselves with the myths of monogamy. We retain romantic attachments to these myths despite the pain and disillusion these unexamined beliefs are bound to bring us. If we are lucky enough to avoid divorce, we must still confront the strong probability that our marriages will be touched by an extramarital relationship at some point, either our own or our spouse's. When that does happen, the effect is often negligible until the other spouse becomes aware of it. This fact has largely failed to enter our consciousness. As far back as 1953, Kinsey reported that "extramarital relationships had least often caused difficulty when the spouse had not known of them."[11] Most women in his study reported their husbands presumably did not know of their involvements. In a 1979 study of men's involvements, three-quarters of wives remained unaware of their husbands' activities.[12] It is only when a spouse's extramarital involvement becomes known that difficulties are likely to occur, which suggests that we react more to traditional meanings than to the actual impact upon us of our spouse's involvement.[13]

Most people tend to react to knowledge of their spouses' involvements with feelings of anger, jealousy, lack of trust, and sometimes the impulse to divorce because these are the "feeling rules" built into traditional attitudes about extramarital sex.[14] In other words, whatever the meaning of the outside relationship, whether it be casual or serious, regardless of when the relationship occurred, in the distant past or the here and now, the tendency is to react with the same set of emotions. We do this because in our culture, these are the only correct emotions to feel when discovering our spouses' infidelity. We do not yet have any feeling rules to cover the changes in the incidence and meaning of modern extramarital sex. Clearly, our feeling rules, built upon traditional attitudes about extramarital behavior, have a great deal to do with our perception of damage to us. This structured emotional reaction and our continuing disapproval of extramarital relations, despite the rising incidence, suggest that Americans are still unwilling or unable to come to terms with the reality of extramarital relations.

There are several possible approaches to employ in resolving this gap between our ideals of exclusivity and our extramarital behavior. Using a *moral* approach, we can continue to condemn extramarital relations and make more zealous attempts to live "faithfully" for life. While this will be successful for some, and possibly desired by most, it is unlikely to be a workable solution for the majority of Americans. In terms of the personal satisfactions we are looking for, our expectations of marriage are too unrealistic to have them all be met in an exclusive framework. And the diverse social forces propelling us toward new marital traditions are too strong to be repelled solely by the force of moral conviction.

Recognizing the impact of these rising personal expectations and changing social pressures, a group of scholars on the family recommend a *'futuristic'* approach.[15] They advocate a new marital ideology that would, in effect, change our ideals to conform with our behavior. They see the need for a new marital ethic which recognizes the value of alternatives to exclusivity. They do not feel we should abandon monogamy, but that we should recognize its inadequacy as a life-long marriage plan for most people. They propose a new ideological perspective on marriage, one that includes the possibility of choosing from a variety of exclusive and non-exclusive alternatives over a lifetime.

ANOTHER APPROACH, A *PSYCHOLOGICAL* ONE, has been used, especially in the past, to lay the blame for the causes of extramarital behavior in individual weaknesses and deficiencies. There is, undoubtedly, some truth to this explanation, but it can hardly explain all incidences of extramarital involvement. In 1967, psychologist Albert Ellis distinguished between healthy and sick reasons for having extramarital sex, thereby beginning to remove moral taint from psychological understanding. While not all psychologists would agree with a nonjudgmental view, the trend is in this direction. For example, psychologist J. D. Block, in a recent book entitled *The Other Man, The Other Woman,* offers therapeutic suggestions for understanding and coping with the emotional needs and reactions associated with extramarital involvements.

A *sociological* perspective . . . complements the psychological focus on the individual by exploring the *social* factors associated with extramarital involvements. When large numbers of people are engaged in any behavior, it ceases to be strictly a private issue. It becomes a public and social concern. From a sociological perspective come such questions as: "What changes in society that are beyond the control of the individual contribute to the rising incidence of extramarital sex?" "What common patterns are to be found in extramarital involvements?" "Are there differences in the extramarital relations of women and men?" "What are the consequences, good and bad, of extramarital relations on marriages and on individuals?" "Are the feeling rules we have still appropriate to the incidence and meanings of today's extramarital sex?"

A SOCIOLOGICAL FOCUS ATTEMPTS TO move individuals beyond thinking that personal problems have only personal causes, to a consciousness that their problems are similar to what others are experiencing and why. Sociological information can aid us in understanding behavior by exposing and clarifying the connections between individuals and the society they live in. A sociological approach does not evaluate what is right or wrong behavior, but it can help us grasp what it means to be living at a particular time in human history. It can help us understand that what we are doing and feeling and thinking has roots beyond our personal motivations, desires, and values. A sociological understanding can aid us in decoding the meaning of our existence.

One of the conditions of modern existence is that we have become increasingly freed from the control of church and state, and as a consequence of this freedom we are personally responsible for more and more decisions that shape our private lives. We no longer are told whom to marry; instead we choose a mate that we hope will prove pleasing to us. We are no longer confined to the same occupation as our parents had; instead we select a career that we believe will prove satisfying and lucrative. We no longer are expected to belong to one religion; instead we can change it as we mature, or even reject religion entirely. We no longer must become parents after we marry; instead we are free to choose whether to have children or not.

And now we no longer are forced by external constraints to be monogamous in marriage. It is now something we must choose instead of having it imposed upon us. President Carter recognized this in his famous *Playboy* interview, when he admitted to lusting in his heart after other women. We have this choice "to be or not to be monogamous," whether we want it or not. Ironically, one advantage modern life does not give us is the choice of not having to make choices.

In having to make choices in so many areas of modern life, we often depend on available information. But we need accurate information to make responsible and intelligent decisions in the situations which confront us every day. The custom of dating arose so that we could get to know people and gain information about them in order to decide whether to marry them or not. We try to find out what various jobs are like and what our own interests are in order to choose the right career for ourselves. Often contemporary married couples read articles and books on the pros and cons of parenthood before deciding whether or not to have children.

Similarly, knowledge of people's extramarital behavior can help us understand this contemporary addition to the institution of marriage. Learning about others' extramarital experiences, and the positive and negative consequences of that behavior, may help us assess these experiences for our own marriages. If we are never tempted, or are at most uncertain, knowledge of others' involvements can confirm the validity of our own decisions. If we, too, have had or think about having extramarital experiences, then that knowledge can deepen understanding of our own decisions and behavior by being able to compare them with others.

Whatever the extramarital decisions individuals make, when they exhibit enough similarity to constitute a pattern, and when they show enough continuity to endure over time, they will become part of the mosaic of modern sexual morality. As our ancestors developed a code of strict monogamy to fit the social needs of their era, so, too, are we developing new traditions to mirror the many possibilities in marriage styles taking shape today.

One example of this creation of new cultural patterns of intimacy is in the area of premarital sexuality. For many years the same hypocrisy characterized attitudes toward premarital sex as currently exists with extramarital sexuality. Gradually, over a period of decades, this attitude-behavior gap is being eliminated. Starting with the 1960's, attitudes became more permissive, so that by 1978 only 41% of a representative sample of Americans thought that premarital sex was "always wrong" or "almost always wrong." Those who disapproved were mostly in the older and less well educated segments of the population. Eighty percent of the 18–29 age group approved of premarital sex.[16] According to the most recent study, 80% of that same group have also experienced premarital sex.[17]

While there is an unmistakable trend toward convergence of attitudes and behavior in the area of premarital sex, there is as yet no firm evidence for a similar trend in extramarital sex. One clue to the possibility of this happening lies in the attitudes of highly educated young adults, a group that often suggest trends indicating where the rest of the population will be going. Of this group, age 18–29 and with more than twelve years of formal education, 40% approve of extramarital sex.[18] This is insufficient data on which to base a prediction, so we must wait for the future to reveal how the tension between extramarital attitudes and behavior will be resolved.

The purpose of this [article] is to report on and discuss extramarital behavior as it is occurring today. The intent is to further understanding, free of past mythologies and traditional moral condemnation. Many will disagree with interpretations of this study, but that is to be expected on any controversial issue, especially in the area of sexuality. Studies of sex, from Kinsey to Masters and Johnson, have stimulated powerful responses because of the conflicting sexual attitudes Americans hold, and because sexuality is such an emotional topic in our society.

Any interpretation of extramarital behavior reflects, and is colored by, the viewpoint of the onlooker. I am no exception. I view extramarital relations from a feminist perspective, and I'm doing so for several reasons.[19]

First, this research and analysis will focus mainly on women, for it is among women, more so than men, that rates of extramarital participation are rising dramatically. Second, feminism is often the inspiration behind the spectrum of change being painted across the lives of women today. Women's renewed interest in social equality has gained them new opportunities in areas as diverse as work, education, religion, politics, and sports. Women are redesigning their lives and redefining their selves. This pervasive new consciousness affects every facet of living, and sexuality is no exception.

Third, women's sexuality, both in its physical and social expression, has long been shaped by stereotyped ideas. Although these myths and ideas are rooted in the anti-female bias of early Western culture,[20] writers, researchers, and scholars have supported and perpetuated them into the present. A number of familiar beliefs make up the social construction of traditional female sexuality. Among these is the idea that female sexuality is rooted in emotions rather than sexual desire, activated by love rather than physical attraction. Another idea is that women's sexuality takes years to develop and reaches its peak when women are in their late thirties or forties. By contrast,

male sexuality, it is said, reaches its peak in adolescence. Women have also been thought to be less interested in sex than men. And in the ultimate of myths, Freud sought to physically relocate women's "mature" orgasm from the clitoris to the vagina.[21]

Beyond these physical "facts" about their sexuality, there is also a traditional model of the social aspects of women's sexuality. This model assumes women are passive sexually, lack autonomy in sexual decision-making, equate sexual expression with love, and perceive sexuality as a form of service to others rather than something they do for their own enjoyment.[22]

It is impossible to know precisely how many women have tried to live up to these culturally dominant notions or how many have succeeded in living up to them, and at what cost to themselves. Feminist theorists, new research findings, and women themselves are all challenging these traditional sexual stereotypes. Masters and Johnson's work in 1966 on *Human Sexual Response* showed there was no physical evidence for the theory of separate vaginal and clitoral orgasms. Moreover, they found women to be more sexual than men if the capacity for multiple orgasms is used as a measure. Mary Jane Sherfey, a feminist psychiatrist, concludes from Masters and Johnson's evidence that women have the capacity to be sexually insatiable.[23] Women have also begun to rely on their own experience to define their sexual capacity and preferences. *The Hite Report* gives self-accounts of the sexuality of some 3,000 women.[24] Such books are necessary in this transitional era to provide information on what those experiences are, both for women who want to know about and compare themselves with others, and for scholars who wish to understand the phenomena of female sexual behavior.

The relatively small amount of research that has been done on the extramarital sexuality of women has tended to reflect the traditionally dominant beliefs. For instance, Kinsey attributed the lesser number of women's extramarital partners (as compared to men's) to their lesser needs, explaining it biologically by referring to innate differences in the nervous system of women.[25] Morton Hunt, a journalist who published his extensive exploration of extramarital "affairs" in 1969, reported that women are "less prone to react quite so strongly" to successful experiences outside of marriage. He implied that cultural definitions are responsible, since "sexual ability is not so closely identified with success as it is for men."[26] In a discussion of reasons for extramarital relationships, sociologist Robert Bell saw the process of aging and its associated need for evidence of physical attractiveness as a motivation for females, but not for males.[27] Overall, the stereotypical model of women's extramarital relations has been characterized by falling in love, motivated by unsatisfactory marriage, rationalized as being beyond personal control, and accompanied by considerable guilt.

But feminist sociologists have taken a different view. They would agree with Jessie Bernard, an eminent woman sociologist, who commented that

it seems to me that a new kind of woman is emerging . . . and one of the distinguishing characteristics of this woman is that she can be casual about sex . . . as casual about sexual relations in or out of marriage as men. They (women) can accept sex at some point without conflict. Even a regular extramarital relationship

does not faze them or in fact interfere with their marriage.[28]

Which of these two opposing pictures of women more accurately captures the reality of women's lives today? Do the increased numbers of women having extramarital relations do so because they fall in love with another man? Because they're unhappily married and seeking an easy way out of their dissatisfaction? Do they feel too guilty to enjoy the extra sex? Are older women doing it only because they fear they're losing their physical attractiveness?

The most recent research suggests that the stereotypical view of women's extramarital behavior is mistaken or at least out-of-date. In 1975 one study of 2,262 women by sociologists Bell, Turner, and Rosen reported that women with low-rated marriages were most likely to have extramarital sex, *but that many happily married women also had sex outside of marriage.* Therefore, they concluded, "this would suggest that for many women extramarital coitus is influenced by a number of personal or social values that go beyond how they evaluate their marriage."[29] One of the personal or social values they found associated with extramarital sex was a liberal sexual attitude. By that they meant women who enjoyed oral-genital sexual contact, and women who often initiated sex within their marriage. Thus, a tendency to engage in extramarital sex may be part of the liberalization of the entire package of women's sexual behavior.

Some similar findings emerged from a study of 100,000 women who answered a questionnaire published in *Redbook* magazine. More than half of the women who had extramarital sex said they were happily married. When Robert Levin, an editor of the magazine, analyzed the data to determine why these happily married women were involved extramaritally, he found that

> when the satisfied-experimental wives were compared to *all* women who took part in the survey in terms of education, income, political outlook, employment status, religious affiliation and even intensity of religious belief, *the statistical differences are negligible.* From a sociological point of view, the average satisfied-experimental wife does not seem too unlike the average women who answered the questionnaire.[30]

Sociology traditionally relies on demographic variables like education, income, employment, and religion partially to explain human behavior. But the *Redbook* magazine results suggest that we have to look elsewhere for explanations of contemporary extramarital behavior. That "elsewhere" is not to be found in the happiness or unhappiness of marriage, according to the Bell and *Redbook* studies.

NOTES

Full identification of sources mentioned in the text and in the following notes will be found in the Bibliography.

1. National Opinion Research Center, 1977.
2. The data on extramarital relations are very limited. We have no truly representative information on the American population as a whole because of the numerous difficulties in doing this kind of research. In the absence of exact data, we must rely on the existing studies of portions of the population to provide the most accurate estimates available. See DeLora and Warren (1977) for an examination of the problems in sexual research and Libby (1977) for an extensive critique of the literature on extramarital sex.
3. Yablonsky, 1979, p. 16.
4. Pietropinto and Simenauer, 1977, p. 312.
5. Levin, 1975.
6. Bell, Turner and Rosen, 1975; Levin, 1975.
7. Pickett, 1978.
8. Harper, 1961, p. 384. Reiss (1981, p. 289) alternatively suggests that the explanation lies in

the child-rearing responsibilities of the female role.
9. Scanzoni, 1972, p. 13.
10. Libby, 1977: xxi–xxii.
11. Kinsey, 1975, p. 433.
12. Yablonsky, 1979.
13. This finding first emerged in Kinsey and has been replicated by others, including Yablonsky, 1979; Hunt, 1969; Cuber and Harroff, 1965; and Levin, 1975.
14. See Hochschild, 1979, for a discussion of the way social structure affects the emotions we display.
15. These scholars include, among others, Robert T. and Anna K. Francoeur, 1974; Rustum and Della Roy, 1970; Lonny Myers and Hunter Leggitt, 1975; Herbert Otto, 1970; and George and Nena O'Neill, 1972a.
16. National Opinion Research Center, 1977.
17. Hunt, 1974.
18. National Opinion Research Center, 1977.
19. See Laws and Schwartz, 1977, for a detailed discussion of a feminist approach to female sexuality.
20. See Bullough and Bullough, 1974, for a historical account of this bias.
21. These stereotypes are/were so well accepted that they formed the assumptions of best-selling marriage manuals from 1950–1970. See Gordon and Shankweiler, 1971.
22. See, for instance, Ehrmann, 1964, p. 600; Gagnon and Simon, 1973, p. 182.
23. Sherfey, 1966, p. 99.
24. Hite, 1976.
25. Kinsey, et al., 1953, p. 589.
26. Hunt, 1969, p. 131.
27. Bell, 1971b, p. 70.
28. Bernard, 1969, p. 44.
29. Bell, et al., 1975.
30. Levin, 1975, p. 5.

BIBLIOGRAPHY

Bell, Robert R. *Marriage and Family Interaction.* Homewood, Illinois: Dorsey, 1971(b).

Bell, Robert R., Turner, Stanley, and Rosen, Lawrence. "A multivariate analysis of female extramarital coitus." *Journal of Marriage and the Family,* 37, May 1975, pp. 375–384.

Bernard, Jessie. "Two clinicians and a sociologist." In *Extramarital Relations,* Gerhard Neubeck, ed. Englewood Cliffs, N.J.: Prentice-Hall, 1969, pp. 25–53.

Bullough, Vern L. and Bullough, Bonnie. *The Subordinate Sex: A History of Attitudes Toward Women.* Baltimore: Penguin, 1974.

Cuber, John F. and Harroff, Peggy B. *The Significant Americans.* New York: Appleton-Century-Crofts, 1965.

DeLora, Joann S. and Warren, Carol A. B. *Understanding Sexual Interaction*. Boston: Houghton Mifflin, 1977.

Ehrmann, W. W. "Marital and nonmarital sexual behavior." In *Handbook of Marriage and the Family*, H. T. Christensen, ed. Chicago: Rand-McNally, 1964, pp. 585–622.

Francoeur, Robert T. and Francouer, Anna K., eds. *The Future of Sexual Relations*. Englewood Cliffs, N.J.: Prentice-Hall, 1974.

Gagnon, John H. and Simon, William. *Sexual Conduct: The Social Sources of Human Sexuality*. Chicago: Aldine Publishing, 1973.

Gordon, Michael and Shankweiler, Penelope. "Different equals less: female sexuality in recent marriage manuals." *Journal of Marriage and the Family*, 33, August 1971: pp. 459–465.

Harper, Robert A. "Extramarital sex relations." In *Encyclopedia of Sexual Behavior*. Albert Ellis and Albert Abarbanel, eds. New York: Hawthorne, 1961, p. 384.

Hite, Shere. *The Hite Report*. New York: Dell, 1976.

Hochschild, Arlie Russell. "Emotion work, feeling rules, and social structure." *American Journal of Sociology*, 85: 1979, pp. 551–575.

Hunt, Morton M. *The Affair*. New York: New American Library, 1969.

Hunt, Morton M. "Sexual behavior in the 1970's, part IV: Extramarital and postmarital sex." *Playboy*, 21: 1974, pp. 60–61, 286–287.

Kinsey, Alfred C., Pomeroy, Wardell B., Martin, Clyde, and Gebhard, Paul H. *Sexual Behavior in the Human Female*. Philadelphia: Saunders, 1953.

Laws, Judith Long and Schwartz, Pepper. *Sexual Scripts: The Social Construction of Female Sexuality*. Hinsdale, Illinois: Dryden, 1977.

Levin, Robert J. "The Redbook report on premarital and extramarital sex: The end of the double standard?" *Redbook*, October 1975, pp. 38–44, 190–192.

Myers, Lonny and Leggitt, Hunter. *Adultery and Other Private Matters*. Chicago: Nelson-Hall, 1975.

National Opinion Research Center. "Cumulative Codebook for the 1972–1977 General Social Survey." Chicago: University of Chicago Press, 1977.

O'Neill, Nena and O'Neill, George. *Open Marriage*. New York: M. Evans Company, Inc. 1972(a).

Otto, Herbert. *The Family in Search of a Future*. New York: Appleton-Century-Crofts, 1970.

Pietropinto, Anthony M. D. and Simenauer, Jacqueline. *Beyond the Male Myth*. New York: New American Library, 1977.

Roy, Rustum and Roy, Della. "Is monogamy outdated?" *Humanist*. March, April: 1970, pp. 19–26.

Scanzoni, John. *Sexual Bargaining: Power Politics in the American Marriage*. Englewood Cliffs, N.J.: Prentice-Hall, 1972.

Sherfey, Mary Jane. "A theory of female sexuality." *Journal of American Psychoanalytic Association*, 1966.

Yablonsky, Lewis, *The Extra-Sex Factor*. New York: Times Books, 1979.

NO

Andrew M. Greeley, Robert T. Michael, and Tom W. Smith

AMERICANS AND THEIR SEXUAL PARTNERS

In the absence of responsible social research about human behavior, poor research and media-generated folk lore become conventional wisdom. The assumptions of such conventional wisdom are seldom questioned and rarely tested. In few areas of human behavior is the power of conventional wisdom so pervasive as it is when the subject is sex. In matters of research on sexual behavior, as in other arenas, Gresham's Law applies—bad research seems to drive out good research. And there is good research on sexual behavior, as the recent lengthy and informative review by the National Research Council details. It is just less sensational than much of the poorer research, and thus less successful in shaping public perceptions abut the facts pertaining to our sexual behavior. Perhaps Gresham's Law should be paraphrased in this context as: sensational findings (often the result of poor or superficial research) drive out carefully balanced and less sensational findings, at least from headlines and thus from public perception.

Bad research, like the self-selected reader surveys in popular magazines and non-random samples such as those gathered for the Hite Report, and the popular metaphor of a "sexual revolution" have created a conventional wisdom that "everyone knows" to be true: marital infidelity and sexual experimentation are widespread among Americans.

But if "monogamy" is defined as having no more than one sexual partner during the past year, research based on a scientifically sound national sample indicates that Americans are a most monogamous people. Only 14 percent of all adult Americans interviewed in a 1988 nationwide survey were not monogamous in this sense; and excluding those who were not sexually active, 18 percent were not monogamous. In only one major population group—young men—were a majority not monogamous.

Our study is based on a supplement to NORC's (the National Opinion Research Center) GSS (General Social Survey) given during the winter of

1988 to about 1500 adults who were scientifically selected from a national probability frame of households in the United States. The questions about sexual behavior were included as a self-administered form during the face-to-face interview conducted in the respondent's home. The self-administered form was sealed by the respondent and returned, unopened by the interviewer, with the rest of the survey. This procedure reassured respondents that their answers were confidential and to be used only for statistical purposes such as this article. The response rate on the 1988 GSS was 77.3 percent, and 93.9 percent of those who responded did answer the questions about sexual behavior, well within the range of "item nonresponse" that is typical for a lengthy interview. There is no evidence in this survey that respondents felt the questions about sexual partners were particularly intrusive or inappropriate.

We use two definitions of monogamy. We report the percentage of sexually active people with one sexual partner (M1) and the percentage of all people with zero or one sexual partner (M2). In both definitions we exclude those few (6.1 percent) who did not answer the question. Each of the two definitions has some appeal as a measure of the tendency for adults to be monogamous, for the sexually inactive—those who report having no sexual partner within the past twelve months—can be considered in or out of the definition depending on its purpose. They are not monogamous in the social sense of being committed to a sexual relationship with a sole partner, but from the epidemiological standpoint of risks of contracting sexually transmitted diseases such as AIDS, they belong to the category of the monogamous. We caution that as our questionnaire asked the num-

ber of partners in the preceding twelve months, we cannot distinguish serial monogamy within the year from having two or more partners in the same interval of time. Our definitions of monogamy exclude persons with more than one partner in a twelve-month period, serially or otherwise. Thus our definition of monogamy represents a lower bound estimate of its prevalence in this respect.

Table 1 shows the basic facts. These facts indicate that a vast majority of adults report monogamous behavior. Among all adults 86 percent were monogamous (M2), while among the sexually active 82 percent were monogamous (M2). More women (90 percent) report being monogamous than men (81 percent). More older respondents report being monogamous than do younger ones with the monogamy rate rising from 61 percent among those under 25 to 96 percent and higher among those over 60. Whites (88 percent) have higher monogamy rates than blacks (74 percent), as do residents of smaller sized communities (90 percent) compared to those in large metropolitan areas (75 percent). There appears to be no appreciable difference between Protestants and Catholics or by region of residence in the United States. Marital status has a major influence, as would be expected, with a remarkably high percentage of married persons (97 percent) reporting monogamous behavior. Among sexually active formerly married people, monogamous behavior appears to be the norm as well. Rates of monogamy appear to vary little with educational level (the anomalous high monogamy rate for M2 in Table 1 reflects the large number of elderly people with low levels of education, many of whom are widowed and have no sexual partner). It appears that sexual experimentation ex-

Table 1

**Monogamy in the United States
(Percent of Sexually Active Persons With One Partner
During Previous Twelve Months)**

	M1*	M2*		M1*	M2*
All	82%	86%	Divorced	62%	73%
	(1972)	(1390)		(125)	(178)
Gender**			Separated	78%	81%
Women	86%	90%		(36)	(43)
	(568)	(793)	Never	52%	64%
Men	78%	81%		(205)	(278)
	(504)	(597)	Race**		
Age**			Black	69%	74%
18–24	56%	61%		(144)	(170)
	(144)	(163)	White	84%	88%
25–29	77%	79%		(889)	(1161)
	(157)	(168)	Religion		
30–39	85%	86%	Protestant	83%	87%
	(283)	(308)		(648)	(852)
40–49	86%	88%	Catholic	85%	89%
	(213)	(243)		(281)	(364)
50–59	91%	93%	Region		
	(96)	(132)	North East	82%	86%
60–69	93%	96%		(216)	(274)
	(119)	(194)	North Central	82%	87%
70 +	95%	98%		(288)	(382)
	(59)	(180)	South	82%	86%
Education				(372)	(482)
Grammar	81%	91%	West	83%	87%
	(70)	(146)		(196)	(252)
High	83%	87%	Size**		
	(504)	(644)	12 SMSA	73%	79%
College	81%	84%		(202)	(265)
	(398)	(480)	Other SMSA	87%	90%
Graduate	84%	86%		(353)	(440)
	(99)	(116)	Other Urb	82%	86%
Marital Status**				(400)	(530)
Married	96%	97%	Rural	86%	90%
	(672)	(740)		(117)	(155)
Widowed	71%	93%			
	(34)	(151)			

M1: Monogamy defined as having one partner; people with zero partners, and people who refused to answer are excluded from the sample.
M2: Monogamy defined as having zero or one partner; refusals are excluded.
** Signifies that the percentage differences within this category are significant at the .01 level for M1 and M2. Numbers in parentheses indicate the size of the cell on which the percentage is based.

ists predominantly among the young and the nonmarried.

Age, gender, and marital status are powerful predictors of monogamy, as Table 2 suggests. The rates for monogamy are strikingly high for both married men and married women in all three age groups—over 90 percent of each group reported themselves monogamous.

Table 2

Rates of Monogamy Among the Sexually Active, by Gender, Age, and Type of Relationship

	Women		
Age	Married*	Regular Partner	No Regular Partner
<30*	94% (80)	64% (70)	40% (15)
30–49*	100% (159)	74% (93)	50% (16)
50 +*	97% (109)	91% (23)	67% (3)
Total	98% (348)	73% (186)	47% (34)
	Men		
Age	Married	Regular Partner	No Regular Partner
<30*	91% (44)	47% (62)	23% (30)
30–49*	95% (163)	55% (53)	42% (12)
50 +*	96% (117)	75% (12)	45% (11)
Total	95% (324)	53% (127)	32% (53)

*NB: Row percentages (by partnership for each age group) are statistically significant at the .01 level for all six groups; the column percentages (by age for a given partnership) are significant at the .01 level for only one group, married women.

For those who have a "regular" sexual partner, the rates of monogamy are decidedly lower, typically falling 25 percentage points for women under 50 and about 40 percentage points for men under 50. Other research suggests that the half-life of a cohabitational union in the United States is only about one year, so if many of those reporting a regular partner are cohabiting, it is likely that they have been in that relationship for less than a full year. Their having more than one sexual partner within a year may cover a period different from that of the regular partnership they report. Many unmarried persons with a "regular" sexual partner may have no expectation about sexual exclusivity, so the lower rates of monogamy for these men and women may not indicate any infidelity.

For those who reported having no regular sexual partner, the rates of monogamy are much lower, about 50 percentage points for women and 60 percentage points for men. They range from 23 percent of the young men to 67 percent of the older women. The rates rise with age and are higher for women. Of the sexually active respondents in the survey who were not married and had no regular sex partner, about one-third of the men and half of the women nonetheless reported only one partner within the year.

Even among the *nonmonogamous* sexual license is limited. Fifty-seven percent of these women and 32 percent of these men report only two sexual partners. Men, more than women, are likely to report having a large number of partners—and hence to be the primary targets for sexually transmitted diseases. (A quarter of the men who have more than one sexual partner report in fact that they have had at least five such partners and only 8 percent of women had five or more partners.) If we project to life cycle patterns from our cross sectional data, when young people marry or reach the age of thirty or so, a large majority adopt monogamy as their lifestyle.

To see which of these demographic variables had independent effects on monogamy we carried out multiple regression analysis on the M1 definition of monogamy. The regressions were run separately for men and for women. They indicate that older people are more likely to be monogamous, that black men (but not black women) are less likely to be monogamous, that those in large cities are less likely to be monogamous, and that compared to the married men and women, those with and those without a regular sex partner are far less likely to be monogamous. The regressions also included information on education level, religion, household age structure, and ethnicity (Hispanics), but none of these variables had any statistically discernible effect on the rate of monogamy.

It is interesting to note, too, that when we reran these regressions on only the persons who were married, there were no significant variables for the women, and only the race variable was significant for the men. That is, marriage is the dominant determinant of the monogamy rate, and within the married population, none of the other factors we looked at—education, city size, household composition, religion, age, (except for race for men)—had an influence that was statistically notable. Again, marital status is clearly the dominant determinant of the monogamy propensity in these data.

One issue that deserves attention, but which we doubtless cannot fully address, is whether the GSS respondents are telling the truth about their sexual behavior.

Might they be lying about the number of their sexual partners? Two points can be made. Survey data from the United Kingdom in 1986 reported comparable proportions of the adult population with zero, one and two or more partners. The similarity of these two quite independent surveys provides some face validity for each. The experience of those who have undertaken surveys of sexual behavior is that respondents tend to be remarkably candid. Phrases like "the new permissiveness," "the playboy philosophy," and "open marriage" have become so fashionable and discussions of marital infidelity in popular journals are so commonplace that respondents might be inclined to exaggerate their sexual accomplishments to keep up with the "trends" rather than understate them. Also, if the respondents to the GSS are falsifying accounts of their sexual behavior because of mores which demand monogamy (a circumstance we do not think is the case), then at a minimum they are demonstrating that those mores still strongly support monogamy.

Are the monogamy rates described above "high" by standards of the recent past? Might the situation of widespread monogamy described by our data reflect a response to the fears created by the AIDS epidemic? Does the high rate of monogamy represent a "retreat" from a previous state of "permissiveness" or "liberation"? Have fear and caution made sexual restraint popular?

As our data is only a snapshot about behavior in the past twelve months, it cannot help us determine directly if the fear of AIDS has affected sexual behavior. Finding that monogamy is relatively rare among young men who have never been married and who do not have a regular sexual partner does not inform us, for they might have had even more partners before they became aware of the AIDS danger.

One way our data might indirectly address this question is if we assume that knowing an AIDS victim inhibits sexual permissiveness. We can compare the sexual behavior of those who do know an AIDS victim with the behavior of those who do not know anyone with AIDS, and that can indicate the magnitude of the behavioral response. But those who do know a victim are significantly less likely to be monogamous. Among all adults 76 percent of those knowing an AIDS victim were monogamous, while 87 percent of those not knowing anyone with AIDS were monogamous. Even those who know an AIDS victim who has died are somewhat less likely to report themselves monogamous (70 percent) than those personally unaware of any AIDS fatalities (80 percent). The direction of causation here is probably that those who are not monogamous, and have a lifestyle that exposes them to greater risks of AIDS and other sexually transmitted diseases, are acquainted with more people who are also at greater risk of contracting those diseases. So this line of inquiry is not revealing.

There is, however, no evidence in our data to support a hypothesis that the current high level of monogamy is the result of fear of AIDS. The demographic correlates of monogamy suggest that sexual behavior varies greatly by gender, age, and especially marital status; these powerful predictors may explain much more of the variation in sexual behavior than does fear of AIDS.

But what might the fear of AIDS have added to the levels of monogamy that had already existed among married peo-

ple? If there were a more permissive attitude among married people towards infidelity five or ten years ago, how great was this permissiveness? Data from prior years of the General Social Survey (with independent national samples of adults) can inform us about how that attitude has changed over the past 15 years. It suggests that norms against extramarital sex were strong even 15 years ago. Studying the trend in attitude toward marital infidelity in the annual GSS questionnaire since 1972, there has been a statistically significant increase in opposition to infidelity. There was an increase from 84 percent to 91 percent of the adult population saying that extramarital sex was always or almost always wrong, as Figure 1 indicates. This hardly indicates a dramatic increase in sexual restraint, especially since disapproval of extramarital sex was quite high in the early 1970s when the GSS was first conducted.

It is worth noting that this increase in opposition to extramarital sex has occurred at the same time as there has been a statistically significant increase in tolerance for premarital sex (an increase in tolerance from 53 percent to 64 percent). The notion that social change is always unidimensional and unidirectional rarely is sustained by empirical data. "Revolutions" in which there is uniformity unmarred by complexity usually exist only in newspaper articles and not in the real world.

Three independent national surveys provide data that enables us to gauge the impact of fear of AIDS on American monogamy. A CBS study in 1986 based on 823 cases reported that 11 percent of Americans said that they had changed their behavior because of AIDS. NBC studies conducted in 1986 and 1987 indicated that 7.3 and 7.4 percent, re-

Figure 1

Attitude Toward Nonmarital Sexual Relations, GGS Annual Survey 1972–1988 (Percent Saying Always or Almost Always Wrong)

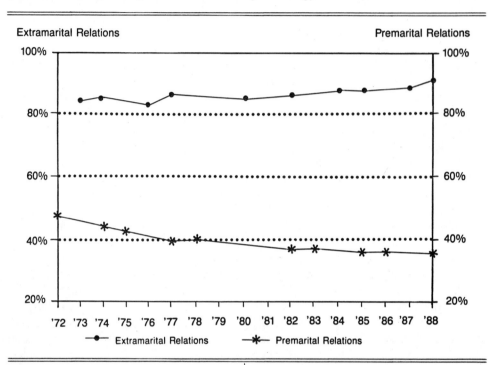

spectively, said they had modified their behavior.

These levels, when reported, were commonly seen as indicating that people were not reacting responsibly to the risks of AIDS, but our findings suggest another interpretation. If many fewer people were engaged in sexual behavior that was risky, it may be quite sensible that few altered their behavior. This is further supported by a 1987 Gallup survey in which 68 percent indicated that no change in their sexual behavior had been made because they did not need to change their behavior. We cannot be sure, and do not intend to be Pollyannas, but our findings that relatively few adults report having sex with many partners may be

one reason only about 10 percent of adults report changing their behavior. Another cautionary note—we focus on only the number of partners, and there are several other dimensions of sexual behavior that one might change in response to the risks of AIDS (e.g., care in the selection of partners, avoidance of high-risk sexual practices, use of condoms, etc.), and these are beyond the scope of our survey.

The details of the reported change in behavior motivated by fear of AIDS conform quite well to the details in the GSS tables reported above about which groups are most at risk: in the Gallup survey 7 percent of the married people and 22 percent of the never married reported a change of behavior; 10 percent of the whites and 22 percent of the blacks reported a change in behavior, as did 13 percent of the men and 9 percent of the women, 19 percent of those under 25 and 10 percent of those between 35 and 50. The changes for married people are compatible with the change in attitudes towards extramarital sex during the years Americans have been conscious of AIDS. So one can tentatively estimate that, even in the absence of AIDS, the monogamy rate for married men and women would not be less than 90 percent. For the whole population the rate, without the AIDS scare, might be between 75 percent and 80 percent. We note again the face validity here: those groups who report the lower monogamy rates in the GSS—men compared to women, non-married compared to married—are those who report in the Gallup survey the biggest change in behavior for fear of contracting AIDS.

The fear of AIDS may have increased monogamy especially among unmarried people and most especially if they are young, but the rates appear to us to have been quite high in any case. Despite the fear of AIDS the promiscuity rate among the young is still high, especially among young, unmarried men, with resultant dangers to themselves and their future partners.

A SEXUAL REVOLUTION?

Like all metaphors the phrase "sexual revolution" is apt for some dimensions of social behavior over the past couple decades, but by no means all of it. It might be useful to review a few changes in recent years in demographic features such as marriage and divorce as well as to speculate on how they might have affected the rate of monogamy in the United States as measured by our variables M1 and M2.

Consider the changes in marital status. The divorce rate in the United States (per 1000 married women) rose from 9.2 in 1960 to 14.9 in 1970, 22.6 in 1980, and then declined slightly to 21.5 in recent years. As a result, despite a rise in remarriage rates, the proportion of the adult population currently divorced also rose dramatically from 3.2 percent in 1970 to 7.8 percent in 1986. Divorced adults are much less likely to be monogamous than are married adults, so this trend probably has decreased the number of adults with one sex partner and increased the number with more than one partner and the number with no partner, thus lowering M1 but not necessarily M2.

The median age at first marriage for women in the United States has risen over the past two decades from 20.6 in 1970 to 22.8 in 1984. As a result, the proportion of 20–24 (25–29) year-old men who have never been married rose from 54.7 percent (19.1 percent) in 1970 to 75.5 percent (41.4 percent) in 1986, and for women that proportion for the same age groups rose from 35.8 percent (10.5 percent) in 1970 to 58.5 percent (26.4 percent) in 1986. These are traditionally sexually active ages and the dramatic increases in the proportions still single probably accompany an increase in the average number of sex partners among the sexually active subsets for these growing segments of the population, thus lowering M1.

There has been a relatively large increase in the rate of cohabitation in the United States, from 0.8 percent in 1970 to 2.8 percent in 1988. This rise among young single couples and among the divorced may offset the tendency toward lower rates of monogamy somewhat, if, as the regressions above imply, the rate of monogamy among those with a "regular" sex partner is higher than among those without such a "regular" partner even though it is lower than among those who are formally married. This would tend to lower M1.

Another dimension of the issue is addressed by the earlier onset of sexual activity by teenagers in the United States. For 17-year-old urban women, the proportion who had premarital intercourse rose from 28 percent in 1971 to 41 percent by 1982. The early onset of sexual activity presumably is associated with a decrease in the monogamy rate for the population as a whole. The trends toward earlier age of beginning sexual activity and toward later age of first marriage lengthen the interval of the life cycle in which sexual activity is most associated with multiple sex partners. The resulting increase in premarital sexual activity mirrors the increased acceptance of that behavior, as reflected in the trends in attitude noted above. It probably lowers M1 and also reduces the discrepancy between M1 and M2.

The changes in fertility control through medical technology (such as the oral contraceptive) and legally accepted practices (such as abortion) have dramatically altered the risks of an unwanted birth associated with sexual behavior. That lower risk surely has had some influence, at the margin at least, on the inclination to engage in nonmarital sexual activity. This, too, may lower M1 and reduce the discrepancy between M1 and M2.

The baby boom of the fifties and early sixties resulted in a disproportionate number of young adults in their twenties over the past decade. As men and women in this age tend to exhibit less monogamy than those in older ages, that demographic bulge itself has tended to lower the overall incidence of monogamy. (This is a trend that can be anticipated with some clarity and as the size of the new cohorts of young adults for the next decade or so will be disproportionately small, this should tend to raise the incidence of monogamy over the next several years, and thus raise M1.)

As this sketchy review of demographic events indicates, there have been several social phenomena that have probably lowered the incidence of monogamy in the past decade or so. Whether these forces have helped create a "sexual revolution" or not, we cannot say. One fact is clear: the high rates of monogamous behavior in the United States exhibited in the GSS data for 1988 do not support the notion that the "revolution," if it occurred, has resulted in a society that does not value or adhere to monogamy.

POSTSCRIPT

Are Extramarital Relationships Becoming More Frequent?

Although Greeley et al. conclude that a sexual revolution has not taken place, their criteria for monogamy, the "within-the-last-12-months" time frame they use, and the complex way they intertwine the concepts of monogamy, sexual exclusiveness, and extramarital behavior do not necessarily help clarify their data. The research reviewed by Atwater would seem to indicate that there is more extramarital sexual activity than there was in earlier times and that women are becoming more like their male counterparts with regard to extramarital experiences. Yet the data are not always clear because of problems related to how questions are worded; how open, willing, and able to answer the respondents are; and whether the respondents who do participate in the studies adequately represent the population at large. For example, are people who respond to surveys on extramaritality doing so to brag? Are those who do not respond more or less extramaritally active? Do other factors such as religion, social class, and education influence the kinds of responses obtained by the research?

There have been few large-scale, representative sex surveys in the past 10 years. Governmental funding through the health service agencies, even on topics as significant as those related to AIDS, has rarely been granted and has often been actively turned down by administrative policymakers as being too politically sensitive. Much of what is known or reported tends to come from surveys printed in magazines, and thus relies on the readership of those magazines for representativeness. Would different results be obtained if the same survey were printed in *Time, Playboy,* and *Reader's Digest?*

SUGGESTED READINGS

A. C. Kinsey, W. B. Pomeroy, and C. E. Martin, *Sexual Behavior in the Human Male* (W. B. Saunders, 1948).

A. C. Kinsey, W. B. Pomeroy, C. E. Martin, and P. H. Gebhard, *Sexual Behavior in the Human Female* (W. B. Saunders, 1953).

K. M. Marett, "Extramarital Affairs: A Birelational Model for Their Assessment," *Family Therapy,* 17 (1990): 21–28.

A. M. Rubin and J. R. Adams, "Outcomes of Sexually Open Marriages," *Journal of Sex Research,* 22 (1986): 311–319.

C. J. Taylor, "Extramarital Sex: Good for the Goose? Good for the Gander?" *Women and Therapy,* 5 (1986): 289–296.

D. L. Weiss, "Marital Exclusivity and the Potential for Future Marital Conflict," *Social Work,* 32 (1987): 45–49.

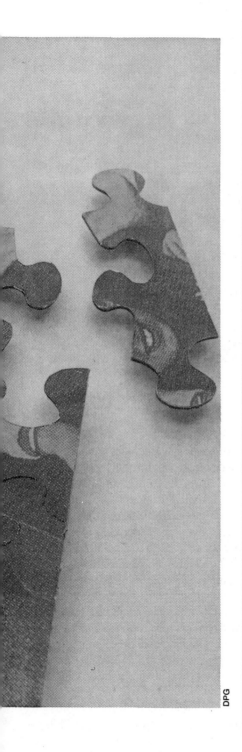

PART 5

Forming New Relationships: Divorce and Remarriage

Statistics show that almost one out of every two marriages will end in divorce. In addition to the former husband and wife, divorce affects many other people: the couple's children, their friends, their extended families, their future spouses if they choose to remarry, and society itself. The extent of the effects of divorce, however, remains a controversy among experts. There is disagreement, for example, on whether or not children of divorce and stepchildren are at greater risk than other children of acquiring emotional and developmental problems as a result of their changed family situations. Whether or not a successful remarriage can follow a divorce is also a topic on which experts do not agree. The discussions in this section focus on the impact of divorce and remarriage on the family and its members.

Children of Divorce: Are They at Greater Risk?

Do Stepchildren Need Special Policies and Programs on Their Behalf?

Is the Success of Remarriage Doomed?

DPG

ISSUE 15

Children of Divorce: Are They at Greater Risk?

YES: Judith S. Wallerstein, from "Children of Divorce: The Dilemma of a Decade," in Elam W. Nunnally, Catherine S. Chilman, and Fred M. Cox, eds., *Troubled Relationships* (Sage Publications, 1988)

NO: David H. Demo and Alan C. Acock, from "The Impact of Divorce on Children," *Journal of Marriage and the Family* (August 1988)

ISSUE SUMMARY

YES: Clinician and researcher Judith S. Wallerstein contends that children whose parents divorce are at greater risk of mental and physical health problems than are children whose families are intact.
NO: Sociologists David H. Demo and Alan C. Acock argue that much of the research on children of divorce is theoretically or methodologically flawed and, consequently, the findings cannot always be trusted.

Despite a stabilization of divorce rates in the 1980s, it has been estimated that at the present rate well over half of the current first marriages in the United States will end in divorce. Over the past two decades the number of children involved in divorce has more than tripled. Current literature suggests that over 60 percent of children will experience life in a single-parent family before they reach age 18. The rates are even higher for black children.

Because divorce significantly changes the lives of parents and their children, many people have expressed great concern over the well-being of children of divorce. Some even predict that significant numbers of children of divorce may remain dysfunctional for much of their adolescence and young adulthood. Although the majority of children of divorce do experience periods of extreme anxiety and stress, some family researchers maintain that the effects of divorce may be less harmful for children than the effects of living in a conflict-ridden home environment. Other researchers point out that much of the research on these children is flawed, either because it is based on clinical studies or because it has theoretical and methodological problems that render it unreliable.

Clinical research is usually developed and implemented by family professionals in applied fields of study (counselors or therapists, family life educators, and clergy, for example), who tend to focus on providing assistance to families with particular problems. Thus, much of the available data are based on studies of children with the most severe reactions to divorce, because such children and their parents make up the researchers' clientele. Although this research is often very useful to other clinicians and helping professionals, it is less useful to advancing knowledge about the majority of children of divorce, who often have less severe problems. Much of the clinical research concentrates on the problems and failures of the research participants and spends little time on the more positive ways in which children and their families adapt or cope with the problems of divorce. On the plus side, clinical research usually focuses more strongly on the long-term developmental changes that affect children of divorce.

Another problem with research in the area of children and divorce is that there has been a tendency for researchers to use a "deficit-family" framework to explain their findings. This means that researchers compare children of divorce to children in intact families (where the two biological parents are present), with the expectation that deviations from the intact family will result in major problems for the children. Such a problem-oriented approach to research narrows the focus of studies and prevents identification of the diversity of factors that affect children after divorce.

Other limitations of the literature on children of divorce include using nonrepresentative samples and then generalizing the findings to all children. Researchers often fail to study income level or social class as factors that affect children's coping abilities and ignore the developmental nature of children's reactions to the divorce process.

In the following selections, Judith S. Wallerstein, while acknowledging certain limitations with the accumulated research on children of divorce, contends that these children are at great risk. She argues that increased attention to education, treatment, and prevention programs is needed for this special population of children. David H. Demo and Alan C. Acock discuss various limitations in the way children of divorce are usually studied, summarize the conclusions from studies they feel are more reliable, and call for future research that pays more attention to the current theoretical and methodological problems of past studies.

YES

Judith S. Wallerstein

CHILDREN OF DIVORCE:
THE DILEMMA OF A DECADE

It is now estimated that 45% of all children born in 1983 will experience their parents' divorce, 35% will experience a remarriage, and 20% will experience a second divorce (A. J. Norton, Assistant Chief, Population Bureau, United States Bureau of the Census, personal communication, 1983). . . .

Although the incidence of divorce has increased across all age groups, the most dramatic rise has occurred among young adults (Norton, 1980). As a result, children in divorcing families are younger than in previous years and include more preschool children. . . .

Although many children weather the stress of marital discord and family breakup without psychopathological sequelae, a significant number falter along the way. Children of divorce are significantly overrepresented in outpatient psychiatric, family agency, and private practice populations compared with children in the general population (Gardner, 1976; Kalter, 1977; Tessman, 1977; Tooley, 1976). The best predictors of mental health referrals for school-aged children are parental divorce or parental loss as a result of death (Felner, Stolberg, & Cowen, 1975). A national survey of adolescents whose parents had separated and divorced by the time the children were seven years old found that 30% of these children had received psychiatric or psychological therapy by the time they reached adolescence compared with 10% of adolescents in intact families (Zill, 1983).

A longitudinal study in northern California followed 131 children who were age 3 to 18 at the decisive separation. At the 5-year mark, the investigators found that more than one-third were suffering with moderate to severe depression (Wallerstein & Kelly, 1980a). These findings are especially striking because the children were drawn from a nonclinical population and were accepted into the study only if they had never been identified before the divorce as needing psychological treatment and only if they were performing at age-appropriate levels in school. Therefore, the deterioration observed in these children's adjustment occurred largely following the family breakup. . . .

From Judith S. Wallerstein, "Children of Divorce: The Dilemma of a Decade," in Elam W. Nunnally, Catherine S. Chilman, and Fred M. Cox, eds., *Troubled Relationships* (Sage, 1988). Copyright © 1988 by Sage Publications. Reprinted by permission.

Divorce is a long, drawn-out process of radically changing family relationships that has several stages, beginning with the marital rupture and its immediate aftermath, continuing over several years of disequilibrium, and finally coming to rest with the stabilization of a new postdivorce or remarried family unit. A complex chain of changes, many of them unanticipated and unforeseeable, are set into motion by the marital rupture and are likely to occupy a significant portion of the child or adolescent's growing years. As the author and her colleague have reported elsewhere, women in the California Children of Divorce study required three to three-and-one-half years following the decisive separation before they achieved a sense of order and predictability in their lives (Wallerstein & Kelly, 1980a). This figure probably underestimates the actual time trajectory of the child's experience of divorce. A prospective study reported that parent–child relationships began to deteriorate many years prior to the divorce decision and that the adjustment of many children in these families began to fail long before the decisive separation (Morrison, 1982). This view of the divorcing process as long lasting accords with the perspective of a group of young people who reported at a 10-year follow-up that their entire childhood or adolescence had been dominated by the family crisis and its extended aftermath (Wallerstein, 1978).

Stages in the Process

The three broad, successive stages in the divorcing process, while they overlap, are nevertheless clinically distinguishable. *The acute phase* is precipitated by the decisive separation and the decision to divorce. This stage is often marked by steeply escalating conflict between the adults, physical violence, severe distress, depression accompanied by suicidal ideation, and a range of behaviors reflecting a spilling of aggressive and sexual impulses. The adults frequently react with severe ego regression and not unusually behave at odds with their more customary demeanor. Sharp disagreement in the wish to end the marriage is very common, and the narcissistic injury to the person who feels rejected sets the stage for rage, sexual jealousy, and depression. Children are generally not shielded from this parental conflict or distress. Confronted by a marked discrepancy in images of their parents, children do not have the assurance that the bizarre or depressed behaviors and moods will subside. As a result, they are likely to be terrified by the very figures they usually rely on for nurturance and protection.

As the acute phase comes to a close, usually within the first 2 years of the divorce decision, the marital partners gradually disengage from each other and pick up the new tasks of reestablishing their separate lives. *The transitional phase* is characterized by ventures into new, more committed relationships; new work, school, and friendship groups; and sometimes new settings, new lifestyles, and new geographical locations. This phase is marked by alternating success and failure, encouragement and discouragement, and it may also last for several years. Children observe and participate in the many changes of this period. They share the trials and errors and the fluctuations in mood. For several years life may be unstable, and home may be unsettled.

Finally, *the postdivorce phase* ensues with the establishment of a fairly stable single-parent or remarried household. Eventually three out of four divorced women and four out of five divorced men reenter wedlock (Cherlin, 1981). Unfortunately, though, remarriage does not bring immediate tranquility into the lives of the family members. The early years of the remarriage are often encumbered by ghostly presences from the earlier failed marriages and by the actual presences of children and visiting parents from the prior marriage or marriages. Several studies suggest widespread upset among children and adolescents following remarriage (Crohn, Brown, Walker, & Beir, 1981; Goldstein, 1974; Kalter, 1977). A large-scale investigation that is still in process reports long-lasting friction around visitation (Jacobson, 1983).

Changes in Parent–Child Relationships
Parents experience a diminished capacity to parent their children during the acute phase of the divorcing process and often during the transitional phase as well (Wallerstein & Kelly, 1980a). This phenomenon is widespread and can be considered an expectable, divorce-specific change in parent–child relationships. At its simplest level this diminished parenting capacity appears in the household disorder that prevails in the aftermath of divorce, in the rising tempers of custodial parent and child, in reduced competence and a greater sense of helplessness in the custodial parent, and in lower expectations of the child for appropriate social behavior (Hetherington, Cox, & Cox, 1978; 1982). Diminished parenting also entails a sharp decline in emotional sensitivity and support for the child; decreased pleasure in the parent–child relationship; decreased attentiveness to the child's needs and wishes; less talk, play, and interaction with the child; and a steep escalation in inappropriate expression of anger. One not uncommon component of the parent–child relationship

coincident with the marital breakup is the adult's conscious or unconscious wish to abandon the child and thus to erase the unhappy marriage in its entirety. Child neglect can be a serious hazard.

In counterpoint to the temporary emotional withdrawal from the child, the parent may develop a dependent, sometimes passionate, attachment to the child or adolescent, beginning with the breakup and lasting throughout the lonely postseparation years (Wallerstein, 1985). Parents are likely to lean on the child and turn to the child for help, placing the child in a wide range of roles such as confidante, advisor, mentor, sibling, parent, caretaker, lover, concubine, extended conscience or ego control, ally within the marital conflict, or pivotal supportive presence in staving off depression or even suicide. This expectation that children should not only take much greater responsibility for themselves but also should provide psychological and social support for the distressed parent is sufficiently widespread to be considered a divorce-specific response along with that of diminished parenting. Such relationships frequently develop with an only child or with a very young, even a preschool, child. Not accidentally, issues of custody and visitation often arise with regard to the younger children. While such disputes, of course, reflect the generally unresolved anger of the marriage and the divorce, they may also reflect the intense emotional need of one or both parents for the young child's constant presence (Wallerstein, 1985).

Parents may also lean more appropriately on the older child or adolescent. Many youngsters become proud helpers, confidantes, and allies in facing the difficult postdivorce period (Weiss, 1979b). Other youngsters draw away from close involvement out of their fears of engulf-ment, and they move precipitously out of the family orbit, sometimes before they are developmentally ready. . . .

CHILDREN'S REACTIONS TO DIVORCE

Initial Responses

Children and adolescents experience separation and its aftermath as the most stressful period of their lives. The family rupture evokes an acute sense of shock, intense anxiety, and profound sorrow. Many children are relatively content and even well-parented in families where one or both parents are unhappy. Few young-sters experience any relief with the di-vorce decision, and those who do are usually older and have witnessed physi-cal violence or open conflict between their parents. The child's early responses are governed neither by an understand-ing of issues leading to the divorce nor by the fact that divorce has a high inci-dence in the community. To the child, divorce signifies the collapse of the struc-ture that provides support and protec-tion. The child reacts as to the cutting of his or her lifeline.

The initial suffering of children and adolescents in response to a marital sep-aration is compounded by realistic fears and fantasies about catastrophes that the divorce will bring in its wake. Children suffer with a pervasive sense of vul-nerability because they feel that the pro-tective and nurturant function of the family has given way. They grieve over the loss of the noncustodial parent, over the loss of the intact family, and often over the multiple losses of neighborhood, friends, and school. Children also worry about their distressed parents. They are concerned about who will take care of the parent who has left and whether the custodial parent will be able to manage alone. They experience intense anger to-ward one or both parents whom they hold responsible for disrupting the fam-ily. Some of their anger is reactive and defends them against their own feelings of powerlessness, their concern about being lost in the shuffle, and their fear that their needs will be disregarded as the parents give priority to their own wishes and needs. Some children, espe-cially young children, suffer with guilt over fantasied misdeeds that they feel may have contributed to the family quar-rels and led to the divorce. Others feel that it is their responsibility to mend the broken marriage (Wallerstein & Kelly, 1980a).

The responses of the child also must be considered within the social context of the divorce and in particular within the loneliness and social isolation that so many children experience. Children face the tensions and sorrows of divorce with little help from anybody else. Fewer than 10% of the children in the California Children of Divorce study had any help at the time of the crisis from adults out-side the family although many people, including neighbors, pediatricians, min-isters, rabbis, and family friends, knew the family and the children (Wallerstein & Kelly, 1980a). Thus, another striking feature of divorce as a childhood stress is that it occurs in the absence of or falling away of customary support.

Developmental factors are critical to the responses of children and adoles-cents at the time of the marital rupture. Despite significant individual differences in the child, in the family, and in par-ent–child relations, the child's age and developmental stage appear to be the most important factors governing the initial response. The child's dominant needs, his or her capacity to perceive and understand family events, the central psychological preoccupation and conflict, the available repertoire of defense and coping strategies, and the dominant patterning of relationships and expectations all reflect the child's age and developmental stage.

A major finding in divorce research has been the common patterns of response within different age groups (Wallerstein & Kelly, 1980a). The age groups that share significant commonalities in perceptions, responses, underlying fantasies, and behaviors are the preschool ages 3 to 5, early school age or early latency ages 5½ to 8, later school age or latency ages 8 to 11, and, finally, adolescent ages 12 to 18 (Kelly & Wallerstein, 1976; Wallerstein, 1977; Wallerstein & Kelly, 1974; 1975; 1980a). These responses, falling as they do into age-related groupings, may reflect children's responses to acute stress generally, not only their responses to marital rupture.

Observations about preschool children derived from longitudinal studies in two widely different regions, namely, Virginia and northern California, are remarkably similar in their findings (Hetherington, 1979; Hetherington et al., 1978; 1982; Wallerstein & Kelly, 1975, 1980a). Preschool children are likely to show regression following one parent's departure from the household, and the regression usually occurs in the most recent developmental achievement of the child. Intensified fears are frequent and are evoked by routine separations from the custodial parent during the day and at bedtime. Sleep disturbances are also frequent, with preoccupying fantasies of many of the little children being fear of abandonment by both parents. Yearning for the departed parent is intense. Young children are likely to become irritable and demanding and to behave aggressively with parents, with younger siblings, and with peers.

Children in the 5- to 8-year-old group are likely to show open grieving and are preoccupied with feelings of concern and longing for the departed parent. Many share the terrifying fantasy of replacement. "Will my daddy get a new dog, a new mommy, a new little boy?" were the comments of several boys in this age group. Little girls wove elaborate Madame Butterfly fantasies, asserting that the departed father would some day return to them, that he loved them "the best." Many of the children in this age group could not believe that the divorce would endure. About half suffered a precipitous decline in their school work (Kelly & Wallerstein, 1979).

In the 9- to 12-year-old group the central response often seems to be intense anger at one or both parents for causing the divorce. In addition, these children suffer with grief over the loss of the intact family and with anxiety, loneliness, and the humiliating sense of their own powerlessness. Youngsters in this age group often see one parent as the "good" parent and the other as "bad," and they appear especially vulnerable to the blandishments of one or the other parent to engage in marital battles. Children in later latency also have a high potential for assuming a helpful and empathic role in the care of a needy parent. School performances and peer relationships suffered a decline in approximately one-half of these children (Wallerstein & Kelly, 1974).

Adolescents are very vulnerable to their parents' divorce. The precipitation of acute depression, accompanied by suicidal preoccupation and acting out, is frequent enough to be alarming. Anger can be intense. Several instances have been reported of direct violent attacks on custodial parents by young adolescents who had not previously shown such behavior (Springer & Wallerstein, 1983). Preoccupied with issues of morality, adolescents may judge the parents' conduct during the marriage and the divorce, and they may identify with one parent and do battle against the other. Many become anxious about their own future entry into adulthood, concerned that they may experience marital failure like their parents (Wallerstein & Kelly, 1974). By way of contrast, however, researchers have also called attention to the adolescent's impressive capacity to grow in maturity and independence as they respond to the family crisis and the parents' need for help (Weiss, 1979a). . . .

Long-Range Outcomes

The child's initial response to divorce should be distinguished from his or her long-range development and psychological adjustment. No single theme appears among all of those children who enhance, consolidate, or continue their good development after the divorce crisis has finally ended. Nor is there a single theme that appears among all of those who deteriorate either moderately or markedly. Instead, the author and her colleague (Wallerstein & Kelly, 1980a) have found a set of complex configurations in which the relevant components appear to include (a) the extent to which the parent has been able to resolve and put aside conflict and anger and to make use of the relief from conflict provided by the divorce (Emery, 1982; Jacobson, 1978 a, b, c); (b) the course of the custodial parent's handling of the child and the resumption or improvement of parenting within the home (Hess & Camara, 1979); (c) the extent to which the child does not feel rejected by the noncustodial or visiting parent and the extent to which this relationship has continued regularly and kept pace with the child's growth; (d) the extent to which the divorce has helped to attenuate or dilute a psychopathological parent–child relationship; (e) the range of personality assets and deficits that the child brought to the divorce, including both the child's history in the predivorce family and his or her capacities in the present, particularly intelligence, the capacity for fantasy, social maturity, and the ability to turn to peers and adults; (f) the availability to the child of a supportive human network (Tessman, 1977); (g) the absence in the child of continued anger and depression; and (h) the sex and age of the child. . . .

FUTURE DIRECTIONS

Despite the accumulating reports of the difficulties that many children in divorced families experience, society has on the whole been reluctant to regard children of divorce as a special group at risk. Notwithstanding the magnitude of the population affected and the widespread implications for public policy and law, community attention has been very limited; research has been poorly supported; and appropriate social, psychological, economic, or preventive measures have hardly begun to develop. Recently the alarm has been sounded in the national press about the tragically unprotected and foreshortened childhoods of children of divorce and their subsequent difficulties in reaching maturity (Winn,

1983). Perhaps this reflects a long-over-due awakening of community concern.

The agenda for research on marital breakdown, separation, divorce, and remarriage and the roads that families travel between each of these way stations [are] long and [have] been cited repeatedly in this [article]. The knowledge that we have acquired is considerable but the knowledge that we still lack is critical. More knowledge is essential in order to provide responsible advice to parents; to consult effectively with the wide range of other professionals whose daily work brings them in contact with these families; to design and mount education, treatment, or prevention programs; and to provide guidelines for informed social policy.

AUTHOR'S NOTE: The Center for the Family in Transition, of which the author is the Executive Director, is supported by a grant from the San Francisco Foundation. The Zellerback Family Fund supported the author's research in the California Children of Divorce Project, one of the sources for this [article]. A slightly different version of this paper has been published in *Psychiatry Update: The American Psychiatric Association Annual Review, Vol. III.* L. Grinspoon (Ed.), pp. 144–158, 1984.

REFERENCES

Cherlin, A. J. (1981). *Marriage, divorce, remarriage.* Cambridge, MA: Harvard University Press.

Crohn, H., Brown, H., Walker, L., & Beir, J. (1981). Understanding and treating the child in the remarried family. In I. R. Stuart & L. E. Abt (Eds.), *Children of separation and divorce: Management and treatment.* New York: Van Nostrand Reinhold.

Emery, R. E. (1982). Interparental conflict and children of discord and divorce. *Psychological Bulletin, 92,* 310–330.

Felner, R. D., Stolberg, A. L., & Cowen, E. L. (1975). Crisis events and school mental health referral patterns of young children. *Journal of Consulting and Clinical Psychology, 43,* 303–310.

Gardner, R. A. (1976). *Psychotherapy and children of divorce.* New York: Jason Aronson.

Goldstein, H. S. (1974). Reconstituted families: The second marriage and its children. *Psychiatric Quarterly, 48,* 433–440.

Hess, R. D., & Camara, K. A. (1979). Post-divorce relationships as mediating factors in the consequences of divorce for children. *Journal of Social Issues, 35,* 79–96.

Hetherington, E. (1979). Divorce: A child's perspective. *American Psychology, 34,* 79–96.

Hetherington, E., Cox, M., & Cox, R. (1978). The aftermath of divorce. In H. Stevens & M. Mathews (Eds.), *Mother–child relations.* Washington, DC: National Association for the Education of Young Children.

Hetherington, E. M., Cox, M., & Cox, R. (1982). Effects of divorce on parents and children. In M. E. Lamb (Ed.), *Nontraditional families: Parenting and child development.* Hillsdale, NJ: Lawrence Erlbaum Associates.

Jacobson, D. (1978a). The impact of marital separation/divorce on children: I. Parent–child separation and child adjustment. *Journal of Divorce, 1,* 341–360.

Jacobson, D. (1978b). The impact of marital separation/divorce on children: II. Interparent hostility and child adjustment. *Journal of Divorce, 2,* 3–20.

Jacobson, D. (1978c). The impact of marital separation/divorce on children: III. Parent–child communication and child adjustment, and regression analysis of findings from overall study. *Journal of Divorce, 2,* 175–194.

Jacobson, D. S. (1983). *Conflict, visiting and child adjustment in the stepfamily: A linked family system.* Paper presented at annual meeting of the American Orthopsychiatric Association, Boston.

Kalter, N. (1977). Children of divorce in an outpatient psychiatric population. *American Journal of Orthopsychiatry, 47,* 40–51.

Kelly, J. B., & Wallerstein, J. S. (1976). The effects of parental divorce: Experiences of the child in early latency. *American Journal of Orthopsychiatry, 46,* 20–32.

Kelly, J. B., & Wallerstein, J. S. (1979). The divorced child in the school. *National Principal, 59,* 51–58.

Morrison, A. L. (1982). *A prospective study of divorce: Its relation to children's development and parental functioning.* Unpublished dissertation, University of California at Berkeley.

Norton, A. J. (1980). The influence of divorce on traditional life cycle measures. *Journal of Marriage and the Family, 42,* 63–69.

Springer, C., & Wallerstein, J. S. (1983). Young adolescents' responses to their parents' divorces. In L. A. Kurdek (Ed.), *Children and divorce*. San Francisco: Jossey-Bass.

Tessman, L. H. (1977). *Children of parting parents*. New York: Jason Aronson.

Tooley, K. (1976). Antisocial behavior and social alienation post divorce: The "man of the house" and his mother. *American Journal of Orthopsychiatry, 46*, 33–42.

Wallerstein, J. S. (1977). Responses of the preschool child to divorce: Those who cope. In M. F. McMillan & S. Henao (Eds.), *Child psychiatry: Treatment and research*. New York: Brunner/Mazel.

Wallerstein, J. S. (1978). Children of divorce: Preliminary report of a ten-year follow-up. In J. Anthony & C. Chilland (Eds.), *The child in his family* (Vol. 5). New York: Wiley.

Wallerstein, J. S. (1985). Parent–child relationships following divorce. In E. J. Anthony & G. Pollock (Eds.), *Parental influences in health and disease* (pp. 317–348). Boston: Little, Brown.

Wallerstein, J. S., & Kelly, J. B. (1974). The effects of parental divorce: The adolescent experience. In J. Anthony & C. Koupernik (Eds.), *The child in his family: Children at psychiatric risk* (Vol. 3). New York: Wiley.

Wallerstein, J. S., & Kelly, J. B. (1975). The effects of parental divorce: The experiences of the preschool child. *American Journal of Orthopsychiatry, 46*, 256–269.

Wallerstein, J. S., & Kelly, J. B. (1980a). *Surviving the breakup: How children and parents cope with divorce*. New York: Basic Books.

Weiss, R. S. (1979a). *Going it alone: The family life and social situation of the single parent*. New York: Basic Books.

Weiss, R. S. (1979b). Growing up a little faster. *Journal of Social Issues, 35*, 97–111.

Winn, M. (8 May 1983). The loss of childhood. *The New York Times Magazine*.

Zill, N. (22 March 1983). *Divorce, marital conflict, and children's mental health: Research findings and policy recommendations*. Testimony before Subcommittee on Family and Human Services, United States Senate Subcommittee on Labor and Human Resources.

NO

David H. Demo and
Alan C. Acock

THE IMPACT OF DIVORCE ON CHILDREN

The purpose of this article is to review and assess recent empirical evidence on the impact of divorce on children, concentrating on studies of nonclinical populations published in the last decade. We also direct attention to a number of important theoretical and methodological considerations in the study of family structure and youthful well-being. . . .

It logically follows that departures from the nuclear family norm are problematic for the child's development, especially for adolescents, inasmuch as this represents a crucial stage in the developmental process. Accordingly, a large body of research literature deals with father absence, the effects of institutionalization, and a host of "deficiencies" in maturation, such as those having to do with cognitive development, achievement, moral learning, and conformity. This focus has pointed to the crucial importance of both parents' presence but also has suggested that certain causes for parental absence may accentuate any negative effects. . . .

EXISTING RESEARCH

A substantial amount of research has examined the effects of family structure on children's social and psychological well-being. Many studies document negative consequences for children whose parents divorce and for those living in single-parent families. But most studies have been concerned with limited dimensions of a quite complex problem. Specifically, the research to date has typically (a) examined the effects of divorce or father absence on children, ignoring the effects on adolescents; (b) examined only selected dimensions of children's well-being; (c) compared intact units and single-parent families but not recognized important variations (e.g., levels of marital instability and conflict) within these structures; and (d) relied on cross-sectional designs to assess developmental processes.

Social and psychological well-being includes aspects of personal adjustment, self-concept, interpersonal relationships, antisocial behavior, and cognitive functioning. . . .

From David H. Demo and Alan C. Acock, "The Impact of Divorce on Children," *Journal of Marriage and the Family*, vol. 50, no. 3 (August 1988). Copyright © 1988 by the National Council on Family Relations, 3989 Central Avenue, NE, Suite #550, Minneapolis, MN 55421. Reprinted by permission. Notes omitted.

Personal Adjustment

Personal adjustment . . . includes such variables as self-control, leadership, responsibility, independence, achievement orientation, aggressiveness, and gender-role orientation. . . . [T]he overall pattern of empirical findings suggests temporary deleterious effects of parental divorce on children's adjustment, with these effects most common among young children (Desimone-Luis, O'Mahoney, and Hunt, 1979; Hetherington, Cox, and Cox, 1979; Kurdek, Blisk, and Siesky, 1981; Wallerstein and Kelly, 1975, 1980a). Kurdek and Siesky (1980b; c) suggest that older children adjust more readily because they are more likely to discuss the situation with friends (many of whom have had similar experiences), to understand that they are not personally responsible, to recognize the finality of the situation, to appreciate both parents for their positive qualities, and to recognize beneficial consequences such as the end of parental fighting and improved relations with parents.

On the basis of her review of research conducted between 1970 and 1980, Cashion (1984: 483) concludes: "The evidence is overwhelming that after the initial trauma of divorce, the children are as emotionally well-adjusted in these [female-headed] families as in two-parent families." Investigations of long-term effects (Acock and Kiecolt, 1988; Kulka and Weingarten, 1979) suggest that, when socioeconomic status is controlled, adolescents who have experienced a parental divorce or separation have only slightly lower levels of adult adjustment. . . .

While their findings are not definitive, Kinard and Reinherz speculate that either "the effects of parental divorce on children diminish over time; or that the impact of marital disruption is less severe for preschool-age children than for school-age children" (1986: 291). Children's age at the time of disruption may also mediate the impact of these events on other dimensions of their well-being (e.g., self-esteem or gender-role orientation) and thus will be discussed in greater detail below. . . . But two variables that critically affect children's adjustment to divorce are marital discord and children's gender.

Marital discord. . . . [E]xtensive data on children who had experienced their parents' divorce indicated that, although learning of the divorce and adjusting to the loss of the noncustodial parent were painful, children indicated that these adjustments were preferable to living in conflict. Many studies report that children's adjustment to divorce is facilitated under conditions of low parental conflict—both prior to *and* subsequent to the divorce (Guidubaldi, Cleminshaw, Perry, Nastasi, and Lightel, 1986; Jacobson, 1978; Lowenstein and Koopman, 1978; Porter and O'Leary, 1980; Raschke and Raschke, 1979; Rosen, 1979).

Children's gender. Children's gender may be especially important in mediating the effects of family disruption, as most of the evidence suggests that adjustment problems are more severe and last for longer periods of time among boys (Hess and Camara, 1979; Hetherington, 1979; Hetherington, Cox, and Cox, 1978, 1979, 1982; Wallerstein, 1984; Wallerstein and Kelly, 1980b). Guidubaldi and Perry (1985) found, controlling for social class, that boys in divorced families manifested significantly more maladaptive symptoms and behavior problems than boys in intact families. Girls differed only on the dimension of locus of control; girls in divorced households scored significantly higher than their counterparts in intact households. . . .

While custodial mothers provide girls with same-sex role models, most boys have to adjust to living without same-sex parents. In examining boys and girls living in intact families and in different custodial arrangements, Santrock and Warshak (1979) found that few effects could be attributed to family structure per se, but that children living with opposite-sex parents (mother-custody boys and father-custody girls) were not as well adjusted on measures of competent social behavior. . . .

Along related lines, a number of researchers have examined gender-role orientation and, specifically, the relation of father absence to boys' personality development. Most of the evidence indicates that boys without adult male role models demonstrate more feminine behavior (Biller, 1976; Herzog and Sudia, 1973; Lamb, 1977a), except in lower-class families (Biller, 1981b). A variety of studies have shown that fathers influence children's gender role development to be more traditional because, compared to mothers, they more routinely differentiate between masculine and feminine behaviors and encourage greater conformity to conventional gender roles (Biller, 1981a; Biller and Davids, 1973; Bronfenbrenner, 1961; Heilbrun, 1965; Lamb, 1977b; Noller, 1978). . . . But it should be reiterated that these effects have been attributed to father absence and thus would be expected to occur among boys in all female-headed families, not simply those that have experienced divorce. . . .

[M]ost of the research on boys' adjustment fails to consider the quality or quantity of father-child contact or the availability of alternative male role models (e.g., foster father, grandfather, big brother, other male relatives, coach, friend, etc.), which makes it difficult to assess the impact of changing family structure on boys' behavior. There are also limitations imposed by conceptualizing and measuring masculinity-femininity as a bipolar construct (Bem, 1974; Constantinople, 1973; Worell, 1978), and there is evidence that boys and girls in father-absent families are better described as androgynous (Kurdek and Siesky, 1980a).

Positive outcomes of divorce. . . . [T]he tendency of children in single-parent families to display more androgynous behavior may be interpreted as a beneficial effect. Because of father absence, children in female-headed families are not pressured as strongly as their counterparts in two-parent families to conform to traditional gender roles. These children frequently assume a variety of domestic responsibilities to compensate for the absent parent (Weiss, 1979), thereby broadening their skills and competencies and their definitions of gender-appropriate behavior. Divorced parents also must broaden their behavioral patterns to meet increased parenting responsibilities, thereby providing more androgynous role models. Kurdek and Siesky (1980a: 250) give the illustration that custodial mothers often "find themselves needing to acquire and demonstrate a greater degree of dominance, assertiveness, and independence while custodial fathers may find themselves in situations eliciting high degrees of warmth, nurturance, and tenderness."

Aside from becoming more androgynous, adolescents living in single-parent families are characterized by greater maturity, feelings of efficacy, and an internal locus of control (Guidubaldi and Perry, 1985; Kalter, Alpern, Spence, and Plunkett, 1984; Wallerstein and Kelly, 1974; Weiss, 1979). For adolescent girls this maturity stems partly from the status and responsibilities they acquire in peer and confidant relationships with custodial mothers. . . .

There is evidence (Kurdek et al., 1981) that children and adolescents with an internal locus of control and a high level of interpersonal reasoning adjust more easily to their parents' divorce and that children's divorce adjustment is related to their more global personal adjustment.

Self-Concept . . .

Marital discord. . . . [F]amily structure is unrelated to children's self-esteem (Feldman and Feldman, 1975; Kinard and Reinherz, 1984; Parish, 1981; Parish, Dostal, and Parish, 1981), but parental discord is negatively related (Amato, 1986; Berg and Kelly, 1979; Cooper, Holman, and Braithwaite, 1983; Long, 1986; Raschke and Raschke, 1979; Slater and Haber, 1984). Because this conclusion is based on diverse samples of boys and girls of different ages in different living arrangements, the failure to obtain effects of family structure suggests either that family composition really does not matter for children's self-concept or that family structure alone is an insufficient index of familial relations. Further, these studies suggest that divorce per se does not adversely affect children's self-concept. Cashion's (1984) review of the literature indicates that children living in single-parent families suffer no losses to self-esteem, except in situations where the child's family situation is stigmatized (Rosenberg, 1979). . . .

Cognitive Functioning

. . . Many . . . studies find that family conflict and disruption are associated with inhibited cognitive functioning (Blanchard and Biller, 1971; Feldman and Feldman, 1975; Hess and Camara, 1979; Kinard and Reinherz, 1986; Kurdek, 1981;

Radin, 1981). . . . In this section we summarize the differential effects of family disruption on academic performance by gender and social class and offer some insights as to the mechanisms by which these effects occur.

Children's gender. Some studies suggest that negative effects of family disruption on academic performance are stronger for boys than for girls (Chapman, 1977; Werner and Smith, 1982), but most of the evidence suggests similar effects by gender (Hess and Camara, 1979; Kinard and Reinherz, 1986; Shinn, 1978). While females traditionally outscore males on standardized tests of verbal skills and males outperform females on mathematical skills, males who have experienced family disruption generally score higher on verbal aptitude (Radin, 1981). Thus, the absence of a father may result in a "feminine" orientation toward education (Fowler and Richards, 1978; Herzog and Sudia, 1973). But an important and unresolved question is whether this pattern results from boys acquiring greater verbal skills in mother-headed families or from deficiencies in mathematical skills attributable to father absence. The latter explanation is supported by evidence showing that father-absent girls are disadvantaged in mathematics (Radin, 1981).

Children's race. . . . [M]ost studies show academic achievement among black children to be unaffected by family structure (Hunt and Hunt, 1975, 1977; Shinn, 1978; Solomon, Hirsch, Scheinfeld, and Jackson, 1972). Svanum, Bringle, and McLaughlin (1982) found, controlling for social class, that there are no significant effects of father absence on cognitive performance for white or black children. Again, these investigations focus on family composition and demonstrate that the effects of family structure on academic performance do not vary as much by race as by social class, but race differences in the impact of divorce remain largely unexplored. . . .

Family socioeconomic status. . . . When social class is controlled, children in female-headed families fare no worse than children from two-parent families on measures of intelligence (Bachman, 1970; Kopf, 1970), academic achievement (Shinn, 1978; Svanum et al., 1982), and educational attainment (Bachman, O'Malley, and Johnston, 1978). . . . In order to disentangle the intricate effects of family structure and SES [socioeconomic status] on children's cognitive performance, family researchers need to examine the socioeconomic history of intact families and those in which disruption occurs, to examine the economic resources available to children at various stages of cognitive development, and to assess changes in economic resources and family relationships that accompany marital disruption.

Family processes. . . . First, family disruption alters daily routines and work schedules and imposes additional demands on adults and children living in single-parent families (Amato, 1987; Furstenberg and Nord, 1985; Hetherington et al., 1983; Weiss, 1979). Most adolescents must assume extra domestic and child care responsibilities, and financial conditions require some to work part-time. These burdens result in greater absenteeism, tardiness, and truancy among children in single-parent households (Hetherington et al., 1983). Second, children in recently disrupted families are prone to experience emotional and behavioral problems such as aggression, distractibility, dependency, anxiety, and withdrawal (Hess and Camara, 1979; Kinard and Reinherz, 1984), factors that may help to explain problems in school conduct and the pro-

pensity of teachers to label and stereotype children from broken families (Hess and Camara, 1979; Hetherington et al., 1979, 1983). Third, emotional problems may interfere with study patterns, while demanding schedules reduce the time available for single parents to help with homework. . . .

Interpersonal Relationships . . .

Peer relations. Studies of preschool children (Hetherington et al., 1979) and preadolescents (Santrock, 1975; Wyman, Cowen, Hightower, and Pedro-Carroll, 1985) suggest that children in disrupted families are less sociable: they have fewer close friends, spend less time with friends, and participate in fewer shared activities. Stolberg and Anker (1983) observe that children in families disrupted by divorce exhibit psychopathology in interpersonal relations, often behaving in unusual and inappropriate ways. Other studies suggest that the effects are temporary. Kinard and Reinherz (1984) found no differences in peer relations among children in intact and disrupted families, but those in recently disrupted families displayed greater hostility. Kurdek et al. (1981) conducted a two-year follow-up of children whose parents had divorced and showed that relationships with peers improved after the divorce and that personal adjustment was facilitated by opportunities to discuss experiences with peers, some of whom had similar experiences. . . .

Dating patterns. Hetherington (1972) reported that adolescent girls whose fathers were absent prior to age 5 had difficulties in heterosexual relations, but Hainline and Feig's (1978) analyses of female college students indicated that early and later father-absent women could not be distinguished on measures of romanticism and heterosexual attitudes.

An examination of dating and sexual behavior among female college students found that women with divorced parents began dating slightly later than those in intact families, but women in both groups were socially active (Kalter, Riemer, Brickman, and Chen, 1985). Booth, Brinkerhoff, and White (1984) reported that, compared to college students with intact families, those whose parents were divorced or permanently separated exhibited higher levels of dating activity, and this activity increased further if parental or parent-child conflict persisted during and after the divorce. . . . Regarding adolescent sexual behavior, the findings consistently demonstrate that males and females not living with both biological parents initiate coitus earlier than their counterparts in intact families (Hogan and Kitagawa, 1985; Newcomer and Udry, 1987). But Newcomer and Udry propose that, because parental marital status is also associated with a broad range of deviant behaviors, these effects may stem from general loss of parental control rather than simply loss of control over sexual behavior. Studies of antisocial behavior support this interpretation.

Antisocial Behavior

Many studies over the years have linked juvenile delinquency, deviancy, and antisocial behavior to children living in broken homes (Bandura and Walters, 1959; Glueck and Glueck, 1962; Hoffman, 1971; McCord, McCord, and Thurber, 1962; Santrock, 1975; Stolberg and Anker, 1983; Tooley, 1976; Tuckman and Regan, 1966). Unfortunately, these studies either relied on clinical samples or failed to control for social class and other factors related to delinquency. However, . . . a number of studies involving large representative samples and controlling for social class

provide similar findings (Dornbusch, Carlsmith, Bushwall, Ritter, Leiderman, Hastorf, and Gross, 1985; Kalter et al., 1985; Peterson and Zill, 1986; Rickel and Langner, 1985). Kalter et al. (1985) studied 522 teenage girls and found that girls in divorced families committed more delinquent acts (e.g., drug use, larceny, skipping school) than their counterparts in intact families. Dornbusch et al. (1985) examined a representative national sample of male and female youth aged 12–17 and found that adolescents in mother-only households were more likely than their counterparts in intact families to engage in deviant acts, partly because of their tendency to make decisions independent of parental input. The presence of an additional adult (a grandparent, an uncle, a lover, a friend) in mother-only households increased control over adolescent behavior and lowered rates of deviant behavior, which suggests that "there are functional equivalents of two-parent families—nontraditional groupings that can do the job of parenting" (1985: 340). . . .

A tentative conclusion based on the evidence reviewed here is that antisocial behavior is less likely to occur in families where two adults are present, whether as biological parents, stepparents, or some combination of biological parents and other adults. Short-term increases in antisocial behavior may occur during periods of disruption, however, as children adjust to restructured relationships and parents struggle to maintain consistency in disciplining (Rickel and Langner, 1985). . . . Peterson and Zill (1986) demonstrated that, when social class was controlled, behavior problems were as likely to occur among adolescents living in intact families characterized by persistent conflict as among those living in disrupted families. . . . Peterson and Zill found that "poor parent-child relationships lead to more negative child behavior, yet maintaining good relationships with parents can go some way in reducing the effects of conflict and disruption" (1986: 306). Hess and Camara's (1979) analyses of a much smaller sample yielded a similar conclusion: aggressive behavior in children was unrelated to family type but was more common in situations characterized by infrequent or low-quality parent-child interaction and parental discord. . . .

LIMITATIONS OF PRIOR RESEARCH

In this section we discuss some of the principal limitations of research assessing the impact of divorce on children. . . .

Nonrepresentative Samples

Sampling is a virtually universal dilemma for researchers. . . .

Among the most problematic nonrepresentative samples are those that rely on clinical populations. While these studies are crucial to our understanding of children and adolescents who are most severely influenced by divorce, they tell us little or nothing about the typical experience following divorce. Since most children whose parents divorce do not receive professional help, such studies can be very misleading about the consequences of divorce for the majority of youth.

While nonrepresentative samples have shortcomings, national surveys typically involve reanalysis of data collected for other purposes and for which the effects of divorce are not a central concern. Because these surveys are not designed to investigate the consequences of divorce, many theoretically important variables are either excluded or poorly operationalized and important control variables are often absent.

What Family Structures Are Being Compared?

Generally, investigations of family structure rely on classification schemes, such as father absence, in which the types derive from different events. For example, many military families are classified as father-absent, but the absence is temporary, the father's income is available to the family, and no social stigma is attached. Alternatively, a single-parent household may consist of a 25-year-old never-married woman and her five children. Other families are father-absent as the result of death, permanent separation, or divorce. A central problem in identifying the effects of family structure is that all of these families are frequently classified as one monolithic family form called "father-absent." . . .

Failure to Control for Income or Social Class

. . . With very few exceptions . . . studies rely on samples of children in one socioeconomic category, usually the middle class, for whom the economic consequences of divorce are dissimilar to those of children in lower socioeconomic categories. As a result, it is impossible to distinguish the effects of divorce and family structure from those of socioeconomic conditions. . . .

Economic factors are important considerations in explicating causal processes for several reasons (see Greenberg and Wolf, 1982; Hill and Duncan, 1987; Kinard and Reinherz, 1984; McLanahan, 1985). First, low-income, single-parent mothers are more likely to work and, as a result, may provide inadequate supervision (Colletta, 1979). Children's behavioral problems associated with "mother-absence" (Hill, Augustyniak, and Ponza, 1986) may therefore be attributable to low income and the need for maternal employment rather than being the result of single-parent family structure per se. Second, the effects of marital disruption on children may be indirect, operating through the economic and emotional impact of divorce on custodial mothers (Longfellow, 1979; Shinn, 1978). As mothers adjust to divorce, single-parenthood, and lower economic status, their anxiety and emotional distress may induce anxiety and stress in children, which in turn may hinder children's academic performance (Kinard and Reinherz, 1986). Failure to examine socioeconomic variation in single-parent families thus obscures the specific processes through which marital disruption affects children. Third, children in single-parent households are more likely to assume adult roles at an early age—for example, working full-time and being responsible for younger siblings, responsibilities that require many adolescents to leave school (Kelly and Wallerstein, 1979; Weiss, 1979). The effects (both positive and negative) of these accelerated life course transitions are consequences of economic deprivation. . . .

Single-parent families precipitated by divorce may be poor as a result of a sudden loss of income. Dramatic changes in lifestyle, financial instability, and loss of status may affect children indirectly through custodial parents' loss of control and altered childrearing practices. Increased labor force participation or increased transfer payments may help, but the net effect is still a dramatic loss of income (Cherlin, 1981; Hoffman, 1977; Weitzman, 1985).

While many families lose a stable middle-class environment and encounter stigmatization and financial instability, other families experience relatively minor changes. Santrock and Warshak (1979) report that postdivorce income losses were severe for mother-custody families but not for father-custody families. Further, the source of income is an important consideration, in that welfare dollars may stigmatize the poor and child support payments are unreliable (Bould, 1977). . . .

The long-term positive effect of divorce on the earning power of women needs to be recognized and may explain why most of the adverse effects of divorce diminish over time. Employed single mothers may provide stronger role models than dependent mothers in intact families, fostering egalitarian sex role attitudes among both women and men whose parents divorced (Kiecolt and Acock, 1988).

Failure to Examine Contextual Factors

A number of contextual factors that distinguish the living conditions of children in intact and disrupted families may be linked to behavioral differences between the two groups. Glenn and Supancic (1984) note that divorced persons participate less in church activities than married persons. . . . If children living in single-parent households are systematically less likely to be exposed to other children who are active in a church, this may have a substantial impact on their adjustment. . . .

Another contextual variable is urban residence. Single-parent households are far more common in urban areas. Urban areas provide a different environment for children than do suburbs, rural areas, or small towns. The quality of the educational system and the exposure to deviant subcultures are two correlates of residential patterns that may affect children who live in a female-headed household. . . . Other contextual factors that influence children include the number of fatherless children in their school, neighborhood SES, presence of a gang subculture, presence of peer groups using drugs (Blechman, Berberian, and Thompson, 1977), and the geographic mobility of peers. . . .

Lack of Longitudinal Designs

Among the hundreds of studies on children of divorce, there are only a pair of widely cited longitudinal studies (Hetherington et al., 1978, 1979; Wallerstein and Kelly, 1980b), and even these studies have serious methodological limitations (Blechman, 1982, Cherlin, 1981). Yet adjustment to changes in family structure is a developmental process. . . . [T]ypical cross-sectional comparisons of children living in disrupted families with children in intact families provide very little, if any, information on the socioeconomic history of these families, level of family conflict, parent-child relations, and so on. If, for example, children from single-parent households were formerly in two-parent households that were poor and conflict-ridden, any problems the children now have may be scars from long ago rather than a direct consequence of the divorce. . . .

CONCLUSIONS

. . . It is simplistic and inaccurate to think of divorce as having uniform consequences for children. The consequences of divorce vary along different dimensions of well-being, characteristics of children (e.g., predivorce adjustment, age at the time of disruption) and characteristics of families (e.g., socioeconomic history, pre- and postdivorce level of conflict, parent-child relationships, and maternal employment). Most of the evidence reviewed here suggests that some sociodemographic characteristics of children, such as race and gender, are not as important as characteristics of families in mediating the effects of divorce. Many studies report boys to be at a greater disadvantage, but these differences usually disappear when other relevant variables are controlled. At present, there are too few methodologically adequate studies comparing white and black children to conclude that one group is more damaged by family disruption than the other.

Characteristics of families, on the other hand, are critical to youthful well-being. Family conflict contributes to many problems in social development, emotional stability, and cognitive skills (Edwards, 1987; Kurdek, 1981), and these effects continue long after the divorce is finalized. Slater and Haber (1984) report that ongoing high levels of conflict, whether in intact or divorced homes, produce lower self-esteem, increased anxiety, and a loss of self-control. . . . Rosen (1979) concludes that parental separation is more beneficial for children than continued conflict. . . . Such conflict and hostility may account for adolescent adjustment problems whether the family in question goes through divorce or remains intact (Hoffman, 1971). . . .

Maternal employment is another variable mediating the consequences of divorce for children. Divorced women often the dual responsibilities of provider and parent to be stressful (Bronfenbrenner, 1976). But studies indicate that women who work prior to the divorce do not find continued employment problematic (Kinard and Reinherz, 1984); the problem occurs for women who enter the labor force after the divorce and who view the loss of time with their children as another detriment to the children that is caused by the divorce (Kinard and Reinherz, 1984). As a practical matter, the alternative to employment for single-parent mothers is likely to be poverty or, at best, economic dependency. . . .

Other bases of social support for single-parent mothers and their children must also be examined. The presence of strong social networks may ease the parents' and, presumably, the child's adjustment after a divorce (Milardo, 1987; Savage et al., 1978). . . . Kinship ties are usually stained, as both biological parents and parents-in-law are more critical of the divorce than friends are (Spanier and Thompson, 1984). . . .

Methodologically, research in support of the family composition hypothesis has been flawed in a number of respects (Blechman, 1982). As described above, most studies (a) rely on simplistic classifications of family structure; (b) overlook potentially confounding factors such as income and social class; (c) use nonrepresentative samples; (d) examine limited dimensions of social and psychological well-being; (e) fail to assess possible beneficial effects deriving from different family structures; and (f) rely on non-longitudinal designs to detect developmental processes.

REFERENCES

Acock, Alan C., and K. Jill Kiecolt. 1988. "Is it family structure or socioeconomic status: Effects of family structure during adolescence on adult adjustment." Paper presented at the annual meetings of the American Sociological Association, Atlanta.

Amato, Paul R. 1986. "Marital conflict, the parent-child relationship, and child self-esteem." Family Relations 35: 403–410.

Amato, Paul R. 1987. "Family processes in one-parent, stepparent, and intact families: The child's point of view." Journal of Marriage and the Family 49: 327–337.

Bachman, Jerald G. 1970. Youth in Transition, Vol. 2: The Impact of Family Background and Intelligence on Tenth Grade Boys. Ann Arbor, MI: Survey Research Center, Institute for Social Research.

Bachman, Jerald G., Patrick M. O'Malley, and Jerome J. Johnston. 1978. Youth in Transition, Vol. 6: Adolescence to Adulthood: A Study of Change and Stability in the Lives of Young Men. Ann Arbor, MI: Survey Research Center, Institute for Social Research.

Bandura, Albert, and Richard H. Walters. 1959. Adolescent Aggression. New York: Ronald Press.

Bem, Sandra L. 1974. "The measurement of psychological androgyny." Journal of Consulting and Clinical Psychology 42: 155–162.

Berg, Berthold, and Robert Kelly. 1979. "The measured self-esteem of children from broken, rejected, and accepted families." Journal of Divorce 2: 363–369.

Biller, Henry B. 1976. "The father and personality development: Paternal deprivation and sex-role development." Pp. 89–156 in Michael E. Lamb (ed.), The Role of the Father in Child Development. New York: Wiley.

Biller, Henry B. 1981a. "The father and sex role development." Pp. 319–358 in Michael E. lamb (ed.), The Role of the Father in Child Development (2nd ed.). New York: Wiley.

Biller, Henry B. 1981b. "Father absence, divorce, and personality development." Pp. 489–552 in Michael E. Lamb (ed.), The Role of the Father in Child Development (2nd ed.). New York: Wiley.

Biller, Henry B., and Anthony Davids. 1973. "Parent-child relations, personality development and psychopathology." Pp. 48–77 in Anthony Davids (ed.), Issues in Abnormal Child Psychology. Monterey, CA: Wadsworth.

Blanchard, Robert W., and Henry B. Biller. 1971. "Father availability and academic performance among third-grade boys." Developmental Psychology 4: 301–305.

Blechman, Elaine A. 1982. "Are children with one parent at psychological risk? A methodological review." Journal of Marriage and the Family 44: 179–195.

Blechman, Elaine A., Rosalie M. Berberian, and W. Douglas Thompson. 1977. "How well does number of parents explain unique variance in self-reported drug use?" Journal of Consulting and Clinical Psychology 45: 1182–1183.

Booth, Alan, David B. Brinkerhoff, and Lynn K. White. 1984. "The impact of parental divorce on courtship." Journal of Marriage and the Family 46: 85–94.

Bould, Sally. 1977. "Female-headed families: Personal fate control and provider role." Journal of Marriage and the Family 39: 339–349.

Bronfenbrenner, Urie. 1961. "The changing American child: A speculative analysis." Journal of Social Issues 17: 6–18.

Bronfenbrenner, Urie. 1976. "Who cares for America's children?" Pp. 3–32 in Victor C. Vaugh and T. Berry Brazelton (eds.), The Family—Can It Be Saved? Chicago: Yearbook Medical Publishers.

Cashion, Barbara G. 1984. "Female-headed families: Effects on children and clinical implications." Pp. 481–489 in David H. Olson and Brent C. Miller (eds.), Family Studies Review Yearbook. Beverly Hills, CA: Sage.

Chapman, Michael. 1977. "Father absence, stepfathers, and the cognitive performance of college students." Child Development 48: 1155–1158.

Cherlin, Andrew J. 1981. Marriage, Divorce, Remarriage. Cambridge, MA: Harvard University Press.

Colletta, Nancy D. 1979. "The impact of divorce: Father absence or poverty?" Journal of Divorce 3: 27–35.

Constantinople, Anne. 1973. "Masculinity-femininity: An exception to a famous dictum?" Psychological Bulletin 80: 389–407.

Cooper, Judith E., Jacqueline Holman, and Valerie A. Braithwaite. 1983. "Self-esteem and family cohesion: The child's perspective and adjustment." Journal of Marriage and the Family 45: 153–159.

DeSimone-Luis, Judith, Katherine O'Mahoney, and Dennis Hunt. 1979. "Children of separation and divorce: Factors influencing adjustment." Journal of Divorce 3: 37–42.

Dornbusch, Sanford M., J. Merrill Carlsmith, Steven J. Bushwall, Philip L. Ritter, Herbert Leiderman, Albert H. Hastorf, and Ruth T. Gross. 1985. "Single parents, extended households, and the control of adolescents." Child Development 56: 326–341.

Edwards, John N. 1987. "Changing family structure and youthful well-being: Assessing the future." Journal of Family Issues 8: 355–372.

Feldman, Harold, and Margaret Feldman. 1975. "The effects of father absence on adolescents." Family Perspective 10: 3–16.

Fowler, Patrick D., and Herbert C. Richards. 1978. "Father absence, educational preparedness, and academic achievement: A test of the confluence model." Journal of Educational Psychology 70: 595–601.

Furstenberg, Frank F., Jr., and Christine Winquist Nord. 1985. "Parenting apart: Patterns of child-rearing after marital disruption." Journal of Marriage and the Family 47: 893–904.

Glenn, Norval, and Michael Supancic. 1984. "The social and demographic correlates of divorce and separation in the United States: An update and reconsideration." Journal of Marriage and the Family 46: 563–576.

Glueck, Sheldon, and Eleanor Glueck. 1962. Family Environment and Delinquency. Boston: Houghton Mifflin.

Greenberg, David, and Douglas Wolf. 1982. "The economic consequences of experiencing parental marital disruption." Child and Youth Services Review 4: 141–162.

Guidubaldi, John, Helen K. Cleminshaw, Joseph D. Perry, Bonnie K. Nastasi, and Jeanine Lightel. 1986. "The role of selected family environment factors in children's post-divorce adjustment." Family Relations 35: 141–151.

Guidubaldi, John, and Joseph D. Perry. 1985. "Divorce and mental health sequelae for children: A two-year follow-up of a nationwide sample." Journal of the American Academy of Child Psychiatry 24: 531–537.

Hainline, Louise, and Ellen Feig. 1978. "The correlates of childhood father absence in college-aged women." Child Development 49:37–42.

Heilbrun, A. B. 1965. "An empirical test of the modeling theory of sex-role learning." Child Development 36: 789–799.

Herzog, Elizabeth, and Cecilia E. Sudia. 1973. "Children in fatherless families." Pp. 141–232 in B. M. Caldwell and N. H. Riccuiti (eds.), Review of Child Development Research (Vol. 3). Chicago: University of Chicago Press.

Hess, Robert D., and Kathleen A. Camara. 1979. "Post-divorce family relationships as mediating factors in the consequences of divorce for children." Journal of Social Issues 35: 79–96.

Hetherington, E. Mavis. 1972. "Effects of father absence on personality development in adolescent daughters." Developmental Psychology 7: 313–326.

Hetherington, E. Mavis. 1979. "Divorce: A child's perspective." American Psychologist 34: 851–858.

Hetherington, E. Mavis, Kathleen A. Camara, and David L. Featherman. 1983. "Achievement and intellectual functioning of children in one-parent households." Pp. 205–284 in Janet T. Spence (ed.), Achievement and Achievement Motives: Psychological and Sociological Approaches. San Francisco: Freeman.

Hetherington, E. Mavis, Martha Cox, and Roger Cox. 1978. "The aftermath of divorce." In J. H. Stevens, Jr., and M. Mathews (eds.), Mother-Child, Father-Child Relations. Washington, DC: National Association for the Education of Young Children.

Hetherington, E. Mavis, Martha Cox, and Roger Cox. 1979. "Play and social interaction in children following divorce." Journal of Social Issues 35: 26–49.

Hetherington, E. Mavis, Martha Cox, and Roger Cox. 1982. "Effects of divorce on parents and young children." In M. Lamb (ed.), Nontraditional Families: Parenting and Child Development. Hillsdale, NJ: Erlbaum.

Hill, Martha S., Sue Augustyniak, and Michael Ponza. 1986. "Adolescent years with parents divorced or separated: Effects on the social and economic attainments of children as adults." Paper presented at the meetings of the Population Association of America, Detroit.

Hill, Martha S., and Greg J. Duncan. 1987. "Parental family income and the socioeconomic attainment of children." Social Science Research 16:39–73.

Hoffman, Martin L. 1971. "Father absence and conscience development." Developmental Psychology 4: 400–406.

Hoffman, Saul. 1977. "Marital instability and the economic status of women." Demography 14: 67–76.

Hogan, Dennis P., and Evelyn M. Kitagawa. 1985. "The impact of social status, family structure, and neighborhood on the fertility of black adolescents." American Journal of Sociology 90: 825–855.

Hunt, Janet G., and Larry L. Hunt. 1977. "Race, daughters, and father-loss: Does absence make the girl grow stronger?" Social Problems 25: 90–102.

Hunt, Larry L., and Janet G. Hunt. 1975. "Race and the father-son connection: The conditional relevance of father absence for the orientations and identities of adolescent boys." Social Problems 23: 35–52.

Jacobson, Doris S. 1978. "The impact of marital separation/divorce on children: II. Interparent hostility and child adjustment." Journal of Divorce 2: 3–19.

Kalter, Neil, Dana Alpern, Rebecca Spence, and James W. Plunkett. 1984. "Locus of control in children of divorce." Journal of Personality Assessment 48: 410–414.

Kalter, Neil, Barbara Riemer, Arthur Brickman, and Jade Woo Chen. 1985. "Implications of parental divorce for female development." Journal of the American Academy of Child Psychiatry 24: 538–544.

Kelly, Joan B., and Judith Wallerstein. 1979. "Children of divorce." National Elementary Principal 59: 51–58.

Kiecolt, K. Jill, and Alan C. Acock. 1988. "The long-term effects of family structure on gender-role attitudes." Journal of Marriage and the Family 50: 709–717.

Kinard, E. Milling, and Helen Reinherz. 1984. "Marital disruption: Effects of behavioral and emotional functioning in children." Journal of Family Issues 5: 90–115.

Kinard, E. Milling, and Helen Reinherz. 1986. "Effects of marital disruption on children's school aptitude and achievement." Journal of Marriage and the Family 48: 285–293.

Kopf, Kathryn E. 1970. "Family variables and school adjustment of eighth grade father-absent boys." Family Coordinator 19: 145–151.

Kulka, Richard A., and Helen Weingarten. 1979. "The long-term effects of parental divorce in childhood on adult adjustment." Journal of Social Issues 35: 50–78.

Kurdek, Lawrence A. 1981. "An integrative perspective on children's adjustment." American Psychologist 36: 856–866.

Kurdek, Lawrence A., Darlene Blisk, and Albert E. Siesky, Jr. 1981. "Correlates of children's long-term adjustment to their parents' divorce." Developmental Psychology 17: 565–579.

Kurdek, Lawrence A., and Albert E. Siesky, Jr. 1980a. "Sex role self-concepts of single divorced parents and their children." Journal of Divorce 3: 249–261.

Kurdek, Lawrence A., and Albert E. Siesky, Jr. 1980b. "Children's perceptions of their parents' divorce." Journal of Divorce 3: 339–378.

Kurdek, Lawrence A., and Albert E. Siesky, Jr. 1980c. "Effects of divorce on children: The relationship between parent and child perspectives." Journal of Divorce 4: 85–99.

Lamb, Michael E. 1977a. "The effects of divorce on children's personality development." Journal of Divorce 1: 163–174.

Lamb, Michael E. 1977b. "The development of mother- and father-infant attachments in the second year of life." Developmental Psychology 13: 637–648.

Long, Barbara H. 1986. "Parental discord vs. family structure: Effects of divorce on the self-esteem of daughters." Journal of Youth and Adolescence 15: 19–27.

Longfellow, Cynthia. 1979. "Divorce in context: Its impact on children." Pp. 287–306 in George K. Levinger and Oliver C. Moles (eds.), Divorce and Separation: Context, Causes, and Consequences. New York: Basic Books.

Lowenstein, Joyce S., and Elizabeth J. Koopman. 1978. "A comparison of the self-esteem between boys living with single-parent mothers and single-parent fathers." Journal of Divorce 2: 195–208.

McCord, Joan, William McCord, and Emily Thurber. 1962. "Some effects of parental absence on male children." Journal of Abnormal and Social Psychology 64: 361–369.

McLanahan, Sara S. 1985. "Family structure and the reproduction of poverty." American Journal of Sociology 90: 873–901.

Milardo, Robert M. 1987. "Changes in social networks of women and men following divorce: A review." Journal of Family Issues 8: 78–96.

Newcomer, Susan, and J. Richard Udry. 1987. "Parental marital status effects on adolescent sexual behavior." Journal of Marriage and the Family 49: 235–240.

Noller, Patricia. 1978. "Sex differences in the socialization of affectionate expression." Developmental Psychology 14: 317–319.

Parish, Thomas S. 1981. "The Impact of divorce on the family." Adolescence 16 (63): 577–580.

Parish, Thomas S., Judy W. Dostal, and Jocelyn G. Parish. 1981. "Evaluations of self and parents as a function of intactness of family and family happiness." Adolescence 16 (61): 203–210.

Peterson, James L., and Nicholas Zill. 1986. "Marital disruption, parent-child relationships, and behavior problems in children." Journal of Marriage and the Family 48: 295–307.

Porter, Beatrice, and K. Daniel O'Leary. 1980. "Marital discord and childhood behavior problems." Journal of Abnormal Child Psychology 8: 287–295.

Radin, Norma. 1981. "The role of the father in cognitive, academic, and intellectual development." Pp. 379–427 in Michael E. Lamb (ed.), The Role of the Father in Child Development (2nd ed.). New York: Wiley.

Raschke, Helen J., and Vernon J. Raschke. 1979. "Family conflict and the children's self-concepts." Journal of Marriage and the Family 41: 367–374.

Rickel, Annette U., and Thomas S. Langner. 1985. "Short-term and long-term effects of marital disruption on children." American Journal of Community Psychology 13: 599–611.

Rosen, Rhona. 1979. "Some crucial issues concerning children of divorce." Journal of Divorce 3: 19–25.

Rosenberg, Morris. 1979. Conceiving the Self. New York: Basic Books.

Santrock, John W. 1975. "Father absence, perceived maternal behavior, and moral development in boys." Child Development 46: 753–757.

Santrock, John W., and Richard A. Warshak. 1979. "Father custody and social development in boys and girls." Journal of Social Issues 35: 112–125.

Savage, James E., Jr., Alvis V. Adair, and Phillip Friedman. 1978. "Community-social variables related to black parent-absent families." Journal of Marriage and the Family 40: 779–785.

Shinn, Marybeth. 1978. "Father absence and children's cognitive development." Psychological Bulletin 85: 295–324.

Slater, Elisa J., and Joel D. Haber. 1984. "Adolescent adjustment following divorce as a function of familial conflict." Journal of Consulting and Clinical Psychology 52: 920–921.

Solomon, Daniel, Jay O. Hirsch, Daniel R. Scheinfeld, and John C. Jackson. 1972. "Family characteristics and elementary school achievement in an urban ghetto." Journal of Consulting and Clinical Psychology 39: 462–466.

Spanier, Graham B., and Linda Thompson. 1984. Parting: The Aftermath of Separation and Divorce. Beverly Hills, CA: Sage.

Stolberg, Arnold L., and James M. Anker. 1983. "Cognitive and behavioral changes in children resulting from parental divorce and consequent environmental changes." Journal of Divorce 7: 23–41.

Svanum, Soren, Robert G. Bringle, and Joan E. McLaughlin. 1982. "Father absence and cognitive performance in a large sample of six- to eleven-year-old children." Child Development 53: 136–143.

Tooley, Kay. 1976. "Antisocial behavior and social alienation post divorce: The 'man of the house' and his mother." American Journal of Orthopsychiatry 46: 33–42.

Tuckman, J., and R. A. Regan. 1966. "Intactness of the home and behavioral problems in children." Journal of Child Psychology and Psychiatry 7: 225–233.

Wallerstein, Judith S. 1984. "Children of divorce: Preliminary report of a ten-year follow-up of young children." American Journal of Orthopsychiatry 54: 444–458.

Wallerstein, Judith S., and Joan B. Kelly. 1974. "The effects of parental divorce: The adolescent experience." In E. James Anthony and Cyrille Koupernik (eds.), The Child in His Family, (Vol 3). New York: Wiley.

Wallerstein, Judith S., and Joan B. Kelly. 1975. "The effects of parental divorce. The experiences of the preschool child." Journal of the American Academy of Child Psychiatry 14: 600–616.

Wallerstein, Judith S., and Joan B. Kelly. 1980a. "Children and divorce: A review." Social Work 24: 468–475.

Wallerstein, Judith S., and Joan B. Kelly. 1980b. Surviving the Breakup: How Children and Parents Cope with Divorce. Basic Books: New York.

Weiss, Robert S. 1979. "Growing up a little faster: The experience of growing up in a single-parent household." Journal of Social Issues 35: 97–111.

Weitzman, Lenore. 1985. The Divorce Revolution: The Unexpected Social and Economic Consequences for Women and Children in America. New York: Free Press.

Werner, Emmy E., and Ruth S. Smith. 1982. Vulnerable but Not Invincible: A Study of Resilient Children. New York: McGraw-Hill.

Worell, J. 1978. "Sex roles and psychological well-being: Perspectives on methodology." Journal of Consulting and Clinical Psychology 46: 777–791.

Wyman, Peter A., Emory L. Cowen, A. Dirk Hightower, and JoAnne L. Pedro-Carroll. 1985. "Perceived competence, self-esteem, and anxiety in latency-aged children of divorce." Journal of Clinical Child Psychology 14: 20–26.

POSTSCRIPT

Children of Divorce: Are They at Greater Risk?

Divorce is typically a painful experience for children. The question is, do children become debilitated for long periods of their lives or do they gradually adapt to their changed family situations? Wallerstein contends that divorce influences long-lasting social and psychological problems for many children, but other scholars argue that the most troublesome symptoms diminish within about two years as parents settle into a routine and as family members learn to cope with the realities of their new life situations.

Demo and Acock maintain that it is inaccurate and simplistic to think that divorce has identical effects on all children. They caution that factors such as the child's age, how she or he reacts to the divorce from the time it is announced or the parents separate through the actual divorce, the family's income before the divorce, the mother's income after the divorce (if the mother becomes the main caregiver), the amount of conflict between the parents before and after the divorce, and the relationship between the child and each parent before and after the divorce should all be considered. They claim that most studies to date have been flawed because they relied on nonrepresentative samples, examined only a few of the many factors that affect adjustment to divorce, overlooked any beneficial aspects of divorce on children, and failed to perform follow-up research on the children after the initial study.

If Wallerstein's conclusions about children of divorce are more accurate, should educational and treatment programs be established and social policies that would help such children be promoted? Or should more reliable information be sought, as Demo and Acock suggest, to counter the prevailing attitude that single-parent families, compared to dual-parent families, are less able to rear healthy children?

In an interview with Jane E. Brody in the *New York Times* (June 23, 1991), Wallerstein discussed her review of several longitudinal studies on children of divorce that appeared in the May 1991 issue of the *Journal of the American Academy of Child and Adolescent Psychiatry*. After reading the research she concludes that although many children "do manage to pull their lives together . . . for about half the children of divorce, the unhappy baggage of their parents' battles remain a lasting legacy." She also asserts that "[w]e are allowing our children to bear the psychological, economic and moral brunt of divorce."

In the June 1991 issue of *Science*, Lindsay Chase-Lansdale and Andrew J. Cherlin caution against making hasty judgments. Their report is based on a sample of over 17,000 British children, age 7, and a follow-up study of 239 of these children whose parents had divorced within four years of the initial interview (the children were then age 11). They found that many of the adverse effects perceived in the children that were previously attributed to divorce actually were present before the divorce. Chase-Lansdale and Cherlin claim that strain caused by marital conflict before the divorce or other *unrelated* problems affecting the children at the time were apparently misinterpreted by other researchers as strictly the result of divorce.

One problem to consider is whether the alleviation of children's negative reactions to divorce is a societal problem or one that is better solved by the parents themselves. How should parents help their children successfully adapt to divorce?

SUGGESTED READINGS

T. M. Cooney and P. Uhlenberg, "The Role of Divorce in Men's Relations With Their Adult Children After Midlife," *Journal of Marriage and the Family*, 52 (1990): 677–688.

R. E. Emery, *Marriage, Divorce, and Children's Adjustment* (Sage Publications, 1988).

E. M. Hetherington, "Coping With Family Transitions: Winners, Losers, and Survivors," *Child Development*, 60 (1989): 1–14.

E. M. Hetherington and J. Arasteh, eds., *The Impact of Divorce, Single Parenting and Stepparenting on Children* (Lawrence Erlbaum, 1988).

S. McLanahan and K. Booth, "Mother-Only Families: Problems, Prospects, and Politics," *Journal of Marriage and the Family*, 51 (1989): 557–580.

J. S. Wallerstein, *Second Chances: Men, Women and Children a Decade After Divorce* (Ticknor & Fields, 1989).

S. A. Wolchik and P. Karoly, eds., *Children of Divorce: Empirical Perspectives on Divorce* (Gardner, 1988).

ISSUE 16

Do Stepchildren Need Special Policies and Programs on Their Behalf?

YES: Margaret Crosbie-Burnett and Ada Skyles, from "Stepchildren in Schools and Colleges: Recommendations for Educational Policy Changes," *Family Relations* (January 1989)

NO: Lawrence H. Ganong and Marilyn Coleman, from " A Comparison of Clinical and Empirical Literature on Children in Stepfamilies," *Journal of Marriage and the Family* (May 1986)

ISSUE SUMMARY

YES: Margaret Crosbie-Burnett, associate professor of educational and psychological studies, and Ada Skyles, a J. D. candidate at Northwestern University School of Law, maintain that stepchildren face uniquely stressful problems related to their family situations that require special educational policies and programs.

NO: Professors of family studies Lawrence H. Ganong and Marilyn Coleman argue that the information currently available on stepchildren and their families is theoretically and methodologically flawed. As a consequence, inaccurate images of stepchildren and their families as deviant and dysfunctional are perpetuated.

What images does the word *family* bring to mind? Does the word *stepfamily* evoke similar kinds of images? Are the images of the stepfamily all positive, all negative, or mixed? Where do people's attitudes and beliefs about stepfamilies originate?

Currently over half of all marriages in the United States eventually end in divorce. In the future, it is projected that a significant number of American children will experience a family divorce. Most children of divorce will also experience the remarriage of at least one of their parents and will live in a stepfamily. The majority of stepfamily members say that their family relationships are good to excellent and that they are managing stepfamily life in a satisfactory manner. But there is a tendency for Americans to idealize the nuclear or "traditional" family and thus to think of stepfamilies as somehow defective or problematic.

Stepfamilies are indeed different from the "traditional" family, but being different does not automatically mean being deviant. Stepfamilies, for example, are more complex than most other families because they involve more than one household and contain a wider circle of relatives with whom family members may interact. This complexity does increase stress for family members. The stress that stems from creating a "new" family from what was originally two different families comes from the pressure of meeting new challenges rather than from the need to protect oneself from imminent harm or danger. This type of stress does produce anxiety, but as family members adapt to the new family situation, they implement various coping mechanisms that reduce feelings of stress and increase feelings of competence and satisfaction. This process may not be easy, but neither is it so difficult that family members become permanently dysfunctional.

Of all stepfamily members, children are most often portrayed as being at risk and are usually the focus of concern in books and articles on step-families. In the following selections, Margaret Crosbie-Burnett and Ada Skyles contend that stepchildren are at risk of having special problems and difficulties. They argue that the education system should be aware of the unique concerns of stepfamilies and should develop and implement programs in their behalf. Lawrence H. Ganong and Marilyn Coleman do not agree with that position, and they suggest that much of the research conducted on stepchildren is flawed and that the misperceptions and stereotypes promoted by this research need to be corrected. They advocate initiating new research studies that take into account the biases of past studies before using the results to promote particular viewpoints or programs.

YES

Margaret Crosbie-Burnett
and Ada Skyles

STEPCHILDREN IN SCHOOLS AND COLLEGES: RECOMMENDATIONS FOR EDUCATIONAL POLICY CHANGES

Our schools and colleges are social institutions. As such, their policies and practices are based on ideologies about life in America. Those policies and practices that relate to students' families assume nuclear, intact, biological families because historically this family structure has been the norm, statistically and culturally. However, the demographic character of American family life has been changing rapidly and educational institutions have not made adequate adjustment to these changes that currently affect such large numbers of students. Unfortunately there has been a reluctance to acknowledge the existence of stepfamilies as an integral part of contemporary life. As a result, schools do not usually consider the unique needs of stepchildren and their families in their policy planning, but relate to all two-parent families as though they were intact, nuclear families. . . .

BACKGROUND

Demographic statistics confirm that stepchildren are a growing population in schools. Ten million children, or 13% of all minor children, are stepchildren who live with a remarried parent (Glick, 1985). These figures underestimate the numbers of children in extended stepfamily networks, however, because they do not include children who have stepparents in the households of their nonresidential parents, or children who have stepparents who are not legally married to their biological parents. Nor do the figures include stepchildren in the first marriages of previously unwed parents; the exact numbers are not known because the children are not identified through the census data collection methods. Also, 18- to 22-year-old stepchildren who are attending college are not included even though many of these young adults are still structurally, psychologically, and financially dependent stepchildren in their

From Margaret Crosbie-Burnett and Ada Skyles, "Stepchildren in Schools and Colleges: Recommendations for Educational Policy Changes," *Family Relations*, vol. 38, no. 1 (January 1989). Copyright © 1989 by the National Council on Family Relations, 3989 Central Avenue, NE, Suite #550, Minneapolis, MN 55421. Reprinted by permission.

stepfamilies. It is likely that the numbers of stepchildren will continue to increase because it is estimated that young Americans have a 50% chance of living in a stepfamily during their lifetime (Furstenberg, 1980).

RESEARCH

. . . Becoming a stepchild is often a stressful transition for children (Hetherington, Cox, & Cox, 1985; Wallerstein & Kelly, 1980), adolescents (Duberman, 1975; Lutz, 1983; Strother & Jacobs, 1984), and young adults (Crosbie-Burnett, 1987). Marriage of a parent means an expansion of one's family into a more complex family system, with the many concomitant financial, psychological, and emotional adjustments (Crosbie-Burnett, Skyles, & Becker-Haven, 1988; Sager et al., 1983; Visher & Visher, 1979). Making this adjustment more difficult for children is the lack of understanding about and support for their concerns. Children rarely get permission from parents or other adults to express anxiety or unhappiness about parental marriage because marriage, by definition, is supposed to be a happy occasion in our culture. Schools are in a position to help support children during this life transition by giving them a safe place to express and explore their feelings, questions, and concerns about parental marriage.

Effects of parental remarriage. Children have legitimate cause for concern. A panel study (Ahrons & Wallisch, 1987) found deterioration of the relationship between divorced biological parents after the remarriage of either parent, but particularly the father. Also, biological parents reported that acquiring stepchildren or having new babies in a remarriage was associated with less involvement with both custodial and noncustodial children, and that having new babies actually created problems with one's children. Clinical evidence corroborates these findings (Rosenberg & Hajal, 1985). For some children parental remarriage exacerbates problems of divided loyalties between the households of parents (Wallerstein & Kelly, 1980). There is growing evidence that parental remarriage is more problematic for girls than for boys. Stepdaughters are reported to have more psychosocial problems (Crosbie-Burnett, in press; Hetherington, Cox, & Cox, 1985), more stress (Lutz, 1983), and more difficult relationships with stepparents (Clingempeel, Ievoli, & Brand, 1984; Clingempeel & Segal, 1986; Peterson & Zill, 1986) than stepsons.

Abuse and neglect of stepchildren. Evidence suggests that children in stepfamilies experience a disproportionately high occurrence of abuse and neglect when compared with children intact, nuclear families (Husain & Chapel, 1983; Lightcap, Kurland, & Burgess, 1982; Russell, 1984; Wilson, Daly, & Weghorst, 1980). Both the bonding that usually occurs between biological parents and children and the incest taboos are lacking between stepparents and stepchildren; these factors have been suggested as reasons for the vulnerability of stepchildren to abuse and neglect (Mead, 1970; Wilson et al., 1980). School personnel need to be aware that stepchildren are at higher risk because they are instrumental in identifying and reporting abuse and neglect of children.

Biases against stepfamilies. Although images of and text about single-parent families are now scattered throughout many textbooks, mention of stepfamilies is noticeably absent (Crosbie-Burnett, 1988). Schools are in a powerful position to request that publishers expand family images and text to include stepfamilies.

More blatant bias was identified in a study of the attitudes of counselors and social workers (Bryan, Ganong, Coleman & Bryan, 1985). Rating written descriptions of family members, in which family structure was identified as either intact family or stepfamily, subjects rated stepchildren and stepparents more negatively than children and parents from intact families.

Functioning of stepchildren in schools. Utilizing a representative national sample, one recent study has revealed that adolescents in stepfamilies are earning lower grades than adolescents in intact, nuclear families, and that stepparents are less active than biological parents in school affairs (Dornbusch, Ritter, Leiderman, Roberts, & Fraleigh, 1987). In other studies of teachers' reports of children's behavior problems, stepchildren were reported to have more behavior problems than children in intact, nuclear families (Crosbie-Burnett, 1988; Touliatos & Lindholm, 1980), yet parents in stepfamilies reported less face-to-face contact with teachers than did parents of intact, nuclear families or single-parent families (Crosbie-Burnett, 1988). The latter study also found that school counselors had more contact with stepchildren than with children from intact, nuclear families or single-parent families. Clinicians and researchers alike have concluded that while teachers are in the important position of providing continued structure and support for children who are adjusting to the restructuring of their families, school counselors can play a crucial role in helping stepchildren function successfully in school and, to some extent, at home (Appel, 1985; Poppen & White, 1984; Strother & Jacobs, 1984; Wallerstein & Bundy, 1984). . . .

School-based interventions. The focus of school-based interventions has been small, time-limited, structured support groups conducted by counselors, social workers, or psychologists for children experiencing family change. . . .

A recent study of the effects of an intervention with counselors, teachers, and elementary students found that even a 2-hour classroom intervention (Crosbie-Burnett & Pulvino, in press) and a 4-hour training session with teachers and counselors can increase family-related communication between stepchildren and teachers (Crosbie-Burnett, 1988). After the intervention teachers and counselors reported feeling more knowledgeable about stepchildren's family experiences and more competent about handling problems and issues that stepchildren might bring to them. In addition, teachers reported that the classroom intervention "stimulated good feelings and respect among kids from all family types" and that there was "a lot of information giving and sharing" after the intervention.

Pressure for change in schools. In addition to the above research, specific information about stepchildren for teachers (Coleman, Ganong, & Henry, 1984) and counselors (Gardner, 1984; Poppen & White, 1984), suggestions for change in school services for stepchildren (Pasley & Ihinger-Tallman, 1986), and suggestions for integrating remarriage and stepfamily living into the college curriculum (Coleman & Ganong, 1983) are now available. It is clear that the time has come for education to take a pro-active stance toward responding to the unique needs of stepchildren and their families. The home-school relationship for stepfamilies is at risk because that relationship depends on mutual trust and understanding; at present most administrators, teachers, and other school professionals lack knowledge of, and skills in relating to, non-nuclear families (Shea, 1982).

CURRENT SITUATION AND BASIS FOR POLICY CHANGE

Society's conceptualization of stepfamilies and the language used to define them has an inherent bias that must be changed before new policy strategies can be devised. A revealing example can be found in the use of the term "reconstituted" family, meaning a family in which a single parent has remarried. The word "reconstituted" reveals how we conceptualize remarried families. The concept suggests that we see remarriage as recreating the "real" family again, after the family has been in an incomplete, nonviable, temporary state—the single-parent household. This view was somewhat more accurate historically when nearly all stepparents *replaced* a deceased parent; however, today 90% of remarried families are formed after the divorce of two living parents. Furthermore, the lack of recognition that first marriages for unwed parents who marry someone other than their child's biological parent create stepfamilies rather than nuclear biological families suggests that the label "stepfamily" means *deviant* and is to be avoided. In both cases *this "recreation of the intact, nuclear family" myth denies the distinct structural and psychological differences between two-biological-parent families and stepfamilies, which contain only one biological parent.* Grouping both family types together under "two-parent families" is the basis for inappropriate policy or, as is more often the case, no policy for stepfamilies, because they become invisible when not perceived as unique and different.

Many families that have parental figures who are not legally married to the biological single parent are structurally and psychologically similar to stepfamilies, but are inappropriately categorized as single-parent families. These include: single parents who cohabit with a partner in a committed relationship; single parents who share parenting with extended family members (e.g., two divorced brothers rearing their children in one home); and homosexual stepfamilies, families in which a homosexual parent recouples but cannot legally marry. In all of these family types, the family structure is certainly different from a single parent living alone with offspring, and the second parental figure may be an important psychological parent to the child.

All of this suggests that society seems "uncomfortable" with the many variant family structures in which children live today. Rather than broadening the concept of family to include the variety of structures, our society appears to camouflage some variant family forms under "real" family (e.g., heterosexual stepfamilies) and define the others as deviant (e.g., homosexual families, single-parent families). Policy has been made in all of our social institutions on this outdated and distorted view of family life in America. It is necessary to modify our policies to reflect the reality of family life today and to demonstrate support for all families in the educational community.

The development of new family-related policy in education requires a fundamental change in our conceptualization of family composition. We can no longer define "family" for all students as the members of the household of a student's primary residence. For increasing numbers of students, the "immediate family" is comprised of persons in two or more households that are linked together by primary parent-child relations and/or sibling relations. In the post-divorce situation these families have been called *binuclear* families (Ahrons, 1984). This word is designed to describe the reality of a child's family situation in which the child spends time in both parents' households. This term is also applicable to the households of two biological parents who were never married but share the parenting of their child.

If one or both of the biological parents marries or cohabits with a partner and thereby brings a stepparent into one of the households, the student then lives in an *extended stepfamily network*. This term was created to denote a group of households that are connected to one another through biology or marriage; it is a combination of the traditional extended family of grandparents, aunts, uncles, cousins, and the modern extended family that is formed by the interrelated households of coparents, at least one of whom has taken a new partner (Crosbie-Burnett et al., 1988).

While we need to take a more expansive view of "family," we also need more consistency in school relations with stepparents. At present, legally married stepparents are conceptualized as replacements of biological parents for purposes of financial policies (e.g., college financial aid), yet they are denied the legal rights and responsibilities of biological parents in other policies (e.g., school permission slips, medical emergency release forms, access to school records, signing report cards) (Stenger, 1986). School policies regarding stepparents do not validate their rather significant contributions to stepchildren's development and, instead, convey a message of their unimportance in school issues. While stepchildren are often taught to respect a stepparent at home, they learn that their stepparents are not respected as parental figures by the schools; this can be detrimental to young children and erode the already fragile stepparent-stepchild relationships.

Before new policies can be developed there are four changes from current conceptualizations that must occur:

1. *The change from the assumption of hostility and "break-up" in the parental relationship when the marital relationship ends to an assumption and encouragement of enduring cooperative coparenting by the biological parents.* Even if this cooperation is not a reality for many coparents, the power of the school as a social institution in making the assumption of cooperation may promote this behavior of both coparents.

2. *A change in thinking about nonresidential parental involvement from the dichotomous categories "involved" versus "uninvolved" to thinking about involvement as many dimensions on a continuum.* Involvement occurs in many ways such as actual behavioral involvement with the child, the emotional closeness a child feels for an absent parent, or both. Even a physically absent parent may still function psychologically as a primary parent to a child.

3. *Letting go of "there can be only one mother and one father" ideology and the subsequent change of perceiving the stepparent as a parental replacement to perceiving the stepparent as an additional parental figure.* Even in the situations where there is a stepfather who is very involved with his stepchild and the biological father is nonresidential, the child may still perceive the stepfather as an additional parent, not a replacement.

4. *An expansion of our narrow definition of parent as the biological parent or parents with whom the student lives to significant*

parental figures in the student's extended stepfamily network. Parental figures can include nonresidential biological parents and residential or nonresidential stepparents, grandparents, or other relatives. Educators must recognize that a student's most important *psychological* parent(s) may not be synonymous with residential biological parent(s) and that all of the parental figures have the *potential* to contribute to the student's development in school. Therefore, all significant parental figures should be acknowledged and included formally in family-related policy. These persons are all potential sources of support upon whom the school can call when helping students to maximize their potential.

POLICY RECOMMENDATIONS . . .

For Counselors, Psychologists, Social Workers, Nurses, and Other Support Services Professionals

- Learn about common stepfamily issues and appropriate intervention strategies.
- When working with an individual student, identify the significant parental figures in the student's family and be sensitive to the student's family experience from his/her perspective.
- Include significant parental figures in the assessment of the student's problem and the intervention; solicit their support in working with the student. Help facilitate communication and cooperation between the adults in different households.
- Facilitate discussion groups for parental figures; focus on school-related issues and student-focused problem solving.
- Periodically offer support groups for stepchildren in the schools.

- Identify local counselors, psychologists, and therapists who have training in stepfamily issues for purposes of referral and consultation. Identify any community support services, such as support groups, for stepfamily members who are having problems. . . .

CONCLUSION

Schools are a powerful institution. Second only to the family, they are the most influential institution in the lives of children. Policies and practices that devalue or ignore the unique aspects of stepfamilies have an adverse impact on a growing proportion of students—stepchildren. New policies must be developed to provide an environment of acceptance and inclusion of stepchildren and their families within the educational community.

REFERENCES

Ahrons, C. R. (1984). The binuclear family: Parenting roles and relationships. In I. Koch-Nielsen (Ed.), *Parent-child relationship, post-divorce: A seminar report* (pp. 54–79). Copenhagen, Denmark: The Danish National Institute for Social Research.

Ahrons, C. R., & Wallisch, K. (1987). Parenting in the binuclear family: Relationships between biological and stepparents. In K. Pasley & M. Ihinger-Tallman (Eds.), *Remarriage and stepparenting: Current research and theory* (pp. 225–256). New York: Guilford Press.

Appel, K. W. (1985). America's changing families: A guide for educators. *Fastback 219.* Bloomington, IN: Phi Delta Kappa Educational Foundation.

Bryan, S. H., Ganong, L. H., Coleman, M., & Bryan, L. R. (1985). Counselors' perceptions of stepparents and stepchildren. *Journal of Counseling Psychology, 32,* 279–282.

Clingempeel, W. G., Ievoli, R., & Brand, E. (1984). Structural complexity and the quality of stepfather-stepchild relationships. *Family Process, 23,* 547–560.

Clingempeel, W. G., & Segal, S. (1986). Stepparent-stepchild relationships and the psychological adjustment of children in stepmother and stepfather families. *Child Development, 57,* 474–484.

Coleman, M., & Ganong, L. (1983, October). *Linkages: Adding remarriage and stepfamilies to the college curriculum.* Paper presented at the annual meeting of the National Council on Family Relations, St. Paul, MN.

Coleman, M., Ganong, L., & Henry, J. (1984). What teachers should know about stepfamilies. *Childhood Education, 60,* 306–309.

Crosbie-Burnett, M. (1987, February). *College-aged stepchildren: Understanding their unique stresses.* Paper presented at the Big 10 Counseling Center Conference, University of Wisconsin—Madison, Madison, WI.

Crosbie-Burnett, M. (1988, February). *Schools and students from non-nuclear families.* Paper presented at the Wisconsin School Counselor Internship Conference, Steven's Point, WI.

Crosbie-Burnett, M. (in press). Impact of joint versus maternal legal custody, sex and age of adolescent, and family structure complexity on adolescents in remarried families. *Conciliation Courts Review.*

Crosbie-Burnett, M., & Pulvino, C. (in press). Classroom guidance on non-traditional families. *The School Counselor.*

Crosbie-Burnett, M., Skyles, A., & Becker-Haven, J. (1988). Exploring stepfamilies from a feminist perspective. In S. Dornbusch & M. Strober (Eds.), *Feminism, children and the new families* (pp. 297–326). New York: Guilford Press.

Dornbusch, S. M., Ritter, P. L., Leiderman, P. H., Roberts, D. S., & Fraleigh, M. J. (1987). Relation of parenting to adolescent school performance. *Child Development, 58,* 1244–1257.

Duberman, L. (1975). *The reconstituted family: A study of remarried couples and their children.* Chicago, IL: Nelson-Hall Publishers.

Furstenberg, F. F., Jr. (1980). Reflections on remarriage. *Journal of Family Issues, 1,* 443–453.

Gardner, R. A. (1984). Counseling children in stepfamilies. *Elementary School Guidance and Counseling, 19,* 40–49.

Glick, P. (1985, November). *An update on the demographics of single-parent and stepfamilies.* Paper presented at the Annual Meeting of the National council on Family Relations, Dallas, TX.

Hetherington, E. M., Cox, M., & Cox, R. (1985). Long-term effects of divorce and remarriage on the adjustment of children. *Journal of the American Academy of Child Psychiatry, 24,* 518–530.

Husain, A., & Chapel, J. (1983). History of incest in girls admitted to a psychiatric hospital. *American Journal of Psychiatry, 140,* 591–593.

Lightcap, J., Kurland, J., & Burgess, R. (1982). Child abuse: A test of some predictions from evolutionary theory. *Ethology & Sociobiology, 3,* 61–67.

Lutz, P. (1983). The stepfamily: An adolescent perspective. *Family Relations, 32,* 367–376.

Mead, M. (1970). Anomalies in American post divorce relationships. In P. Bohannan (Ed.), *Divorce and after* (pp. 107–139). New York: Doubleday & Co.

Pasley, K., & Ihinger-Tallman, M. (1986). Stepfamilies: New challenges for the schools. In T. Fairchild (Ed.), *Crisis intervention strategies for school-based helpers* (pp. 70–112). Springfield, IL: Charles C. Thomas.

Peterson, J. L., & Zill, N. (1986). Marital disruption, parent-child relationships, and behavior problems in children. *Journal of Marriage and the Family, 48,* 295–307.

Poppen, W. A., & White, P. N. (1984). Transition to the blended family. *Elementary School Guidance and Counseling, 19*(1), 50–61.

Rosenberg, E. B., & Hajal, F. (1985). Stepsibling relationships in remarried families. *Social Casework, 66,* 287–292.

Russell, D. (1984). The prevalence and seriousness of incestuous abuse: Stepfathers versus biological fathers. *Child Abuse and Neglect, 8,* 15–22.

Sager, C. J., Brown, H. S., Crohn, H., Engel, L., Rodstein, E., & Walker, E. (1983). *Treating the remarried family.* New York: Brunner/Mazel.

Shea, C. A. (1982). *Schools and non-nuclear families: Recasting relationships.* (Eric Document Reproduction Service No. ED234 333 CG 016 927.)

Stenger, R. L. (1986). The school counselor and the law: New developments. *Journal of Law and Education. 15*(1), 105–116.

Strother, J., & Jacobs, L. (1984). Adolescent stress as it relates to stepfamily living: Implications for school counselors. *The School Counselor, 32,* 97–103.

Touliatos, J., & Lindholm, B. W. (1980). Teachers' perceptions of behavior problems in children from intact, single-parent, and stepparent families. *Psychology in the Schools, 17,* 264–269.

Visher, E. B., & Visher, J. S. (1979). *Stepfamilies: A guide to working with stepparents and stepchildren.* New York: Brunner/Mazel.

Wallerstein, J. S., & Bundy, M. L. (1984). Helping children of disrupted families: An interview with Judith S. Wallerstein, *Elementary School Guidance & Counseling, 19*(1), 19–29.

Wallerstein, J. S., & Kelly, J. B. (1980). *Surviving the breakup.* New York: Basic Books.

Wilson, M., Daly, M., & Weghorst, S. J. (1980). Household composition and the risk of child abuse and neglect. *Journal of Biosociological Science, 12,* 333–340.

NO

Lawrence H. Ganong
and Marilyn Coleman

A COMPARISON OF CLINICAL AND EMPIRICAL LITERATURE ON CHILDREN IN STEPFAMILIES

The clinical literature on stepfamilies is almost double the volume of empirical studies and has tended to dominate the field. The predominance of clinical literature may be contributing to commonly perceived negative stereotypes of stepfamilies and stepfamily members (i.e., they are fraught with problems, need assistance, etc.). However, in a previous comprehensive view of empirical studies of stepchildren, we concluded that there were few differences between stepchildren and children from intact nuclear families (Ganong and Coleman, 1984). If, in fact, stepchildren are not "different" in any major way from children in other families, the negative perceptions need to be corrected. . . .

The purpose of this article is to review the literature on stepchildren and compare "clinical" or applied work to "empirical" research in this area. . . . It should be noted that the terms *clinical* and *clinician* are broadly defined to include all family professionals in applied fields (e.g., family life educators, teachers, clergy). Most reviews of stepchildren, stepparents, or stepfamily literature have not distinguished between conclusions of empirical research and those of other writings. . . .

METHODS

This comparative review was limited to literature published in books and journals. References were obtained from computer searches of major resource banks (i.e., National Institutes of Mental Health, ERIC, *Psychological Abstracts*), bibliographies compiled by the Stepfamily Association of America (Bohannon, 1981) and the National Council on Family Relations (Pasley and Ihinger-Tallman, 1983), suggestions from colleagues, and standard library search procedures. Over 350 references were reviewed. Empirical research

From Lawrence H. Ganong and Marilyn Coleman, "A Comparison of Clinical and Empirical Literature on Children in Stepfamilies," *Journal of Marriage and the Family*, vol. 48 (May 1986). Copyright © 1986 by the National Council on Family Relations, 3989 Central Avenue, NE, Suite #550, Minneapolis, MN 55421. Reprinted by permission. Notes omitted.

was selected for this review if the main focus of the study was the effects on children of parental remarriage, having a stepparent, or living in a stepfamily. For the clinical literature the following criteria were used: (a) a main focus was on counseling, educating, or providing assistance to stepchildren and stepfamilies; (b) the report was in a clinically oriented book or journal, was written by a practitioner, or was written for counselors, teachers, or other helping professionals. First-person accounts written by stepparents or stepchildren were excluded, as were publications in popular periodicals. A total of 43 empirical studies and 71 clinical references were included. While these 114 references may not make up the universe of published work on stepchildren, they represent an exhaustive search and adequately serve the purposes of this comparative review. . . .

RESULTS AND DISCUSSION

Theory

Clinicians wrote more often from a theoretical perspective than did researchers. Fifty-one of 71 clinical references discussed stepchildren from clear theoretical positions. . . . The underlying framework for most research, however, was "the deficit-family model" (Marotz-Baden, Adams, Bueche, Munro, and Munro, 1979) or the "deficit-comparison" approach (Ganong and Coleman, 1984). Comparisons are made between stepchildren and children living in an intact nuclear family, with the expectation that stepchildren will be in a deficit position. The primary assumption of this approach is that variations from the "intact" nuclear family (e.g., stepfamilies) produce undesirable effects on children.

Clinicians have demonstrated more awareness of problems inherent in the deficit-comparison perspective and have argued against comparing stepfamilies to nuclear families because of basic structural and developmental differences (Fishman and Hamel, 1981; Pill, 1981; Visher and Visher, 1979; Waldron and Whittington, 1979). Recently, a few researchers have agreed that the deficit-comparison model is limiting and should be abandoned in empirical studies of stepfamilies (Fox and Inazu, 1982; Santrock, Warshak, and Elliott, 1982). . . .

In general, the two groups share a tendency toward perceiving stepfamilies and stepchildren within a problem-oriented framework. Chilman (1983), in an earlier review of literature, contended that

Clinicians particularly tend to view this family form as traumatic because they see the selected group of troubled people who come for counseling. They do *not* see those who are making a relatively trouble-free adjustment to their marriage.

Researchers do see stepchildren and other stepfamily members who are functioning well, but their "deficit-comparison" lens may restrict their vision. This orientation is not conducive to assisting either clinicians or researchers in asking questions that will broaden understanding of stepfamily dynamics, identify stepfamily strengths, and improve clinical practice, but rather leads again and again over well-trod ground. For example, researchers continue to examine such variables as self-esteem and perceptions of stepparents (Raschke and Raschke, 1979), and clinicians continue to discuss "myths of instant love," loyalty conflicts, and loss and mourning (Visher and Visher, 1979). Little is added to our understanding of the effects of parental remarriage on children, and little progress is made toward developing a more fruitful framework for considering stepfamilies.

Methodology

Clinicians and researchers utilize different methods to study stepchildren and their families. . . .

According to a comprehensive review of the empirical literature (Ganong and Coleman, 1984), research on stepchildren is characterized by (a) the tendency to collect self-report data from a single respondent, usually the child (30 studies); (b) a reliance on surveys, with data gathered only once from each respondent (34 studies); (c) use of one method of gathering data (34 studies), especially questionnaires developed by the researchers (18 studies); and (d) nonprobability sampling techniques (30 studies). Empirical data were usually collected in group settings such as school classrooms. The dearth of multitrait-multimethod studies, of longitudinal studies, and of studies obtaining responses from multiple family members has been criticized as a major weakness of this research (Esses and Campbell, 1984; Ganong and Coleman, 1984).

Researchers have shown a great interest in perceptions of stepchildren and their parents (e.g., Halperin and Smith, 1983; Parish and Philip, 1982). . . . [M]uch of this attention reflects the fact that perceptions can be measured easily with a questionnaire. . . . One result is that, by and large, researchers are not examining what clinicians see as important.

For clinicians, articulating the process by which conclusions were drawn appeared to be a secondary concern; seldom did clinical writers explain the sources upon which their information was based. Clinical methodology included descriptions of programs, case studies, literature reviews, interviews, and clinical impressions. Some works were based on more than one method. The most frequent method was clinical impressions; a study was given this code whenever authors made a number of conclusions without either providing their rationale or citing a source. . . .

The primary emphasis of clinicians has been on the stepchild's family (which may include two households). In contrast to researchers, clinicians usually collected data from several family members. Suprafamily influences on children such as school, friends, the legal system, and religious institutions seldom were considered. . . . Societal attitudes (i.e., negative images of stepfamily members) were sometimes mentioned (e.g., Visher and Visher, 1979), but the impact of specific societal systems was not often identified. Researchers were not much better about considering suprafamily influences; most often considered were stepchildren's peers and their relationships in school (Touliatos and Lindholm, 1980). Clinicians focused more on processes in stepfamily interaction than researchers did. Clinicians also referred more to long-term developmental changes in individuals and relationships, and repeated observations were more characteristic of clinical studies. Clinicians also tended to emphasize children's adjustments during the transition period following parental remarriage. Researchers, on the other hand, paid little attention to developmental issues pertaining to individuals and stepfamilies. Consequently, there is an absence of both longitudinal studies of how stepchildren adjust and cohort studies of stepchildren in different stages of stepfamily life.

Clinicians and researchers both tended to use nonprobability samples, though researchers drew from a broader, more "normal" spectrum. Clinicians derived their data about stepchildren and their families from a sample of people seeking help. In spite of this, clinicians typically did not hesitate to generalize conclusions to all stepfamilies.

Types of Stepfamilies

There are many variations of stepfamily structures (Ganong and Coleman, 1984; Pasley and Ihinger-Tallman, 1982; Robinson, 1980). Clinicians generally did a better job than researchers of considering this complexity. Clinical writers frequently pointed out that stepfamilies are complex environments structurally, interpersonally, and emotionally (e.g., Sager, Brown, Crohn, Engel, Rodstein, and Walker, 1983; Visher and Visher, 1979; Wald, 1981). They contended that this complexity distinguishes stepfamilies from other family forms and is a major cause of difficulty for stepchildren's adjustment and adaptation. For example, clinicians frequently discussed differences between stepmother and stepfather households (e.g., Fishman and Hamel, 1981; Schulman, 1972); stepchildren whose parents divorced and those with a deceased parent (e.g., Jones, 1978; Prosen and Farmer, 1982); stepchildren who do and do not have stepsiblings (e.g., Goldner, 1982; Whiteside and Auerbach, 1978); and stepchildren who live full-time with a stepparent and those who live in more than one household (e.g., Fishman and Hamel, 1981; Visher and Visher, 1979).

Researchers, on the other hand, have tended to ignore the complexity of stepfamilies to the point where crucial distinctions between different types of stepfamilies were not made and critical variables were not assessed. Basic variables such as the type of stepfamily household (i.e., stepmother, stepfather, or "complex") and the cause of dissolution of the child's original family (i.e., death of a parent or divorce) were seldom measured. Less than half of the studies included stepchildren from both stepmother and stepfather households, only one included nonresidential stepchildren (Duberman, 1973), and just three assessed children from complex stepfamily households (Burchinal, 1964; Clingempeel, Ievoli, and Brand, 1984; Duberman, 1973). About a third included both children with a deceased parent and those whose parents divorced, a third studied only stepchildren whose parents divorced, and the other third did not measure the cause of family dissolution.

Several other household characteristics and family situations of stepchildren considered significant by clinicians were relatively ignored by researchers. For example, age at dissolution of parents' marriage, years resided in a single-parent household, age at parental remarriage, years resided in the stepfamily household, custody arrangements, residence, birth order, number of siblings, stepparents' age, presence of a half-sibling, stepsiblings, and extended family are among the stepfamily characteristics that were "underexamined" by researchers.

This lack of consideration of complexity reduces the ability of researchers to generalize and raises serious questions about their results. . . .

Conclusions

Differing conclusions were drawn by researchers and clinicians. The research literature, for the most part, did not report significant differences between stepchildren and children from other family structures on such variables as cognitive performance, psychosomatic complaints, personality characteristics, social behavior, family relationships, and social attitudes, despite using a deficit-comparison model as the conceptual base (Ganong and Coleman, 1984). The clinical literature, on the other hand, generally reported that stepchildren and their families inherently are beset by problems and difficulties (e.g., "All stepfamilies begin with great handicaps"; Satir, 1972: 173). Since clinical writers have been more prolific than researchers, their influence on the perception of stepchildren and stepfamilies by family professionals may be commensurately greater. This negative orientation may reinforce an image of stepchildren and stepfamilies as deviant and dysfunctional.

SUMMARY

In summary, we found that few similarities between the empirical and clinical studies could be identified. The primary similarities are the deficit-comparison approach underlying investigations in both areas and a shared appreciation for the influence of family functioning on stepchildren's adjustment. . . .

There is much evidence to indicate that researchers and clinicians interested in stepchildren are professionally segregated and little evidence demonstrating communication between the groups. . . . [G]reater interchange between the two groups of professionals potentially could enhance and stimulate research efforts as well as improve clinical practice.

Greater intercourse also could aid in building a substantial body of knowledge about stepchildren and their families. In the absence of more comprehensive literature, what does exist contributes to a

"Whoozle Effect" (Gelles, 1980). A Whoozle Effect occurs when a particular finding reported in one study is subsequently cited by others without consideration of possible limitations to the study and without efforts to replicate the findings. Frequent citation of a study over the years results in the findings being treated as "facts." The original caveats regarding methodological or sampling characteristics tend to be forgotten, but the findings and conclusions do not (Gelles, 1980).

The literature on stepchildren illustrates the Whoozle Effect. Often the initial investigation is not an empirical study with well-defined sampling and measurement techniques but is rather a report of clinical impressions based on data gleaned via clinical observations from a unique sample of unknown size and characteristics. This means that much of what is "known" about stepchildren is based on clinical data bases. For example, frequent references are made in both clinical and self-help literature (Coleman, Ganong, and Gingrich, 1985) to loyalty conflicts for stepchildren. This assertion has been based on clinical impressions. Not until Lutz's (1983) study of adolescents was this assertion empirically tested, yet this is one of the most well-known "facts" about stepchildren. The Whoozle Effect is enhanced when reviewers neglect to distinguish between results drawn from empirical research and those emanating from clinical work. The failure of most previous reviews on stepchildren and stepfamilies to make such distinctions may contribute to the pervasiveness of the deficit, problem-oriented framework.

What can clinicians learn from researchers? As noted earlier, clinicians seem to rely primarily on observations of stepchildren and their families. Many clinicians consider self-report techniques as unreliable (Schwartz and Breunlin, 1983). It has been reported, however, that self-report scores from well-constructed instruments are sometimes more useful and more accurate than clinical interviews or observations (Olson, 1983). . . .

Findings from clinical works would be elucidated if clinicians took greater care in generalizing from their data. Congruent with this admonishment is another to clinicians to be more explicit in reporting sources of their impressions. In some clinical studies virtually no mention is made regarding the sample (i.e., total sample size, sample composition) or methods by which conclusions are drawn.

Clinicians often seem to develop a skewed image of the world, perhaps because their data base is comprised of individuals or families having troubles. . . .

What can researchers learn from clinicians? From the clinical literature, researchers can gain a greater appreciation of the value of observing and conceptualizing stepfamily interaction and of considering the complexity of stepfamilies. Few empirical studies on stepchildren have utilized multiple methods and fewer still have examined the stepchild in the context of a multilevel family system. Researchers can learn from clinicians the value of looking at the whole family. . . . The consideration of changes within stepfamilies over time would greatly enhance our understanding of the development of stepfamily systems and the effects of transitions on children in stepfamilies.

REFERENCES

Bohannon, Paul. 1981. "Stepfamilies: A partially annotated bibliography." Palo Alto, CA: Stepfamily Association of America.

Burchinal, Lee G. 1964. "Characteristics of adolescents from unbroken, broken, and reconstituted families." Journal of Marriage and the Family 26: 44–50.

Chilman, Catherine S. 1983. "Remarriage and stepfamilies: Research results and implications." Pp. 147–163 in Eleanor D. Macklin and R. H. Rubin (eds.), Contemporary Families and Alternative Lifestyles. Beverly Hills, CA: Sage.

Clingempeel, Glenn, R. Ievoli, and E. Brand. 1984. "Structural complexity and the quality of stepfather-stepchild relationships." Family Relations 33: 465–473.

Coleman, Marilyn, L. Ganong, and R. Gingrich, 1985. "Stepfamily strengths: A review of the popular literature." Family Relations 34: 583–589.

Duberman, Lucille. 1973. "Step-kin relationships." Journal of Marriage and the Family 35: 283–292.

Espinoza, Ronald, and Y. Newman. 1979. Stepparenting (DHEW Publication No. ADM 78-579). Washington, DC: U.S. Government Printing Office.

Esses, Lillian M., and C. Campbell. 1984. "Challenges in researching the remarried." Family Relations 33: 415–424.

Fishman, Barbara, and B. Hamel. 1981. "From nuclear to stepfamily ideology: A stressful change." Alternative Lifestyles 4(2): 181–204.

Fox, Greer L., and J. K. Inazu. 1982. "The influence of mother's marital history on the mother-daughter relationship in black and white households." Journal of Marriage and the Family 44: 143–153.

Ganong, Lawrence H., and M. Coleman. 1984. "Effects of remarriage on children: A review of the empirical literature." Family Relations 33: 389–406.

Gelles, Richard J. 1980. "Violence in the family: A review of research in the seventies." Journal of Marriage and the Family 42: 873–885.

Goldner, Virginia. 1982. "Remarriage family: Structure, system, future." Pp. 187–206 in James C. Hansen and L. Messenger (eds.), Therapy with Remarried Families. Rockville, MD: Aspen.

Halperin, Sandra, and T. Smith. 1983. "Differences in stepchildren's perceptions of their stepfathers and natural fathers: Implications for family therapy." Journal of Divorce 7: 19–30.

Jones, Shirley, M. 1978. "Divorce and remarriage: A new beginning, a new set of problems." Journal of Divorce 2: 217–227.

Lutz, Patricia. 1983. "The stepfamily: An adolescent perspective." Family Relations 32: 367–375.

Marotz-Baden, Ramona, G. Adams, N. Bueche, B. Munro, and G. Munro. 1979. "Family form or family process? Reconsidering the deficit family model approach." Family Coordinator 28: 5–14.

Olson, David. 1983. "Family systems–behavioral medicine: Emerging research and methodology." Paper presented at the Family Systems-Behavioral Medicine Workshop, Wayzata, MN (October).

Parish, Thomas, and M. Philip. 1982. "The self-concepts of children from intact and divorced families: Can they be affected in school settings?" Education 103 (Fall): 60–63.

Pasley, Kay, and M. Ihinger-Tallman. 1982. "Remarried family life: Supports and constraints." Pp. 367–383 in Nick Stinnett et al. (eds.), Family Strengths IV: Positive Support Systems. Lincoln: University of Nebraska Press.

Pasley, Kay and Ihinger-Tallman. 1983. "Remarriage and stepparenting: A comprehensive bibliography." Unpublished manuscript.

Pill, Cynthia J. 1981. "A family life education group for working with stepparents." Social Casework 62: 159–166.

Prosen, Selina S., and J. H. Farmer. 1982. "Understanding stepfamilies: Issues and Implications for counselors." Personnel and Guidance Journal 60: 393–397.

Robinson, Margaret. 1980. "Stepfamilies: A reconstituted family system." Journal of Family Therapy 2: 45–69.

Sager, Clifford, H. S. Brown, H. Crohn, T. Engel, E. Rodstein, and E. Walker. 1983. Treating the Remarried Family. New York: Brunner/Mazel.

Santrock, John, R. Warshak, and G. L. Elliott. 1982. "Social development and parent-child interaction in father-custody and stepmother families." Pp. 289–314 in Michael E. Lamb (ed.), Non-traditional Families: Parenting and Child Development. Hillsdale, NJ: Erlbaum.

Satir, Virginia. 1972. Peoplemaking. Palo Alto, CA: Science and Behavior Books.

Schulman, Gerda. 1972. "Myths that intrude on the adaptation of the stepfamily." Social Casework 53: 131–139.

Schwartz, Richard C., and D. Breunlin. 1983. "Research: Why clinicians should bother with it." Family Therapy Networker 7 (July/August): 23–27, 57–59.

Touliatos, John, and B. W. Lindholm. 1980. "Teachers' perceptions of behavior problems in children from intact, single-parent, and stepparent families." Psychology in the Schools 17: 264–269.

Visher, Emily B., and J. S. Visher. 1979. Stepfamilies: A Guide to Working with Stepparents and Stepchildren. New York: Brunner/Mazel.

Wald, Esther. 1981. The Remarried Family: Challenge and Promise. New York: Family Service Association of America.

Waldron, Jane A., and R. Whittington. 1979. "The stepparent/stepfamily." Journal of Operational Psychiatry 10: 47–50.

Whiteside, Mary, and L. S. Auerbach. 1978. "Can a daughter of my father's new wife be my sister? Families of remarriage in family therapy." Journal of Divorce 1: 271–283.

POSTSCRIPT

Do Stepchildren Need Special Policies and Programs on Their Behalf?

Crosbie-Burnett and Skyles claim that children in stepfamilies are under considerable stress, which is related to the emotional, psychological, and economic adjustments that these children must make as members of stepfamilies. They maintain that stepfamily life is difficult for children because it lacks needed family support and because of societal biases against stepfamilies. Their solution is to implement school-based interventions—to change policies and practices at school to reflect greater support of stepchildren and their families.

Ganong and Coleman maintain that stepchildren are not really much different from other children and that much of the research on stepchildren is biased and unreliable. They compare studies done by clinicians with those of other researchers. Although they see some benefits to the clinical studies, Ganong and Coleman argue that such studies consistently present stepchildren as deviant and stepfamily life as problematic. A primary reason for this portrayal is that clinicians regularly rely on their own troubled clients for research information. Ganong and Coleman conclude that clinicians view stepchildren as having multiple concerns that need resolving and hastily present these children as having an exaggerated risk of developing psychological problems. They believe that society has developed many negative stereotypes toward stepchildren partly because clinicians publish most of the research on these children and their families along with their unfavorable conclusions.

One clinical team that advocates considering the strengths and rewards of stepfamily life is Emily B. Visher and John S. Visher. In their book *Old Loyalties, New Ties: Therapeutic Strategies with Stepfamilies* (Brunner-Mazel, 1988), they caution therapists that only "a few of the total number of stepfamilies will ever seek therapeutic help. . . . They turn to therapy as a valuable tool to help create a rewarding family life for themselves and their children." Visher and Visher discuss how most stepfamilies claim to have good to excellent family relationships, and they describe seven "stepfamily tasks" that they believe lead to successful adaptation to stepfamily life.

With regard to stepfamilies and the methods by which they are studied, how might clinicians and other researchers study stepfamilies without bias? How does using a deficit-comparison approach bias the results of studies on stepchildren? How do myths and stereotypes about stepchildren affect these children's lives? Are there other institutions besides schools where changing policies and practices could aid stepchildren? Do some of the typical problems that stepchildren experience stem mainly from being in a stepfamily or do they appear earlier, such as before the divorce, during the divorce process, or during the single-parent phase?

SUGGESTED READINGS

J. Barney, "Stepfamilies: Second Chance or Second-Rate?" *Phi Delta Kappan*, 140 (1990): 144–148.

A. C. Brown, R. J. Green, and J. Druckman, "A Comparison of Stepfamilies With and Without Child-Focused Problems," *American Journal of Orthopsychiatry*, 60 (1990): 556–567.

M. Coleman and L. H. Ganong, "Remarriage and Stepfamily Research in the 1980s," *Journal of Marriage and the Family*, 52 (1990): 925–940.

P. Glick, "Remarried Families, Stepfamilies, and Stepchildren: A Brief Demographic Analysis," *Family Relations*, 38 (1989): 24–27.

M. Hetherington and J. Arasteh, eds., *Impact of Divorce, Single Parenting and Stepparenting on Children* (Lawrence Erlbaum, 1988).

A. Levine, "The Second Time Around: Realities of Remarriage," *U.S. News & World Report*, 108 (January 1990): 50–53.

ISSUE 17

Is The Success of Remarriage Doomed?

YES: Andrew Cherlin, from "Remarriage as an Incomplete Institution," *American Journal of Sociology* (November 1978)

NO: Ann Goetting, from "The Six Stations of Remarriage: Developmental Tasks of Remarriage After Divorce," *Family Relations* (April 1982)

ISSUE SUMMARY

YES: Professor of sociology Andrew Cherlin discusses a number of reasons why remarriage is less successful than marriage and proposes that this is primarily because remarriage in its present form has not been accepted in the larger society.

NO: Professor of sociology Ann Goetting argues that remarriage is a process and that for it to be successful it must progress through a series of developmental stages.

In earlier times, remarriage typically involved people whose spouses had died. Although remarriage was permitted by some communities, not all found it acceptable, perhaps taking the stance that marriage is for life, and that it is inappropriate to remarry after the death of one's partner and violate the sanctity of that marriage. More recently, remarriage has become a status more often entered into by persons who have been divorced, and it has been met with varying degrees of success. Remarriages are often less successful than first marriages in terms of subsequent rates of divorce. With divorce figures still indicating that as many as 40 to 50 percent of marriages will terminate before the death of either spouse, it seems that efforts need to be made to assist people in making both marriage and remarriage work, assuming that the institution of marriage is still valued by society.

In his selection, Andrew Cherlin indicates that society has not institutionalized remarriage after divorce, or made it acceptable to most people in the larger community. If such is the case, remarriages are likely to receive much less social support and services than first marriages, even though they are likely to be a much more complex and complicated form of marriage and may require more outside assistance.

Explanations for the lack of community and social support are often based on public perceptions, or misperceptions, like "divorced persons are emotionally unstable" or "divorced persons are more cautious based on their previous marital experience and are more likely to divorce again." In such cases the *label* "divorced" has a significant role to play in the status of the individuals involved, partly because it tends to carry with it some negative connotations.

Finances may also play a part in the breakdown of remarriage, as many new (remarried) families find themselves juggling alimony or child support in addition to everyday household expenses.

Andrew Cherlin depicts remarriage as an incomplete institution, one currently fraught with problems both internal and external to the marital union. In her selection, Ann Goetting uses P. Bohannon's classic framework for the divorce process as the basis for a positive, developmental life cycle approach to working through the tasks of remarriage. Her positive views of remarriage provide a sharp contrast to Cherlin.

YES

Andrew Cherlin

REMARRIAGE AS AN INCOMPLETE INSTITUTION

The higher divorce rate for remarriages after divorce than for first marriages, it is argued, is due to the incomplete institutionalization of remarriage after divorce in the United States. Persons who are remarried after a divorce and have children from previous marriages face problems unlike those encountered in first marriages. The institution of the family provides no standard solutions to many of these problems, with the result that the unity of families of remarriages after divorce often becomes precarious. The incomplete institutionalization of remarriage shows us, by way of contrast, that family unity in first marriages is still supported by effective institutional controls, despite claims that the institutional nature of family life has eroded in the 20th century. Some suggestions for future research on remarriage and on the institutionalization of married life are presented.

Sociologists believe that social institutions shape people's behavior in important ways. Gerth and Mills (1953, p. 173) wrote that institutions are organizations of social roles which "imprint their stamps upon the individual, modifying his external conduct as well as his inner life." More recently, Berger and Luckmann (1966) argued that institutions define not only acceptable behavior, as Gerth and Mills believed, but also objective reality itself. Social institutions range from political and economic systems to religion and language. And displayed prominently in any sociologist's catalogue of institutions is a fundamental form of social organization, the family.

The institution of the family provides social control of reproduction and child rearing. It also provides family members with guidelines for proper behavior in everyday family life, and, presumably, these guidelines contribute to the unity and stability of families. But in recent years, sociologists have de-emphasized the institutional basis of family unity in the United States. According to many scholars, contemporary families are held together more by consensus and mutual affection than by formal, institutional controls.

The main source of this viewpoint is an influential text by Ernest Burgess and Harvey Locke which appeared in 1945. They wrote:

The central thesis of this volume is that the family in historical times has been, and at present is, in transition from an institution to a companionship. In the past, the important factors unifying the family have been external, formal, and authoritarian, as the law, the mores, public opinion, tradition, the authority of the family head, rigid discipline, and elaborate ritual. At present, in the new emerging form of the companionship family, its unity inheres less and less in community pressures and more and more in such interpersonal relationships as the mutual affection, the sympathetic understanding, and the comradeship of its members. [P. vii]

In the institutional family, Burgess and Locke stated, unity derived from the unchallenged authority of the patriarch, who was supported by strong social pressure. But, they argued, with urbanization and the decline of patriarchal authority, a democratic family has emerged which creates its own unity from interpersonal relations.

Many subsequent studies have retained the idea of the companionship family in some form, such as the equalitarian family of Blood and Wolfe (1960) or the symmetrical family of Young and Wilmott (1973). Common to all is the notion that patriarchal authority has declined and sex roles have become less segregated. Historical studies of family life demonstrate that the authority of the husband was indeed stronger in the preindustrial West than it is now (see, e.g., Ariès 1962; Shorter 1975). As for today, numerous studies of "family power" have attempted to show that authority and power are shared more equally between spouses (see Blood and Wolfe 1960). Although these studies have been criticized (Safilios-Rothschild 1970), no one has claimed that patriarchal authority is as strong now as the historical record indicates it once was. Even if we believe that husbands still have more authority than wives, we can nevertheless agree that patriarchal authority seems to have declined in the United States in this century.

But it does not follow that institutional sources of family unity have declined also. Burgess and Locke reached this conclusion in part because of their assumption that the patriarch was the transmitter of social norms and values to his family. With the decline of the patriarch, so they believed, a vital institutional link between family and society was broken. This argument is similar to the perspective of Gerth and Mills, who wrote that a set of social roles becomes an institution when it is stabilized by a "head" who wields authority over the members. It follows from this premise that if the head loses his authority, the institutional nature of family life will become problematic.

Yet institutionalized patterns of behavior clearly persist in family life, despite the trend away from patriarchy and segregated sex roles. As others have noted (Dyer and Urban 1958; Nye and Berardo 1973), the equalitarian pattern may be as firmly institutionalized now as the traditional pattern was in the past. In the terms of Berger and Luckmann, most family behavior today is habitualized action which is accepted as typical by all members—that is, it is institutionalized behavior. In most everyday situations, parents and children base their behavior on social norms: parents know how harshly to discipline their children, and children learn from parents and friends which parental rules are fair and which to protest. These sources of institutionalization in the contemporary American family have received little attention from students of family unity, just as family members themselves pay little attention to them.

The presence of these habitualized patterns directly affects family unity. "Habitualization," Berger and Luckmann wrote, "carries with it the important psychological gain that choices are narrowed" (1966, p. 53). With choices narrowed, family members face fewer decisions which will cause disagreements and, correspondingly, have less difficulty maintaining family unity. Thus, institutional support for family unity exists through the routinization of everyday behavior even though the husband is no longer the unchallenged agent of social control.

Nowhere in contemporary family life is the psychological gain from habitualization more evident than in the families of remarried spouses and their children, where, paradoxically, habitualized behavior is often absent. We know that the unity of families of remarriages which follow a divorce is often precarious—as evidenced by the higher divorce rate for these families than for families of first marriages (U.S. Bureau of the Census 1976). And in the last few decades, remarriage after divorce—as opposed to remarriage after widowhood—has become the predominant form of remarriage. In this paper, I will argue that the higher divorce rate for remarriages after divorce is a consequence of the incomplete institutionalization of remarriage after divorce in our society. The institution of the family in the United States has developed in response to the needs of families of first marriages and families of remarriages after widowhood. But because of their complex structure, families of remarriages after divorce that include children from previous marriages must solve problems unknown to other types of families. For many of these problems, such as proper kinship terms, authority to discipline stepchildren, and legal relationships, no institutionalized solutions have emerged. As a result, there is more opportunity for disagreements and divisions among family members and more strain in many remarriages after divorce.

The incomplete institutionalization of remarriage after divorce reveals, by way of contrast, the high degree of institutionalization still present in first marriages. Family members, especially those in first marriages, rely on a wide range of habitualized behaviors to assist them in solving the common problems of family life. We take these behavioral patterns for granted until their absence forces us to create solutions on our own. Only then do we see the continuing importance of institutionalized patterns of family behavior for maintaining family unity.

I cannot provide definitive proof of the hypothesis linking the higher divorce rate for remarriages after divorce to incomplete institutionalization. There is very little quantitative information concerning remarriages. In fact, we do not even know how many stepparents and stepchildren there are in the United States. Nor has there ever been a large, random-sample survey designed with families of remarriages in mind. (Bernard's 1956 book on remarriage, for example, was based on information supplied nonrandomly by third parties.) There are, nevertheless, several studies which do provide valuable information, and there is much indirect evidence bearing on the plausibility of this hypothesis and of alternative explanations. I will review this evidence, and I will also refer occasionally to information I collected through personal interviews with a small, nonrandom sample of remarried couples and family counselors in the northeast. Despite the lack of data, I believe that the problems of families of remarriages are worth examining, especially given the recent increases in divorce and remarriage rates. In the hope that his article will stimulate further investigations, I will also present suggestions for future research.

THE PROBLEM OF FAMILY UNITY

Remarriages have been common in the United States since its beginnings, but until this century almost all remarriages followed widowhood. In the Plymouth Colony, for instance, about one-third of all men and one-quarter of all women who lived full lifetimes remarried after the death of a spouse, but there was little divorce (Demos 1970). Even as late as the 1920s, more brides and grooms were remarrying after widowhood than after divorce, according to estimates by Jacobson (1959). Since then, however, a continued increase in divorce (Norton and Glick 1976) has altered this pattern. By 1975, 84% of all brides who were remarrying were previously divorced, and 16% were widowed. For grooms who were remarrying in 1975, 86% were previously divorced (U.S. National Center for Health Statistics 1977). Thus, it is only recently that remarriage after divorce has become the predominant form of remarriage.

And since the turn of the century, remarriages after divorce have increased as a proportion of all marriages. In 1900 only 3% of all brides—including both the single and previously married—were divorced (Jacobson 1959). In 1930, 9% of all brides were divorced (Jacobson 1959), and in 1975, 25% of all brides were divorced (U.S. National Center for Health

Statistics 1977). As a result, in 7 million families in 1970 one or both spouses had remarried after a divorce (U.S. Bureau of the Census 1973). Most of this increase is due to the rise in the divorce rate, but some part is due to the greater tendency of divorced and widowed adults to remarry. The remarriage rate for divorced and widowed women was about 50% higher in the mid-1970s than in 1940 (Norton and Glick 1976).

At the same time, the percentage of divorces which involved at least one child increased from 46% in 1950 to 60% in 1974 (U.S. National Center for Health Statistics 1953, 1977). The increase in the percentage of divorces which involve children means that more families of remarriages after divorce now have stepchildren. Although it is not possible with available data to calculate the exact number of families with stepchildren, we do know that in 1970 8.9 million children lived in two-parent families where one or both parents had been previously divorced (U.S. Bureau of the Census 1973). Some of these children—who constituted 15% of all children living in two-parent families—were from previous marriages, and others were from the remarriages.

Can these families of remarriages after divorce, many of which include children from previous marriages, maintain unity as well as do families of first marriages? Not according to the divorce rate. A number of studies have shown a greater risk of separation and divorce for remarriages after divorce (Becker, Landes, and Michael 1976; Bumpass and Sweet 1972; Cherlin 1977; Monahan 1958). Remarriages after widowhood appear, in contrast, to have a lower divorce rate than first marriages (Monahan 1958). A recent Bureau of the Census report (U.S. Bureau of the Census 1976) estimated that about

33% of all first marriages among people 25–35 may end in divorce, while about 40% of remarriages after divorce among people this age may end in divorce. The estimates are based on current rates of divorce, which could, of course, change greatly in the future.[1]

Conventional wisdom, however, seems to be that remarriages are more successful than first marriages. In a small, non-random sample of family counselors and remarried couples, I found most to be surprised at the news that divorce was more prevalent in remarriages. There are some plausible reasons for this popular misconception. Those who remarry are older, on the average, than those marrying for the first time and are presumably more mature. They have had more time to search the marriage market and to determine their own needs and preferences. In addition, divorced men may be in a better financial position and command greater work skills than younger, never-married men. (Divorced women who are supporting children, however, are often in a worse financial position—see Hoffman [1977].)

But despite these advantages, the divorce rate is higher in remarriages after divorce. The reported differences are often modest, but they appear consistently throughout 20 years of research. And the meaning of marital dissolution for family unity is clear: when a marriage dissolves, unity ends. The converse, though, is not necessarily true: a family may have a low degree of unity but remain nominally intact. Even with this limitation, I submit that the divorce rate is the best objective indicator of differences in family unity between remarriages and first marriages.

There are indicators of family unity other than divorce, but their meaning is less clear and their measurement is more difficult. There is the survey research tradition, for example, of asking people how happy or satisfied they are with their marriages. The invariable result is that almost everyone reports that they are very happy. (See, e.g., Bradburn and Caplovitz 1965; Glenn 1975; Campbell, Converse, and Rodgers 1976.) It may be that our high rate of divorce increases the general level of marital satisfaction by dissolving unsatisfactory marriages. But it is also possible that the satisfaction ratings are inflated by the reluctance of some respondents to admit that their marriages are less than fully satisfying. Marriage is an important part of life for most adults—the respondents in the Campbell et al. (1976) national sample rated it second only to health as the most important aspect of their lives—and people may be reluctant to admit publicly that their marriage is troubled.

Several recent studies, nevertheless, have shown that levels of satisfaction and happiness are lower among the remarried, although the differences typically are small. Besides the Campbell et al. study, these include Glenn and Weaver (1977), who found modest differences in marital happiness in the 1973, 1974, and 1975 General Social Surveys conducted by the National Opinion Research Center. They reported that for women, the difference between those who were remarried and those who were in a first marriage was statistically significant, while for men the difference was smaller and not significant. In addition, Renne (1971) reported that remarried, previously divorced persons were less happy with their marriages than those in first marriages in a probability sample of 4,452 Alameda County, California, households. Again, the differences were modest, but they were consistent within categories of age, sex, and race. No tests of significance were reported.

The higher divorce rate suggests that maintaining family unity is more difficult for families of remarriages after divorce. And the lower levels of marital satisfaction, which must be interpreted cautiously, also support this hypothesis. It is true, nevertheless, that many remarriages work well, and that the majority of remarriages will not end in divorce. And we must remember that the divorce rate is also at an all-time high for first marriages. But there is a difference of degree between remarriages and first marriages which appears consistently in research. We must ask why families of remarriages after divorce seem to have more difficulty maintaining family unity than do families of first marriages. Several explanations have been proposed, and we will now assess the available evidence for each.

PREVIOUS EXPLANATIONS

One explanation, favored until recently by many psychiatrists, is that the problems of remarried people arise from personality disorders which preceded their marriages (see Bergler 1948). People in troubled marriages, according to this view, have unresolved personal conflicts which must be treated before a successful marriage can be achieved. Their problems lead them to marry second spouses who may be superficially quite different from their first spouse but are characterologically quite similar. As a result, this theory states, remarried people repeat the problems of their first marriages.

If this explanation were correct, one would expect that people in remarriages would show higher levels of psychiatric symptomatology than people in first marriages. But there is little evidence of this. On the contrary, Overall (1971) reported that in a sample of 2,000 clients seeking help for psychiatric problems, currently remarried people showed lower levels of psychopathology on a general rating scale than persons in first marriages and currently divorced persons. These findings, of course, apply only to people who sought psychiatric help. And it may be, as Overall noted, that the differences emerged because remarried people are more likely to seek help for less serious problems. The findings, nevertheless, weaken the psychoanalytic interpretation of the problems of remarried life.

On the other hand, Monahan (1958) and Cherlin (1977) reported that the divorce rate was considerably higher for people in their third marriages who had divorced twice than for people in their second marriages. Perhaps personality disorders among some of those who marry several times prevent them from achieving a successful marriage. But even with the currently high rates of divorce and remarriage, only a small proportion of all adults marry more than twice. About 10% of all adults in 1975 had married twice, but less than 2% had married three or more times (U.S. Bureau of the Census 1976).

Most remarried people, then, are in a second marriage. And the large number of people now divorcing and entering a second marriage also undercuts the psychoanalytic interpretation. If current rates hold, about one-third of all young married people will become divorced, and about four-fifths of these will remarry. It is hard to believe that the recent increases in divorce and remarriage are due to the sudden spread of marriage-threatening personality disorders to a large part of the young adult population. I conclude, instead, that the psycho-analytic explanation for the rise in divorce and the difficulties of remarried spouses and their children is at best incomplete.[2]

A second possible explanation is that once a person has divorced he or she is less hesitant to do so again. Having divorced once, a person knows how to get divorced and what to expect from family members, friends, and the courts. This explanation is plausible and probably accounts for some of the difference in divorce rates. But it does not account for all of the research findings on remarriage, such as the finding of Becker et al. (1976) that the presence of children from a previous marriage increased the probability of divorce for women in remarriages, while the presence of children from the new marriage reduced the probability of divorce. I will discuss the implications of this study below, but let me note here that a general decrease in the reluctance of remarried persons to divorce would not explain this finding. Moreover, the previously divorced may be more hesitant to divorce again because of the stigma attached to divorcing twice. Several remarried people I interviewed expressed great reluctance to divorce a second time. They reasoned that friends and relatives excused one divorce but would judge them incompetent at marriage after two divorces.

Yet another explanation for the higher divorce rate is the belief that many remarried men are deficient at fulfilling their economic responsibilities. We know that divorce is more likely in families where the husband has low earnings (Goode 1956). Some remarried men, therefore, may be unable to earn a sufficient amount of money to support a family. It is conceivable that this inability to be a successful breadwinner could account for all of the divorce rate differential, but statistical studies of divorce suggest otherwise. Three recent multivariate analyses of survey data on divorce have shown that remarried persons still had a higher probability of divorce or separation, independent of controls for such socioeconomic variables as husband's earnings (Becker et al. 1976), husband's educational attainment (Bumpass and Sweet 1972), and husband's and wife's earnings, employment status, and savings (Cherlin 1977). These analyses show that controlling for low earnings can reduce the difference in divorce probabilities, but they also show that low earnings cannot fully explain the difference. It is possible, nevertheless, that a given amount of income must be spread thinner in many remarriages, because of child-support or alimony payments (although the remarried couple also may be receiving these payments). But this type of financial strain must be distinguished from the questionable notion that many remarried husbands are inherently unable to provide for a wife and children.

INSTITUTIONAL SUPPORT

The unsatisfactory nature of all these explanations leads us to consider one more interpretation. I hypothesize that the difficulties of couples in remarriages after divorce stem from a lack of institutionalized guidelines for solving many common problems of their remarried life. The lack of institutional support is less serious when neither spouse has a child from a previous marriage. In this case, the family of remarriage closely resembles families of first marriages, and most of the norms for first marriages apply.

But when at least one spouse has children from a previous marriage, family life often differs sharply from first marriages. Frequently, as I will show, family members face problems quite unlike those in first marriages—problems for which institutionalized solutions do not exist. And without accepted solutions to their problems, families of remarriages must resolve difficult issues by themselves. As a result, solving everyday problems is sometimes impossible without engendering conflict and confusion among family members.

The complex structure of families of remarriages after divorce which include children from a previous marriage has been noted by others (Bernard 1956; Bohannan 1970; Duberman 1975). These families are expanded in the number of social roles and relationships they possess and also are expanded in space over more than one household. The additional social roles include stepparents, stepchildren, stepsiblings, and the new spouses of noncustodial parents, among others. And the links between the households are the children of previous marriages. These children are commonly in the custody of one parent—usually the mother—but they normally visit the noncustodial parent regularly. Thus they promote communication among the divorced parents, the new stepparent, and the noncustodial parent's new spouse.

Family relationships can be quite complex, because the new kin in a remarriage after divorce do not, in general, replace the kin from the first marriage as they do in a remarriage after widowhood. Rather, they add to the existing kin (Fast and Cain 1966). But this complexity alone does not necessarily imply that problems of family unity will develop. While families of remarriages may appear complicated to Americans, there are many societies in which complicated kinship rules and family patterns coexist with a functioning, stable family system (Bohannan 1963; Fox 1967).

In most of these societies, however, familial roles and relationships are well defined. Family life may seem complex to Westerners, but activity is regulated by established patterns of behavior. The central difference, then, between families of remarriages in the United States and complicated family situations in other societies is the lack of institutionalized social regulation of remarried life in this country. Our society, oriented toward first marriages, provides little guidance on problems peculiar to remarriages, especially remarriages after divorce.

In order to illustrate the incomplete institutionalization of remarriage and its consequences for family life, let us examine two of the major institutions in society: language and the law. "Language," Gerth and Mills (1953, p. 305) wrote, "is necessary to the operations of institutions. For the symbols used in institutions coordinate the roles that compose them, and justify the enactment of these roles by the members of the institution." Where no adequate terms exist for an important social role, the institutional support for this role is deficient, and general acceptance of the role as a legitimate pattern of activity is questionable.

Consider English terms for the roles peculiar to remarriage after divorce. The term "stepparent," as Bohannan (1970) has observed, originally meant a person who replaced a dead parent, not a person who was an additional parent. And the negative connotations of the "stepparent," especially the "stepmother," are well known (Bernard 1956; Smith 1953). Yet there are no other terms in use. In some situations, no term exists for a child to use in addressing a stepparent. If the child calls her mother "mom," for example, what should she call her stepmother? This lack of appropriate terms for parents in remarriages after divorce can have negative consequences for family functioning. In one family I interviewed, the wife's children wanted to call their stepfather "dad," but the stepfather's own children, who also lived in the household, refused to allow this usage. To them, sharing the term "dad" represented a threat to their claim on their father's attention and affection. The dispute caused bad feelings, and it impaired the father's ability to act as a parent to all the children in the household.

For more extended relationships, the lack of appropriate terms is even more acute. At least the word "stepparent," however inadequate, has a widely accepted meaning. But there is no term a child living with his mother can use to describe his relationship to the woman his father remarried after he divorced the child's mother. And, not surprisingly, the rights and duties of the child and this woman toward each other are unclear. Nor is the problem limited to kinship terms. Suppose a child's parents both remarry and he alternates between their households under a joint custody arrangement. Where, then, is his "home"? And who are the members of his "family"? These linguistic inadequacies correspond to the absence of widely accepted definitions for many of the roles and relationships in families of remarriage. The absence of proper terms is both a symptom and a cause of some of the problems of remarried life.

As for the law, it is both a means of social control and an indicator of accepted patterns of behavior. It was to the law, for instance, that Durkheim turned for evidence on the forms of social solidarity. When we examine family law, we find a set of traditional guidelines, based on precedent, which define the rights and duties of family members. But as Weitzman (1974) has shown, implicit in the precedents is the assumption that the marriage in question is a first marriage. For example, Weitzman found no provisions for several problems of remarriage, such as balancing the financial obligations of husbands to their spouses and children from current and previous marriages, defining the wife's obligations to husbands and children from the new and the old marriages, and reconciling the competing claims of current and ex-spouses for shares of the estate of a deceased spouse.

Legal regulations concerning incest and consanguineal marriage are also inadequate for families of remarriages. In all states marriage and sexual relations are prohibited between persons closely related by blood, but in many states these restrictions do not cover sexual relations or marriage between other family members in a remarriage—between a stepmother and a stepson, for example, or between two stepchildren (Goldstein and Katz 1965). Mead (1970), among others, has argued that incest taboos serve the important function of allowing children to develop affection for and identification with other family members without the risk of sexual exploitation. She suggested that current beliefs about incest—as embodied in law and social norms—fail to provide adequate security and protection for children in households of remarriage.[3]

The law, then, ignores the special problems of families of remarriages after divorce. It assumes, for the most part, that remarriages are similar to first marriages. Families of remarriages after divorce, consequently, often must deal with problems such as financial obligations or sexual relations without legal regulations or clear legal precedent. The law, like the language, offers incomplete institutional support to families of remarriages.

In addition, other customs and conventions of family life are deficient when applied to remarriages after divorce. Stepparents, for example, have difficulty determining their proper disciplinary relationship to stepchildren. One woman I interviewed, determined not to show favoritism toward her own children, disciplined them more harshly than her stepchildren. Other couples who had children from the wife's previous marriage reported that the stepfather had difficulty establishing himself as a disciplinarian in the household. Fast and Cain (1966), in a study of about 50 case records from child-guidance settings, noted many uncertainties among stepparents about appropriate role behavior. They theorized that the uncertainties derived from the sharing of the role of parent between the stepparent and the noncustodial, biological parent. Years ago, when most remarriages took place after widowhood, this sharing did not exist. Now, even though most remarriages follow divorce, generally accepted guidelines for sharing parenthood still have not emerged.

There is other evidence consistent with the idea that the incomplete institutionalization of remarriage after divorce may underlie the difficulties of families of remarriages. Becker et al. (1976) analyzed the Survey of Economic Opportunity, a nationwide study of approximately 30,000 households. As I mentioned above, they found that the presence of children from a previous marriage increased the probability of divorce for women in remarriages, while the presence of children from the new marriage reduced the probability of divorce. This is as we would expect, since children from a previous marriage expand the family across households and complicate the structure of family roles and relationships. But children born into the new marriage bring none of these complications. Consequently, only children from a previous marriage should add to the special problems of families of remarriages.[4]

In addition, Goetting (1978a, 1978b) studied the attitudes of remarried people toward relationships among adults who are associated by broken marital ties, such as ex-spouses and the people ex-spouses remarry. Bohannan (1970) has called these people "quasi-kin." Goetting presented hypothetical situations involving the behavior of quasi-kin to 90 remarried men and 90 remarried women who were white, previously divorced, and who had children from previous marriages. The subjects were asked to approve, disapprove, or express indifference about the behavior in each situation. Goetting then arbitrarily decided that the respondents reached "consensus" on a given situation if any of the three possible response categories received more than half of all responses. But even by this lenient definition, consensus was not reached on the proper behavior in most of the hypothetical situations. For example, in situations involving conversations between a person's present spouse and his or her ex-spouse, the only consensus of the respondents was that the pair should say "hello." Beyond that, there was no consensus on whether they should engage in polite conversation in public places or on the telephone or whether the ex-spouse should be invited into the new spouse's home while waiting to pick up his or her children. Since meetings of various quasi-kin must occur regularly in the lives of most respondents, their disagreement is indicative of their own confusion about how to act in common family situations.

Still, there are many aspects of remarried life which are similar to life in first marriages, and these are subject to established rules of behavior. Even some of the unique aspects of remarriage may be regulated by social norms—such as the norms concerning the size and nature of wedding ceremonies in remarriages (Hollingshead 1952). Furthermore, as Goode (1956) noted, remarriage is itself an institutional solution to the ambiguous status of the divorced (and not remarried) parent. But the day-to-day life of remarried adults and their children also includes many problems for which there are no institutionalized solutions. And since members of a household of remarriage often have competing or conflicting interests (Bernard 1956), the lack of consensual solutions can make these problems more serious than they otherwise would be. One anthropologist, noting the lack of relevant social norms, wrote, "the present situation approaches chaos, with each individual set of families having to work out its own destiny without any realistic guidelines" (Bohannan 1970, p. 137).

DISCUSSION AND SUGGESTIONS FOR RESEARCH

The lack of institutionalized support for remarriage after divorce from language, the law, and custom is apparent. But when institutional support for family life exists, we take it for granted. People in first marriages rarely stop to notice that a full set of kinship terms exists, that the law regulates their relationships, or that custom dictates much of their behavior toward spouses and children. Because they pay little attention to it, the institutional nature of everyday life in first marriages can be easily underestimated. But such support contributes to the unity of first marriages despite the decline of the patriarch, who was the agent of social control in past time. Institutional guidelines become manifest not only through the transmission of social pressure by a family head but also through the general acceptance of certain habitual behavior patterns as typical of family life. Since this latter process is an ongoing characteristic of social life, the pure "companionship" family—which, in fairness, Burgess and Locke defined only as an ideal type—will never emerge. We have seen this by examining the contrasting case of remarriage after divorce. In this type of marriage, institutional support is noticeably lacking in several respects, and this deficiency has direct consequences for proper family functioning. I have tried to show how the incomplete institutionalization of remarriage after divorce makes the maintenance of family unity more difficult.

One of the first tasks for future research on remarriage is to establish some basic social demographic facts: what proportion of remarried couples have children present from a previous marriage, what proportion have children present from the remarriage, how many children visit noncustodial parents, how frequent these visits are, and so on. As I mentioned, there is no reliable information on these questions now. The U.S. Bureau of the Census, for example, has not discriminated in most of its surveys between parents and stepparents or between children and stepchildren. Yet until figures are available, we can only guess at the number of families which face potential difficulties because of complex living arrangements.

And if we reinterviewed families of remarriage some time after obtaining this information from them, we could begin to test the importance of institutional support for family unity. It follows from the argument advanced here that the more complex the family's situation—the more quasi-kin who live nearby, the more frequently adults and children interact with quasi-kin, the more likely each remarried spouse is to have children from a previous marriage—the more serious becomes the lack of institutional guidelines. Thus, adults in remarriages with a more complex structure should be more likely to divorce or separate in the future, other things being equal. Also, a more complex structure might increase the financial strain on family members, so their earnings and financial obligations should be carefully assessed.

But beyond collecting this fundamental information, we need to discover, by a variety of means, what norms are emerging concerning remarriage and how they emerge. Content analyses of literature, for example, or close study of changes in the language and the law may be illuminating. Just in the past few years, discussion groups, adult education courses, newletters, and self-help books for remarried parents have proliferated. Whether these developments are central to the institutionalization of remarriage remains to be seen, but they represent possible sources of information about institutionalization which should be monitored. In addition, detailed ethnographic studies could allow us to uncover emerging patterns of institutionalization among families of remarriages.

And in all these investigations of the institutionalization of remarried life, we must develop a perspective different from that of traditional family research. In much past research—starting with the work of Burgess and others—family sociologists have been concerned primarily with the interpersonal relations of family members, especially of husbands and wives (Lasch 1977). But sociologists' theories—and their research strategies—have assumed, for the most part, that interpersonal relations in families can be accounted for without many references to social institutions. Thus, Burgess and Locke (1945) popularized the notion of the companionship family, whose stability depended largely on what went on within the household. And Locke (1951) measured marital adjustment through a questionnaire which focused largely on such personal characteristics as adaptability and sociability. Yet in order to understand family life—whether in first marriages or remarriages—we must explicitly consider the influences of social institutions on husbands and wives and on parents and children.

We need to know what the institutional links are between family and society which transmit social norms about everyday behavior. That is, we need to know exactly how patterns of family behavior come to be accepted and how proper solutions for family problems come to be taken for granted. And the recent rise in the number of remarriages after divorce may provide us with a natural laboratory for observing this process of institutionalization. As remarriage after divorce becomes more common, remarried parents and their children probably will generate standards of conduct in conjunction with the larger society. By observing these developments, we can improve our understanding of the sources of unity in married—and remarried—life.

ACKNOWLEDGEMENT

I wish to thank Doris Entwisle, George Levinger, Valerie Oppenheimer, and Richard Rubinson for comments on earlier drafts.

NOTES

1. A study by McCarthy (1977), however, suggests that remarriages may be more stable than first marriages for blacks. Using life-table techniques on data from 10,000 women under age 45 collected in the 1973 Survey of Family Growth, McCarthy reported that the probability of separation and divorce during the first 15 years of marriage is lower for blacks in remarriages than in first marriages, but is about 50% higher for whites in remarriages than for whites in first marriages.

2. Despite the lack of convincing evidence, I am reluctant to discount this explanation completely. Clinical psychologists and psychiatrists with whom I have talked insist that many troubled married persons they have treated had made the same mistakes twice and were in need of therapy to resolve long-standing problems. Their clinical experience should not be ignored, but this "divorce-proneness" syndrome seems inadequate as a complete explanation for the great problems of remarried people.

3. Bernard (1956) noted this problem in the preface to the reprinted edition of her book on remarriage. "Institutional patterns," she wrote, "are needed to help remarried parents establish relationships with one another conducive to the protection of their children."

4. In an earlier paper (Cherlin 1977), I found that children affected the probability that a woman in a first marriage or remarriage would divorce only when the children were of preschool age. But the National Longitudinal Surveys of Mature Women, from which this analysis was drawn, contained no information about whether the children of remarried wives were from the woman's previous or current marriage. Since the Becker et al. (1976) results showed that this distinction is crucial, we cannot draw any relevant inferences about children and remarriage from my earlier study.

REFERENCES

Ariès, Philippe, 1962. *Centuries of Childhood.* New York: Knopf.

Becker, G., E. Landes, and R. Michael. 1976. "Economics of Marital Instability." Working Paper no. 153. Stanford, Calif.: National Bureau of Economic Research.

Berger, Peter L., and Thomas Luckmann. 1966. *The Social Construction of Reality.* New York: Doubleday.

Bergler, Edmund. 1948. *Divorce Won't Help.* New York: Harper & Bros.

Bernard, Jessie. 1956. *Remarriage.* New York: Dryden.

Blood, Robert O., and Donald M. Wolfe. 1960. *Husbands and Wives.* New York: Free Press.

Bohannan, Paul. 1963. *Social Anthropology.* New York: Holt, Rinehart & Winston.

———. 1970. "Divorce Chains, Households of Remarriage, and Multiple Divorces." Pp. 127n39 in *Divorce and After,* edited by Paul Bohannan. New York: Doubleday.

Bradburn, Norman, and David Caplovitz. 1965. *Reports on Happiness.* Chicago: Aldine.

Bumpass, L. L., and A. Sweet, 1972. "Differentials in Marital Instability: 1970." *American Sociological Review* 37 (December): 754–66.

Burgess, Ernest W., and Harvey J. Locke. 1945. *The Family: From Institution to Companionship.* New York: American.

Campbell, Angus, Philip E. Converse, and Willard L. Rodgers. 1976. *The Quality of American Life.* New York: Russell Sage.

Cherlin, A. 1977. "The Effects of Children on Marital Dissolution." *Demography* 14 (August): 265–72.

Demos, John. 1970. *A Little Commonwealth: Family Life in Plymouth Colony.* New York: Oxford University Press.

Duberman, Lucile. 1975. *The Reconstituted Family.* Chicago: Nelson-Hall.

Dyer, W. G., and D. Urban. 1958. "The Institutionalization of Equalitarian Family Norms." *Journal of Marriage and Family Living* 20 (February): 53–58.

Fast, I., and A. C. Cain. 1966. "The Stepparent Role: Potential for Disturbances in Family Functioning." *American Journal of Orthopsychiatry* 36 (April): 485–91.

Fox, Robin. 1967. *Kinship and Marriage.* Baltimore: Penguin.

Gerth, Hans, and C. Wright Mills. 1953. *Character and Social Structure.* New York: Harcourt, Brace & Co.

Glenn, N. 1975. "The Contribution of Marriage to the Psychological Well-Being of Males and Females." *Journal of Marriage and the Family* 37 (August): 594–601.

Glenn, N., and C. Weaver. 1977. "The Marital Happiness of Remarried Divorced Persons." *Journal of Marriage and the Family* 39 (May): 331–37.

Goetting, Ann. 1978a. "The Normative Integration of the Former Spouse Relationship." Paper presented at the annual meeting of the American Sociological Association, San Francisco, September 4–8.

____. 1978b. "The Normative Integration of Two Divorce Chain Relationships." Paper presented at the annual meeting of the Southwestern Sociological Association, Houston, April 12–15.

Goldstein, Joseph, and Jay Katz. 1965. *The Family and the Law.* New York: Free Press.

Goode, William J. 1956. *Women in Divorce.* New York: Free Press.

Hoffman, S. 1977. "Marital Instability and the Economic Status of Women." *Demography* 14 (February): 67–76.

Hollingshead, A. B. 1952. "Marital Status and Wedding Behavior." *Marriage and Family Living* (November), pp. 308–11.

Jacobson, Paul H. 1959. *American Marriage and Divorce.* New York: Rinehart.

Lasch, Christopher. 1977 *Haven in a Heartless World: The Family Besieged.* New York: Basic.

Locke, Harvey J. 1951. *Predicting Adjustment in Marriage: A Comparison of a Divorced and a Happily Married Group.* New York: Holt.

McCarthy, J. F. 1977. "A Comparison of Dissolution of First and Second Marriages." Paper presented at the 1977 annual meeting of the Population Association of America, St. Louis, April 21–23.

Mead, M. 1970. "Anomalies in American Postdivorce Relationships." Pp. 107–25 in *Divorce and After,* edited by Paul Bohannan. New York: Doubleday.

Monahan, T. P. 1958. "The Changing Nature and Instability of Remarriages." *Eugenics Quarterly* 5:73–85.

Norton, A. J., and P. C. Glick. 1976. "Marital Instability: Past, Present, and Future." *Journal of Social Issues* 32 (Winter): 5–20.

Nye, F. Ivan, and Felix M. Berardo. 1973. *The Family: Its Structure and Interaction.* New York: Macmillan.

Overall, J. E. 1971. "Associations between Marital History and the Nature of Manifest Psychopathology." *Journal of Abnormal Psychology* 78 (2): 213–21.

Renne, K. S. 1971. "Health and Marital Experience in an Urban Population." *Journal of Marriage and the Family* 33 (May): 338–50.

Safilios-Rothschild, Constantina. 1970. "The Study of Family Power Structure: A Review 1960-1969." *Journal of Marriage and the Family* 32 (November): 539–52.

Shorter, Edward. 1975. *The Making of the Modern Family.* New York: Basic.

Smith, William C. 1953. *The Stepchild.* Chicago: University of Chicago Press.

U.S. Bureau of the Census. 1973. *U.S. Census of the Population: 1970. Persons by Family Characteristics.* Final Report PC(2)-4B. Washington, D.C.: Government Printing Office.

____. 1976 *Number, Timing, and Duration of Marriages and Divorces in the United States: June 1975.* Current Population Reports, Series P-20, No. 297. Washington, D.C.: Government Printing Office.

U.S. National Center for Health Statistics. 1953. *Vital Statistics of the United States, 1950.* Vol. 2. *Marriage, Divorce, Natality, Fetal Mortality, and Infant Mortality Data.* Washington, D.C.: Government Printing Office.

____. 1977. *Vital Statistics Report. Advance Report. Final Marriage Statistics, 1975.* Washington, D.C.: Government Printing Office.

Weitzman, L. J. 1974. "Legal Regulation of Marriage: Tradition and Change." *California Law Review* 62:1169–1288.

Young, Michael, and Peter Wilmott. 1973. *The Symmetrical Family.* New York: Pantheon.

NO

Ann Goetting

THE SIX STATIONS OF REMARRIAGE: DEVELOPMENTAL TASKS OF REMARRIAGE AFTER DIVORCE

As the incidence of divorce and subsequent remarriage in the United States continues to increase, the problems associated with the developmental tasks of such remarriage become more relevant. An analysis of causal explanations for the increasingly common nature of remarriage after divorce is followed by a description of six developmental tasks which are faced by persons approaching the status passage from divorced to remarried. This developmental process is a extension of Paul Bohannan's six stations of divorce and consists of the emotional, psychic, community, parental, economic, and legal stations of remarriage.

Remarriage is emerging as a common form of marriage. Currently, remarriages represent 32% of all marriages in the United States (Price-Bonham & Balswick, 1980). As the divorce rate continues to rise and the rate of remarriage remains high—it recently has been estimated that 80% of Americans who are currently obtaining divorces will eventually remarry (Glick, 1975a)—an increasing number of people are finding themselves immersed in a marital structure quite different from the one with which they are familiar. As Schlesinger (1970) pointed out, a remarriage "possesses its own constructs, characteristics, and possibilities" (p. 101). Some of the most important differences between a first marriage and a remarriage are based on the ties each partner has to the previous marriage through children, through financial and custodial settlement, through the family and friends of the former spouse, and through continued commitment and/or attachment to the former spouse. It is probably true that the single visible factor which most differentiates a remarriage from a first marriage is the presence of children from a former marriage. Cherlin (1978) indicated that when neither spouse had a child from a previous marriage, the family of remarriage closely resembled families of first marriage and most of the norms for first marriages applied.

From Ann Goetting, "The Six Stations of Remarriage: Developmental Tasks of Remarriage After Divorce," *Family Relations*, vol. 31, no. 2 (April 1982). Copyright © 1982 by the National Council on Family Relations, 3989 Central Avenue, NE, Suite #550, Minneapolis, MN 55421. Reprinted by permission.

Though it has been suggested that remarriages are happier and more successful than first marriages (Rollin, 1971), the best available evidence has consistently indicated over the last two decades that while most remarriages do remain intact until death, the risk of marital dissatisfaction and divorce is somewhat greater than that associated with first marriages (Cherlin, 1978; McCarthy, 1978). It is estimated that one third of first marriages will end in divorce while close to one half of remarriages will do so (U.S. Bureau of the Census, 1976).

Furstenberg (1979) pointed out that the rate of conjugal stability in remarriage is only slightly lower than that in first marriage and might well be accounted for, not by greater difficulties inherent in the structure of remarriage, but by the fact that remarriages include a disproportionately greater number of individuals who accept divorce as a solution to an unsatisfactory marital situation. While this may be true, while remarriage may not require a *more difficult* lifestyle or adjustment process than first marriage, it can be assumed to require one that is *different* and therefore worthy of consideration because of the unique nature of remarriage.

The main purpose of this paper is to examine remarriage as a process. More specifically, the concern is to explore the various developmental tasks associated with the status passage from divorced to remarried. The question addressed here is: what are the situations which a person may expect to encounter upon entering and participating in remarried life? Furstenberg introduced the concept "normative schedule" to describe demographic processes that become relatively constant over time. As marriage, divorce and subsequent remarriage become routinized, they become part of a normative schedule, part of the life course. While the processes of marriage and divorce have been charted (Berger & Kellner, 1964; Bohannan, 1970; Vaughan, 1978), the final component of this marital normative schedule, that is remarriage, virtually has been overlooked in the family literature. A descriptive model of this status passage from divorced to remarried could aid the practitioner in guiding clients through the developmental tasks associated with their transition into remarriage after divorce.

Before addressing the developmental tasks of remarriage, attention is turned to the divorce and remarriage trends which are the sources of this emerging marital form. The concern here is with why divorce and subsequent remarriage have become increasingly common. Why are more and more people accepting divorce as a solution to an unsatisfactory marriage? And why do so many, though the proportion is declining (Norton & Glick, 1976), find their way back into the marriage market and eventually recommitted to matrimony?

EXPLANATIONS FOR DIVORCE AND REMARRIAGE

Divorce

The divorce rate in the United States has been rising almost continuously since data were first collected by the United States Census Bureau. It is estimated that about 37% of first marriages currently being contracted will end in divorce if the present conditions affecting divorce continue (Glick, 1973). In the past when divorce was relatively rare it was blamed on individual deficiencies. With the dramatic increase during the middle

1960's when divorce was chosen as a solution to marital problems by a broader spectrum of the population, however, emphasis has turned away from the deviance perspective and toward societal-level explanations. One recent analysis blamed the long term divorce increase on five components of our social structure: (1) the doctrine of individualism; (2) the trend toward equality of sexes; (3) the trend toward a general acceptance of divorce; (4) growing systemness; and, (5) affluence (Goetting, 1979). While this analysis is quite comprehensive, other components could be added to constitute a long list of factors fostering divorce. For example, Glick (1975b, p. 8) suggested that the following factors contribute to marital disruption: (1) social disruption such as the Vietnam war and inflation; (2) the secularization of life which dilutes the influence of organized religion in discouraging divorce; (3) education for marriage and family life in churches, schools and colleges which fosters more objective evaluation of marriage and divorce; and, (4) marriage and divorce counseling which assist incompatible couples in dissolving intolerable marriages. Also, divorce has been blamed on the socialization process which teaches men and women to have different and even opposing interests and social orientations. The result is that they have difficulty as adults becoming the companions required by the modern marriage ethic (Goetting, 1981).

Remarriage

Unlike divorce, little attention has been devoted to the high rate of remarriage after divorce. While single isolated explanations are scattered throughout the family literature, no attempt has been made to integrate these ideas into a comprehensive set of societal-level explanations. An attempt here to do so yields four: (1) the value of romantic love; (2) social exchange—satiation and alternatives; (3) social norms; and, (4) norm ambiguity and role instability.

Romantic Love. Romantic love was conceptualized by Goode (1959) to mean a strong emotional attachment between adolescents or adults, consisting of at least the components of sex desire and tenderness. In American society it has been taught that being romantically in love and having this love reciprocated is a major goal in life. The individual who "has no one" is pitied or at least considered to be in this way unfulfilled. Furthermore it has been taught that appropriate fulfillment of the need for romantic love is found within the institution of marriage. Biegel (1951) and Goode (1959) suggested that while romantic love serves important functions for social stability, it is based on temporary personal need satisfaction, and therefore is unstable. A marriage based on such fragile ground is conducive to divorce. Biegel stated that the "burning craving" of romantic love cannot last. Goode agreed that the passion of romantic love dies in the marital relationship. He stated that the "antithesis of romantic love is 'conjugal' love, the love between a settled couple" (Goode, 1959, p. 39). Synthesizing this series of ideas on romantic love, it is suggested here that romantic love leads to marriage, which in turn leads to conjugal love, a non-romantic form of love. If this simple process is extended, some implications for remarriage can be suggested. The individual is taught to strive for romantic love and seek satisfaction within marriage. But then marriage destroys the romantic elements of the relationship and replaces them with a relationship based on responsibility. Therefore, married individuals who are no longer romantically involved with each other would be left unfulfilled and once again in pursuit of romantic love. Extramarital romantic love relationships or at least desires or fantasies of such would then stimulate divorce and ultimately result in remarriage.

Benson (Note 1) suggested that most married individuals avoid this cycle of remarriage probably because of a lack of ambition in the continuing search for love. Because they are influenced by various social controls (for example, norms disapproving extramarital romantic involvements), they in fact remain unfulfilled romantically.

Social Exchange—Satiation and Alternatives. Exchange theory offers another cyclical scheme explaining serial monogamy. Theories of social exchange view humans as reward-seeking, punishment-avoiding creatures. The theories perceive human interaction to be analogous to economic markets, though humans can exchange things which are not measured by money. People are motivated toward profit—that is, an excess of reward (something valuable) over cost (something punishing or loss or reward). From the perspectives of Homans (1961) and Thibaut and Kelley (1959) divorce and subsequent remarriage can be viewed as the exchange between marital partners, and explained in the following way: A and B choose to interact with one another (marry) because each obtains the highest profit (such as companionship, romantic love or whatever is valuable) relative to interacting with alternative persons in that kind of relationship. But eventually satiation will weaken that relationship. This is based on the assumption that the more of a rewarding activity

a person receives from another, the less valuable the further units of that activity ("diminishing returns"). At the same time that the relationship is becoming weakened due to satiation, it is becoming further weakened because of the increase in alternative marriage partners resulting from social changes including industrialization, urbanization, the doctrine of individualism, and the increased proportion of women in the labor force. The many alternative spouses raise what Thibaut and Kelley refer to as the "comparison level for alternatives." Therefore, because of the satiation of marital rewards and the increase in alternative spouses, A and B will divorce and both find new partners who will again offer them the best profit (remarriage) until once again satiation sets in and a better alternative presents itself.

While under the principle of satiation it is assumed that the individual seeks rewards from interacting with a variety of people, a person *may* get such variety of interaction while being married. The need for variety may be satisfied by interacting with family, friends, colleagues or an extramarital lover. This is how exchange theorists would explain the marriages that last. If the spouses do not limit themselves to interacting with each other, that is, if they spend time together as well as time with others, satiation does not occur and so alternatives are less attractive. Thibaut and Kelley (1959) devoted a chapter to nonvoluntary relationships. They suggested that some below-comparison-level relationships (relationships that are below the person's standards of satisfaction) are maintained because alternatives are unacceptable. In other words, the marriage may provide too little reward, but the costs of divorce (one alternative) outweigh its rewards.

Social Norms. Another explanation for remarriage after divorce is that it represents an adaptation to social norms. One such norm is Farber's (1964) "permanent availability." Like romantic love, permanent availability is useful in explaining divorce and remarriage. According to Farber the norm of permanent marriage is being replaced by the norm of permanent availability. This notion implies that divorce can be explained by greater attractions to new spouses. It implies an expectation to better one's lot in society by progressing on to more attractive marital partners in somewhat the same way that one would move to a new position that offered a higher salary or better working conditions.

Another norm which has implications for remarriage is that of success in marriage. To the extent that divorce represents some kind of failure, marriage represents success. While there is social pressure on both sexes for success in marriage, such pressure is greater for women because the marriage and family have traditionally been her primary domain of responsibility. Whether a marriage is a "success" or "failure" is commonly largely attributed to the wife's "expressive" skills in maintaining the marriage. After an individual becomes divorced, the sense of failure can often be relieved by success within subsequent remarriage. In this sense, divorce carries within it the seeds of remarriage. Remarriage is an attempt to alleviate feelings of failure.

The third and final norm to be considered here which is conducive to remarriage after divorce is that of marriage itself. Marriage is the "normal" life-style, and society tends to organize social life on the basis of couples and families. Duberman (1974) stated: "Ours is a two-by-two world, and there is little room in it for the unaccompanied individual. . . . To justify their own state, married people think of marriage as 'natural' and anyone who does not conform to this point of view is challenging the social values" (p. 115). Being without a spouse places one in an awkward position often resulting in a truncated social life. Single persons may be excluded from social affairs because of their proverbial "fifth wheel" status. Adult singleness, not necessarily the divorced status, represents deviance from the norm, and in that way exerts social pressure toward marriage.

The pressure to become "normal" in terms of becoming a partner in marriage may be greater for parents than for other categories of singles because there are more individuals involved in the striving for a normal family life. Single parents may feel added pressure in terms of accomplishing normal lives not for only themselves but for their children.

Norm Ambiguity and Role Instability. In contrast to the view that remarriage after divorce is an adaptation to social norms is Goode's argument that such remarriage represents adaptation to norm ambiguity associated with the status of divorce. In his classic volume *Women in Divorce*, Goode (1956) suggested that the lack of norms associated with the status of being divorced created pressures toward remarriage, and in this way minimized social disruption caused by divorce. It was his contention that such norm ambiguity provided institutional pressures conducive to remarriage which allowed a high divorce rate to exist while kinship institutions were maintained and major societal disruption was avoided. Goode (1956) described the following four areas of norm ambiguity associated with the divorced status:

1. There are no ethical imperatives for relatives or friends to furnish needed material or emotional support during and after the crisis to divorcees *as* divorcees.

2. Issues are unclear concerning the readmission of divorcees into their former kinship structure or into a new one. We are not at all clear as to where members of the divorcing family ought to go. Families of orientation are under no obligation to take them back, nor are former in-laws, even though in the case of the woman, they all have surnames in common.

3. There are no clear avenues for the formation of new families. It is unclear as to what constitutes appropriate behavior in terms of finding a second husband or wife. Such norm ambiguity permeates the relationships of the divorcees with parents, friends and children.

4. There is no clear definition concerning the general proper behavior and emotional attitudes of the divorced. They don't know whether they should be grieved or relieved. Lacking specification of behavior expectations, divorcees are subject to criticism by some regardless what they do.

It was Goode's assumption that the norm ambiguity associated with divorce places sufficient stress on most divorcees to pressure them back into the comfortably norm-regulated state of marriage. He believed that the lack of institutionalization of post-divorce adjustment functions to create pressures toward new marriages, which in turn maintain the kinship structures necessary for the survival of society. It should be noted that while such norm ambiguity could create pressure toward remarriage, it could instead lead to the development of clear norms for the divorced.

Bernard (1956) argued along the same general lines as Goode in her explanation of the high rate of remarriage after divorce. She referred to the inherent instability in the status of "divorced" and the resulting drive toward remarriage. She contended that even if divorced persons have no children, they cannot resume the status of being single because marriage has fundamentally altered their self-images, daily habits and leisure activities, relations with friends and family and even their identities.

> Dissolution of marriage disrupts a complex integration of role, which requires a corresponding role to be played by someone in the outside world . . . his need for a partner who will play a complementary role and thus render functional a long-standing role of one's own is undoubtedly a strong motivational drive toward remarriage. (p. 125)

THE STATIONS OF REMARRIAGE

While there are clear factors favoring remarriage after divorce such as experience and maturity, it remains a trying experience for most who pursue it. As suggested earlier, a great portion of the problems associated with remarriage are related to the complexities introduced by children from former marriages. The complexity of an institution in itself need not present problems, but if society fails to provide guidelines for the relationships involved, the outcome may be one of chaos and conflict. For lack of such guidelines in Western culture, the remarried pair is often expected to function in the same way as does a first married pair, despite the fact that in addition to the new husband and wife there may be two former spouses, two sets of children, four sets of grandparents, and numerous other relatives and friends associated with a former marriage. In addition, there may be many unresolved feelings carried over into the new marriage.

Undoubtedly, remarriage after divorce is a complex process with several interrelated components. That process is described here through use of Bohannan's (1970) model outlining developmental tasks of divorce. His six "stations" of divorce consist of those tasks which must be mastered in order to exit successfully from an existing marriage. They include the emotional, legal, economic, coparental, community and psychic divorces. Those stations are revisited here in the course of moving from divorce to remarriage. As Furstenberg (1979) pointed out, a successful remarriage must involve undoing or refashioning many of the adaptations made to a successful divorce. As is true of the divorce stations, all six stations of remarriage need not necessarily occur to all remarrying people with the same intensity and in the same order. In fact, some individuals may avoid some stations altogether. The six stations of remarriage are ordered here in such a way that the first three can occur independent of the existence of children from a former marriage, while the last three assume the involvement of such children.

Emotional Remarriage

Typically the remarriage process begins with the emotional remarriage. This is the often slow process by which a divorced person reestablishes a bond of attraction, commitment and trust with a member of the opposite sex. After having experienced severe disappointment in a previous relationship, the divorcee learns to release emotions in an effort to once again secure comfort and love. Often this process is wrought with the fear that this emotional investment will lead to loss and rejection. Such fears may justifiably be intense because an additional failure at relationships threatens not only to leave the individual once again disappointed and alone, but also to damage identity and self-concept. Another divorce could strongly suggest to others as well as self a deficiency in those skills, whatever they may be, which are necessary to sustain a marriage. While there is always ambiguity in terms of cause and fault with one divorce—possibly it was at least partially the fault of the other spouse, or maybe the divorce could be blamed on a situation which surrounded that particular marriage—additional failures begin to single out an individual as a "loser." Due to the loss, rejection and failure that are typically associated with divorce, the emotional remarriage is a unique and often arduous and volatile process which is not satisfactorily completed by all who attempt it.

Psychic Remarriage

Psychic remarriage is the process of changing one's conjugal identity from individual to couple. It involves relinquishing the personal freedom and autonomy established by the psychic divorce, and resuming a lifestyle in which a person is expected to be viewed as one component of a partnership.

The psychic remarriage affects different individuals in different ways. For example, men and women are likely to differ in the amount of stress experienced in their respective transitions in conjugal identity. In general the psychic remarriage may represent less change for men than for women, and therefore mean less potential for difficulties in adjustment. Since the role of adult male in our society dictates a primary identity with occupational status thereby de-emphasizing conjugal identity, men are likely to experience a relatively mild identity shift as they pass from the status of single person to that of mate. In other words, since the social status and therefore personal identity of a man is relatively independent of his marital status, a shift in his marital status would not represent an extreme alteration in personal identity. But the situation may be very different for women, who in accordance with traditional gender roles, identify strongly with their marital status. While the occupational sphere tends to be the domain of the man, the conjugal sphere is seen as the domain of the woman. It is the woman, then, who is faced with the more extreme identity shift when there is an alteration in marital status.

But the shift is not of equal intensity among all women. Changes in marital status would seemingly have a greater effect on women who hold traditional gender role attitudes than on those who hold nontraditional attitudes. The traditional women would suffer a great loss with psychic divorce, a true identity crisis. But upon remarriage these women would adjust easily in the psychic realm. For them psychic remarriage represents the recovery of their valued identity as wife. Non-traditional women, on the other hand, are likely to view the psychic divorce in positive terms as a period of growth into autonomous identity, an opportunity to do away with the restraints of couple identity. It is these women who are likely to have adjustment problems associated with psychic remarriage. To them the wife role is less important, and psychic remarriage represents loss of the more highly valued independence and freedom. It is interesting to note that

the suggestion presented here that non-traditional women, when compared with traditional women, are likely to discover satisfaction in psychic divorce and severe stress in psychic remarriage has some empirical support in 1970 census statistics. Those data indicate that women with five or more years of college education (an index of non-traditional attitude) are divorcing more often than other divorced men and women (Glick, 1975b).

It becomes clear that psychic remarriage represents a different kind of process for different categories of people, but it safely can be assumed that in most, if not all, cases it represents some disruption and the consequent need for adjustment.

Community Remarriage

The community remarriage like the community divorce represents an alteration which a person often must make in relationships with a community of friends. Where the community divorce involves breaking away from the world of couples, entering what Hunt (1966) called "the world of the formerly married," the community remarriage involves re-entrance into the couple's world. Like the community divorce, the community remarriage may be a turbulent process. Unmarried friends are typically lost for lack of a common lifestyle, especially friends of the opposite sex. These friends are replaced by married couples, often remarried couples with whom remarrieds share important aspects of biography.

In some ways the process of community remarriage has potential for being more strenuous than does the process of community divorce because it can result in the loss of closer friends. With the community divorce one must give up couples, that is *pairs* of friends who were shared with a spouse. Often the friend-ships had not been intimate. Instead, they were secondary to, convenient to, and dependent upon, the marital rela-tionship. They were not one's own friends, selected as a reflection of one's interests and needs. They were relation-ships based on the combined interests and needs of the spouses. But with the community remarriage, one may be put in a position of severing the close person-ally-tailored ties established while di-vorced, and replacing them with less intimate, couple-oriented relationships. Furthermore, those bonds of friendship established during that period of time when one was divorced may be partic-ularly valuable because they lent support at a time of personal crisis. These were the friends who were there to help the individual through the typically devas-tating experiences associated with the divorce process.

So the community remarriage, while representing re-entrance into the "nor-mality" of the couples' world, also may mean the eventual loss of valuable friend-ship bonds. Married life is often intol-erant of relationships with unmarried friends. Its structure discourages those connections with the past, those ties with the world of the formerly married.

Parental Remarriage

The parental remarriage is necessary if there are children. It is the union of an individual with the children of this new spouse. Parental remarriage may be the most difficult developmental task of re-marriage as suggested by one . . . study (Messinger, 1976). It is certainly the one that has received the most attention in the literature as is indicated by the fact that a series of bibliographies on step-relationships, the product of parental re-

marriage, is periodically compiled and distributed for the use of social scientists (Sell, 1977). Unprecedented numbers of people find themselves living with other peoples' children, and many view the process of combining with them to form a family unit as challenging at best.

Fast and Cain (1966) suggested that the problems of stepparenthood are based on the fact that the role definition of stepparent in this society is poorly artic-ulated, and implies contradictory expec-tations as "parent," "stepparent" and "nonparent." The stepparent cannot fully assume any of these roles, and therefore must individually work out behavior pat-terns for interacting with one's spouse's children. Folk tradition describes the stepmother as wicked and cruel—in a word, unparentlike—so to enact that role would be socially unacceptable. Instead, the stepparent is encouraged to assume the role of parent, for which there is legal support in the explication of the rights and duties entailed by the "in loco par-entis" relationship. But the stepparent cannot totally assume the role of father or mother. The natural parent is typically still active in the parental role, which requires that the stepparent gracefully accede to the parental rights of another and behave as nonparent. The step-parent and the natural parent are placed in a position of sharing the residential, educational, financial, health, and moral decisions incumbent on the parental role. Society provides no guidelines for this sharing of rights and responsibilities which can easily lead to confusion, frus-tration, and resentment.

Another explanation for the difficulties associated with parental remarriage and the associated steprelationships is that marital role expectations between hus-band and wife are not worked out prior to the assumption of parental roles. Spouses are not allowed the opportunity to develop workable and comfortable marital relationships and to establish a primary husband-wife bond prior to the birth of children. Marital and parental adjustment must be confronted simultaneously which could encourage the inappropriate involvement of children in marital dissention. Marital and parental problems could easily confound one another. The natural parent's prior relationship to his child can serve as a threat to the establishment of a primary husband-wife bond. In that way it may detract from the integration of the new family unit.

One problem relating to stepparenthood that appears often in the literature is discipline. The stepparent is often reluctant to provide discipline because the clear authority vested in a natural parent is lacking. If the stepparent does actually attempt to discipline, such action may not be well-received by the child or may not be interpreted as acceptable by the spouse. This problem of discipline would seemingly be more common for stepfathers than stepmothers, since children typically stay with their mothers after divorce. It is the stepfather who most often enters a formerly single-parent family unit and who, therefore, actually experiences daily interaction with his stepchildren. The stepmother, on the other hand, usually spends limited time with her visiting stepchildren.

Another specific problem associated with parental remarriage concerns children as a link to the former marriage, and was expressed by Messinger's (1976) subjects. Some felt that continued ties through the children with previous family members made it more difficult for the new spouse to integrate into the new family unit. In this way they saw the children as a source of marital disruption. New mates frequently felt that such continued ties made them feel as though they were outsiders.

Economic Remarriage

The economic remarriage is the reestablishment after divorce of a marital household as a unit of economic productivity and consumption. Like the parental remarriage, it is a particularly difficult developmental task of remarriage, as evidenced by the Messinger study, which suggested that the problem of finances in remarriage was surpassed in severity only by problems associated with children. The economic remarriage as a developmental task can be considered as being an extension of the parental remarriage in that its main difficulties stem from the existence of children from a former marriage. When there are such children involved, the economic remarriage becomes complex in that it emerges as an open system, dependent on or at least interrelated with the economic behavior of individuals other than the two spouses.

Typically the standard of living increases at remarriage due to the simple fact that financial resources which had formerly maintained two residences are combined to support only one. So the problem is not so much one of insufficient funds as it is one of financial instability and resource distribution. One source of instability stems from the sporadic nature of incoming child support payments, especially after the mother has remarried. Many reconstituted families are simply unable to predict how much money will be available from month to month because of the uncertainty associated with the arrival of child support payment. Information* collected in 1978 from a sample of United States women indicates that continuity of support payments declined somewhat with the remarriage of the mother; only 43% of the remarried wives reported having received their payments always, as opposed to 51% of the divorced but not remarried. Not knowing whether that next payment will arrive can introduce significant inconvenience into the remarriage household. A second source of economic instability lies in the unpredictable nature of the needs of the husband's children, who typically reside with their mother. While outgoing child support payments may be constant, the possibility of unexpected needs requiring extra financial cost (medical, educational, etc.) can loom as a dark cloud over the remarriage. It can bring the same kind of uncertainty and consequent inconvenience into the remarriage household as lack of continuity associated with incoming child support payments.

The problem of resource distribution refers to the issue of how the money should be spent; who should get how much of what is available? For example, if *his* daughter is given ballet lessons, should not *her* son be allowed tennis lessons, even though the sources of support for the two children are quite different? If the resources available to her son from her ex-spouse preclude such tennis lessons, should the stepfather finance such lessons for the sake of equity? Messinger (1976) reported frequent statements of discomfort and embarrassment on the part of mothers over the financial

*These data were obtained from a combination of the March and April 1979 Current Population Surveys conducted by the United States Bureau of the Census. Although the information has not been published by the Bureau, it has been made available on computer tapes.

cost incurred for her new husband on behalf of her children. Society fails to provide guidelines for these kinds of situations, which can lead to stress in the remarital relationship.

The economic remarriage unites individuals from two different family systems and two different generations who have learned different and possibly opposing earning and spending habits. The problems involved in integrating such persons into a smooth functioning economic unit may provide a true challenge for all involved.

Legal Remarriage

Remarriage as a form of marriage is a creature of the law. Since it is such a relatively newly recognized way of life, its legal ramifications are only beginning to be explored. By the time a remarriage takes place, alimony, child support, and the division of property have already been set regarding the former marriage. The new marriage may cause additional legal considerations concerning responsibility toward relationships from the former marriage. The complexity of what Bohannan (1970) referred to as the pseudokinship system created by remarriage after divorce requires decisions regarding his and her financial resources, his and her former spouses, and his, her, and their children. In consideration of all of these, people need to evaluate their legal responsibilities and to decide how they want their resources distributed. Remarriage after divorce does not mean that a person exchanges one family for another; instead it means that the individual takes on an additional family. Since legal responsibilities associated with this action have not been clearly charted, individuals are left to base legal decisions on their own moral guidelines. For some this can be a difficult process because it involves assigning weights of importance to members of their complicated pseudokinship networks. Such questions arise as to which wife deserves the life and accident insurance, medical coverage, retirement benefits, pension rights and property rights. Is it the former wife who played a major role in building the estate or is it the current wife who has contributed less but is currently in his "good graces"? Also, to which children should he lend support for college education—his children, her children or their children? Since state inheritance laws typically favor a person's current spouse and natural children, inheritance rights need to be clearly defined at the point of legal remarriage if the person wishes to will benefits to a former spouse or to stepchildren.

Until the time that state legal codes respond to the needs of the remarried, individuals will continue to be left to work out the legal problems and decisions of remarriage after divorce. The imposition of structure by the state in this area not only would make the legal remarriage logistically simpler, but might contribute to increased affability for the relationships involved. The implementation of a standard procedure for the distribution of resources, for example, would eliminate the sense of competition and jealousy which is now encouraged by the lack of guidelines. If, for example, it was predetermined by the state that the resources of remarried persons would be divided among all of their surviving spouses in proportions corresponding to the length of each marriage, bitterness on the part of any of those spouses toward one another before or after death regarding equity in inheritance rights might be reduced. The burden of respon-

sibility for distribution of resources would have been lifted from the individual by the state. Such legal structure could relieve tension among spouses, former spouses, parent-child relationships and steprelationships, and therefore contribute to the maintenance of the complex pseudokinship structure created by remarriage after divorce.

CONCLUDING STATEMENT

As divorce and subsequent remarriage become increasingly common, adjustment to their developmental tasks becomes a greater concern for family practitioners. While individuals face different tasks in varying orders, it has been suggested here that the six developmental tasks of divorce outlined by Bohannan are also important developmental tasks of remarriage. Remarriage can be a complex process, and its adjustment accordingly difficult. The problems associated with remarital adjustment are often heightened by the fact that partners in remarriage may still be adjusting to their divorces. At remarriage, a person may be compelled to commence the stations of remarriage while having not yet completed the stations of divorce. For example, as an individual struggles with establishing bonds of affection, commitment and trust with a new partner, he or she may still be contending with the severance of emotional ties with the former spouse. In order to be able to provide guidance and support to individuals in the throes of remarital adjustment, the practitioner needs to be familiar, first, with the general complexity of remarriage after divorce and, second, with the specific developmental tasks which can be anticipated as part of the adjustment process.

NOTE

1. Benson, L. Personal communication, 1969.

REFERENCES

Berger, P. L., & Kellner, H. Marriage and the construction of reality, *Diogenes*, 1964, **46**, 1–23.

Bernard, J. *Remarriage: A study of marriage.* New York: Dryden Press, 1956.

Biegel, H. Romantic love. *American Sociological Review.* 1951, **16**, 326–334.

Bohannan, P. The six stations of divorce. I. P. Bohannan (Ed.), *Divorce and after.* New York: Doubleday and Co., Inc., 1970.

Cherlin, A. Remarriage as an incomplete institution. *American journal of Sociology,* 1978, **84**, 634–650.

Duberman, L. *Remarriage and its alternatives.* New York: Praeger, 1974.

Farber, B. *Family: Organization and interaction.* San Francisco: Chandler Publishing Co., 1964.

Fast, I., & Cain, A. C. The stepparent role: Potential for disturbances in family functioning. *American Journal of Orthopsychiatry,* 1966, **36**, 485–491.

Furstenberg, F. F. Recycling the family. *Marriage and Family Review,* 1979, **2** (3), 1, 12–22.

Glick, P. C. Dissolution of marriage by divorce and its demographic consequences. *International Population Conference.* Liege, Belgium: International Union for the Scientific Study of Population, 1973, **2**, 65–69.

Glick, P. C. A demographer looks at American families. *Journal of Marriage and the Family,* 1975, **31**, 15–26. (a)

Glick, P. C. Some recent changes in American families. *Current Population Reports: Special Studies,* Series P-23, no. 52. Washington, D.C.: U.S. Government Printing Office, 1975. (b).

Goetting, A. Some societal-level explanations for the rising divorce rate. *Family Therapy,* 1979, **VI** (2), 71–87.

Goetting, A. Divorce outcome research: issues and perspectives. *Journal of Family Issues.* 1981, **2**, 350–378.

Goode, W. J. *Women in divorce.* New York: Free Press, 1956.

Goode, W. J. The theoretical importance of love. *American Sociological Review,* 1959, **24**, 38–47.

Homans, G. C. *Social behavior: Its elementary forms.* New York: Harcourt, Brace and World, Inc., 1961.

Hunt. M. M. *The world of the formerly married.* New York: McGraw-Hill Book Co., 1966.

McCarthy, J. A comparison of the probability of the dissolution of first and second marriages. *Demography,* 1978, **15** (3), 345–359.

Messinger, L. Remarriage between divorced people with children from previous marriages: A proposal for preparation for remarriage. *Journal of Marriage and Family Counseling,* 1976, **38**, 193–200.

Norton, A. J., & Glick, P. C. Marital instability: Past, present and future. *Journal of Social Issues,* 1976, **32**, 5–20.

Price-Bonham, S., & Balswick, J. O. The non-institutions: Divorce, desertion and remarriage. *Journal of Marriage and the Family,* 1980, **42**, 959–972.

Rollin, B. The American way of marriage: Remarriage. *Look,* September 21, 1971, 62–67.

Schlesinger, B. Remarriage as family reorganization for divorced persons: A Canadian study. *Journal of Comparative Family Studies,* 1970, **1** (1), 101–118.

Sell, K. D. *Divorce in the 1970's.* Salisbury, N.C.: Department of Sociology, Catawba College, 1977.

Thibaut, J. W., and Kelley, H. H. *The social psychology of groups.* New York: Wiley, 1959.

U.S. Bureau of the Census. Number, timing and duration of marriages and divorces in the United States: June, 1975. *Current Population Reports,* Series P-20, No. 297. Washington, D.C.: U.S. Government Printing Office, 1976.

Vaughan, D. Uncoupling: The social construction of divorce. In H. Robboy, S. L. Greenblatt, & C. Clark (Eds.), *Social interaction: Introductory readings in sociology.* New York: St. Martins. 1978.

POSTSCRIPT

Is the Success of Remarriage Doomed?

Although remarriage was previously regarded as an uncommon and generally unacceptable practice, today we find many people marrying second or subsequent times, regardless of the circumstances surrounding their earlier marital dissolutions. Counselors and therapists now talk about premarital, remarital counseling and contracting for remarriage, two relatively new ideas that are based on refocused and updated ideas not so new to marriage counseling. In the relatively short history of marital counseling, much of the early practice was oriented towards helping people become aware of their values, responsibilities, and religious obligations with regard to the impending union. Some of the counseling was legally focused, and premarital contracts were sometimes developed, not only to protect property but also to protect children and to reinforce roles in marriage, family, and the larger community. Other premarital work had a religious focus and was oriented toward the expectations and requirements the religion set forth regarding the union. Today the new focus is upon those remarrying, which indicates a growing acceptance of the fact that people do divorce and remarry.

Marriage, remarriage, and family relationships do not just happen. They are generally planned for, learned about, and negotiated, either formally or informally. Many courses are offered in colleges and universities on the topic of marriage. Mental health associations and family service agencies offer workshops related to marriage and family life. Many books are available that offer advice on how to have a happy marriage, raise well-adjusted children, and have family financial assets grow. If there is a willingness on the part of those involved to work on issues and tasks and, if necessary, to seek outside assistance, the chances of successful remarriage can be enhanced.

SUGGESTED READINGS

P. Bohannon, "The Six Stations of Divorce," in P. Bohannon, ed., *Divorce and After* (Doubleday, 1970).

M. Coleman and L. H. Ganong, "Remarriage and Stepfamily Research in the 1980s: Increased Interest in an Old Family Form," *Journal of Marriage and the Family*, **52** (1990): 925–940.

C. Hobart and D. Brown, "Effects of Prior Marriage Children on Adjustment in Remarriage: A Canadian Study," *Journal of Comparative Family Studies*, **19** (1988): 381–396.

M. F. Whiteside, "Family Rituals as a Key to Kinship Connections in Remarried Families," *Family Relations*, **38** (1989): 34–39.

CONTRIBUTORS TO THIS VOLUME

EDITORS

GLORIA W. BIRD is an associate professor of family studies in the Department of Family and Child Development at Virginia Polytechnic Institute and State University. An active member of the National Council on Family Relations and the International Society for the Study of Personal Relationships, Professor Bird's research has focused on stress and coping and dual-career families. Her work has appeared most recently in such journals as the *Journal of Marriage and the Family* and *Family Relations*. Professor Bird received a B.S. and M.S. from Kansas State University and a Ph.D. in Family and Consumer Enviromental Studies from Oklahoma State University. She is presently at work with Keith Melville on the fifth edition of *Marriage and Family Today* (McGraw-Hill; tentatively scheduled for publication in 1993).

MICHAEL J. SPORAKOWSKI is a professor of family development at Virginia Polytechnic Institute and State University, where he has taught since 1970. He is a licensed professional counselor. A life member of the American Association for Family Therapy, he also holds memberships in the American Psychological Association, the National Council on Family Relations, and the Virginia Council on Family Relations, among other organizations. Professor Sporakowski's major research interests include intergenerational studies of marital and family life, population-related issues, and long-term marriages, specifically those lasting 50 years or more. He received a B.S. and M.Ed. from Pennsylvania State University, and a Ph.D. in the Interdivisional Program in Marriage and Family Living from Florida State University. His work has appeared in such journals as *Family Relations* and *Marriage and Family Review*.

STAFF

Marguerite L. Egan   Program Manager
Brenda S. Filley   Production Manager
Whit Vye   Designer
Libra Ann Cusack   Typesetting Supervisor
Juliana Arbo   Typesetter
David Brackley   Copy Editor
David Dean   Administrative Assistant
Diane Barker   Editorial Assistant
David Filley   Graphics

AUTHORS

ALAN C. ACOCK is a professor in and the chair of the Department of Human Development and Family Sciences at Oregon State University in Corvallis, Oregon.

LYNN ATWATER is an associate professor of sociology at Seton Hall University in South Orange, New Jersey. She is a member of the National Council on Family Relations, the International Council on Family Relations, and the American Sociological Association.

DEBORAH BELLE is an assistant professor of psychology at Boston University and the William T. Grant Foundation Faculty Scholar in the Mental Health of Children. She is the editor of *Lives in Stress: Women and Depression* (Sage Publications, 1982).

P. LINDSAY CHASE-LANSDALE is an assistant professor in the Irving B. Harris Graduate School of Public Policy Studies at the University of Chicago and a fellow of developmental and family research in the University of Chicago's Chapin Hall Center for Children.

ANDREW CHERLIN is a professor of sociology at Johns Hopkins University and a member of the National Academy of Sciences Committee on Child Development Research and Public Policy. He is the coauthor, with Frank F. Furstenberg, Jr., of *Divided Families: What Happens to Children When Parents Part* (Harvard University Press, 1991).

BRYCE J. CHRISTENSEN is the director of The Rockford Institute Center on the Family in America in Rockford, Illinois. He is the author of *Utopia Against the Family* and the editor of *The Retreat from Marriage: Causes and Consequences*.

MARILYN COLEMAN is a professor in and the chair of the Department of Human Development and Family Studies at the University of Missouri in Columbia. She coteaches a graduate course on remarriage and stepfamilies and conducts workshops for professionals and for stepfamily members.

MARGARET CROSBIE-BURNETT is an associate professor of educational and psychological studies at the University of Miami in Coral Gables, Florida. A licensed psychologist in Wisconsin, she cochairs the National Council on Family Relations Focus Group on Remarriage and Stepfamilies and serves on the editorial board for the journal *Family Relations*.

DAVID H. DEMO is an associate professor in the Department of Sociology at Virginia Polytechnic Institute and State University in Blacksburg, Virginia.

MICAELA DI LEONARDO is an associate professor of anthropology and women's studies at Northwestern University and a fellow of Northwestern University's Urban Affairs Center. She is the author of *Varieties of Ethnic Experience: Kinship, Class, and Gender Among California Italian-Americans* (Cornell University Press, 1984).

R. EMERSON DOBASH is a professor at the University of Stirling in Scotland. He is the coauthor, with Russell P. Dobash, of *Violence Against Wives* (Free Press, 1979).

RUSSELL P. DOBASH is a professor at the University of Stirling in Scotland. He is the coauthor, with R. Emerson Dobash, of *Violence Against Wives* (Free Press, 1979) and a coauthor of *The Imprisonment of Women* (Basil Blackwell, 1986).

ANN DRUYAN, a writer and television producer, is Secretary of the Federation of American Scientists—founded in 1945 to combat the misuse of science and technology.

FRANKLYN W. DUNFORD is a research associate in the Institute of Behavioral Science at the University of Colorado at Boulder. He is currently studying the correlates of domestic assault among cases known to the police.

BARBARA EHRENREICH, a feminist and socialist party leader, is a writer and a contributing editor to *Ms.* magazine. She has authored or coauthored numerous books and articles, including *The Worst Years of Our Lives: Irreverent Notes from a* *Decade of Greed* (Pantheon Books, 1990).

DELBERT S. ELLIOTT is the associate director of the Program on Problem Behavior in the Institute of Behavioral Science at the University of Colorado at Boulder. He is a coauthor, with David Huizinga and Suzanne S. Ageton, of *Explaining Delinquency and Drug Use* (Sage Publications, 1985).

DEIRDRE ENGLISH is a free-lance writer and lecturer. A feminist and a former executive editor of *Mother Jones*, she has collaborated with Barbara Ehrenreich on several books, including *For Her Own Good: 150 Years of the Experts' Advice to Women* (Doubleday, 1978).

CYNTHIA FUCHS EPSTEIN is a professor in the Department of Sociology, Graduate Center, at the City College of New York, where she has taught since 1975. She is an editor of *Sex Roles*, a quarterly journal, and the author of *Deceptive Distinctions: Sex, Gender, and the Social Order* (Yale University Press, 1988).

PAULA L. ETTELBRICK is associated with the Lambda Legal Defense and Education Fund, a nonprofit, tax-exempt organization located in New York City, which works nationally to defend and extend the rights of homosexuals through test case litigation and public information.

NAOMI FARBER is an assistant professor in the Graduate School of

Social Work and Social Research at Bryn Mawr College in Bryn Mawr, Pennsylvania.

LAWRENCE H. GANONG is a professor in the Department of Human Development and Family Studies and in the School of Nursing at the University of Missouri in Columbia. He has coauthored over 80 articles and book chapters, most of which are on remarriage and stepfamily issues.

ANN GOETTING is a professor in the Department of Sociology at Western Kentucky University in Bowling Green, Kentucky.

STEVEN GOLDBERG is an associate professor in and acting chair of the Department of Sociology at City College, City University of New York, where he has taught since 1970. He is the author of *The Inevitability of Patriarchy* (William Morrow & Co., 1973).

JEAN M. GRANGER is a professor and the coordinator for the undergraduate program in the Department of Social Work at California State University, Huntington Beach.

ANDREW M. GREELEY, a sociologist, novelist, journalist, and Roman Catholic priest, is the director of the Center for the Study of American Pluralism at the University of Chicago's National Opinion Research Center and a professor of sociology at the University of Arizona in Phoenix.

ORRIN G. HATCH, senator (R) from Utah (1977–present; term ends 1995), has been very active in the movement for implementing a Human Life Amendment to the U.S. Constitution. He has chaired the Labor and Human Resources Committee, which has oversight responsibilities for the Department of Labor, the Department of Health and Human Services, and the Department of Education.

LIZ HODGKINSON is a free-lance writer living in London, England, whose book *Sex is Not Compulsory* attracted worldwide media interest and established her as an expert on the subject of sexual and other relationships.

DAVID HUIZINGA is a research associate in the Institute of Behavioral Science at the University of Colorado in Boulder, Colorado. He is a coauthor, with Delbert S. Elliott and Scott Menard, of *Multiple Problem Youth: Delinquency, Substance Use, and Mental Health Problems* (Springer-Verlag, 1989).

PAUL WILLIAM KINGSTON is a professor at the University of Virginia in Charlottesville, Virginia. He is a coauthor, with Sheila B. Kamerman and Alfred J. Kahn, of *Maternity Policies and Working Women* (Columbia University Press, 1983).

HERBERT T. KRIMMEL is a professor of jurisprudence and bioethics at Southwestern University

School of Law in Los Angeles, California, where he has been teaching since 1977. He has recently been appointed to the advisory panel of the California Joint Legislative Committee on Surrogate Parenting.

JOSEPH A. LUCCA is a professor in the Department of Physical Therapy at the University of Delaware in Newark, Delaware.

JOAN MEIER is an attorney with the Public Citizen Litigation Group and a member of the board of directors of the Washington, D.C., Coalition Against Domestic Violence.

ROBERT T. MICHAEL is an economist and the dean of the Graduate School of Public Policy Studies at the University of Chicago. He is a former director of the University of Chicago's National Opinion Research Center.

STEVEN L. NOCK is a professor of sociology at the University of Virginia in Charlottesville, Virginia. His current research focuses on surveillance and other methods of establishing reputations among young people who do not live in families.

JOSEPH H. PLECK is the Luce Professor of Families, Change, and Society at Wheaton College in Norton, Massachusetts. His publications include *Working Wives, Working Husbands* (Sage Publications, 1985).

JOHN A. ROBERTSON is the Thomas Watt Gregory Professor of Law at the University of Texas at Austin and a fellow of the Hastings Center. He has served on a federal task force on organ transplantation and on the Ethics Committee of the American Fertility Society.

CARL SAGAN is one of the most widely known scientists in America and a controversial author in the fields of astronomy and space exploration. He is the director of the Cornell University Laboratory for Planetary Studies and president of Carl Sagan Productions, Inc., which specializes in scientific books and supplies.

IRVING SARNOFF is a professor of psychology at New York University in New York City. His numerous writings center around his interests in the fields of personality and social psychology, and since 1980 he has teamed with his wife, Suzanne Sarnoff, to lecture in courses on Human Sexual Love and the Psychology of Marriage.

SUZANNE SARNOFF, a lecturer on psychology at New York University in New York City, has lectured in courses on Human Sexual Love and the Psychology of Marriage with her husband, Irving Sarnoff, since 1980. The Sarnoffs have coauthored *Sexual Excitement/Sexual Peace: The Place of Masturbation in Adult Relationships* (M. Evans, 1979).

FELICE N. SCHWARTZ is the president and founder of Catalyst, a not-for-profit research and advisory organization that works with corporations to foster the career and leadership development of women.

ADA SKYLES is currently pursuing a J.D. degree at the Northwestern University School of Law. She is a former director of the Office of Child Support for Wisconsin's Department of Health and Social Services, and she has received the American Public Welfare Association Award for successful projects initiative in implementing child support reform in Wisconsin. Her publications have appeared in *Family Relations* and *Public Welfare*.

TOM W. SMITH is a survey researcher and historian, and the director of the General Social Survey at the University of Chicago's National Opinion Research Center.

SUZANNE K. STEINMETZ is a professor in and the chair of the Department of Sociology at Indiana University-Purdue University at Indianapolis.

ANDREW SULLIVAN, a former editor of *The New Republic*, is a doctoral candidate in government at Harvard University.

RONALD L. TAYLOR is an associate professor in and a former chairman of the Department of Sociology at the University of Connecticut, Storrs. His research on black self-esteem, ethnicity, and social change in black communities

has appeared in *Social Science Quarterly, American Journal of Sociology,* and the *American Journal of Orthopsychiatry.*

J. E. VEEVERS is a professor in the Department of Sociology at the University of Victoria in Victoria, British Columbia, Canada.

MARIS A. VINOVSKIS is a professor of history at the University of Michigan in Ann Arbor, Michigan.

JUDITH S. WALLERSTEIN is a lecturer in social welfare at the University of California, Berkeley, the senior consultant to Marin County Community Mental Health Center, and the executive director of the Center for the Family in Transition.

INDEX

abortion: 114, 117, 130, 131, 140, 149; controversy over, 90–108; teenage, 157, 158, 211

accountability, mutual, pregnancy and, 118–120

achievement, ambivalence toward, and childlessness, 133

Acock, Alan C., on the impact of divorce on children, 276–289

activity-focused relationships, male participation in, 19, 20

acute phase, in the divorcing process, 269

adolescents: 20, 22; black, controversy over government programs for, 210–221; controversy over marriage of, 156–173; see also, children

adoption: 104; of babies born to teens, 158, 211; childlessness and, 126, 128, 129, 131–132; homosexuals and, 76, 78; vs. surrogate motherhood, 138–139, 141, 143, 147, 148

adultery, see extramarital relationships; infidelity

African American family policy, vs. national family policy, 215–221

agency adoption, 138–139, 140

aggression: in children of divorce, 277, 280; as male trait, 5–13, 62, 229

AIDS, 62, 64, 78, 255, 258, 259, 260, 261

Akron v. Akron Center for Reproductive Health, 106

alcohol abuse, 213, 230, 239

alimony, 318, 336

AMA (American Medical Association), abortion and, 90–91

androgynous, today's woman as, 195, 203

antisocial behavior, in children of divorce, 281–282

anxiety: 55, 199; in children of divorce, 271, 280, 283, 284

Archer, Jeffrey, marriage of, 63–65, 68

arrest, role of, in domestic violence, 181, 182, 184, 185, 186–189

artificial insemination, 138, 139, 141, 144, 145, 146, 147, 150

attainment, as male trait, 5–13

Atwater, Lynn, on extramarital relationships, 244–262

availability, permanent, and remarriage after divorce, 330

baby boom, 59, 196, 262

Baby Doe controversy, 144

battered wives, see domestic violence

behavior problems, in children of divorce, 280, 282, 296, 305

Belle, Deborah, on gender differences in the social moderators of stress, 18–27

biases, textbook, against stepfamilies, 295–296

binuclear families, 298

biological clock, women's, 194, 203

birth control, 94, 116, 127, 140

birth defects, surrogate motherhood and, 143–144, 148–149

black youth, controversy over government programs for, 210–221

blaming the victim: and domestic violence, 238; and problems of black youth, 210

blended families, 138, 142

Bohannan, Paul, theory of, on six stations of divorce, 326, 327, 332, 336

brain development, in abortion controversy, 96, 97, 105–106

breadwinner, traditional male role of, 40, 66, 204, 318

Burgess, Ernest, 312, 313, 322

cancer, effect of marriage on, 54, 55, 56

career-primary women, vs. career-and-family women, 197–198, 199, 200, 202, 203

central nervous system, gender differences and, 6, 7

Chase-Lansdale, P. Lindsay, on teenage marriage, 156–163

Cherlin, Andrew: 326, 327; on remarriage as an incomplete institution, 312–325

child abuse: 9, 229; in stepfamilies, 295

child care: visibility of women's nonmarket activities in, 28, 29, 30, 31, 32, 33, 34, 39, 40, 41, 42, 45, 46, 47; for working women, 200, 202, 205, 217, 218–219

child support, 318, 335–336

childbirth: 194, 195, 203; and controversy over teen marriage, 156–173; marriage and, 112, 121–123, 140

childlessness, 19, 58, 59, 123, 126–134

children: 20, 54, 69, 183; of divorce, controversy over, 58, 268–289; and domestic violence, 230–231; effect of surrogate motherhood on, 140, 141–142, 143–144; and mothers, 19, 22, 24–25, 32, 56, 57; of teen mothers, 161–162; see also, adolescents; families; fathers; mothers; stepchildren

Christiansen, Bryce J., on the costly retreat from marriage, 54–59

class, social, as an issue in controversy on teenage marriage, 156–173

clinical and empirical literature on children in stepfamilies, comparison of, 301–307

cognitive functioning, children's, effect of divorce on, 276, 279–280, 296, 305

cohabitation, 59, 123, 234, 257, 261, 296

Coleman, Marilyn, on a comparison of clinical and empirical literature on children in stepfamilies, 301–307

collaborative reproduction, see surrogate mothers

colleges and schools, special programs for stepchildren in, 294–300

commitment, in marriage, 62, 70, 76, 77, 131–134

community remarriage, 326, 333–334

"companionship" family, 322, 323

conceive, couple's decision to, 113–115, 115–117

conception, as beginning of life, 92, 93, 106

Conflict Tactics Scale (CTS), use of, in domestic violence research, 236–237

conjugal love, 328

consanguineal marriage, 320

conservatives, views of, on government programs for black youth, 219, 220

constitutional amendment, on abortion, 99, 106, 107

contraception, 94, 114, 116, 118, 157, 211, 262

courts, attitude of, toward domestic violence, 181, 184

crime: and black youth, 210, 211, 212, 213; gender differences in, 10

crisis lines, for battered spouses, 232, 238

Crosbie-Burnett, Margaret, on special programs for stepchildren in schools and colleges, 294–300

culture: gay, 80; gender differences and, 7, 34; male corporate, 204

custody, child, in a divorce, 270, 304, 320, 326

cyclical aspect, of family violence, 228

dating patterns, of adolescents from single-parent families, 280–281

deficit-family model vs. deficit-comparison approach to research on stepfamilies, 302, 305

Demo, David H., on the impact of divorce on children, 276–289

Democrats, views of, on government programs for black youth, 219, 220

depression, 18, 39, 40, 55, 60–61, 141; in children of divorce, 268, 269, 273

developmental stages, fetal, 95–96, 105

di Leonardo, Michaela, on women, families, and the work of kinship, 28–34

discipline, stepparents and, 313, 314, 320, 335

disengagement, subculture of, among black youth, 212–213

divorce: 62, 66, 130, 150, 227, 229, 316; controversy over children of, 268–289; and extramarital relationships, 246, 261; and family social networks, 20, 21, 29; health and, 54, 55, 57, 58, 59; teen, 156, 159, 161; see also, remarriage; stepchildren

Dobash, R. Emerson and Russell P., on battered women, 233–240

domestic partnership laws, 76, 77, 78, 84

domestic violence: 60, 61, 69, 71; controversy over, 180–185, 226–260

dominance, as male trait, 5–13, 80

drug abuse, black youth and, 210, 213

Druyan, Ann, on abortion, 90–98

dual-income families, see two-earner families

Dunford, Franklyn W., on domestic violence, 186–189

economic remarriage, 326, 335–336

education: end of, for teenage parents, 158, 160, 161, 167, 218; parent/child, 43, 44, 45, 46

egg, human, 93, 94, 95, 116, 138, 139, 142, 149

Ehrenreich, Barbara, on the "mommy track," 202–205

ejaculate, 116

elderly, the: 20, 84, 220; care of, by women, 28, 31, 34; institutionalization of, 57–58

Elliott, Delbert S., on domestic violence, 186–189

embryo transfer, 138, 141

emotional intimacy, stress and, 18, 19, 20, 21, 23–24, 32

emotional remarriage, 326, 332

empirical and clinical literature on children in stepfamilies, comparison of, 301–307 endocrine system, gender differences and, 6, 7

English, Deidre, on the "mommy track," 201–204

ensoulment, as beginning of life, 94, 95, 97

environment, as cause for gender differences, 4–13

Epstein, Cynthia Fuchs, on gender differences and prejudice, 9–13

Equal Rights Amendment, 107–108

equality, in marriage, 66, 67, 120–121, 236, 328

ethics: marital, 247–248; of surrogate motherhood, 138, 145–146

ethnographic studies: of gender differences, 5, 6; of remarriage, 323

Ettelbrick, Paula A., on gay and lesbian marriage, 80–84

extended family, 30, 32, 62, 216, 294, 297, 298

extramarital relationships, controversy over, 244–262, 329

family: black, controversy over government programs for, 210–221; definition of, and same-sex marriage, 76, 77; definition of, and surrogate motherhood, 139, 142, 150; health and sense of, 54, 55, 57; and teen marriage, 157–158, 165, 168–169, 169–170; see also, blended family; children; divorce; domestic violence; fathers; kin keepers; mothers; nuclear family; reconstituted family; remarriage; single-parent families; stepfamilies; two-earner families

fantasies: in children of divorce, 270, 271; sexual, 68, 71

Farber, Naomi, on the significance of race and class in marital decisions among unmarried adolescent mothers, 164–173

fathers: and children, 19, 22, 45–46, 203, 205; and controversy over men's family roles, 38–48; teen, 159, 161, 162, 163, 165–166, 167–168, 170; see also, children; families; mothers

fears, of children of divorce, 270, 271

fecundity, decline of, childlessness and, 131–132

femininity, 4, 278

feminism: 6, 29, 34, 39, 55, 80, 195, 202, 203, 204, 236, 250, 251

fidelity, sexual, in marriage: 63, 64, 75, 68; see also, extramarital relationships; infidelity

financial security: in marriage, 66, 68–69, 76, 77, 195; problems with, in remarriage, 335–336

flexibility, job-related, working women's need for, 196, 199–200, 202, 204, 205

freedom of choice, abortion and, 90–92

friendships: 22, 245; loss of, in divorce, 333–334; in marriage, 66, 67; men's, 19, 20

fun, parent/child, 43, 44, 46, 47

Furstenberg, Frank, 159–160, 161, 162–163, 326, 332

futuristic approach, to marital ethics, 247

Ganong, Lawrence H., on a comparison of clinical and empirical literature on children in stepfamilies, 301–307

gay men, controversy over marriage for, 76–84

Gelles, R. J., 228, 230, 236, 237, 305

gender differences: 20; as present at birth, controversy over, 4–13; in psychological distress, 39–41; and women as victims in their roles, controversy over, 18–34

gender-role orientation, effect of divorce on children's, 277, 278, 284

glass ceiling, for working women, 196, 204

Goetting, Ann: 321; on the six stations of remarriage, 326–338

Goldberg, Steven: 9–10, 12; on gender differences as present at birth, 4–8

Granger, Jean M., on the difference between African American family policy and national family policy, 215–221

Greeley, Andrew M., on American sexual behavior, 254–260

grief, in children of divorce, 271, 272

GSS (General Social Survey), NORC's (National Opinion Research Center), on sexual behavior, 254–260

handicapped children: abortion of, 102–103; and surrogate mothers, 144, 145

hardship, abortion to avoid, 102–103

Harris v. McRae, 107

Hatch, Orrin G., on abortion, 99–108

health, effect of marriage on, 54–59

heart disease, effect of marriage on, 54, 55, 57

helplessness, learned, in marriage, 40, 61

help-seeking, as female activity, 19, 21

hierarchical dominance, men and, 5, 6, 10, 11

Hite Report, The (Hite), 250, 254

Hodgkinson, Liz, on marriage today, 60–72

holiday celebrations, importance of, in women's work of kinship, 29, 30, 31, 32, 34

homicide, 213, 215, 226, 229

homosexuals: 297; see gay men; lesbians

housework, visibility of women's nonmarket activities in, 28, 29, 30, 31, 32, 33, 34, 39, 40, 41, 43, 44, 45, 46, 47

Huizinga, David, on domestic violence, 186–189

hunter-gatherer societies, 12–13, 94

husbands: reliance on, of wives, for emotional support, 20–21, 22, 24; see also, divorce; domestic violence; marriage; remarriage

identity confusion: in children of surrogate mothers, 142; of divorced women, 333

illegitimate children: 56, 57, 140; and controversy over teen marriage, 156–173

immediate family, changing definition of, 297–298

incest: 92, 94; in stepfamilies, 295, 320

incomplete institution, remarriage as, 312–325

independent adoption, 139, 140

individual interests, in marriage, 66, 68

individualism, divorce and, 328, 329

infanticide, 105, 226

infertility: 59, 68, 117; see also, adoption; surrogate mothers

infidelity, sexual, in marriage: 62–63, 68, 69–70; controversy over, 244–262

in-laws, 30, 31, 34, 62, 226

insemination, artificial, 138, 139, 141, 144, 145, 146, 147, 150

intercourse, sexual, for conception, 115–117

interdependence, marital, parenthood and, 114, 115, 117, 118, 124

intimacy, emotional, stress and, 18, 19, 20, 21, 23–24, 32

Italian-American community, as example of women's work of kinship, 18–34

kin keepers, women as, 22, 24, 28–34, 330, 331

Kingston, Paul William, on the impact of couples' work-time commitment on children, 42–48

Kinsey, Alfred, study of, on American male sexual behavior, 244, 245, 246, 250, 251

kinship terms, lack of, for stepfamilies, 314, 319–320, 322

Krimmel, Herbert T., on surrogate parenting, 145–152

language, as illustration of the incomplete institutionalization of remarriage, 319–320, 322, 323

law, as illustration of the incomplete institutionalization of remarriage, 319, 320, 322, 323

learned helplessness, in marriage, 40, 61

legal station of remarriage, 326, 336–337

lesbians, marriage for: 65; controversy over, 76–84

liberals, views of, on government programs for black youth, 219, 220

Locke, Harvey, 312, 313, 322

logically abstract thinking, as male trait, 7, 8

love: and marriage, 63, 66, 68, 70, 71, 112, 114, 123, 124, 125, 246; romantic, remarriage and, 328–329, 330

loyalties, children's divided, and parental remarriage, 295, 302

Lucca, Joseph S., on husband battering, 226–232

maidenhood, prolonged, for today's teenagers, 156–157

marriage: as a good thing, controversy over, 54–72; controversy over extramarital relations and, 244–262; controversy over parenthood as necessary to good, 112–134; controversy over teen, 156–173; emotional intimacy in, 20–21, 24, 25, 29; see also, divorce; domestic violence; remarriage

masculinity, 4, 19, 120–121, 278

Masters and Johnson, 116, 250

maternity leave, 194, 196, 198, 199, 200, 202, 204

mathematics aptitude, gender differences in, 7–8, 279

meals, eating, as parent/child activity, 43, 44, 46

mediation, role of, in domestic violence, 186–189

Medicaid, 57, 58, 59

medical profession, abortion and, 90–91

Medicare, 57, 58

Meier, Joan, on domestic violence, 180–185

men: friendships of, 19, 20, 21; see also, domestic violence; fathers; gender differences; husbands

mental health, marriage and, 54, 55, 57

Michael, Robert M., on Americans and their sexual partners, 254–260

Minneapolis Domestic Violence Experiment, 186, 188

"mommy track," controversy over, 194–204

money, as motive for surrogate motherhood, 141, 146, 151

monogamy: 246, 256, 257, 258, 262; serial, 62, 255, 329

moral approach, to marital ethics, 247

mortality rates, effect of marriage on, 24, 54, 55

mothers: and children, 19, 22, 24–25, 29, 46–47; teen, and controversy over teen marriage, 156–173; working, 38, 40, 42–48, 194–204; see also, children; family; fathers; mommy track; surrogate mothers

mother's life, abortion to protect, 102–103, 106

motive, importance of, in surrogate motherhood, 146–148, 151

murder: abortion as, 62, 95, 96, 104, 108; spousal, and controversy over domestic violence, 180–189

myths: abortion, 99–108; about extramarital relationships, 246, 249

national family policy, vs. African American family policy, 215–221

Nazis: 9; medical ethics of, 147–148

nervous system, central, gender differences and, 6, 7

networks: kinship, 28–34; social, stress and, 18, 19–20

Nock, Stephen L., on the impact of couples' work-time commitments on children, 42–48

no-fault divorce, 57, 227

Noncompeting Agreement, in domestic violence research, 238–239

Noonan, John, 102, 108

NORC's (National Opinion Research Center), GSS (General Social Survey) of, on sexual behavior, 254–260

norm ambiguity, as reason for remarriage, 328, 330–331

nuclear family: 12, 29, 32, 77, 216, 217, 276; vs. stepfamilies, 294, 296, 297, 301, 302

nurturing, as mirror of marital development, 123–125

Omaha police experiment, and the role of arrest in domestic violence, 186–189

oppression, of blacks, 215, 216; patriarchy as, 9

orgasm, 116, 122, 250

out-of-wedlock births, and controversy over teenage marriage, 156–173

pain, fetal, and abortion controversy, 105–106

parentage, definition of, and surrogate motherhood, 138, 141–142

parental coverage, 44, 48

parenthood, as necessary for a good marriage, controversy over, 112–134

part-time jobs, for working women, 199, 200, 202

patriarchy, 5, 6, 9, 12, 80, 227, 235, 238, 313, 322

peer relationships, trouble with, in children of divorce, 272, 280

personality disorders, as reason for divorce and remarriage, 317–318

physiology, gender differences and, 4, 6, 7

plateauing, career, for working women, 194, 196

play, parent/child, 43, 44, 45

Pleck, Joseph H., on men's increasing time in family roles, 38–41

police, attitude of, toward domestic violence, 181–183, 184, 185, 186–189

postdivorce phase, in the divorce process, 269–270

postponement: childlessness and, 126–134; of teen marriage, 165–166

poverty: 164, 285; and black youth, 210, 211, 212, 213, 215, 216

pregnancy: effect of, on marriage, 112, 118–121; teen, 156–173, 210, 211, 212, 215; see also, abortion; mothers; surrogate mothers

prejudice, gender differences and, 9–13

premarital sexuality, 249, 262

pro-life vs. pro-choice, in abortion controversy, 90–108

prostitutes, 63, 67, 183, 245

pseudokinship system, of remarriage, 336

psychic remarriage, 326, 332–333

psychoanalytic explanation, for divorce and remarriage, 317, 318

psychological approach, to marital ethics, 247–248

quality time, with children, 42, 46

quasi-kin, 321, 322

quickening, of a fetus, 90, 94, 96, 118

race: effect of, on cognitive functioning of children of divorce, 279–280, 284; as an issue in controversy over teen marriage, 156–173

racism, 210, 215

reconstituted family, 297, 335

Redbook questionnaire, on sexual behavior, 251–252

religion: abortion and, 94–95, 100–101, 104; divorce and, 328

remarriage: 268, 269–270, 274; controversy over, 312–338; *see also,* stepchildren

reproduction, collaborative, *see* surrogate mothers

reproductive freedom, and the abortion controversy, 90–108

Republicans, views of, on government programs for black youth, 219, 220

right to life, abortion and, 93–94

Robertson, John A., on surrogate mothers, 138–144

Roe v. Wade, 90, 97, 98, 102

role instability, as reason for remarriage, 328, 330–331

romantic love, as reason for remarriage, 328–329

Sagan, Carl, on abortion, 90–98

same-sex marriages: 65; controversy over, 76–84

Sarnoff, Irving and Suzanne, on marriage and parenthood, 112–125

SAT (Scholastic Aptitude Test) math scores, gender differences in, 7–8

school performance, decline in, in children of divorce, 272, 279, 280

schools and colleges, special programs for stepchildren in, 294–300

Schwartz, Felice N.: on the "mommy track," 194–201; reaction to views of, 202–205

security, marriage and, 64, 66, 68–69, 78, 133–134

self-esteem: 18, 40, 142, 231; in children of divorce, 277, 278, 284, 302

separation: marital, 54, 60, 270, 274, 282; role of, in domestic violence, 186–189

serial monogamy, 62, 255, 329

sex, importance of, in marriage, 66, 68

sex differences, *see* gender differences

sex hormones, gender differences and, 12–13

sexism, in the workplace, 198, 204

sexual activity, among adolescents, and controversy over teenage marriage, 156–173

sexual revolution, 261–262

sexually transmitted diseases, 117, 255, 257

shelters, for battered women, 232, 234, 238

single people: 62, 330, 333; health of, 55, 56, 57

single-parent families: 57, 147, 204, 216, 229, 269, 276, 278, 280, 283, 296, 297, 304; teen, 158, 163, 164–173

Skyles, Ada, on special programs for stepchildren in schools and colleges, 294–300

Smith, Tom W., on Americans and their sexual partners, 254–260

social exchange, as reason for remarriage, 328, 329

social networks: stress and, 18, 19–20, 23–25; women's, 18–34

social norms, as reason for remarriage, 328, 330

Social Security, 57, 217, 220

socialization, as cause for gender differences, 4–13

sociobiologists, 9, 10, 11, 12

socioeconomic status (SES), effect of, on children of divorce, 280, 281–282, 282–283, 284

sociological approach, to marital ethics, 248

sperm, 93, 94, 95, 116, 117, 138, 142, 147, 149

stability, in teenage marriages, 159–160, 162

Stack, Carol B., 32, 33

status, occupational, men and, 5, 6, 7

Steinmetz, Suzanne K.: 236, 237, 239; on husband battering, 226–232

stepchildren: 314, 315, 318, 321, 323, 327, 331–332, 334; controversy over special educational policies and programs for, 294–307

stereotypes: gender, and the "mommy track," 195, 196, 198, 204; negative, and the "mommy track," 301, 303, 319, 334

stress: 40, 41, 198, 229, 272, 283, 295; gender differences in the social moderators of, 18–27

suicide: 40, 213, 215, 240; in children of divorce, 268, 273

Sullivan, Andrew, on gay and lesbian marriage, 76–79

support groups: for battered spouses, 231; school, for stepchildren, 299

Supreme Court, *see* individual cases

surrogate mothers, controversy over, 138–152

talking, as parent/child activity, 43

Taylor, Ronald L., on black youth as an endangered generation, 210–214

teenagers, *see* adolescents

television, watching, as parent/child activity, 43, 46, 47

thought, human, beginning of, in abortion debate, 96, 97, 98

Thurman, Tracy, 184

transitional phase, in the divorce process, 269

turnover, employee, and working women, 194, 200

two-earner families, 40–41, 43–44, 47, 48, 58

two-tier system, marriage as, 83, 84

Umberson, Deborah, 55, 56

unemployment: among black youth, 210, 211, 212, 215; among teen parents, 158, 167, 171

unity, family, in stepfamilies, 314, 315–317, 323

urban black youth, controversy over government programs for, 210–221

uterus, 117, 138, 139

vasectomy, 128, 130, 131

Veevers, J. E., on childlessness, 126–134

viability, fetal, and the abortion controversy, 97–98, 102, 105

victim, blaming the: and domestic violence, 238; and problems of black youth, 210

victims, controversy over women's role as, 18–34

Vinovskis, Maris A., on teenage marriage, 156–173

violence, domestic, see domestic violence

Wallerstein, Judith S.: 277, 284, 295; children of divorce, 268–275

welfare, 58, 158, 210, 218, 219, 283

Whoozle Effect, in empirical and clinical studies, 305

widows and widowers, 24, 54, 59, 62, 255, 314, 315, 321

wives: as emotional support of husbands, 20–21, 22, 24; see also, divorce; domestic violence; marriage; remarriage

women: as victims in their roles, controversy over, 18–34; see also, abortion; domestic violence; mommy track; mothers; pregnancy; surrogate mothers; wives

working women: 38, 40, 194–204; impact on children of, 42–48